SPATIAL ANALYSIS USING BIG DATA

Spatial Econometrics and Spatial Statistics

SPATIAL ANALYSIS USING BIG DATA

Methods and Urban Applications

Edited by

YOSHIKI YAMAGATA

Center for Global Environmental Research
National Institute for Environmental Studies
Tsukuba, Ibaraki, Japan

HAJIME SEYA

Departments of Civil Engineering
Graduate School of Engineering Faculty of Engineering
Kobe University, Kobe, Hyogo, Japan

ELSEVIER

ACADEMIC PRESS

An imprint of Elsevier

Academic Press is an imprint of Elsevier
125 London Wall, London EC2Y 5AS, United Kingdom
525 B Street, Suite 1650, San Diego, CA 92101, United States
50 Hampshire Street, 5th Floor, Cambridge, MA 02139, United States
The Boulevard, Langford Lane, Kidlington, Oxford OX5 1GB, United Kingdom

Library of Congress Cataloging-in-Publication Data
A catalog record for this book is available from the Library of Congress

British Library Cataloguing-in-Publication Data
A catalogue record for this book is available from the British Library

ISBN: 978-0-12-813127-5

For information on all Academic Press publications visit our website at https://www.elsevier.com/books-and-journals

Publisher: Candice Janco
Acquisition Editor: Scott J Bentley
Editorial Project Manager: Redding Morse
Production Project Manager: Debasish Ghosh
Cover Designer: Matthew Limbert

Typeset by TNQ Technologies

Contents

Contributors

Toshihiro Hirano
Kanto Gakuin University, Yokohama, Kanagawa, Japan

Daisuke Murakami
The Institute of Statistical Mathematics, Tachikawa, Tokyo, Japan

Hajime Seya
Departments of Civil Engineering, Kobe University, Kobe, Hyogo, Japan

Yoshiki Yamagata
Center for Global Environmental Research, National Institute for Environmental Studies, Tsukuba, Ibaraki, Japan

Takahiro Yoshida
Center for Global Environmental Research, National Institute for Environmental Studies, Tsukuba, Ibaraki, Japan

Preface

The world today is experiencing a technological revolution caused by the internet of things (IoT), big data, and artificial intelligence (AI). Consequently, interest in using spatial big data for practical purposes has boomed in recent years. Hundreds of new applications are emerging over a wide variety of areas such as weather forecasting, car navigation, restaurant/hotel recommendation, and so forth. New types of data are also becoming available through IoT applications and the scope of spatial analysis models being drastically enhanced by AI and machine-learning techniques.

In the urban context, these technologies are often associated with another international interest—smart cities. The implementation of a combination of these technologies in urban environments could exceed our original expectations. Managing these systems requires spatial statistical researchers to take on the responsibility of data scientists analyzing complex urban spatial big data, addressing new societal challenges, and contending with real-world issues like climate change by developing new applications.

The purpose of this book is to provide graduate-level students and urban researchers alike with the basic theories and methods of spatial statistics and spatial econometrics necessary for developing new urban analytic applications utilizing spatial big data. Therefore, in the beginning emphasis is centered on mathematical formulation of spatial statistical and econometric methods, complemented with new developments for analyzing spatial big data. Initially more attention is given to describing the fundamental theories in an illustrative manner, to be useful for applied researchers (*Methods*). Utilizing programming illustrations, using R code, we describe how to empirically implement the methodologies presented in the previous chapters (*Implementations*). Following this, varieties of empirical application examples relating to the spatial big data analytical methods are explained with special emphasis placed on climate change mitigation issues in the urban spatial planning context (*Applications*).

We believe by combining foundational methods of spatial statistics and spatial econometrics with practical empirical applications, researchers and practitioners may have a better understanding of how spatial big data analysis can be applied to facilitate evidence-based urban spatial planning. In the empirical part of this book, the focus is on models exemplifying these concepts, shown being utilized for climate change mitigation solutions in cities in Japan. The research methods presented in this book are general enough to be applicable for addressing other different type of issues in different cities as well as other multispatial scales such as regional or national levels. The authors also believe that this book's contents can contribute to supporting researchers, practitioners, and students in conducting practical spatial analyses using big data for their studies or others.

Spatial statistics (econometrics) refers to statistical (econometric) analysis conducted on data with position coordinates, that is, spatial data. The utilization of spatial aspects of data in statistical analyses can enhance and improve the reliability of our models and analysis. One of the key concepts in spatial statistics and spatial econometrics is spatial dependency or spatial autocorrelation, defined in Tobler's first law of geography:"Everything is related to everything else, but near things are more related than distant things." Although historically the most popular academic areas for spatial autocorrelation analysis were, and are, ecology and genetics; the scope of application for spatial statistics has expanded substantially to include geography and regional science, medicine and epidemiology (Waller and Gotway, 2004), criminology (Townsley, 2009), image analysis (Curran and various studies in Atkinson, 1998), remote sensing (Cressie, 2018), minology (Journel and Huijbregts, 1978), soil science (Goovaerts, 1999), climate science (Elsner et al., 2011), and the water field (Ver Hoef et al., 2006), among others, reinforcing the fact that knowledge is cumulative.

First, let us briefly trace the lineage of spatial autocorrelation analysis. The first use of spatial autocorrelation analysis is often attributed to John Snow's cholera map in the mid 19th century. Snow created a disease map for the Soho area of London, in which the distribution of cholera patients and the distribution of water pumps were superimposed onto the city map. In doing so he found that the data was concentrated and distributed, with cholera patients clustered around water pumps in Broadstreet. This is 30 years before the discovery of *Vibrio cholerae* by Robert Koch. Snow's analysis, which acquired useful information by mapping spatial accumulation and autocorrelation of cholera, is considered to be the first real case of spatial data analysis. It would take 100 years before Moran's development of the *I* statistic (1948; 1950), and Geary's *C* statistic (1954) made it possible to quantitatively evaluate the presence or absence of spatial autocorrelation.

In the 1960 and 1970s, in the field of quantitative geography, spatial autocorrelation was regarded as one of the most basic and important problems, leading researchers to develop stronger analytical modeling methods for spatial data (e.g., Curry, 1966; Cliff and Ord, 1973). Building on these techniques, the scientific field of spatial econometrics, which examines the relationship between data in discrete spaces (zones of cities, towns, etc.) and flows of econometric geography, emerges in regional science. However, the field of econometrics has now become an independent field of study, with many articles published in mainstream econometrics journals (Anselin, 2010; Arbia, 2011).

Separately, another form of spatial statistics arose in the field of natural sciences. This academic field was established from mining science and treated spatial data as a continuous quantity in space (Matheron, 1963). In geostatistics, the dependency between data is described as a direct function of distance. Once a function is identified, the dependency between data at any location can be expressed using it, which enables spatial prediction of data at any point. This is a major feature of modeling in geostatistics.

Regardless of field, according to Cressie (1993), spatial data may be categorized into:

(1) geostatistical data
(2) lattice data
(3) point patterns

The term *spatial statistics* is sometimes used to represent an academic discipline dealing with geostatistical data or point patterns. However, spatial statistics, as a comprehensive system of analysis, is better defined in relation to all three data types noted by Cressie (1993). Among these, our book deals only with the spatial data categorized in geostatistical and lattice data. , We have little experience with point patterns; therefore, for more detail we refer to comprehensive texts such as Diggle (2013). Further, several key topics fall outside our scope including spatial data acquiring, sampling, handling, processing, and mining. Our focus is on spatial data *analysis* (or modeling).

Methods for processing geostatistical data were developed from geostatistics, whereas lattice data analysis arose from spatial econometrics (Anselin, 1988). Although there are many similarities in modeling techniques of geostatistics and spatial econometrics, Anselin (1986) describes it as "each approach tends to be self-contained, with little cross-reference shown in published articles." Different development histories make it relatively rare for either field to reference the other's papers. Compounding this is a sort of mutually exclusive entry barrier resulting from different designations being used for the same model, depending on the field, causing confusion. In fact, texts that cover methods of spatial econometrics and geostatistics are limited to Haining (1990, 2003) and Chun and Griffith (2013), for example. Brunsdon and Comber (2018) cover the implementation of R code in both fields but have few theoretical descriptions. Thus, in this book, using our latest research, we explain the methods employed by both fields as much as possible while supporting their implementation using R coding.

Moreover, facilitating the need for better modeling techniques for spatial big data, beyond just reviewing recent efforts, we introduce implementation methods utilizing R. This book consists of three parts: *Methods* (Chapters 2–6), *Implementations* (Chapter 7), and *Applications* (Chapters 8–11). The content of each chapter is briefly explained as follows.

Chapter 1: Defines spatial data and its two major features, "spatial autocorrelation" and "spatial heterogeneity." It provides a solid foundation upon which all subsequent chapters are built.

Chapter 2: Provides the basic mathematical preparation necessary for spatial statistical and econometric analysis. We describe the classical regression model that is the basis of this book followed by explanations about the applied regression models, generalized linear model and additive model. Of course, readers who are familiar with regression models may skip this chapter. In addition, since spatial statistical models in recent years are often subjected to theoretical development based on Bayesian statistics, it is also explained here.

Chapter 3: Introduces measures (test statistics) related to the *existence* of spatial autocorrelation in data called global indicators of spatial association, followed by reviews on the measures related to *where* the spatial autocorrelation occurs, called local indicators of spatial association (LISA). Also, the spatial weight matrix, which is an important tool for spatial econometrics, is explained.

Chapters 4 and 5: Explain the modeling techniques of the geostatistical data and lattice data, respectively. For the latter, it especially focuses on spatial econometrics. Applications to spatial big data is also discussed.

Chapter 6: Introduces geographically weighted regression (GWR) and eigenvector spatial filtering approaches that have been developed in quantitative geography. Their recent advances, especially in terms of computation, are also explained.

Chapter 7: Provides implementations with R. We chose R because of its barrier-free nature (available for free and easy to learn), which is important for students, as well as the existence of a lot of excellent *packages* that include many specialized functions for analyzing spatial big data.

As examples of spatial data, we use well-known housing price data in Lucas county (Ohio, USA), available through spData package of R. The data size is 25,357, thus medium-sized.

Chapters 8–11 illustrate the application of spatial statistical/econometrics techniques for urban planning issues, especially focusing on climate change mitigation. Each chapter uses various original data, and in this sense our application chapters do not offer current standard applications. However, we believe such applications would become more and more important in the future as aforementioned. The details of each chapter is explained as follows:

Chapter 8: Illustrates spatial modeling by combining multiple spatial data. This kind of topic is becoming important today as an increasing number of spatial data in different forms are available. We first introduce a geostatistical approach to estimate temperatures in an intraurban scale by combining weather monitoring data and geo-tagged tweets relating to heat. Then, this approach is employed in an empirical study in Tokyo.

Chapter 9: Illustrates two GPS data analyses to quantify goodness of walking environment. The first study applies a quantitative geographic approach (GWR model; see Chapter 6) to investigate local determinants of a walking environment, focusing on the impact of a pedestrian network structure on the number of pedestrians. The second analysis applies LISA (see Chapter 3) to quantify the heat-wave risk for pedestrians in an intraurban scale.

Chapter 10: Applies a spatial econometric approach to a spatially explicit downscaling of socioeconomic scenarios; the resulting socioeconomic scenarios by 0.5-degree grids are useful to evaluate regional climate risks in the future. We first apply the spatial econometric model to project city population growth in several future scenarios. Then, the result is used in the downscaling.

Chapter 11: Illustrates an estimation of quasi real-time energy consumption in each building using Google's popular time data, which records quasi real-time human locations/activities collected from users of Google Map on smartphones. We apply the geostatistical compositional kriging model to the popular time data for a ward in central Tokyo.

Although this book is as self-comprehensive as possible, a basic (undergraduate level) knowledge of statistics and econometrics is useful. Therefore, readers who are not familiar with statistics and econometrics are encouraged to familiarize themselves with these topics before reading this book. After reading our book, readers who are interested in spatial statistics and spatial econometrics may also refer to more advanced textbooks such as Cressie and Wikle (2011) for spatial statistics, and Kelejian and Piras (2017) for spatial econometrics.

Yoshiki YAMAGATA and Hajime SEYA
May 1, 2019

References

Anselin, L., 1986. Some further notes on spatial models and regional science. Journal of Regional Science 26 (4), 799–802.

Anselin, L., 1988. Spatial Econometrics: Methods and Models. Kluwer Academic Publishers, Dordrecht.

Anselin, L., 2010. Thirty years of spatial econometrics. Papers in Regional Science 89 (1), 3–25.

Arbia, G., 2011. A lustrum of SEA: recent research trends following the creation of the Spatial Econometrics Association (2007–2011). Spatial Economic Analysis 6 (4), 377–395.

Brunsdon, C., Comber, L., 2018. An Introduction to R for Spatial Analysis and Mapping, second ed. SAGE Publications Ltd, London.

Chun, Y., Griffith, D.A., 2013. Spatial Statistics and Geostatistics: Theory and Applications for Geographic Information Science and Technology. SAGE Publications Ltd, Thousand Oaks.

Cliff, A.D., Ord, J.K., 1973. Spatial Autocorrelation. Pion, London.

Cressie, N.A.C., 1993. Statistics for Spatial Data, Revised Edition. Wiley, New York.

Cressie, N.A.C., Wikle, C.K., 2011. Statistics for Spatio-Temporal Data. Wiley, New York.

Cressie, N.A.C., 2018. Mission CO2ntrol: a statistical scientist's role in remote sensing of atmospheric carbon dioxide. Journal of the American Statistical Association 113 (521), 152–168.

Curran, P.J., Atkinson, P.M., 1998. Geostatistics and remote sensing. Progress in Physical Geography 22 (1), 61–78.

Curry, L., 1966. A note on spatial association. The Professional Geographer 18 (2), 97–99.

Diggle, P.J., 2013. Statistical Analysis of Spatial and Spatio-Temporal Point Patterns. third ed. CRC Press, Boca Raton, FL.

Elsner, J.B., Hodges, R.E., Jagger, T.H., 2011. Spatial grids for hurricane climate research. Climate Dynamics 39 (1–2), 21–36.

Geary, R.C., 1954. The contiguity ratio and statistical mapping. The Incorporated Statistician 5 (3), 115–145.

Goovaerts, P., 1999. Geostatistics in soil science: state-of-the-art and perspectives. Geoderma 89 (1–2), 1–45.

Haining, R., 1990. Spatial Data Analysis in the Social and Environmental Sciences. Cambridge University Press, Cambridge.

Haining, R., 2003. Spatial Data Analysis: Theory and Practice. Cambridge University Press, Cambridge.

Journel, A.G., Huijbregts, C.J., 1978. Mining Geostatistics. Academic Press, London.

Kelejian, H.H., Piras, G., 2017. Spatial Econometrics. Academic Press, Cambridge.

Matheron, G., 1963. Principles of geostatistics. Economic Geology 58 (8), 1246–1266.

Moran, P.A.P., 1948. The interpretation of statistical maps. Journal of the Royal Statistical Society B 10 (2), 243–251.

Moran, P.A.P., 1950. A test for the serial dependence of residuals. Biometrika 37 (1–2), 178–181.

Townsley, M., 2009. Spatial autocorrelation and impacts on criminology. Geographical Analysis 41 (4), 452–461.

Ver Hoef, J.M., Peterson, E., Theobald, D., 2006. Spatial statistical models that use flow and stream distance. Environmental and Ecological Statistics 13 (4), 449–464.

Waller, L.A., Gotway, C.A., 2004. Applied Spatial Statistics for Public Health Data. Wiley, New York.

CHAPTER ONE

Introduction

Yoshiki Yamagata[1], Hajime Seya[2]
[1]Center for Global Environmental Research, National Institute for Environmental Studies, Tsukuba, Ibaraki, Japan
[2]Departments of Civil Engineering, Kobe University, Kobe, Hyogo, Japan

Contents

1.1 The definition of spatial data

Data relating to geospatial information is used in our everyday lives. In this book, based on the Japanese *Basic Act on the Advancement of Utilizing Geospatial Information* promulgated in 2007, we define the term geospatial information as

(1) information that represents the position of a specific point or area in geospace (including temporal information pertaining to said information, hereinafter referred to as positional information); and/or

(2) any information associated with this information.

We term the data, which relates to geospatial information, as *spatial data*. In addition, the aforementioned geospatial and geographic information are taken to have the same meaning. Naturally, there are various other methods of defining spatial data (e.g., Waller and Gotway, 2004, pp. 38–39).

Currently, the single most important book concerning spatial statistics is, undoubtedly, Cressie (1993). This great work spans 900 pages, and has served as a "dictionary" in this field for many years. The first chapter classified spatial

Spatial Analysis Using Big Data
ISBN: 978-0-12-813127-5
https://doi.org/10.1016/B978-0-12-813127-5.00001-1

data into geostatistical data, lattice data, and point patterns.[1] We begin this section with an outline of these data.

Let $\Re$ be the whole set of real numbers, and let $\mathbf{s} \in \Re^d$ be a spatial position in Euclidean space of dimension d (usually $d = 2$ or 3)[2] and let $\mathbf{Y}(\mathbf{s})$ be a random (possibly multivariate) quantity at position $\mathbf{s}$. The spatial process[3] is defined as $\{\mathbf{Y}(\mathbf{s}): \mathbf{s} \in D\}$ ($D \subset \Re^d$ shows the domain). $d = 2$ corresponds to two-dimensional spatial coordinates (e.g., x and y planar coordinates), and $d = 3$ is where the height dimension is added to this (e.g., elevation).

As previously described, spatial data is data with location and attributes. Here, the term data is frequently used to correspond with observed values. In this book, the realization of the spatial process $\mathbf{Y}(\mathbf{s})$, namely the observed value, is expressed as $\mathbf{y}(\mathbf{s})$.[4] Cressie and Wikle (2011) have developed a clear discussion by clearly separating a *data model* (DM) relating to $\mathbf{y}(\mathbf{s})$ and a *process model* (PM) relating to $\mathbf{Y}(\mathbf{s})$. In this book, DM and PM are used separately when needed, and the three types of spatial data are defined as follows.

- Geostatistical data $\mathbf{y}(s)$ are the realized values obtained from the geostatistical process $\mathbf{Y}(\mathbf{s})$, where $\mathbf{s}$ varies continuously within a fixed domain D. For example, elevation corresponds to this data type.
- Lattice data $\mathbf{y}(s)$ are the realized values from the lattice process $\mathbf{Y}(\mathbf{s})$, where $\mathbf{s}$ varies on a countable subdomain of a fixed domain D. For example, socioeconomic data gathered from areas such as municipalities and satellite remote sensing image data at the pixel level correspond to this data type.
- Spatial point patterns data $\mathbf{y}(\mathbf{s})$ are the realized values from the spatial point process, which is a spatial process relating to the position of a randomly occurring event where D itself is random. Event data, such as crime, correspond to this type.

In addition, following Cressie and Wikle (2011, p.18), we assume a spatio-temporal process that adopts a time axis, expressing where t moves continuously within $T \subset \Re$ as $\{\mathbf{Y}(\mathbf{s}; t): \mathbf{s} \in D, t \in T\}$ and where it moves discretely as $\{\mathbf{Y}_t(\mathbf{s}): \mathbf{s} \in D, t \in T\}$.

[1] Note that among the standard texts with some reputation, Banerjee et al. (2014) refer to (a) and (b) as point-referenced and areal data, respectively, while Schabenberger and Gotway (2005) present (b) as lattice/regional data (other classification names are identical).

[2] $d > 3$ is often used in the field of computer experiments.

[3] Often also called a random field.

[4] Arbia (2006) discusses the importance of distinguishing between $Y(\mathbf{s})$ and $y(\mathbf{s})$. However, there seems to be little awareness of this point in applied research.

However, our book basically focuses on spatial process/data, not spatio-temporal process/data. Now, observation points are taken to be $\mathbf{s}_i$ ($i = 1, \ldots, N$). In this book, the univariate random variable is expressed as either $Y(\mathbf{s}_i)$ or Y_i, and its actual value as $y(\mathbf{s}_i)$ or y_i.

1.2 Characteristics of spatial data: spatial autocorrelation and spatial heterogeneity

According to Anselin (1988), the characteristics of spatial data are spatial autocorrelation and spatial heterogeneity. The term spatial dependence is also often used to mean the former of the two. Naturally, autocorrelation and dependency are not identical terms. However, in practice, both are often used to mean autocorrelation, and in this book, we advance the argument that they are mutually interchangeable, as in Anselin and Bera (1998, p. 240). In addition, although the term spatial correlation is often used, it is more appropriate to use the term autocorrelation rather than correlation for the correlation that occurs due to spatial positioning in the same variable (Getis, 2008).

1.2.1 Spatial autocorrelation

Spatial autocorrelation, as shown in Fig. 1.2.1, is generally classified into *positive* spatial autocorrelation, in which neighboring data show similar trends, and *negative* spatial autocorrelation, in which neighboring data show notably different values. These are known as Tobler's (1970) First Law of Geography—*everything is related to everything else, but near things are more related than distant things.* The latter, shown in a checkerboard pattern in Fig. 1.2.1, is not always easy to explain intuitively; however, when considering, for example, the spatial distribution of forests or crops, negative spatial autocorrelation may occur if appropriate thinning is not performed

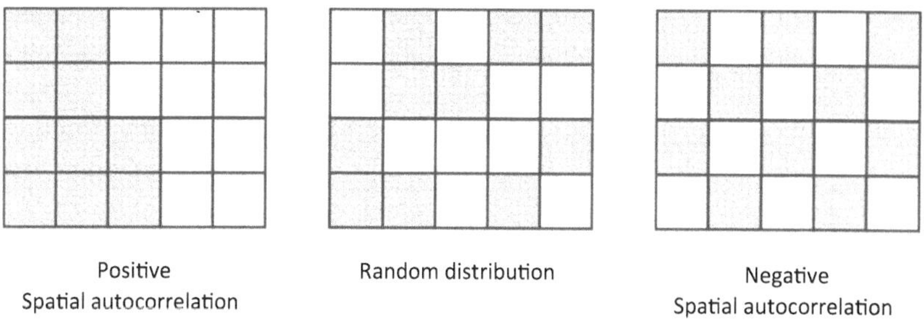

Figure 1.2.1 A representation of spatial autocorrelation □ and ▨ are binary variables taking 1 and 0, respectively.

due to competition for necessary nutrients. See Griffith and Arbia (2010) for details concerning negative spatial autocorrelation.

Mathematically, spatial autocorrelation is expressed by the following moment condition (Anselin and Bera, 1998):

$$Cov(y_i, y_j) = E(y_i y_j) - E(y_i) \cdot E(y_j) \neq 0, \forall i \neq j. \quad (1.1)$$

Here, y_i and y_j show data at points $\mathbf{s}_i \in D, \mathbf{s}_j \in D$. Various phenomena showing spatial autocorrelation exist around us. Let us take an example of the official land prices (Land Market Price Publication) in Japan, published by the Ministry of Land, Infrastructure, Transport and Tourism. One method used by real estate surveyors is transaction comparison, where land is evaluated by comparing the surrounding transaction prices. As a result, there is the possibility of spatial autocorrelation occurring in appraisal value (Tsutsumi and Seya, 2009). In another example, in the field of spatial epidemiology, the visualization and detection of disease clustering is of particular interest. For example, while it is known that the risk of each disease occurring depends on the region (because of aspects like region-specific foods and culture), a positive spatial autocorrelation is evident where this kind of risk is spatially concentrated. Since illness is a type of event (number) data, a specific method is required to test for spatial concentration (e.g., Waller and Gotway, 2004).

Here, we wish to briefly describe the difference between spatial autocorrelation and temporal autocorrelation. The dependency relationship of time series is modeled on the idea that the causal chain between the prior phenomenon and the phenomenon of interest follows the direction of progress, and that the phenomenon at a given point in time exerts no influence on those prior to that point in time. Conversely, spatial autocorrelation is characterized by simultaneous occurrence in multiple directions with accompanying feedback (Anselin, 2009). Although the details are described later, this relationship complicates the estimations and inferences.

1.2.2 Spatial heterogenity

Spatial heterogeneity refers to the uneven distribution of a trait, event, or relationship across a region (Anselin, 2010). From a statistical point of view, it results in unstable model structure in space (function form and/or regression coefficient). One example is the segmented market of real estate (e.g., Islam and Asami, 2009).

In a cross section, however, care needs to be taken since there are many cases in which spatial heterogeneity is indistinguishable from spatial autocorrelation. For example, when the residuals from a regression analysis form positive spatial clusters, this can be interpreted as both spatial heterogeneity (group level variance heterogeneity) and spatial autocorrelation (concentration of similar residuals) (Anselin, 2001). Therefore, in spatial econometrics, it is common to impose structure on the problem through the specification of a model, coupled with extensive specification testing for potential departures from the null model (Anselin and Bera, 1998). However, approaches nonparametrically specifying unknown patterns of spatial heterogeneity have also been developed (Kelejian and Piras, 2017), which will also be explained in this book.

References

Anselin, L., 1988. Spatial Econometrics: Methods and Models. Kluwer Academic Publishers, Dordrecht.

Anselin, L., 2001. Spatial econometrics. In: Baltagi, B. (Ed.), A Companion to Theoretical Econometrics. Blackwell, Oxford, pp. 310–330.

Anselin, L., 2009. Spatial regression. In: Fotheringham, S., Rogerson, P. (Eds.), The SAGE Handbook of Spatial Analysis. Sage Publications Inc, Los Angeles, pp. 255–276.

Anselin, L., 2010. Thirty years of spatial econometrics. Papers in Regional Science 89 (1), 3–25.

Anselin, L., Bera, A.K., 1998. Spatial dependence in linear regression models with an introduction to spatial econometrics. In: Ullah, A., Giles, D.E. (Eds.), Handbook of Applied Economic Statistics. Marcel Dekker, New York, pp. 237–289.

Arbia, G., 2006. Spatial Econometrics: Statistical Foundations and Applications to Regional Growth Convergence. Springer, New York.

Banerjee, S., Carlin, B.P., Gelfand, A.E., 2014. Hierarchical Modeling and Analysis for Spatial Data, second ed. Chapman & Hall/CRC, Boca Raton.

Cressie, N.A.C., 1993. Statistics for Spatial Data, Revised Edition. Wiley, New York.

Cressie, N.A.C., Wikle, C.K., 2011. Statistics for Spatio-Temporal Data. Wiley, New York.

Getis, A., 2008. A history of the concept of spatial autocorrelation: a geographer's perspective. Geographical Analysis 40 (3), 297–309.

Griffith, D.A., Arbia, G., 2010. Detecting negative spatial autocorrelation in georeferenced random variables. International Journal of Geographical Information Science 24 (3), 417–437.

Islam, K.S., Asami, Y., 2009. Housing market segmentation: a review. Review of Urban & Regional Development Studies 21 (2–3), 93–109.

Kelejian, H.H., Prucha, I.R., 2007. HAC estimation in a spatial framework. Journal of Econometrics 140 (1), 131–154.

Schabenberger, O., Gotway, C.A., 2005. Statistical Methods for Spatial Data Analysis. Chapman & Hall/CRC, Boca Raton.

Tobler, W., 1970. A computer movie simulating urban growth in the Detroit region. Economic Geography 46 (2), 234–240.

Tsutsumi, M., Seya, H., 2009. Hedonic approaches based on spatial econometrics and spatial statistics: application to evaluation of project benefits. Journal of Geographical Systems 11 (4), 357–380.

Waller, L.A., Gotway, C.A., 2004. Applied Spatial Statistics for Public Health Data. Wiley, New York.

PART ONE

Methods

CHAPTER TWO

Mathematical preparation

Hajime Seya[1], Yoshiki Yamagata[2]
[1]Departments of Civil Engineering, Kobe University, Kobe, Hyogo, Japan
[2]Center for Global Environmental Research, National Institute for Environmental Studies, Tsukuba, Ibaraki, Japan

Contents

2.1 Definitions of notations

In this book, scalars are shown in fine italics a, and vectors and matrices are shown in bold $\mathbf{a}$ (there are instances of lowercase characters and uppercase characters). Moreover, when $\mathbf{a}$ is a column vector and $\mathbf{A}$ is a matrix, a_i is the ith component of $\mathbf{a}$, $\mathbf{a}_{-i}$ is a vector from $\mathbf{a}$ with the ith component removed, $\mathbf{A}_i$ is the ith row of $\mathbf{A}$, $A_{i,j}$ is the component on row i column j of $\mathbf{A}$, and $\mathbf{A}_{-i}$ is a matrix from $\mathbf{A}$ with the ith row removed. Furthermore, $\mathbf{I}$ expresses an identity matrix, $\mathbf{O}$ a square matrix from 0, $\mathbf{1}$ a column vector of 1, $\mathbf{0}$ a column vector of 0, and $\mathbf{A}^{-1}$ and $\mathbf{A}'$ are the inverse matrix of $\mathbf{A}$ and the transposed matrix of $\mathbf{A}$, respectively. Dimensions of matrices and vectors are omitted, where obvious, from the context. However, depending on their necessity, these are written as $\mathbf{A}_{[n]}$ for an nth order square matrix and $\mathbf{A}_{[n \times m]}$ for a matrix with n rows and m columns. In addition, as much as

Spatial Analysis using Big Data
ISBN: 978-0-12-813127-5
https://doi.org/10.1016/B978-0-12-813127-5.00002-3

possible, mathematical notations will follow the standard form given by Abadir and Magnus (2002).

2.2 The classical linear regression model

Before explaining spatial statistics and spatial econometrics, we explain the basis of the classical linear regression (CLR) model. Also, the generalized linear model (GLM), the additive model, and Bayesian statistics are introduced here. Particularly, in recent years, many statistical estimations, inferences, and predictions with regression models have been based on the Bayesian statistical theory, and therefore it is desirable to understand its basic principles. In fact, Banerjee et al. (2014) (for geostatistics or spatial statistics) and LeSage and Pace (2009) (for spatial econometrics), two of the standard texts, have developed theories that are reliant mostly upon Bayesian statistics.

2.2.1 The classical linear regression model and violation of typical assumptions

In the CLR model, the following relationship is established for all observed values y_i at position $\mathbf{s}_i$ ($i = 1, \ldots, N$):

$$y_i = \beta_1 + \sum_{k=2}^{K} x_{k,i}\beta_k + \varepsilon_i. \tag{2.2.1}$$

where, y_i denotes a dependent variable, $x_{k,i}$ ($k = 2, \ldots, K$) denotes an exogenous explanatory variable, β_1 is a constant, β_k is the regression coefficient corresponding to $x_{k,i}$, and ε_i is the error term. Expressing Eq. (2.2.1) as a matrix yields the following equation:

$$\begin{pmatrix} y_1 \\ y_2 \\ \vdots \\ y_N \end{pmatrix} = \beta_1 \begin{pmatrix} 1 \\ 1 \\ \vdots \\ 1 \end{pmatrix} + \left(\begin{bmatrix} x_{2,1} & \cdots & x_{K,1} \\ \vdots & \ddots & \vdots \\ x_{2,N} & \cdots & x_{K,N} \end{bmatrix} \right) \begin{pmatrix} \beta_2 \\ \beta_3 \\ \vdots \\ \beta_K \end{pmatrix} + \begin{pmatrix} \varepsilon_1 \\ \varepsilon_2 \\ \vdots \\ \varepsilon_N \end{pmatrix}, \tag{2.2.2}$$

or

$$\mathbf{y} = \beta_1 1 + \mathbf{x}\boldsymbol{\beta}_2 + \boldsymbol{\varepsilon}.$$

where $\mathbf{y}$ is an $N \times 1$ dependent variable vector containing y_i, $\mathbf{1}$ is an $N \times 1$ vector containing 1, $\mathbf{x}$ is an $N \times (K-1)$ exogenous explanatory variables matrix consisting of $x_{k,i}$, $\boldsymbol{\beta}_2$ is a $(K-1) \times 1$ regression coefficient vector consisting of β_k, and $\boldsymbol{\varepsilon}$ is an $N \times 1$ error term vector consisting of ε_i. If we rearrange such that $\mathbf{X} \equiv [1;\mathbf{x}]$, $\boldsymbol{\beta} \equiv [\beta_1;\boldsymbol{\beta}'_2]'$, we have

$$\mathbf{y} = \mathbf{X}\boldsymbol{\beta} + \boldsymbol{\varepsilon}. \tag{2.2.3}$$

In the CLR model, the following four assumptions are usually made:

(1) $\mathbf{X}$ is exogenous.

(2) Given $\mathbf{X}$, the conditional expected value of $\mathbf{y}$ is $\mathbf{X}\boldsymbol{\beta}$, and the conditional expected value of $\boldsymbol{\varepsilon}$ is $\mathbf{0}$. That is, $E[\boldsymbol{\varepsilon}|\mathbf{X}] = 0$.

(3) Given $\mathbf{X}$, the error term $\boldsymbol{\varepsilon}$ satisfies:

$$Var[\boldsymbol{\varepsilon}|\mathbf{X}] = \sigma_\varepsilon^2 \mathbf{I}_{[N]} = \begin{pmatrix} \sigma_\varepsilon^2 & 0 & \cdots & 0 \\ 0 & \sigma_\varepsilon^2 & \ddots & \vdots \\ \vdots & \ddots & \ddots & 0 \\ 0 & \cdots & 0 & \sigma_\varepsilon^2 \end{pmatrix}. \tag{2.2.4}$$

Eq. (2.2.4) implies independent and identically distributed error terms.

(4) The rank of $\mathbf{X}$ is K. That is, an inverse matrix exists in $(\mathbf{X'X})$.

In addition to these four assumptions, the following assumption is typically made:

(5) $\boldsymbol{\varepsilon} \sim N(\mathbf{0}\sigma_\varepsilon^2 \mathbf{I}_{[N]})$; that is, normal distributed error terms in population.

This assumption implies

$$y \sim N\left(\mathbf{X}\boldsymbol{\beta}, \sigma_\varepsilon^2 \mathbf{I}_{[N]}\right). \tag{2.2.5}$$

With assumption (5), the ordinary least squares (OLS) estimator of $\boldsymbol{\beta}$ follows the normal distribution, making it possible to perform a hypothesis test on its significance when the number of observations in a sample is rather small (when large, we can apply the central limit theorem).

The OLS estimator $\widehat{\boldsymbol{\beta}}_{ols}$ of the CLR model is obtained by minimizing the sum of squares $\widehat{\boldsymbol{\varepsilon}}'_{ols}\widehat{\boldsymbol{\varepsilon}}_{ols}$ of residual vector:

$$\widehat{\boldsymbol{\varepsilon}}_{ols} = \mathbf{y} - \mathbf{X}\widehat{\boldsymbol{\beta}}_{ols} \tag{2.2.6}$$

The first-order condition of optimization yields

$$\mathbf{X}'\mathbf{y} = \mathbf{X}'\mathbf{X}\widehat{\boldsymbol{\beta}}_{ols} \tag{2.2.7}$$

With assumption (4), there is an inverse matrix in $(\mathbf{X'X})$, and therefore the OLS estimator of $\boldsymbol{\beta}$ can be obtained from

$$\widehat{\boldsymbol{\beta}}_{ols} = (\mathbf{X}'\mathbf{X})^{-1}\mathbf{X}'\mathbf{y} \tag{2.2.8}$$

Also, the variance of $\widehat{\boldsymbol{\beta}}_{ols}$ is given by:

$$\mathrm{Var}\left(\widehat{\boldsymbol{\beta}}_{ols}\right) = \sigma_{\varepsilon}^{2}(\mathbf{X}'\mathbf{X})^{-1} \tag{2.2.9}$$

Since σ_{ε}^{2} is usually unknown, we substitute σ_{ε}^{2} with the estimator

$$\widehat{\sigma}_{\varepsilon,ols}^{2} = \widehat{\boldsymbol{\varepsilon}}'_{ols}\widehat{\boldsymbol{\varepsilon}}_{ols}/(N-K) \tag{2.2.10}$$

Note that the fitted value of $\mathbf{y}$ is given by $\widehat{\mathbf{y}} = \mathbf{X}\widehat{\boldsymbol{\beta}}_{ols}$, and thus if this is substituted into Eq. (2.2.8), we obtain $\widehat{\mathbf{y}} = \mathbf{X}(\mathbf{X}'\mathbf{X})^{-1}\mathbf{X}'\mathbf{y}$. Here, $\mathbf{P}_{\mathbf{X}} = \mathbf{X}(\mathbf{X}'\mathbf{X})^{-1}\mathbf{X}'$ is a projection matrix that produces $\widehat{\mathbf{y}}$ from $\mathbf{y}$, and for this reason, it is termed a hat matrix. Similarly, $\mathbf{M}_{\mathbf{X}} = \mathbf{I}_{[N]} - \mathbf{P}_{\mathbf{X}}$ is an operator that creates a residual from $\mathbf{y}$. These operators are also important in the restricted maximum likelihood (REML) method described elsewhere.

Where assumptions (1)−(4) hold, the OLS estimator becomes the best linear unbiased estimator (BLUE), and this property is known as the Gauss-Markov theorem. Unfortunately, however, it is rare in empirical analyses that all these assumptions are satisfied, and in many cases, violations of assumptions (1)−(3) occur in particular. Therefore, later we explain the consequences of violating assumptions (1)−(3), and the countermeasures to them. Note that with respect to assumption (4), it is possible to satisfy this assumption by removing the explanatory variable(s) that causes perfect multicollinearity.

2.2.2 Endogeneity

When deviating from assumptions (1) and (2) (i.e., when a correlation between the explanatory variable and error term occurs), the OLS estimator lacks both consistency and unbiasedness. Cases where $\mathbf{x}$ has a measurement error, where an important variable is missing from the model (omitted variable bias), and where $\mathbf{x}$ and $\mathbf{y}$ are jointly determined (simultaneity/reverse causality) are regarded as examples of this kind of situation. As a countermeasure to this problem, the instrumental variable (IV) method is applied to obtain consistent estimators for the regression coefficients. The IV(s) must have correlation to the endogenous explanatory variables conditionally on the other covariates, although they cannot have correlation to the error term conditionally on the other covariates. The latter condition rule out any direct effect of the instruments on the dependent variable or any effect running through omitted variables. This is called the *exclusion restriction*. As its generalization, the two-stage least squares (2SLS) method as well as the generalized method of moments (GMM) can also be used.

Since these methods are used for estimating parameters of the spatial econometric models, let us briefly describe their basics here.

We will now explicitly introduce endogenous variables into the CLR model, which we can express as follows:

$$\mathbf{y} = \mathbf{X}\boldsymbol{\beta} + \dot{\mathbf{X}}\dot{\boldsymbol{\beta}} + \boldsymbol{\varepsilon}, \tag{2.2.11}$$

where we take $\mathbf{X}$ to be an $N \times K$ explanatory variable matrix consisting of constant terms and exogenous variables, and $\dot{\mathbf{X}}$ as an $N \times L$ explanatory variable matrix consisting of endogenous variables. In addition, $\boldsymbol{\beta}$ denotes a $K \times 1$ regression coefficient vector corresponding to exogenous variables, and $\dot{\boldsymbol{\beta}}$ denotes an $L \times 1$ regression coefficient vector corresponding to endogenous variables. Here, because $\dot{\mathbf{X}}$ is an endogenous variable, it has a correlation to the error term ($Cov[\varepsilon_i, \dot{x}_{l,i}] \neq 0,\ \forall\ l = 1, \ldots, L$). Hence we may consider introducing IVs, say $\mathbf{Z}_{[N\times P]}$, which correlates with $\dot{\mathbf{X}}$, but does not correlate with $\boldsymbol{\varepsilon}$. For the sake of identification, the degree P of $\mathbf{Z}$ must be greater than or equal to the number of endogenous variables L. Under such a scenario, the IV estimator can be obtained by applying the 2SLS method. That is, when the explanatory variable matrix is rearranged to form $\mathbf{R} \equiv \left[\mathbf{X}; \dot{\mathbf{X}}\right]$, a two-stage estimation is performed, such that $\mathbf{R}$ is projected onto the plane spanned by $\mathbf{S} \equiv [\mathbf{X};\mathbf{Z}]$, uncorrelated to the error term and the estimated $\widehat{\mathbf{R}}$ value obtained, the next $\mathbf{y}$ is regressed on $\widehat{\mathbf{R}}$, not $\mathbf{R}$. This is a simple idea of using $\widehat{\mathbf{R}}$, which does not have correlation to the error term. If a valid IV is used, the 2SLS estimator may be consistent.

The 2SLS estimator of parameter $\ddot{\boldsymbol{\beta}} \equiv \left[\boldsymbol{\beta}'; \dot{\boldsymbol{\beta}}'\right]'$ is finally obtained from

$$\widehat{\ddot{\boldsymbol{\beta}}}_{2sls} = \left(\widehat{\mathbf{R}}'\widehat{\mathbf{R}}\right)^{-1}\widehat{\mathbf{R}}'\mathrm{y}, \tag{2.2.12}$$

$$Var\left[\widehat{\ddot{\boldsymbol{\beta}}}_{2sls}\right] = \sigma_{\varepsilon}^{2}\left(\mathbf{R}'\widehat{\mathbf{R}}\right)^{-1}, \tag{2.2.13}$$

where $\widehat{\mathbf{R}} = (\mathbf{S}'\mathbf{S})^{-1}\mathbf{S}'\mathbf{R}$, and therefore $\ddot{\boldsymbol{\beta}}_{2sls} = \left[\mathbf{R}'\mathbf{S}(\mathbf{S}'\mathbf{S})^{-1}\mathbf{S}'\mathbf{R}\right]^{-1}$ $\mathbf{R}'\mathbf{S}(\mathbf{S}'\mathbf{S})^{-1}\mathbf{S}'\mathbf{y}$. Since σ_{ε}^{2} is unknown, σ_{ε}^{2} can be substituted with an estimate using

$$\widehat{\sigma}_{\varepsilon,2sls}^{2} = \widehat{\boldsymbol{\varepsilon}}'_{2sls}\widehat{\boldsymbol{\varepsilon}}_{2sls}/(N-K), \tag{2.2.14}$$

where

$$\widehat{\boldsymbol{\varepsilon}}_{2sls} = \mathbf{y} - \mathbf{R}\ddot{\widehat{\widehat{\boldsymbol{\beta}}}}_{2sls} \tag{2.2.15}$$

Note the use of $\mathbf{R}$ instead of $\widehat{\mathbf{R}}$. Since the coefficient estimator in the 2SLS method can be obtained asymptotically, it can be divided either by $(N-K)$ or N.

The 2SLS method is also used as the parameter estimation method of the spatial lag model (SLM), which is one of the representative models of the spatial econometrics that will be introduced in Chapter 5. GMM, instead, can be applied for the parameter estimation of the spatial error model (SEM), which is also introduced in Chapter 5.

Now, our explanation turns to the GMM. First let us explain the method of moments (MM), which also can be used as the parameter estimation of the CLR model. The MM is a method of estimating parameters by using moment conditions that a model should satisfy. The moment condition in the CLR model is the absence of correlation between the explanatory variables and the error term; that is,

$$E[\mathbf{X}'_i \varepsilon_i] = \mathbf{0}_{[K\times 1]}, \quad \forall i = 1, \ldots, N \tag{2.2.16}$$

Here, since $\mathbf{X}_i$ is a $1 \times K$ vector expressing the ith row component of $\mathbf{X}$, the conditional expression becomes set K. In matrix form, we can write this condition as

$$E[\mathbf{X}'\boldsymbol{\varepsilon}] = \mathbf{0}_{[K\times 1]} \tag{2.2.17}$$

The corresponding sample moment condition can be obtained as

$$\frac{\mathbf{X}'\boldsymbol{\varepsilon}}{N} = \frac{\mathbf{X}'(\mathbf{y} - \mathbf{X}\boldsymbol{\beta})}{N} = \mathbf{0}_{[K\times 1]}. \tag{2.2.18}$$

Hence with assumption (4), the MM estimator may be given as

$$\widehat{\boldsymbol{\beta}}_{mm} = (\mathbf{X}'\mathbf{X})^{-1}\mathbf{X}'\mathbf{y}, \tag{2.2.19}$$

and thus it is understood to be identical to the OLS estimator.

Here, let us write the moment condition of the CLR model shown in Eq. (2.2.16) in a more general way:

$$E[h(y_i, \mathbf{X}_i, \boldsymbol{\beta})] = \mathbf{0}_{[R\times 1]}, \tag{2.2.20}$$

Here, $h(y_i, \mathbf{X}_i, \boldsymbol{\beta})$ is an $R \times 1$ vector-valued function. If we substitute with the sample moment condition, this becomes:

$$h_s(\mathbf{y}, \mathbf{X}, \boldsymbol{\beta}) = \frac{1}{N}\sum_{i=1}^{N} h_s(y_i, \mathbf{X}_i, \boldsymbol{\beta}), \tag{2.2.21}$$

where $h_s(\mathbf{y},\mathbf{X},\boldsymbol{\beta})$ is also an $R \times 1$ vector-valued function. If the number of the estimand, K, of $\boldsymbol{\beta}$ matches the number of moment conditions R, as in the case of the CLR model, it is possible to obtain those parameters using the MM. However, where $R > K$ the parameters that exactly satisfy Eq. (2.2.21) are generally not present. Therefore, we consider determining parameters that minimize a quadratic form such as

$$h_s(\mathbf{y}, \mathbf{X}, \boldsymbol{\beta})'\mathbf{V}h_s(\mathbf{y}, \mathbf{X}, \boldsymbol{\beta}) \tag{2.2.22}$$

The estimator obtained in this way is a GMM estimator. The GMM estimator is known to have consistency and asymptotic normality under very general conditions (Hayashi, 2000). Here, $\mathbf{V}$ is the weight assigned to each condition and Hansen (1982) showed that under some regularity conditions, the minimum variance of the GMM estimator can be achieved by using the following equation:

$$\mathbf{V} = \left[\frac{1}{N}\sum_{i=1}^{N} h(y_i, \mathbf{X}_i, \boldsymbol{\beta})h(y_i, \mathbf{X}_i, \boldsymbol{\beta})'\right]^{-1} \tag{2.2.23}$$

However, in order to obtain the estimator $\mathbf{V}$ in Eq. (2.2.23), it is necessary to substitute the corresponding estimates for $\boldsymbol{\beta}$. Therefore, a two-step estimation is performed: calculating $\widehat{\boldsymbol{\beta}}^{(0)}_{\text{gmm}}$ using suitable initial value of weight (e.g., identity matrix value), substituting it into Eq. (2.2.23) to obtain $\widehat{\mathbf{V}}^{-1}$, and finally obtaining the GMM estimator by minimizing Eq. (2.2.22).

Here, we can easily show that the 2SLS estimator is a special case of the GMM estimator. Now, let's return to Eq. (2.2.11). When we set the IVs to $\mathbf{Z}_{[N\times P]}$, we can define $\mathbf{S} \equiv [\mathbf{X};\mathbf{Z}]_{[N\times(K+P)]}$. Now, by adding the moment condition relating to $\mathbf{Z}$ to that of the CLR model, the following equation is obtained:

$$E[\mathbf{S}'\boldsymbol{\varepsilon}] = \mathbf{0}_{[(K+P)\times 1]} \tag{2.2.24}$$

Replacing the left side with a sample analogous, we obtain

$$\frac{\mathbf{S}'\left(\mathbf{y} - \mathbf{R}\ddot{\boldsymbol{\beta}}\right)}{N}, \tag{2.2.25}$$

where $\mathbf{R} \equiv \left[\mathbf{X}; \dot{\mathbf{X}}\right]$, $\ddot{\boldsymbol{\beta}} \equiv \left[\boldsymbol{\beta}'; \dot{\boldsymbol{\beta}}'\right]'$. The GMM estimator for $\ddot{\boldsymbol{\beta}}$ is obtained by minimizing the quadratic form

$$h_s\left(\mathbf{y}, \mathbf{X}, \dot{\mathbf{X}}, \mathbf{Z}, \ddot{\boldsymbol{\beta}}\right)'\mathbf{V}h_s\left(\mathbf{y}, \mathbf{X}, \dot{\mathbf{X}}, \mathbf{Z}, \ddot{\boldsymbol{\beta}}\right), \tag{2.2.26}$$

and its sample analogous yields:

$$\left(\frac{\mathbf{S}'(\mathbf{y}-\mathbf{R}\ddot{\boldsymbol{\beta}})}{N}\right)'\mathbf{V}\left(\frac{\mathbf{S}'(\mathbf{y}-\mathbf{R}\ddot{\boldsymbol{\beta}})}{N}\right), \tag{2.2.27}$$

where $\mathbf{V}$ is obtained by:

$$\mathbf{V}=\left(\frac{\sigma_{\varepsilon}^{2}\mathbf{S}'\mathbf{S}}{N}\right)^{-1} \tag{2.2.28}$$

From the first-order condition of optimization, the GMM estimator of $\ddot{\boldsymbol{\beta}}$ is given by:

$$\hat{\ddot{\boldsymbol{\beta}}}_{gmm}=\left[\mathbf{R}'\mathbf{S}(\mathbf{S}'\mathbf{S})^{-1}\mathbf{S}'\mathbf{R}\right]^{-1}\mathbf{R}'\mathbf{S}(\mathbf{S}'\mathbf{S})^{-1}\mathbf{S}'\mathbf{y}. \tag{2.2.29}$$

It is apparent that this equation is identical to the 2SLS estimator (Eq. 2.2.12). In addition, the asymptotic distribution is also consistent with that obtained from the 2SLS method. For further details, please refer to Hayashi et al. (2000).

2.2.3 Spatial autocorrelation of error term and heteroskedastic variance

Next, we examine violations of assumption (3), where the error term does not satisfy homoskedasticity and/or no-autocorrelation. In both cases the OLS estimator is unbiased, but not efficient. Particularly in the case of spatial data, there are many instances where no-autocorrelation does not hold due to spatial autocorrelation stems from unobserved factors. Now, let us expand the CLR model in the following manner:

$$\mathbf{y}=\mathbf{X}\boldsymbol{\beta}+\boldsymbol{u}, \tag{2.2.30}$$

$$Var[\mathbf{u}]=E[\mathbf{u}\mathbf{u}']=\boldsymbol{\Sigma}, \tag{2.2.31}$$

with

$$\boldsymbol{\Sigma}=\begin{pmatrix} Var[u_1] & Cov[u_1,u_2] & \cdots & Cov[u_1,u_N] \\ Cov[u_2,u_1] & Var[u_2] & \cdots & Cov[u_2,u_N] \\ \vdots & \vdots & \ddots & \vdots \\ Cov[u_N,u_1] & \cdots & \cdots & Var[u_N] \end{pmatrix},$$

where, $\boldsymbol{\Sigma}$ is termed a variance–covariance matrix, which is a matrix with variance in the diagonal terms and covariance in nondiagonal terms. If $\boldsymbol{\Sigma}=\sigma_{\varepsilon}^{2}\mathbf{I}$ does not hold, the OLS estimator is not BLUE, and the standard error estimator has bias, which may result in erroneous inference.

Fortunately, however, if the structure of $\boldsymbol{\Sigma}$ is known, using the generalized least squares method, $\boldsymbol{\beta}'$s BLUE can be obtained:

$$\widehat{\beta}_{gls} = \left(X'\sum^{-1}X\right)^{-1} X\prime\sum^{-1}y. \tag{2.2.32}$$

Of course, $\boldsymbol{\Sigma}$ is usually not known, and it is necessary to set $N \times N$ elements of $\boldsymbol{\Sigma}$ with any assumption.

Simply speaking, in the modeling of geostatistical data (geostatistical model), the variance—covariance matrix is directly constructed as a function of distance. Meanwhile, in lattice data modeling (spatial econometric model), it is indirectly constructed through structuring the dependency between the data or error terms (e.g., autoregression type and moving average type). These differences are explained in more detail in Chapters 4 and 5.

2.3 The generalized linear model

In the CLR model introduced in Eq. (2.2.1), if we assume that the error term follows a normal distribution, it can be expressed as:[1]

$$E[y_i] = \mu_i = \mathbf{X}_i\boldsymbol{\beta};\ y_i \sim N\left(\mu_i, \sigma_\varepsilon^2\right), \tag{2.3.1}$$

where $\mathbf{X}_i$ denotes the vector consisting of the ith row of $\mathbf{X}$. Here, needless to say, it is not mandatory to assume normal distribution. The GLM can handle a wide class of distributions called an exponential distribution family, where we have

$$f(E[y_i]) = f(\mu_i) = \mathbf{X}_i\boldsymbol{\beta} \tag{2.3.2}$$

Note that the relationship between μ_i and $\mathbf{X}_i\boldsymbol{\beta}$ are modeled by nonlinear function $f(\bullet)$. The function $f(\bullet)$ is called a link function, and this kind of model is called a generalized linear model. The GLM has the following characteristics:

[1] Dependent variable y_i follows a distribution belonging to the exponential distribution group.

[2] $f(\mu_i)$ and $\mathbf{X}_i\boldsymbol{\beta}$ have a linear relationship.

Poisson distribution and binomial distribution, in addition to the normal distribution, are well-known distributions belonging to exponential distribution family. Commonly used link functions differ, depending on the

[1] For the sake of simplicity, we do not distinguish between the stochastic variable Y_i and its observation y_i.

distribution that we assume. For example, a logarithmic link function is generally used for Poisson distribution and its generalization, negative binominal distribution. These commonly used link functions are called canonical link functions, and are convenient for practical use because the maximum likelihood estimates of parameters can easily be calculated by applying the iterative reweighted least squares (IRLS) method.

In the following, as an example of the GLM, we explain the Poisson regression model, which is often used in spatial statistics. Now, let y_i be the number of occurrences of an event. Events $\{y_1, \ldots, y_N\}$ are assumed to be mutually independent, and it is assumed that the frequency of an event's occurrence is very small. Given such a situation, the probability distribution of y_i is

$$y_i \sim Poisson(\mu_i), \tag{2.3.3}$$

and a Poisson distribution can approximate this situation well. Famous examples of phenomena that can be described by a Poisson distribution include the number of spelling mistakes when writing a page of text, and the number of traffic fatalities in a year in a given region. The probability mass function of the Poisson distribution is given by

$$p(y_i|\mu_i) = \frac{\mu_i^{y_i} \exp(-\mu_i)}{y_i!}, \tag{2.3.4}$$

where $y_i!$ denotes the factorial of y_i. In the Poisson distribution, y_i takes an infinite value with $y_i \in \{0,1,2,\ldots,\infty\}$. An important property of the Poisson distribution is that expected value = variance = μ_i, and since the shape of the distribution is defined by one parameter, μ_i, it has the advantage of being extremely easy to use. In actual data, however, variance > expected value, termed overdispersion, often occurs. In this case it is possible to use a negative binomial distribution that extends the Poisson distribution and assumes that the variations of μ_i follow the gamma distribution. The probability mass function of the negative binomial distribution is given by

$$p(y_i|\mu_i) = \frac{\Gamma(y_i + \upsilon^{-1})}{y_i!\Gamma(\upsilon^{-1})} \left(\frac{\upsilon^{-1}}{\upsilon^{-1} + \mu_i}\right)^{\upsilon^{-1}} \left(\frac{\mu_i}{\upsilon^{-1} + \mu_i}\right)^{y_i}, \tag{2.3.5}$$

and the expected value and variance are μ_i and $\mu_i + \upsilon\mu_i^2$, respectively. It is therefore possible to adjust overdispersion using the parameter υ.

In the Poisson (or negative binomial) distribution, the logarithmic function

$$\ln(\mu_i) = \mathbf{X}_i\boldsymbol{\beta} \tag{2.3.6}$$

is often used as a link function. It follows the mean component given as

$$\mu_i = \exp(\mathbf{X}_i\boldsymbol{\beta}) = \exp\left(\beta_1 + x_{2,i}\beta_2 + \ldots + x_{K,i}\beta_K\right) \tag{2.3.7}$$

Here, we introduce offset term to Eq. (2.3.7). Let n_i be the arbitral total number (e.g., population) of geographical unit i ($i = 1, \ldots, N$), and let y_i be the number of occurrences of events. Then it is natural to think that the larger n_i becomes, the number of event occurrences increases. However, if we set a dependent variable as a dimensionless quantity (i.e., ratio), it is no longer possible to distinguish 1/2 from 2/4 (i.e., information is lost), and it becomes unclear what kind of distribution we should assume for this ratio variable. As an alternative, therefore, we can assume

$$\mu_i = n_i \exp\left(\beta_1 + x_{2,i}\beta_2 + \ldots + x_{K,i}\beta_K\right), \tag{2.3.8}$$

where the expected value of y_i, μ_i, is modeled such that it is proportional to n_i. Taking the natural logarithm of both sides and in vector form, we obtain

$$\ln\mu_i = \ln n_i + \mathbf{X}_i\boldsymbol{\beta}, \tag{2.3.9}$$

where $\ln n_i$ is a constant called an offset term, which is a *known* constant included in the model, and can be easily incorporated in parameter estimation. Parameter $\boldsymbol{\beta}$ of the Poisson regression model can be estimated using the maximum likelihood method via the IRLS method. For more details about GLM, see, for example, Wood (2017).

2.4 The additive model

As we have discussed, the GLM is a *generalized* linear model, in the sense that $E(y_i)$ and linear component $\mathbf{X}_i\boldsymbol{\beta}$ are related using a nonlinear function $f(\bullet)$. However, it is possible that $f(\mu_i)$ and the explanatory variables have nonlinear relationships. Hence natural extension is

$$f(\mu_i) = g(\mathbf{X}_i\boldsymbol{\beta}), \tag{2.4.1}$$

where $g(\bullet)$ is a nonlinear function. Fig. 2.4.1 shows a case in which Seya et al. (2011) constructed a hedonic model in which rent data for Tokyo's 23 wards in FY 2006 were regressed on several explanatory variables, and for one of the explanatory variables, the logarithm of occupied area, a partial residual plot (one index of a nonlinearity judgment by plotting $x_{k,i}\widehat{\beta}_k + \widehat{\varepsilon}_i$ with respect to explanatory variable $x_{k,i}$) was created. From this figure, it can

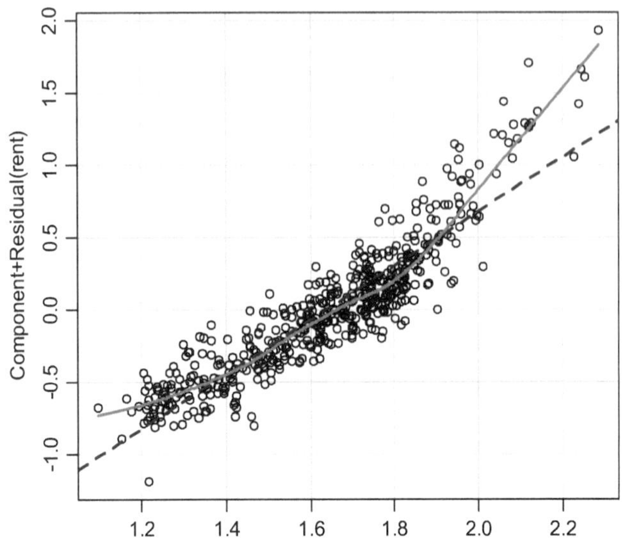

Figure 2.4.1 Partial residual plot (y axis:$x_{k,i}\widehat{\beta}_{k,i} + \widehat{\varepsilon}_i$, x axis:$x_{k,i}$). The R function crPlots (car package) was used for the plot. *Dotted line*: linear estimator; *solid line*: LOESS estimator (smoothing).

be seen that the relationship with rent changes significantly around 1.9 (60—80 m^2 occupied area). Where this kind of nonlinearity exists, in the CLR model, the relationship between the explanatory variable and the data cannot be expressed well.

Now, among the nonlinear functions $g(\bullet)$, a model that expresses the sum of several smoothing functions like

$$f(\mu_i) = \mathbf{X}_i\boldsymbol{\beta} + g_1(x_{1i}) + g_2(x_{2i}) + \ldots, \tag{2.4.2}$$

is comparatively easy to handle, and is termed the generalized additive model (Hastie and Tibshirani, 1990; Wood, 2017). Since this model contains both the parametric term $\mathbf{X}_i\boldsymbol{\beta}$, and the nonparametric term $g_1(x_{1,i})+g_2(x_{2,i})+\ldots$, it can be understood to be a semiparametric regression model (Ruppert et al., 2003). Of these, the nonparametric terms are often specified to use penalized spline functions.

Next, for the sake of simplicity, we will explain the additive model (AM), assuming that $f(\bullet)$ itself is linear ($f(\mu_i) = \mu_i$), and also we assume the case of two explanatory variables.

When data (y_i; $x_{1,i}$; $x_{2,i}$) is obtained, the AM can be formulated as follows:

$$y_i = \beta_0 + x_{1,i}\beta_1 + x_{2,i}\beta_2 + g_1\left(x_{1,i}\right) + g_2\left(x_{2,i}\right) + \varepsilon_i, \tag{2.4.3}$$

where g_1 and g_2 are smoothing functions, respectively, and ε_i is the independent and identically distributed error term. When a smoothing function is specified by a linear spline function, the following equation is obtained:

$$y_i = \beta_0 + x_{1,i}\beta_1 + x_{2,i}\beta_2 + \sum_{h=1}^{Q_1} b_{1,h}\left(x_{1,i} - \kappa_{1,h}\right)_+ \\ + \sum_{h=1}^{Q_2} b_{2,h}\left(x_{2,i} - \kappa_{2,h}\right)_+ + \varepsilon_i, \tag{2.4.4}$$

where $(x-\kappa)_+$ is an operator that is 0 for $x<\kappa$, and $x-\kappa$ for $x \geq \kappa$, and κ expresses a "not." $b_{1,h}$ and $b_{2,h}$ are the corresponding parameters. For example, let us suppose that the relationship between $x_1$and$y$ changes greatly in the vicinity of $x_1 = 0.6$. In this case, with $\kappa_1 = 0.6$, for values less or greater than 0.6, we should attach a difference in the relationship between $x_1$and y (see Ruppert et al., 2003, for an explanation of the figure on this point). Since multiple such points can usually be seen, multiple nots are placed corresponding to each explanatory variable, respectively. In the example of Eq. (2.4.4), Q_1 nots are allocated to the variable x_1, and Q_2 nots are allocated to variable x_2. If there are too many nots Q_1 and Q_2, issues of overfitting the data may occur. Hence we can estimate parameters using the penalized least squares method with restrictions on possible values of $b_{1,h}$ and $b_{2,h}$. There are various methods for this restriction; for example, $\max\left|b_{1,h}\right|\langle\overline{m}, \sum\left|b_{1,h}\right| < \overline{m}, \sum b_{1,h}^2 < \overline{m}(\overline{m}$ is an appropriate constant). The third restriction may lead to a type of ridge estimator.

Expressing Eq. (2.4.4) in a matrix form, we obtain:

$$\mathbf{y} = \mathbf{X}\boldsymbol{\beta} + \mathbf{Z}\mathbf{b} + \boldsymbol{\varepsilon}, \tag{2.4.5}$$

where

$$\mathbf{X} = \begin{bmatrix} 1 & x_{1,1} & x_{2,1} \\ \vdots & \vdots & \vdots \\ 1 & x_{1,N} & x_{2,N} \end{bmatrix}; \ \boldsymbol{\beta} = \left[\beta_0; \beta_1; \beta_2\right]',$$

$$\mathbf{b} = \left[b_{1,1}, \ldots, b_{1,Q_1}; b_{2,1}, \ldots, b_{2,Q_2}\right]'; \ \mathbf{Z} = \left[\mathbf{Z}_1; \mathbf{Z}_2\right],$$

$$\mathbf{Z}_1 = \begin{bmatrix} (x_{1,1}-\kappa_{1,1})_+ & \cdots & (x_{1,1}-\kappa_{1,Q_1})_+ \\ \vdots & \ddots & \vdots \\ (x_{1,N}-\kappa_{1,1})_+ & \cdots & (x_{1,N}-\kappa_{1,Q_1})_+ \end{bmatrix};$$

$$\mathbf{Z}_2 = \begin{bmatrix} (x_{2,1}-\kappa_{2,1})_+ & \cdots & (x_{2,1}-\kappa_{2,Q_2})_+ \\ \vdots & \ddots & \vdots \\ (x_{2,N}-\kappa_{2,1})_+ & \cdots & (x_{2,N}-\kappa_{2,Q_2})_+ \end{bmatrix}.$$

Define $\mathbf{R} \equiv [\mathbf{X};\mathbf{Z}]$; $\ddot{\boldsymbol{\beta}} \equiv [\boldsymbol{\beta}'; \mathbf{b}']'$, and a matrix $\boldsymbol{D}$ as

$$\mathbf{D} = \begin{pmatrix} \mathbf{O}_{[2\times 2]} & \mathbf{O}_{[2\times Q_1]} & \mathbf{O}_{[2\times Q_2]} \\ \mathbf{O}_{[Q_1\times 2]} & \widetilde{\lambda}_1^2 \times \mathbf{I}_{[Q_1\times Q_1]} & \mathbf{O}_{[Q_1\times Q_2]} \\ \mathbf{O}_{[Q_2\times 2]} & \mathbf{O}_{[Q_2\times Q_1]} & \widetilde{\lambda}_2^2 \times \mathbf{I}_{[Q_2\times Q_2]} \end{pmatrix}, \tag{2.4.6}$$

where $\widetilde{\lambda}_1, \widetilde{\lambda}_2 \geq 0$ denotes the Lagrangian multipliers. The penalized least squares estimate for $\ddot{\boldsymbol{\beta}}$ can be obtained by minimizing

$$||\mathbf{y} - \mathbf{R}\ddot{\boldsymbol{\beta}}||^2 + \ddot{\boldsymbol{\beta}}'\mathbf{D}\ddot{\boldsymbol{\beta}}, \tag{2.4.7}$$

where $||\,.\,||$ denotes a vector norm. The optimization yields

$$\widehat{\ddot{\boldsymbol{\beta}}}_{\widetilde{\lambda}} = (\mathbf{R}'\mathbf{R} + \mathbf{D})^{-1}\mathbf{R}'\mathbf{y}. \tag{2.4.8}$$

When $\widetilde{\lambda}_1$ (or $\widetilde{\lambda}_2$) takes a value close to 0, overfitting the data tends to occur. When the value takes a relatively large value, on the other hand, we cannot fully capture the nonlinearity between x_1(or x_2) and y. Hence the calibration of these parameters are very important.

Here, let's consider substituting fixed effects $b_{1,h}$ and $b_{2,h}$ with random effects $u_{1,h} \sim i.i.d.N(0, \sigma_{1u}^2)$ and $u_{2,h} \sim i.i.d.N(0, \sigma_{2u}^2)$, respectively, and formalizing the model as a mixed model. This will smoothen the linear spline function, and avoid data overfitting (Ruppert et al., 2003, p.109). Moreover, a further advantage is that there are many statistical packages for mixed models. Substituting $b_{1,h}$, $b_{2,h}$ by $u_{1,h}$, $u_{2,\,h}$ in Eq. (2.4.7) and dividing by σ_ε^2, we obtain

$$\frac{1}{\sigma_\varepsilon^2}||\mathbf{y} - \mathbf{X}\boldsymbol{\beta} - \mathbf{Z}\mathbf{u}||^2 + \frac{\widetilde{\lambda}_1^2}{\sigma_\varepsilon^2}||\mathbf{u}_1||^2 + \frac{\widetilde{\lambda}_2^2}{\sigma_\varepsilon^2}||\mathbf{u}_2||^2, \tag{2.4.9}$$

where $\mathbf{u} = [\mathbf{u}'_1; \mathbf{u}'_2]'$, $\mathbf{u}_1 = [u_{1,1}, \ldots, u_{1,Q_1}]'$, and$\mathbf{u}_2 = [u_{2,1}, \ldots, u_{2,Q_2}]'$. Here, if we look at $\sigma^2_{1u} = \sigma^2_\varepsilon / \tilde{\lambda}^2_1$, $\sigma^2_{2u} = \sigma^2_\varepsilon / \tilde{\lambda}^2_2$, Eq. (2.4.9) can be no other than the general criterion for obtaining the best linear unbiased predictor (BLUP) of $\boldsymbol{\beta}$ and $\mathbf{u}$ (Ruppert et al., 2003, p.100). In other words, the penalized least squares method of Eq. (2.4.9) is equivalent to finding the BLUP in the mixed model. Hence let us reconstruct the model to be the standard form of the mixed model as

$$\mathbf{y} = \mathbf{X}\boldsymbol{\beta} + \mathbf{Z}\mathbf{u} + \boldsymbol{\varepsilon} = \mathbf{R}\ddot{\boldsymbol{\beta}} + \boldsymbol{\varepsilon}, \tag{2.4.10}$$

$$Cov\begin{bmatrix} \mathbf{u} \\ \boldsymbol{\varepsilon} \end{bmatrix} = \begin{bmatrix} \sigma^2_{1,u}\mathbf{I}_{[Q_1]} & \mathbf{O} & \mathbf{O} \\ \mathbf{O} & \sigma^2_{2,u}\mathbf{I}_{[Q_2]} & \mathbf{O} \\ \mathbf{O} & \mathbf{O} & \sigma^2_\varepsilon \mathbf{I}_{[n]} \end{bmatrix}. \tag{2.4.11}$$

We can estimate $\ddot{\boldsymbol{\beta}}$ with, for instance, the REML (Ruppert et al., 2003, pp.100–101) method. The estimator of $\ddot{\boldsymbol{\beta}}$ can be obtained as

$$\hat{\ddot{\boldsymbol{\beta}}}_{\tilde{\lambda}} = (\mathbf{R}'\mathbf{R} + \mathbf{D})^{-1}\mathbf{R}'\mathbf{y}. \tag{2.4.12}$$

Here, as in the hat matrix in the linear regression model, the matrix $\mathbf{R}(\mathbf{R}'\mathbf{R} + \mathbf{D})^{-1}\mathbf{R}'$, converts an observed value into a fitted value, and its trace gives a degree of freedom to the model. This value can be interpreted as a measure of smoothness of the smoothing function, and it can also be obtained for each explanatory variable (Ruppert et al., 2003, pp.175–176). In this way, the degree of nonlinearity can be quantified. Moreover, whether nonlinearity ought to be considered can be judged statistically using a likelihood ratio test, which is possible to implement using the standard mixed model software.

The AM is a model that forms the foundation of the geo-additive model, which is sometimes used for modeling large spatial data (see Chapter 4). Note that geo-additive model is an extension of the GLM framework using AM; please refer to Wood (2017) in regard to this.

2.5 The basics of Bayesian statistics

2.5.1 Bayes' theorem

In standard statistics (frequentism), we try to estimate parameters by assuming that they have a specific fixed value. However, in the Bayesian statistical framework, we believe parameters to have a (probability) distribution.

This distribution, called a prior distribution, needs to be given to the analyst in advance. In Bayesian estimation, we obtain the posterior distributions by updating the prior distributions using observed data based on the Bayes' theorem, and performing a statistical inference (Bayesian inference) based on that posterior distribution. Since the choice of prior distributions affect the results of parameter estimation there is a position that we should, as much as possible, opt to give noninformative prior distributions. Since now, because of the development of computation techniques including the Markov chain Monte Carlo method (MCMC) and the Hamiltonian Monte Carlo, even when given noninformative prior distributions, it is possible to derive and evaluate the posterior distributions through simulation.

When taking the prior probability density function of parameter $\boldsymbol{\theta}$ ($\boldsymbol{\theta} \subset \Re^J$) to be $p(\boldsymbol{\theta})$, and the likelihood function to be $p(\mathbf{y}|\boldsymbol{\theta})$, the posterior probability density function of $\boldsymbol{\theta}$ is obtained as

$$p(\boldsymbol{\theta}|\mathbf{y}) = \frac{p(\boldsymbol{\theta}, \mathbf{y})}{\int p(\boldsymbol{\theta}, \mathbf{y}) d\boldsymbol{\theta}} = \frac{p(\mathbf{y}|\boldsymbol{\theta})p(\boldsymbol{\theta})}{m(\mathbf{y})} \propto p(\mathbf{y}|\boldsymbol{\theta})p(\boldsymbol{\theta}), \tag{2.5.1}$$

where $p(\boldsymbol{\theta}|\mathbf{y})$ incorporates all prior information and data in the form of the prior distribution and likelihood function, respectively. The $m(\mathbf{y}) = \int p(\boldsymbol{\theta},\mathbf{y}) d\boldsymbol{\theta}$ term is a scaling constant, representing the marginal probability density function of $\mathbf{y}$. Since this term is often difficult to evaluate analytically, and does not depend on $\boldsymbol{\theta}$; it is often abbreviated as in Eq. (2.5.1). In Bayesian estimation, it is possible to perform flexible modeling by incorporating prior beliefs and knowledge about parameters into the model through the prior distribution in this way. In fact, there are also approaches to modeling spatial autocorrelation through prior distribution (see Congdon, 2010).

2.5.2 The Markov chain Monte Carlo method

After obtaining the posterior distribution for $\boldsymbol{\theta}$, statistical inferences may be made about the parameters. To that end, when taking the parameter of interest to be θ_j, it is necessary to use integral calculus to remove nuisance parameters $\boldsymbol{\theta}_{-j}$, in which we have no interest. In this way we obtain a marginal probability density function, such that

$$p(\theta_j|\mathbf{y}) = \int p(\boldsymbol{\theta}|\mathbf{y}) d\boldsymbol{\theta}_{-j}. \tag{2.5.2}$$

By using this marginal probability density, point estimation/interval estimation for $\theta_j$can be performed. Unlike standard statistics, although the obtained parameters have a distribution, there are many cases where the point estimate $\widehat{\theta}_j$is of our interest. For instance, the average, median mode of the marginal posterior distribution is used as the point estimate value. For interval estimation, we can use the Bayesian credible interval $100(1-\alpha)\%$ for example. When $\alpha = 0.05$, the credible interval indicates that parameter $\widehat{\theta}_j$ is included in the interval (l, m) with 95% probability. This concept is more intuitive and easier to understand than confidence intervals in frequentism. In the formula, we define

$$\Pr\left(l < \widehat{\theta}_j < m\right) = \int_l^m p\left(\widehat{\theta}_j | \mathbf{y}\right) d\theta_j = 1 - \alpha, \quad 0 < \alpha < 1. \tag{2.5.3}$$

Parameter inference in the regression model (significance testing) is performed by asking whether or not 0 is included in the credible interval. For example, looking at the 95% credible interval, if $(0.5 < \widehat{\theta}_j < 1.0)$, since 0 is not included within the credible interval, we can judge the parameter as being positively significant. However, since multiple integrations of Eq. (2.5.2) are difficult to perform where $\boldsymbol{\theta}$ has large dimensions, an approximation calculation is often necessary. Various Monte Carlo integration methods have been proposed to date,[2] and in particular, the MCMC method Gelfand and Smith (1990) brought to the statistical sciences has been an epoch-defining method that can efficiently evaluate high-dimensional integration, contributing greatly to the development and practical implementation of Bayesian statistics[3].

The MCMC method, as the name suggests, is a Monte Carlo method using a Markov chain. Prior to the MCMC method, many methods were based on independent sampling from the distribution; however, the MCMC method uses the Monte Carlo method for sample sequences with serial correlation. Here, a Markov chain is used to generate a sample series with a serial correlation. In Markov chains, there is a property that, when repeated a sufficient number of times from an appropriate initial value, the distribution of stochastic samples converges on an invariant distribution under regular conditions. Therefore, by constructing a Markov chain such that this invariant distribution becomes a posterior distribution, stochastic samples of the Markov chain can be used as probability samples from the posterior distribution. Representative algorithms include the Gibbs sampler and the Metropolis–Hastings (MH) algorithm. We explain these next.

[2] Rue and Martino's (2007) integrated nested Laplace approximation method for function approximation without simulation has also seen major development in recent years.

[3] In fact, the first author, Professor Alan Gelfand, is a prominent spatial statistician.

The Gibbs sampler is an algorithm for when a full conditional distribution is available. When the probability density function of the posterior distribution is taken to be $p(\boldsymbol{\theta}|\mathbf{y})$, the density function of the conditional posterior distribution can be expressed as follows:

$$\begin{gathered} p(\theta_1|\mathbf{y},\theta_2,\ldots,\theta_J) \\ p(\theta_2|\mathbf{y},\theta_1,\theta_3,\ldots,\theta_J) \\ \vdots \\ p(\theta_J|\mathbf{y},\theta_1,\ldots,\theta_{J-1}) \end{gathered} \tag{2.5.4}$$

When it is possible to generate random samples from each conditional distribution, we can use the Gibbs sampler as follows:

(0) Set the initial value: $\boldsymbol{\theta}^{(0)} = \left(\theta_1^{(0)}, \theta_2^{(0)}, \ldots, \theta_J^{(0)}\right)'$

(1) **for** $t = 1$ to T **do**

(2) sample $\theta_1^{(t+1)} \sim p\left(\theta_1 \middle| \mathbf{y}, \theta_2^{(t)}, \ldots, \theta_J^{(t)}\right)$

(3) sample $\theta_2^{(t+1)} \sim p\left(\theta_2 \middle| \mathbf{y}, \theta_1^{(t+1)}, \theta_3^{(t)}, \ldots, \theta_J^{(t)}\right)$

(4) ...

(5) sample $\theta_J^{(t+1)} \sim p\left(\theta_J \middle| \mathbf{y}, \theta_1^{(t+1)}, \ldots, \theta_{J-1}^{(t+1)}\right)$

(6) $\boldsymbol{\theta}^{(t+1)} \leftarrow \left(\theta_1^{(t+1)}, \theta_2^{(t+1)}, \ldots, \theta_J^{(t+1)}\right)'$

(7) **end for**

Here, when $T \to \infty$, the empirical distribution of the sample series $\left(\theta_1^{(t)}, \theta_2^{(t)}, \ldots, \theta_J^{(t)}\right)', t = 1, \ldots, T$, converges on a joint distribution (posterior distribution). Now, by extracting the sample series $\left(\theta_j^{(t)}\right), t = 1, \ldots, T$ for a given parameter θ_j, we can calculate a point estimate and credible interval. In practice, the average and standard deviation are obtained for the part that excludes the period that depends on the initial value, termed the burn-in period.

Where sampling from the conditional posterior distribution cannot be done simply, the MH algorithm is used. The MH algorithm is a method of sampling from a proposal distribution $q(\boldsymbol{\theta}^\star|\boldsymbol{\theta}^{(t-1)})$, which approximates in lieu of a conditional posterior distribution, where the generation of random numbers is difficult. In instances where the proposal distribution is a symmetric distribution such as a normal distribution, since

$q\left(\boldsymbol{\theta}^*\middle|\boldsymbol{\theta}_{(t-1)}\right) = q\left(\boldsymbol{\theta}_{(t-1)}\middle|\boldsymbol{\theta}^*\right)$ is established, the simpler Metropolis algorithm can be used. The Metropolis algorithm can be described as follows:

(0) Set the initial value: $\boldsymbol{\theta}^{(0)} = \left(\theta_1^{(0)}, \theta_2^{(0)}, \ldots, \theta_J^{(0)}\right)'$

(1) **for** $t = 1$ to T **do**

(2) sample $\left(\boldsymbol{\theta}^* \text{ from proposal } q\left(\boldsymbol{\theta}^*\middle|\boldsymbol{\theta}_{(t-1)}\right)\right)$

(3) compute ratio $\alpha = \frac{p(\boldsymbol{\theta}^*|\mathbf{y})}{p\left(\boldsymbol{\theta}^{(t-1)}\middle|\mathbf{y}\right)} = \exp\left[\ln\left(p\left(\boldsymbol{\theta}^*\middle|\mathbf{y}\right) - \ln p\left(\boldsymbol{\theta}^{(t-1)}\middle|\mathbf{y}\right)\right]\right.$

(4) if $\alpha \geq 1$,set $\boldsymbol{\theta}^{(t)} = \boldsymbol{\theta}^\star$
else if $\alpha < 1$, set $\boldsymbol{\theta}^{(t)} = \begin{cases} \boldsymbol{\theta}^* & \text{with probability: } \alpha \\ \boldsymbol{\theta}^{(t-1)} & \text{with probability: } (1-\alpha) \end{cases}$

(5) **end if**

(6) **end for**

Since we usually wish to sample many high-probability points in the probability density function, the movement to increase the value of the posterior distribution is accepted with a probability of 1. However, if we reject all movements that decrease the value of the posterior probability distribution, we will be unable to move from the position with the highest probability. Hence we also accept this move with an acceptance ratio α. The ratio should be about 0.2–0.4 (e.g., Brooks et al., 2011, p.424); however, care is required, as this depends on the dimensions of $\boldsymbol{\theta}$.

The normal distribution $q\left(\boldsymbol{\theta}^*\middle|\boldsymbol{\theta}_{(t-1)}\right) = N\left(\boldsymbol{\theta}^*\middle|\boldsymbol{\theta}^{(t-1)}, \mathbf{E}_0\right)$ is often used as the proposal distribution. However, because it is difficult to find a proposal distribution that closely approximates a posterior distribution where there are multiple dimensions, it is more practical to assume a one-dimensional proposal distribution q_j for each parameter, like the Gibbs sampler. For this purpose, the random walk process can be used. Using the random walk process, the proposal distribution $q\left(\theta_j^*\middle|\theta_j^{(t-1)}\right)$ relating to a given parameter θ_j can be expressed thus:

$$q\left(\theta_j^*\middle|\theta_j^{(t-1)}\right) = N\left(\theta_j^*\middle|\theta_j^{(t-1)}, \xi^2\right), \tag{2.5.5}$$

where ξ^2 is an important parameter that determines the acceptance ratio, and is adjusted within the algorithm such that it approaches the appropriate acceptance ratio. For instance if we wish the acceptance ratio to be about 0.4, if the acceptance ratio falls below 0.3, ξ^2 is multiplied by 0.9, and if it exceeds 0.5, is multiplied by 1.1, during the burn-in period (Han and Lee, 2013).

Where it is desirable that the proposal distribution be symmetrical, this kind of random walk process can be used; however, there are many instances where the normal distribution does not match the proposal distribution, such as when there is a positive limit on the state space that the parameter can take (Banerjee et al., 2014). In this case, it is necessary for the proposal distribution to use the asymmetric $q\left(\boldsymbol{\theta}^*\middle|\boldsymbol{\theta}_{(t-1)}\right)$. We use the MH algorithm where it is not symmetrical, which is the generalization of the Metropolis algorithm. The acceptance ratio in the MH algorithm is given by:

$$\alpha = \frac{p(\boldsymbol{\theta}^*|\mathbf{y})q\left(\boldsymbol{\theta}^{(t-1)}\middle|\boldsymbol{\theta}^*\right)}{p\left(\boldsymbol{\theta}^{(t-1)}\middle|\mathbf{y}\right)q\left(\boldsymbol{\theta}^*\middle|\boldsymbol{\theta}^{(t-1)}\right)}. \tag{2.5.6}$$

For details concerning the MCMC method, refer to Brooks et al. (2011).

2.5.3 Bayesian estimation of the classical linear regression model

In this section, we explain Bayesian estimation, taking the CLR model as an example, as follows:

$$\mathbf{y} \sim N\left(\mathbf{X}\boldsymbol{\beta}, \sigma_\varepsilon^2\mathbf{I}\right). \tag{2.5.7}$$

The likelihood of this regression model is given by

$$\begin{aligned} p\left(\mathbf{y}\middle|\boldsymbol{\beta}, \sigma_\varepsilon^2\right) &= \prod_{i=1}^{N} \frac{1}{\sqrt{2\pi\sigma_\varepsilon^2}}\exp\left[-\frac{(y_i - \mathbf{X}_i\boldsymbol{\beta})^2}{2\sigma_\varepsilon^2}\right] \\ &\propto \left(\sigma_\varepsilon^2\right)^{-N/2}\exp\left[-\frac{(\mathbf{y}-\mathbf{X}\boldsymbol{\beta})'(\mathbf{y}-\mathbf{X}\boldsymbol{\beta})}{2\sigma_\varepsilon^2}\right] \end{aligned} \tag{2.5.8}$$

Here, with $\mathbf{y} - \mathbf{X}\beta = \left(\mathbf{y} - \mathbf{X}\widehat{\boldsymbol{\beta}}\right) + \left(\mathbf{X}\widehat{\boldsymbol{\beta}} - \mathbf{X}\beta\right) = \widehat{\boldsymbol{\varepsilon}} + \mathbf{X}\left(\widehat{\boldsymbol{\beta}} - \boldsymbol{\beta}\right)$ and $\mathbf{X}'\widehat{\boldsymbol{\varepsilon}} = \mathbf{0}$, we obtain

$$\begin{aligned} &(\mathbf{y}-\mathbf{X}\boldsymbol{\beta})'(\mathbf{y}-\mathbf{X}\boldsymbol{\beta}) \\ &= \left[\widehat{\boldsymbol{\varepsilon}} + \mathbf{X}\left(\widehat{\boldsymbol{\beta}} - \boldsymbol{\beta}\right)\right]'\left[\widehat{\boldsymbol{\varepsilon}} + \mathbf{X}\left(\widehat{\boldsymbol{\beta}} - \boldsymbol{\beta}\right)\right] \\ &= \widehat{\boldsymbol{\varepsilon}}'\widehat{\boldsymbol{\varepsilon}} + \left(\boldsymbol{\beta} - \widehat{\boldsymbol{\beta}}\right)'\mathbf{X}'\mathbf{X}\left(\boldsymbol{\beta} - \widehat{\boldsymbol{\beta}}\right) \\ &= (N-K)s^2 + \left(\boldsymbol{\beta} - \widehat{\boldsymbol{\beta}}\right)'\mathbf{X}'\mathbf{X}\left(\boldsymbol{\beta} - \widehat{\boldsymbol{\beta}}\right), \end{aligned} \tag{2.5.9}$$

where $\widehat{\boldsymbol{\beta}} = (\mathbf{X}'\mathbf{X})^{-1}\mathbf{X}'\mathbf{y}$, $s^2 = (N-K)^{-1}\left(\mathbf{y}-\mathbf{X}\widehat{\boldsymbol{\beta}}\right)'\left(\mathbf{y}-\mathbf{X}\widehat{\boldsymbol{\beta}}\right)$. By substituting Eq. (2.5.9) into Eq. (2.5.8) we obtain

$$p(\mathbf{y}|\boldsymbol{\beta},\sigma_\varepsilon^2) \propto (\sigma_\varepsilon^2)^{-n/2}\exp\left[-\frac{(N-K)s^2 + \left(\boldsymbol{\beta}-\widehat{\boldsymbol{\beta}}\right)'\mathbf{X}'\mathbf{X}\left(\boldsymbol{\beta}-\widehat{\boldsymbol{\beta}}\right)}{2\sigma_\varepsilon^2}\right] \tag{2.5.10}$$

The posterior distribution can be obtained by combining this likelihood with the prior distribution.

Useful prior distributions, known as conjugate prior distributions, are often used. That is, if the posterior distributions are in the same probability distribution family as the prior probability distribution, the prior is called as conjugate. Now, for the prior distributions of $\boldsymbol{\beta}$ and σ_ε^2, we assume

$$p(\boldsymbol{\beta},\sigma_\varepsilon^2) = p(\boldsymbol{\beta}|\sigma_\varepsilon^2)p(\sigma_\varepsilon^2). \tag{2.5.11}$$

Then, we assume that the conditional prior probability of $\boldsymbol{\beta}$ when given $\sigma_\varepsilon^2$is the normal distribution $\boldsymbol{\beta}|\sigma_\varepsilon^2 \sim N(\boldsymbol{\beta}_0, \sigma_\varepsilon^2\mathbf{E}_0^{-1})$, and that the prior distribution of σ_ε^2 follows the inverse gamma distribution $\sigma_\varepsilon^2 \sim IG(a_0/2, b_0/2)$. Their density functions are given by

$$p(\boldsymbol{\beta}|\sigma_\varepsilon^2) = \frac{1}{(2\pi\sigma_\varepsilon^2)^{k/2}}|\mathbf{E}_0|^{1/2}\exp\left[-\frac{(\boldsymbol{\beta}-\boldsymbol{\beta}_0)'\mathbf{E}_0(\boldsymbol{\beta}-\boldsymbol{\beta}_0)}{2\sigma_\varepsilon^2}\right]; \tag{2.5.12}$$

$$p(\sigma_\varepsilon^2) = \frac{(b_0/2)^{(a_0/2)}}{\Gamma(a_0/2)}(\sigma_\varepsilon^2)^{-(a_0/2+1)}\exp\left(-\frac{b_0}{2\sigma_\varepsilon^2}\right), \tag{2.5.13}$$

respectively. According to Bayes' theorem, because the posterior probability density function becomes $p(\boldsymbol{\beta},\sigma_\varepsilon^2|\mathbf{y}) \propto p(\mathbf{y}|\boldsymbol{\beta},\sigma_\varepsilon^2)p(\boldsymbol{\beta}|\sigma_\varepsilon^2)p(\sigma_\varepsilon^2)$, through a simple calculation, the conditional posterior distributions for each parameter are obtained as

$$\boldsymbol{\beta}|\sigma_\varepsilon^2, \mathbf{y} \sim N(\widetilde{\boldsymbol{\beta}}, \sigma_\varepsilon^2\widetilde{\mathbf{E}}); \tag{2.5.14}$$

$$\sigma_\varepsilon^2|\mathbf{y} \sim IG\left(\widetilde{a}/2, \widetilde{b}/2\right), \tag{2.5.15}$$

where $\widetilde{\boldsymbol{\beta}} = (\mathbf{X}'\mathbf{X}+\mathbf{E}_0)^{-1}\left(\mathbf{X}'\mathbf{X}\widehat{\boldsymbol{\beta}} + \mathbf{E}_0\boldsymbol{\beta}_0\right)\widetilde{\mathbf{E}} = (\mathbf{X}'\mathbf{X}+\mathbf{E}_0)^{-1}\widetilde{a} = a_0 + N$, and $\widetilde{b} = b_0 + \left(N-K\right)s^2 + \left(\boldsymbol{\beta}_0 - \widehat{\boldsymbol{\beta}}\right)'\left[\left(\mathbf{X}'\mathbf{X}\right)^{-1} + \mathbf{E}_0^{-1}\right]^{-1}\left(\boldsymbol{\beta}_0 - \widehat{\boldsymbol{\beta}}\right)$.

Therefore, it is sufficient to perform the Gibbs Sampler based on these conditional distributions. Note that Bayesian estimation is a shrinkage estimator, in the sense that the OLS estimator is corrected to the direction toward average component in the prior distribution.

In these explanations, we assumed that $p(\boldsymbol{\beta}, \sigma_\varepsilon^2) = p(\boldsymbol{\beta}|\sigma_\varepsilon^2)p(\sigma_\varepsilon^2)$. Next, we assume an independent prior distribution as

$$p(\boldsymbol{\beta}, \sigma_\varepsilon^2) = p(\boldsymbol{\beta})p(\sigma_\varepsilon^2), \tag{2.5.16}$$

and we set

$$\boldsymbol{\beta} \sim N(\dot{\boldsymbol{\beta}}, \dot{\mathbf{E}}); \tag{2.5.17}$$

$$\sigma_\varepsilon^2 \sim IG\left(\dot{a}/2, \dot{b}\big/2\right), \tag{2.5.18}$$

Then, the conditional posterior distribution is given as

$$\boldsymbol{\beta}|\sigma_\varepsilon^2, \mathbf{y} \sim N(\ddot{\boldsymbol{\beta}}, \ddot{\mathbf{E}}); \tag{2.5.19}$$

$$\sigma_\varepsilon^2\Big|\boldsymbol{\beta}, \mathbf{y} \sim IG\left(\ddot{a}/2, \ddot{b}\big/2\right), \tag{2.5.20}$$

where $\ddot{\boldsymbol{\beta}} = \left[\sigma_\varepsilon^{-2}\mathbf{X}'\mathbf{X} + \dot{\mathbf{E}}_{-1}\right]^{-1}\left(\sigma_\varepsilon^{-2}\mathbf{X}'\mathbf{y} + \dot{\mathbf{E}}_{-1}\dot{\boldsymbol{\beta}}\right)$, $\ddot{\mathbf{E}} = \left[\sigma_\varepsilon^{-2}\mathbf{X}'\mathbf{X} + \dot{\mathbf{E}}_{-1}\right]^{-1}$, $\ddot{a} = \dot{a} + N$, and $\ddot{b} = \dot{b} + \left(\mathbf{y} - \mathbf{X}\boldsymbol{\beta}\right)'\left(\mathbf{y} - \mathbf{X}\boldsymbol{\beta}\right)$.

Lastly, with $p(\boldsymbol{\beta}, \sigma_\varepsilon^2) = p(\boldsymbol{\beta})p(\sigma_\varepsilon^2)$, we set noninformative priors as

$$p(\boldsymbol{\beta}) \propto 1; \tag{2.5.21}$$

$$p(\sigma_\varepsilon^2) \propto \frac{1}{\sigma_\varepsilon^2}. \tag{2.5.22}$$

With these priors, the conditional posterior distribution is given by

$$\boldsymbol{\beta}\Big|\sigma_\varepsilon^2, \mathbf{y} \sim N\left(\widehat{\boldsymbol{\beta}}, \sigma_\varepsilon^2(\mathbf{X}'\mathbf{X})^{-1}\right); \tag{2.5.23}$$

$$\sigma_\varepsilon^2|\mathbf{y} \sim IG\left((N-K)/2, (N-K)s^2/2\right). \tag{2.5.24}$$

References

Abadir, K., Magnus, J., 2002. Notation in econometrics: a proposal for a standard. The Econometrics Journal 5, 76–90.

Banerjee, S., Carlin, B.P., Gelfand, A.E., 2014. Hierarchical Modeling and Analysis for Spatial Data, second ed. Chapman & Hall/CRC, Boca Raton.

Brooks, S., Gelman, A., Jones, G., Meng, X.L. (Eds.), 2011. Handbook of Markov Chain Monte Carlo. Chapman and Hall/CRC, Boca Raton.

Congdon, P., 2010. Applied Bayesian Hierarchical Methods. Chapman and Hall/CRC, London.

Hayashi, F., 2000. Econometrics. Princeton Univ Pr.

Gelfand, A.E., Smith, A.F.M., 1990. Sampling-based approaches to calculating marginal densities. Journal of the American Statistical Association 85 (410), 398–409.

Han, X., Lee, L.F., 2013. Bayesian estimation and model selection for spatial Durbin error model with finite distributed lags. Regional Science and Urban Economics 43 (5), 816–837.

Hansen, L.P., 1982. Large sample properties of generalized methods of moments estimators. Econometrica 50 (4), 1029–1054.

Hastie, T., Tibshirani, R., 1990. Generalized Additive Models. Chapman & Hall/CRC, London.

Hayashi, F., 2000. Econometrics. Princeton University Press, Princeton.

LeSage, J.P., Pace, R.K., 2009. Introduction to Spatial Econometrics. Chapman & Hall/CRC, Boca Raton.

Rue, H., Martino, S., 2007. Approximate Bayesian inference for hierarchical Gaussian Markov random field models. Journal of statistical planning and inference 137 (10), 3177–3192.

Ruppert, D., Wand, M.P., Carroll, R.J., 2003. Semiparametric Regression (Cambridge Series in Statistical and Probabilistic Mathematics). Cambridge University Press, Cambridge.

Seya, H., Tsutsumi, M., Yoshida, Y., Kawaguchi, Y., 2011. Empirical comparison of the various spatial prediction models: in spatial econometrics, spatial statistics, and semiparametric statistics. Procedia-Social and Behavioral Sciences 21, 120–129.

Wood, S.N., 2017. Generalized Additive Models: An Introduction With R, second ed. Chapman & Hall/CRC, Boca Raton.

CHAPTER THREE

Global and local indicators of spatial associations

Hajime Seya
Departments of Civil Engineering, Kobe University, Kobe, Hyogo, Japan

Contents

3.1 Spatial weight matrix

In Chapter 2, we explained that bias may occur in standard errors of regression coefficient estimates when spatial autocorrelation and/or spatial heterogeneity exists in the residuals of the regression model. To confront this problem, we can use spatial econometric models. A spatial weight matrix, which we describe in the following subsections, is a central tool in spatial econometrics.

Spatial Analysis Using Big Data
ISBN: 978-0-12-813127-5
https://doi.org/10.1016/B978-0-12-813127-5.00003-5

3.1.1 Definition of the spatial weight matrix

The spatial weight matrix is a convenient and easy-to-understand tool for addressing spatial autocorrelation among data. Here, the data may be observed values or residuals obtained from a regression model. First, we introduce the concept of spatial weight matrix with the following definition.

The spatial weight matrix $\mathbf{W}$ of $N \times N$ describes the relationship between the data observed at i and j. Let S_i denote the neighborhood (label) set consisting of areas/points with dependency on area/point i. If there is a dependency between the data y_i and y_j observed at i and j (i.e., $j \in S_i$), the element of $\mathbf{W}$ is given as $w_{ij} \neq 0$; if there is no dependency (i.e., $j \notin S_i$), then it is given as $w_{ij} = 0$.

Let us take an example used in Seya and Tsutsumi (2014). We consider a simple case of five areas $\{1, 2, 3, 4, 5\}$ as shown in Fig. 3.1.1. The coordinates of the central point of each area are given by $\mathbf{s}_1, \mathbf{s}_2, \mathbf{s}_3, \mathbf{s}_4, \mathbf{s}_5$, respectively. Here, for instance, in the case of area 1, if only area 2 is dependent, the neighborhood set of area 1, say S_1 , becomes $\{2\}$ and ($w_{12} \neq 0$), and the remaining $\{3, 4, 5\}$ are excluded from the neighborhood set ($w_{1j} = 0,\ \mathit{for}\ j = 3, 4, 5$). Because a neighborhood set can be considered for each of the areas $\{1, 2, 3, 4, 5\}$, we consider a matrix $\mathbf{W}$ with i rows and j columns, and provide its elements as w_{ij}. To avoid it explaining itself, the elements of the diagonal matrix are usually 0.

Different from time series data, where unidirectional effects from old data → new data can be found, there is no clear *order* in cross-sectional

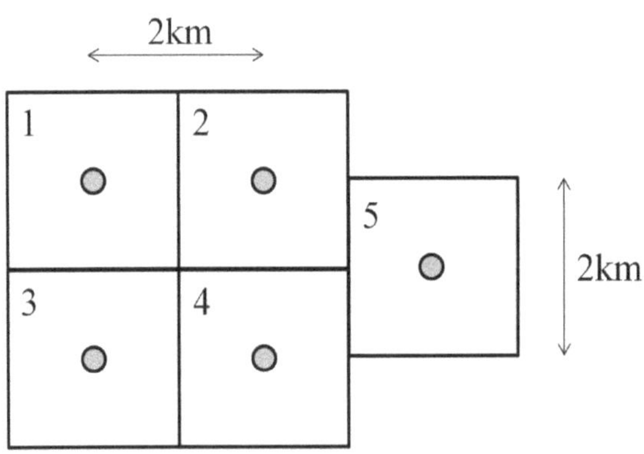

Figure 3.1.1 Virtual area.

spatial data. Hence we typically assume that the relationship is bidirectional, and it can be modeled by setting $\{w_{ij} \neq 0 \text{ and } w_{ji} \neq 0\}$. Of course we can also assume a unidirectional effect in an adhoc manner, for instance, as from large economy to small economy (Seya et al., 2012). So many ways of providing **W** can be considered, but those that are typically used in empirical research are as follows.[1]

- Contiguity-based **W**: it is 1 if the zone boundaries are in contact (shared) and 0 if not in contact (symmetric matrix).

Affecting area
1 2 3 4 5

$$\mathbf{W} = \begin{pmatrix} 0 & 1 & 1 & 0 & 0 \\ 1 & 0 & 0 & 1 & 1 \\ 1 & 0 & 0 & 1 & 0 \\ 0 & 1 & 1 & 0 & 1 \\ 0 & 1 & 0 & 1 & 0 \end{pmatrix}. \tag{3.1.1}$$

1 2 3 4 5 Affected area

- k nearest neighbor (kNN)-based **W**: point j might be less than or equal to kth nearest neighbor of point i, the weight is 1;otherwise, the weight is 0 (asymmetric matrix). For example, if $k = 2$, the following matrix can be obtained.

$$\mathbf{W} = \begin{pmatrix} 0 & 1 & 1 & 0 & 0 \\ 1 & 0 & 0 & 1 & 0 \\ 1 & 0 & 0 & 1 & 0 \\ 0 & 1 & 1 & 0 & 0 \\ 0 & 1 & 0 & 1 & 0 \end{pmatrix} \tag{3.1.2}$$

Notably, the **W** obtained using kNN is not necessarily a symmetrical matrix because i is not necessarily included in the area neighborhood k unit of area j, even if j is included in the area neighborhood k unit of area i. One more point to note is that, in the case of $k = 3$, $\{2, 4\}$ is included in the neighborhood set S_5 of area 5, but it is not obvious which of $\{1, 3\}$ should be included. Therefore, it is necessary to exogenously select one side, or make the selection including both (as weight 1/2, if needed).

[1] The typical spatial weight matrices listed here can be easily implemented using the R spdep package, GeoDa, etc.

- Inverse-distance-based **W** without a distance cutoff:

$$\mathbf{W}=\begin{pmatrix} 0 & 1/2 & 1/2 & 1/(2.83) & 1/(4.12) \\ 1/2 & 0 & 1/(2.83) & 1/2 & 1/(2.24) \\ 1/2 & 1/(2.83) & 0 & 1/2 & 1/(4.12) \\ 1/(2.83) & 1/2 & 1/2 & 0 & 1/(2.24) \\ 1/(4.12) & 1/(2.24) & 1/(4.12) & 1/(2.24) & 0 \end{pmatrix}$$

$$\approx\begin{pmatrix} 0 & 0.50 & 0.50 & 0.35 & 0.24 \\ 0.50 & 0 & 0.35 & 0.50 & 0.45 \\ 0.50 & 0.35 & 0 & 0.50 & 0.24 \\ 0.35 & 0.50 & 0.50 & 0 & 0.45 \\ 0.24 & 0.45 & 0.24 & 0.45 & 0 \end{pmatrix} \quad (3.1.3)$$

It is **W** that uses the inverse of the (typically Euclidean) distance, which does not set a cutoff that takes 0 when exceeding a certain distance. And it is a symmetrical matrix (in case of Euclidean). Here, we set $w_{ij} = (1/d_{ij})^{\alpha}$ with $\alpha = 1$, but in empirical analysis, $\alpha = 2$ is also used in an analogy of gravity models.

However, in recent years, when using a dense matrix in which$w_{ij} \neq 0$ for almost all elements, it is suggested that spatial process may be overly smoothed and spatial correlation parameters are systematically underestimated in the spatial econometric model. Hence it is necessary to pay attention when applying it (see Smith, 2009; Arbia et al., 2019).

- Inverse-distance-based **W** with a distance cutoff

It is **W** using the inverse of the (typically Euclidean) distance with a cutoff that sets the weight to 0 if it exceeds a certain distance and it is a symmetrical matrix (in case of Euclidean). For example, if we set the cutoff to 2.5 km (i.e., 0.40), the following matrix is obtained.

$$\mathbf{W}=\begin{pmatrix} 0 & 0.50 & 0.50 & 0 & 0 \\ 0.50 & 0 & 0 & 0.50 & 0.45 \\ 0.50 & 0 & 0 & 0.50 & 0 \\ 0 & 0.50 & 0.50 & 0 & 0.45 \\ 0 & 0.45 & 0 & 0.45 & 0 \end{pmatrix} \quad (3.1.4)$$

Instead of the Euclidean distance, LeSage and Polasek (2008) use a traffic network distance. In the traffic network distance, **W** need not to be symmetric, if one-way roads exist.

3.1.2 Specification of the spatial weight matrix

The choice of weight matrix **W** affects both estimations and inferences (e.g., Florax and Folmer, 1992; Griffith, 1996; Stakhovych and Bijmolt, 2009). However, currently, there are few guidelines for selecting the correct **W** (Anselin, 2002). Following Stakhovych and Bijmolt (2009), we classified the means of providing **W** into the following three types:

[A] Completely exogenous
[B] Determining from the data
[C] Estimating

[A] is a typical method provided by whether area boundaries are in contact (contiguity-based **W**) as previously mentioned, as well as the inverse distance, Delaunay triangulation, and so forth (LeSage, 1999).

For [B], Aldstadt and Getis (2006) proposed an algorithm termed AMOEBA (a multidirectional optimum ecotope-based algorithm),[2] in which the geometric form of spatial clusters are identified, similar to a region growing algorithm of image segmentation. The distance need not be limited to the geographic one. We can consider other types of distances, including social economic distances (e.g., difference of gross domestic product [GDP]), migration flow (Conway and Rork, 2004), technological similarity (Lychagin et al., 2016), among others. These methods may also be categorized to [B]. However, we need to note that methods for parameter estimations and inferences of spatial econometric models have been developed for exogenous **W**. If **W** is endogenous, we need to rely on recently proposed parameter estimation methods for endogenous **W** (e.g., Qu and Lee, 2015; Zhou et al., 2016). Kostov (2010) noted that the reason why **W** based on geographical distance is often used is that the exogeneity is automatically satisfied.

There are very few studies classified as [C]. Fernández-Vázquez et al. (2009) tried to estimate **W** by generalized maximum entropy and generalized cross-entropy techniques. In a panel setting when the number of time series variables can grow faster than the number of time points for data, studies employed (graphical) LASSO to estimate **W** (Ahrens and Bhattacharjee, 2015; Moscone et al., 2017; Lam and Souza, 2019).

Because research regarding the estimation of the elements of **W** in [C] is still under development, it is common to select the most adequate **W** from prepared candidates. We could mention Kostov (2010) based on boosting and LeSage and Pace (2009), who attempted a model selection using

[2] GIS software that implements AMOEBA is available at the website of the first author (http://www.acsu.buffalo.edu/~geojared/tools.htm). It can also be implemented using the AMOEBA package of R.

posterior model probabilities based on a Bayesian approach.[3] The latter Bayesian approach is useful for the selection of both $\mathbf{X}$ and $\mathbf{W}$ (LeSage and Pace, 2009). Kelejian (2008) and Kelejian and Piras (2011) extended the J-test, which is a representative method of nonnested model selection, to the spatial econometric model. Meanwhile, Mur and Angulo (2009) noted the usefulness of information criterion (comprehensibility and clarity of results in the sense of selecting the unique best model). Similarly, Stakhovych and Bijmolt (2009) stated that using information criterion (e.g., Akaike's information criterion [AIC]) increases the possibility of correct model specification. Seya et al. (2013) attempted to simultaneously select $\mathbf{W}$ and $\mathbf{X}$ to minimize the AIC by applying a technique termed transdimensional simulated annealing that combines reversible jump Markov chain Monte Carlo and simulated annealing. Other attempts include not model selections but model ensembles. We can mention those based on Bayesian model averaging (LeSage and Parent, 2007) and weighted average least squares (WALS) (Seya et al., 2014).[4]

3.1.3 Standardization of the spatial weight matrix

The spatial lag model (SLM), described in Chapter 6, is a representative spatial econometric model. For the maximum likelihood estimation of the parameters of this model, calculation of the term $(\mathbf{I}-\rho\mathbf{W})^{-1}$ is necessary during the process of estimation (here ρ is a parameter that indicates the degree of spatial autocorrelation). In many previous studies, $|\rho| < 1$ is assumed in the analogy of time series models, but the singular point of $(\mathbf{I}-\rho\mathbf{W})$ is not necessarily outside the range of $(-1, 1)$. Therefore, some standardization is typically performed on $\mathbf{W}$ to guarantee the existence of the inverse matrix. The most widely used standardization is row-standardization (also termed row-normalization), in which the elements of each row of $\mathbf{W}$ sum to unity. With the contiguity-based $\mathbf{W}$ (Eq. 3.1.1), row-standardization may be performed as

$$\mathbf{W} = \begin{pmatrix} 0 & 1/2 & 1/2 & 0 & 0 \\ 1/3 & 0 & 0 & 1/3 & 1/3 \\ 1/2 & 0 & 0 & 1/2 & 0 \\ 0 & 1/3 & 1/3 & 0 & 1/3 \\ 0 & 1/2 & 0 & 1/2 & 0 \end{pmatrix} \tag{3.1.5}$$

[3] The Spatial Econometrics Toolbox of Matlab is available at the website of the first author.
[4] See Magnus and De Luca (2016) for details about the WALS.

By using row-standardization, the spatial lag variable $\mathbf{Wy} = \sum_{j=1}^{N} w_{ij}y_j$ becomes the weighted average of the observations in the neighborhood set, hence easy to interpret. In the case of an inverse-distance-based weight, it is also important that the effect of scale (meters, kilometers, etc.) disappears. In addition, when the minimum and maximum eigenvalues of $\mathbf{W}$ are denoted as $\omega_{\min}$ and $\omega_{\max}$ (if all the eigenvalues are real), the term $(\mathbf{I}-\rho\mathbf{W})$ is nonsingular for all $(1/\omega_{\min} < \rho < 1/\omega_{\max})$, but because the maximum eigenvalue of $\mathbf{W}$ after row-standardization is 1, the row-standardization limits the range of possible spatial parameters to $(1/\omega_{\min} < \rho < 1)$. In other words, row-standardization is important to ensure continuous parameter space for estimation.

There is also the problem, however, that the meaning of distance is lost by row-standardization (Anselin, 1988, p. 24). To confront, Kelejian and Prucha (2010) show two alternatives. The simpler one of them is standardizing as

$$\mathbf{W}^* = \frac{\mathbf{W}}{\omega_{\max}} \tag{3.1.6}$$

Because the maximum eigenvalue of $\mathbf{W}^*$ is 1, the parameter space is given as $(1/\omega_{\min} < \rho < 1)$. This standardization is also presented in Corrado and Fingleton (2012). This method does not destroy economic interpretation in terms of distance decay and can be used as long as $\mathbf{W}$ is not too large (e.g., less than 400) to enable an accurate eigenvalue calculation (see Kelejian and Prucha, 1998; Arbia et al., 2019 about this).

3.2 Testing for spatial autocorrelation

The measures (test statistics) related to the *existence* of spatial autocorrelation in data, that is, focusing on whether there is any spatial autocorrelation in the data, is termed global indicators of spatial association (GISA), and the measures (test statistics) related to *where* the spatial autocorrelation occurs is termed local indicators of spatial association (LISA). The latter focuses on identifying local clusters, such as hot spots (accumulation of higher values) and cool spots (accumulation of smaller values) as well as spatial outliers. Here, first we explain about GISA, followed by the explanation about LISA.

3.2.1 Testing for global spatial autocorrelation

The most famous indicators of GISA are Moran's I (Moran, 1948, 1950; Cliff and Ord, 1981) and Geary's C (Geary, 1954). Here, in contrast to

LISA, we term them global Moran and global Geary, respectively. Global Moran is defined by the following equation:

$$I = \frac{N}{S_0} \frac{\sum_{i=1}^{N} \sum_{j=1}^{N} w_{ij} \left(y_i - \overline{y}\right) \left(y_j - \overline{y}\right)}{\sum_{i=1}^{N} \left(y_i - \overline{y}\right)^2}, \tag{3.2.1}$$

where N is the number of samples and $S_0 = \sum_{i=1}^{N} \sum_{j=1}^{N} w_{ij}$; that is, sum of all the elements of the spatial weight matrix $\mathbf{W}$. When the row sum of the weight matrix is standardized to 1, the global Moran is given in a simple form because N and S_0 coincide and the term N/S_0 disappears. $\overline{y}$ is the average of the observed values. Different from the correlation coefficient, unfortunately sometimes it is misunderstood that global Moran does not need to take values from -1 to $+1$ (see Maruyama, 2015). In fact, the value limits are given by $|I| \leq \sqrt{Var[\mathbf{Wy}]/Var[\mathbf{y}]}$. The positive value of global Moran implies the existence of a positive autocorrelation, and conversely, the negative value implies the existence of a negative autocorrelation.

Meanwhile, global Geary is provided by the following equation:

$$C = \frac{N-1}{2S_0} \frac{\sum_{i=1}^{N} \sum_{j=1}^{N} w_{ij} \left(y_i - y_j\right)^2}{\sum_{i=1}^{N} \left(y_i - \overline{y}\right)^2} \tag{3.2.2}$$

Global Geary can take values from 0 to 2. A value near 0 implies the existence of a positive autocorrelation, and conversely, a value near 22 implies the existence of a negative autocorrelation. From Eqs. (3.2.1) and (3.2.2), note that global Moran is defined as the product of deviation from the mean while global Geary is a statistic that focuses on the difference of the value itself. Because of these differences, while global Moran is adept at grasping global spatial autocorrelations, global Geary is a more sensitive statistic in relation to local spatial autocorrelations.

Global Moran and global Geary are often used to diagnose spatial autocorrelation of regression model residuals. This is because if there is a spatial autocorrelation in the error term, there is the problem that the ordinary least squares (OLS) estimator has no consistency and the t values of the regression coefficients have upward bias. Now, when the residuals of the regression model is calculated as $\mathbf{e} = \mathbf{y} - \mathbf{X}\widehat{\boldsymbol{\beta}}$, the global Moran is provided by the following equation:

$$I = \frac{N}{S_0} \frac{e'\mathbf{We}}{e'\mathbf{e}} \tag{3.2.3}$$

Once we can calculate global Moran and global Geary values based on Eqs. (3.2.1)–(3.2.3), the next issue of interest is inferences on I or C. The null hypothesis is that the y_i (or e_i) values are randomly distributed in space (spatial randomness). The distribution of the I or C statistic can be derived under the assumption of normality or randomization. The latter means that each value can equally likely be observed at each location (Cliff and Ord, 1981).

The global Moran (replace I by C in the case of Geary) can be standardized as the following equation using the expected value $E[I]$ and the variance $Var[I]$:

$$Z = \frac{I - E(I)}{\sqrt{Var(I)}} \tag{3.2.4}$$

Because Z follows the standard normal distribution $N(0,1)$ in an asymptotical manner, it is possible to conduct hypothesis testing using the null hypothesis that spatial autocorrelation does not exist under a given **W**. When normality is assumed, the expected value and variance may be given by (Cliff and Ord, 1981):

$$E(I) = \frac{-1}{N-1}; \tag{3.2.5}$$

$$Var(I) = \frac{1}{(N-1)(N+1)S_0^2}\left(N^2 S_1 - NS_2 + 3S_0^2\right) - [E(I)]^2; \tag{3.2.6}$$

$$S_1 = \frac{1}{2}\sum_{i=1}^{N}\sum_{j=1}^{N}(w_{ij} + w_{ji})^2; \ S_2 = \sum_{i=1}^{N}\left(w_i + w_i^*\right)^2; \ w_i = \sum_{j=1}^{N} w_{ij}; \ w_i^* = \sum_{j=1}^{N} w_{ji} \tag{3.2.7}$$

Meanwhile, when normality is assumed, the expected value and variance of global Geary may be given by (Cliff and Ord, 1981):

$$E(C) = 1; \tag{3.2.8}$$

$$Var(C) = \frac{(2S_1 + S_2)(N-1) - 4S_0^2}{2(N+1)S_0^2} \tag{3.2.9}$$

Note that expected value of Moran's I is not exactly zero, though it approaches to zero depending on the increase of N. In the case of residuals, assuming $K = rank(\mathbf{X})$ (the number of explanatory variables including the constant terms), the expected value and variance are given as

$$E(I) = \left(\frac{N}{S_0}\right)\frac{tr(\mathbf{MW})}{N-K}; \tag{3.2.10}$$

$$Var(I) = \left(\frac{N}{S_0}\right)^2 \frac{\left[tr(\mathbf{MWMW}') + tr(\mathbf{MW})^2 + \{tr(\mathbf{MW})\}^2\right]}{(N-K)(N-K+2)} - [E(I)]^2 \tag{3.2.11}$$

If I is sufficiently larger than $E[I]$, the existence of a positive autocorrelation is suggested, and in contrast, if sufficiently small, a negative autocorrelation.

In contrast to analytical derivations aforementioned, a permutation test is also commonly used. In this approach, N observations are randomly assigned to observed points (locations), and statistics (global Moran or global Geary) are repeatedly calculated for a sufficient number of times (99 or 999 times is often used). Then, the original statistics are evaluated using the obtained empirical (reference) distribution. In particular, this approach is useful for small samples where asymptotic normality cannot be used. Note however that the permutation test is inadequate for regression residuals. This is because the OLS residual, provided by $\mathbf{e} = \mathbf{M}\boldsymbol{\varepsilon}$ (where $\mathbf{M} = \mathbf{I} - \mathbf{X}(\mathbf{X}'\mathbf{X})^{-1}\mathbf{X}'$ denotes a projection matrix), by construction, has a correlation (randomization assumption does not hold) as long as $\mathbf{M}$ is not a diagonal matrix (in other words, $\mathbf{X} = \mathbf{1}$), and therefore cannot be regarded as a random sample to be permutated (Anselin and Rey, 1991; Schmoyer, 1994). A possible approach of spatial bootstrap test is proposed in Lin et al. (2011).

Global Moran has the ability to detect not only spatial autocorrelation of residuals, but also spatial autocorrelation (spatial lag) of dependent variables (Anselin and Rey, 1991). In addition, it has been shown that it has the ability to detect heteroscedasticity, which is a difference form the Durbin—Watson ratio (Anselin and Griffith, 1988). Therefore, with global Moran alone, although the existence of spatial autocorrelation can be tested, it is difficult to specify the most desirable model. Because of this, a testing method based on the maximum likelihood method is often simultaneously used, assuming a specific spatial autocorrelation structure in the alternative hypotheses. As typical test methods, the Wald, likelihood ratio, and Lagrangean multiplier (LM) tests are used. The LM test is also termed Rao's score test (Anselin, 2001). We explain these in Chapter 5, because they are related to the spatial econometric models.

Kelejian and Prucha (2001) generalized the global Moran to be applicable to SLM, discrete choice models (binomial and multinomial), tobit models, and error terms in sample selection models. In addition, Jacqmin-Gadda et al. (1997) proposed that for the generalized linear model. Extension to spatio-temporal data is conducted by Griffith (1981) and Lee and Li (2017). Moreover, Liu et al. (2015) developed global and local Moran indexes for a vector, which is applicable to flow data.

A statistic similar to global Moran or global Geary is the Kelejian Robinson statistic (Kelejian and Robinson, 1992). This statistic does not require the assumption of normality. For the relationship between global Moran and the Kelejian Robinson statistic, please see Anselin and Bera (1998).

Very few studies applied global Moran and global Geary to big data. An interesting exception is that of Luo et al. (2019), which compared the performance of these indexes with massive data, and suggested that *the Moran coefficient is more efficient than the Geary ratio because this index has a relatively smaller asymptotic as well as exact variance.*

3.2.2 Testing for local spatial autocorrelation

LISA is one of the tools for exploratory spatial data analysis (ESDA). ESDA is the extension of exploratory data analysis to the problem of detecting spatial properties of data—to detect spatial patterns in data, to formulate hypothesis which are based on, or which are about, the geography of data, and to assess spatial models (Haining et al., 1998). Representative tools for ESDA include kernel density, *K*-functions, Variogram, and LISA. Because kernel density and *K*-functions are used for spatial point process (i.e., event data) we do not deal with them; please refer to Okabe et al. (2009) and Diggle (2013), respectively. Variogram will be explained in Chapter 4. Hence here, we focus on LISA.

3.2.2.1 Local Moran statistic

Anselin (1995) defines that LISA should meet the following two requirements:

(1)The LISA for each observation measures the extent of significant clustering of similar values around the observation.

(2)The sum of LISA for all observations is proportional to a corresponding GISA.

Anselin (1995) proposed the local Moran as a LISA that meets such requirements. The local Moran is defined as

$$I_i = \frac{y_i - \overline{y}}{m_2} \sum_j w_{ij} \left(y_j - \overline{y} \right), \tag{3.2.12}$$

where m_2 is a constant defined as $m_2 = N^{-1} \sum_i \left(y_i - \overline{y} \right)^2$. In this manner, I_i is defined as the similarity between the deviation of its value from the mean value and the deviation from the mean of the observed value in the neighborhood set S_i.[5] In other words, I_i has a large positive value if its own value is similar to that of the surrounding values, and a large negative value if it has a very different value. However, if there is no relationship with the surrounding values, I_i has a value near zero. Anselin (1995) showed that global Moran is an average of local Moran statistics, and thus requirement (2) is satisfied.

The expected value and variance of the local Moran are obtained as follows under the randomization hypothesis:

$$E(I_i) = -w_i/(N-1); \tag{3.2.13}$$

$$\begin{aligned} Var(I_i) = {} & w_{i(2)}(N - b_2)/(N-1) \\ & + 2w_{i(kh)}(2b_2 - N)/\{(N-1)(N-2)\} - w_i^2/(N-1)^2, \end{aligned} \tag{3.2.14}$$

where $w_i = \sum_j w_{ij}$, $b_2 = m_4/m_2^2$, $m_4 = \sum \left(y_i - \overline{y} \right)^4 / N$, $w_{i(2)} = \sum_{j \neq i} w_{ij}^2$, and $2w_{i(kh)} = \sum_{k \neq i} \sum_{h \neq i} w_{ik} w_{ih}$. In this manner, for each observed value, it is possible to conduct a hypothesis test on the existence of spatial autocorrelation, and the range of the spatial cluster can be specified using the Moran scatter plot, which we will describe later.

[5] Note that, as the global Moran, it does not have to be a value from −1 to 1.

3.2.2.2 Local Geary statistic

Anselin (1995) also proposed the local Geary, which was further elaborated by Sokal et al. (1998a,b) and Anselin (2019). The local Geary is defined as follows:

$$C_i = \frac{1}{m_2}\sum_j w_{ij}\left(y_i - y_j\right), \tag{3.2.15}$$

where m_2 is a constant defined as $m_2 = N^{-1}\sum_i\left(y_i - \overline{y}\right)^2$. The expected value of the local Geary is obtained as follows under the randomization hypothesis (Sokal et al., 1998a,b):

$$E[C_i] = 2Nw_i/(N-1) \tag{3.2.16}$$

Although it is possible to develop $Var[C_i]$, Anselin (2019) advocated the use of the permutation test, which was outlined in Anselin (1995). This consisted of creating a reference distribution for each individual location by randomly permuting the remaining values (i.e., all observations except the value at location i) and recomputing the statistic each time.

As an extension of the local Moran, Rusche et al. (2011) uses a bivariate local Moran to conduct an analysis related to industrial coaccumulation. Similarly, Anselin (2019) proposed a multivariate local Geary. All of these methods can be implemented using GeoDa.[6]

3.2.2.3 G_i and G_i* statistics

The G_i and G_i^* statistics of Getis-Ord are also representative LISA. It is also possible to construct the global statistic G proportional to these (Haining, 2003). The G_i and G_i^* statistics in area i are given by the following[7]:

$$G_i = \frac{\sum_{j\neq i} w_{ij} y_j}{\sum_{j\neq i} y_j}; \tag{3.2.17}$$

$$G_i^* = \frac{\sum_j w_{ij} y_j}{\sum_j y_j}, \tag{3.2.18}$$

where y represents the quantity (>0) to pay attention to. G_i and G_i^* always have a value of 0 or more from their definition, and if there are large value

[6] A general-purpose software of spatial econometrics is provided free of charge, which is the research team of Dr. Luc Anselin (https://geodacenter.github.io/). See also Haining (2003, p.265) for bivariate association.

[7] Typical spatial autocorrelation statistics such as (global/local) Moran, Geary, and G_i can be implemented using the spdep package of R.

Table 3.2.1 Characteristics of the G_i statistic.

Statistic name	$G_i (j \neq i)$	$G_i^* (j = i)$
Statistic	$\frac{\sum_{j \neq i} w_{ij} y_j}{\sum_{j \neq i} y_j}$	$\frac{\sum_j w_{ij} y_j}{\sum_j y_j}$
Expected value	$w_i / (N-1)$	w_i^* / N
Variance	$\frac{w_i (N-1-w_i) Q_{i2}}{(N-1)^2 (N-2) Q_{i1}^2}$	$\frac{w_i^* (N-w_i^*) Q_{i2}*}{(N)^2 (N-1) (Q_{i1}*)^2}$
Variable definition	$w_i = \sum_{j \neq i} w_{ij}$ $Q_{i1} = \frac{\sum_{j \neq i} y_j}{(N-1)}$ $Q_{i2} = \frac{\sum_{j \neq i} y_j^2}{(N-1)} - Q_{i1}^2$	$w_i^* = \sum_j w_{ij}$ $Q_{i1}^* = \frac{\sum_j y_j}{N}$ $Q_{i2}^* = \frac{\sum_j y_j^2}{N} - (Q_{i1}^*)^2$

Created by the author based on Table 3.2.1 of Getis, A., Ord, J.K., 1992. The analysis of spatial association by use of distance statistics. Geographical Analysis, 24 (3), 189–206.

data in the neighbor of zone i, a large value is shown (hot spot), and conversely, if there are small value data in the neighbor of zone i, a small value is shown (cool spot). Note that y_j needs to be positive by definition. Here, it is distinguished as the G_i statistic when $j = i$ is not allowed, and the G_i^* statistic when it is allowed. For example, if we want to analyze industrial clusters within a 500-m radius from zone i, the G_i^* statistic has to be used as $w_{ii} = 1$, because our own y_i value should be included.

Expected values and variances of G_i and G_i^* when the distribution is completely random are respectively determined as shown in Table 3.2.1 under the randomization hypothesis. Standardization using expected values and variances enables hypothesis testing on the significance of the hot and cool spots.

Ord and Getis (1995) extended the G_i and G_i^* statistics to the following, such that it could be applied even when including *nonpositive* observations. This enables application of the model residuals. The corrected statistic is provided by the following:

$$G_i = \frac{\sum_{j \neq i} w_{ij} y_j - w_i Q_{i1}}{(Q_{i2})^{1/2} \{ [(N-1) S_i - w_i^2] / (N-2) \}^{1/2}}; \tag{3.2.19}$$

$$G_i^* = \frac{\sum_j w_{ij} y_j - w_i^* Q_{i1}^*}{(Q_{i2}^*)^{1/2} \{ (N S_i - w_i^{*2}) / (N-1) \}^{1/2}}, \tag{3.2.20}$$

with $S_i = \sum_{j \neq i} w_{ij}^2$ and $S_i^* = \sum_j w_{ij}^2$.

Ord and Getis (2001) noted that the performance of LISA deteriorates when global spatial autocorrelation exists and presented a correction method. Boots (2003) proposed LISA for categorical data.

3.2.3 Examples

3.2.3.1 Japanese income data: an application of local Moran

In Tamesue et al. (2013), our research group analyzed recent regional income disparities in Japan using GISA and LISA. Here, we briefly introduce some of these results. The income data used was the per capita income of the population at the municipality unit from 1998 to 2007.[8,9] Regarding the spatial distribution of income disparity, it is considered that municipalities with similar income levels are geographically clustered; in other words, municipalities with low income per capita are near other municipalities with a low income, and municipalities with high income per capita are near other municipalities with high income; for this reason spatial autocorrelation analysis is useful.

Fig. 3.2.1 shows the transition of the global Moran values of income in Japan. For all years, the null hypothesis that spatial autocorrelation does not

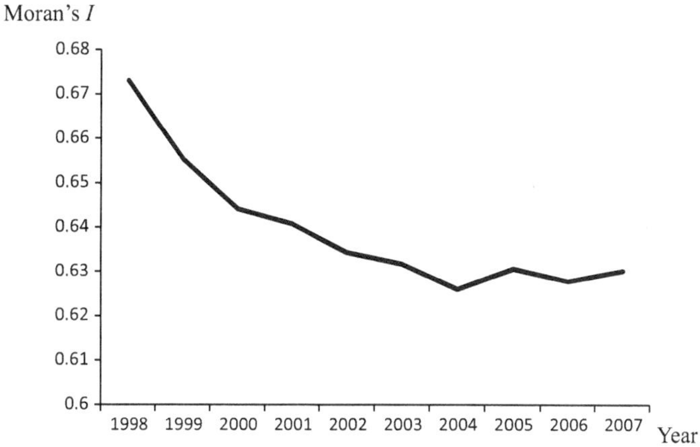

Figure 3.2.1 Transition of global Moran values of income in Japan. *Created by the author based on Figure 4 of Tamesue and Tsutsumi, 2013.*

[8] From the NSC Marketing Database of Nippon Statistics Center Co., Ltd (created based on investigations of the municipal taxation situation etc. conducted by the Ministry of Internal Affairs and Communications).

[9] The aggregated classification of data is as of 2007 after the great merger of municipalities in the Heisei era. However, two municipalities in Okinawa Prefecture had special circumstances in which the per capita income was an abnormally high value compared to other years because of address changes of specific high-income people. Because of this, the analysis was conducted for 1809 municipalities excluding these two.

exist was rejected at a 1% level, indicating the existence of a strong positive spatial autocorrelation. However, the value of the global Moran has gradually decreased since 1998, and it is thought that the degree of spatial autocorrelation has weakened.

Next, Tamesue et al. (2013) used the Moran scatter plot proposed by Anselin (1996) to visualize the spatial distribution of income disparity. In the Moran scatter plot, standardized (average 0, variance 1) observed values were plotted on the x axis and the spatial lag variables of the standardized dependent variables on the y axis. It can be considered that, by the standardization, the origin is the average income level, and then it becomes a high-income level if it is higher than the origin, and a low-income level if it is lower. As a result, the Moran scatter plot can be classified into clusters by considering the relationship between the area and nearby areas by using four divided quadrants (see Fig. 3.2.2). The existing research is mainly aimed at extracting the area of the first quadrant (hot spot: High-High [HH]) and the third quadrant (cool spot: Low-Low [LL]), but Tamesue et al. (2013) also focused on the second and fourth quadrants that show the income level gap with nearby areas; each of them was defined as sole loser (low-high [LH)] and sole winner (high-low [HL]) from their characteristics.

Fig. 3.2.3 shows the geographical distribution of each municipality color-coded by cluster and classified according to the Moran scatter plot (only distribution maps for 1998 and 2007 are shown because of space constraints). There are many hot spots distributed along the Pacific belt and also in Hokuriku. At the same time, there are also areas where there is a sole loser

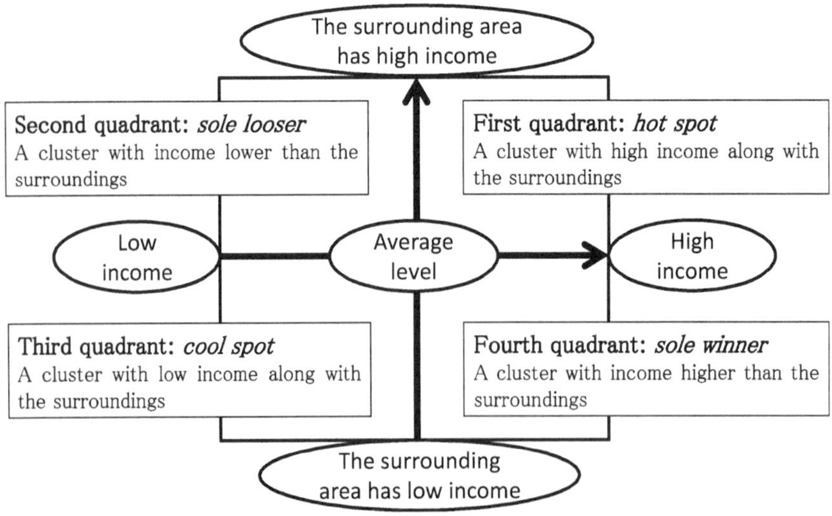

Figure 3.2.2 Image of classification by Moran scatter plot (with income as an example).

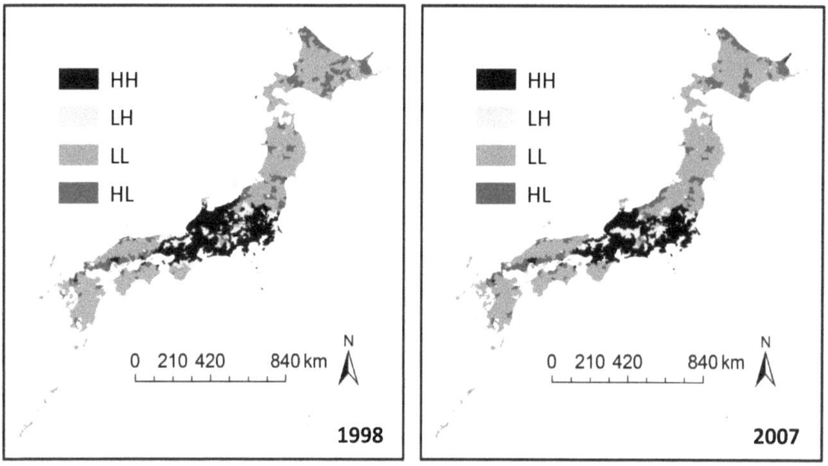

Figure 3.2.3 Spatial distribution of clusters by Moran scatter plot. *Created by the author based on Figure 10 of Tamesue and Tsutsumi, 2013.*

in a cluster of hot spots. As previously mentioned, because a sole loser is a low-income area surrounded by high-income areas, these areas are necessarily around hot spots that are high-income clusters. However, cool spot clusters are distributed in Hokkaido, Tohoku, Chugoku, Shikoku, and Kyushu. In addition, it can be confirmed that many sole winner clusters exist in Hokkaido and along the Seto Inland Sea; these tend to be distributed near the coast.

In this manner, spatial autocorrelation analysis offers a new perspective on income disparity analysis. Please refer to Tamesue et al. (2013) for more details, such as the calculation results of the local Moran statistic. Notably, the income disparity analysis here is simple in the sense that it does not consider the effects of natural variations of income resulting from aging.

3.2.3.2 Japanese population data: an application of local Geary

Different from local Moran, in local Geary, similar neighbors could have either similar high values or similar low values. Moreover, they could also result from two data points that span the mean, but that are very close together in value. Hence Anselin (2019) proposed the categorization by locating the pairs y_i, $\sum w_{ij} y$ in the Moran scatter plot. Then, those pairs that correspond with a significant small value of C_i and that fall clearly in the High-High or Low-Low quadrants can be classified as such. For these pairs falling in the Low-High quadrant, they may be classified as *Other*.

Fig. 3.2.4 shows the results of applying local Moran (left-hand side) and local Geary (right-hand side) to Japanese population data observed at

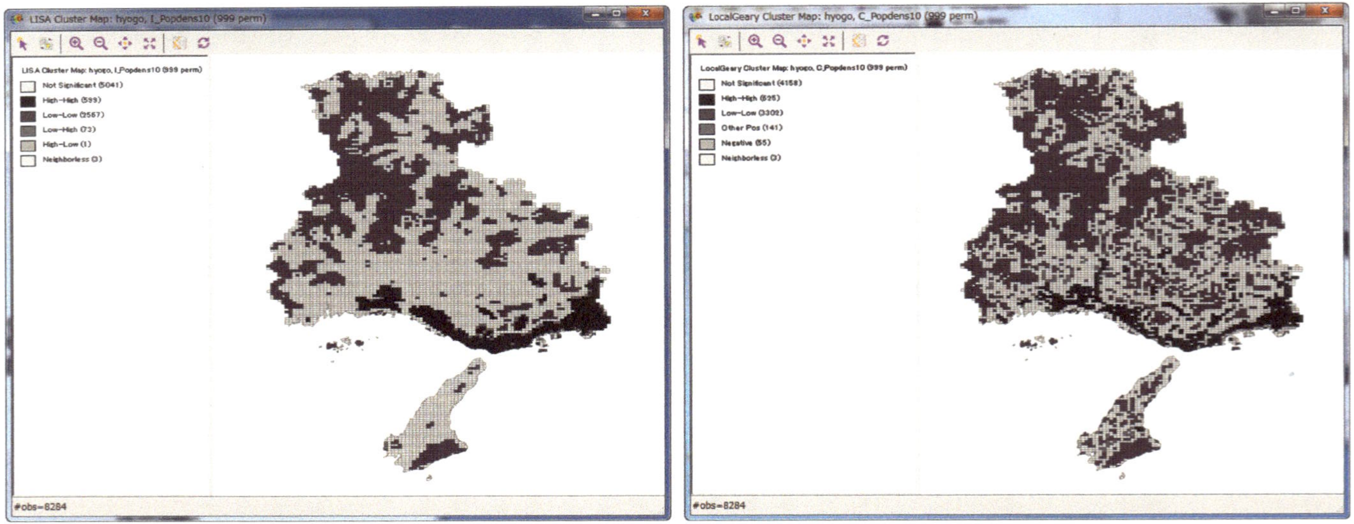

Figure 3.2.4 Spatial distribution of clusters by Moran (Geary) scatter plot (left-hand side for local Moran; right-hand side for local Geary).

(approximately) 1 km^2 squared grid in the year 2010[10] The target area is Hyogo prefecture, of which the capital is Kobe city. In fact, in Hyogo prefecture, population is concentrated to the south, along the bay area. In the result of local Moran, in which observed values are compared to the mean, grids categorized to High-High can be found only around the bay area. On the other hand, in the case of local Geary, it successfully detected some suburban core districts as High-High. Such an interesting finding may suggest the possibility of local Geary as a new tool for ESDA.

3.3 Testing for spatial heterogeneity

3.3.1 Testing for global spatial heterogeneity

As standard econometrics, representative test statistics on heteroscedasticity are Chow statistic and Breusch-Pagan (BP) statistic. However, it has been noted that these test statistics are affected when spatial autocorrelation exists in the error term (Anselin, 1988).[11] Anselin (1988) proposed the spatially adjusted BP test statistic for heteroscedasticity and the spatial Chow test statistic for spatial structural change (spatial stability of regression coefficients) (Anselin, 1988, pp. 122–124). Because the premise of these is the spatial econometric model, we will describe them in Chapter 5.

3.3.2 Testing for local spatial heterogeneity: H_i statistic

Ord and Getis (2012) proposed the local heteroscedasticity statistic H_i as an analogy of the G_i statistic. For example, in crime analysis, when a high crime rate cluster (hot spot) is detected, it is important to distinguish whether the areas are equally dangerous (low dispersion) or if there is a mix of safe and dangerous areas (high dispersion).

[10] Data source is a population census and is available from e-Stat (https://www.e-stat.go.jp/gis). The map was created using the software GeoDa. The number of grids is 8284 and total population of Hyogo prefecture in 2010 is 5,588,133.

[11] It has been shown by Monte Carlo experiments that when strong spatial autocorrelation exists, the rejection probability of the null hypothesis of "there is no heteroscedasticity" in the BP test is two to three times that of the case where spatial autocorrelation does not exist. In the case of the Chow test, there is an opposite direction effect (Anselin, 1988).

Now, let us consider the following 10 × 10 binary data according to Ord and Getis (2012), including a hot spot consisting of 1's.

	0	0	0	0	0	0	0	0	0	0
	0	0	0	0	0	0	0	0	0	0
	0	0	0	0	0	0	0	0	0	0
1 ←	0	0	0	1	1	1	1	0	0	0
	0	0	0	1	1	1	1	0	0	0
	0	0	0	1	1	1	1	0	0	0
	0	0	0	1	1	1	1	0	0	0
	0	0	0	0	0	0	0	0	0	0
	0	0	0	0	0	0	0	0	0	0
	0	0	0	0	0	0	0	0	0	0

Here, if the variance is calculated for every moving 3 × 3 grid, the following result is obtained. (Note that the result is 8 × 8 because 3 × 3 cannot be taken at the endmost. In addition, the result is scaled such that the overall average is 1.[12])

0.00	0.00	0.00	0.00	0.00	0.00	0.00	0.00
0.00	1.00	1.75	2.25	2.25	1.75	1.00	0.00
0.00	1.75	2.50	2.25	2.25	2.50	1.75	0.00
0.00	2.25	2.25	0.00	0.00	2.25	2.25	0.00
0.00	2.25	2.25	0.00	0.00	2.25	2.25	0.00
0.00	1.75	2.50	2.25	2.25	2.50	1.75	0.00
0.00	1.00	1.75	2.25	2.25	1.75	1.00	0.00
0.00	0.00	0.00	0.00	0.00	0.00	0.00	0.00

In this manner, it can be seen that the variance is not constant inside the hot spot. Therefore, we need to consider such local heterogeneity. First, define $\bar{y}_i$ as follows:

$$\bar{y}_i = \frac{\sum_j w_{ij} y_j}{\sum_j w_{ij}} \tag{3.3.1}$$

And we define local residuals in the neighboring area as follows:

$$e_j = y_j - \bar{y}_j, j \in S_i \tag{3.3.2}$$

[12] We calculate the variance in the 3 × 3 moving window in order. Because the average of the results was 0.09877, we scaled it such that the average would be 11 by dividing by this value.

Table 3.3.1 Search for local spatial effects using the G_i and H_i statistics.

	H_i is high	H_i is low
$\lvert G_i^* \rvert$ is large	A hot spot with heterogeneous local conditions	A hot spot with similar surrounding areas
$\lvert G_i^* \rvert$ is small	Heterogeneous local conditions but at a low average level (infrequent)	Homogeneous local conditions and a low average level

Created by the author based on Ord, J.K., Getis, A. 2012. Local spatial heteroscedasticity (LOSH). The Annals of Regional Science 48 (2), 529–539.

The H_i statistic is then provided by the following:

$$H_i = \frac{\sum_j w_{ij} |e_j|^\alpha}{\sum_j w_{ij}} \tag{3.3.3}$$

If $\alpha = 1$, it corresponds to an absolute deviations measure, and if $\alpha = 2$, it corresponds to a variance measure. Of course, other settings are also possible. In addition, whether to allow $i = j$ depends on the objective, similar to the G_i statistic. Here we describe the case where $i = j$ is allowed. Using the G_i and the H_i statistics in combination, it is possible to search for local spatial effects of an object as shown in Table 3.3.1 (Ord and Getis, 2012).

Testing for heteroscedasticity is performed by $Z_i = 2H_i/V_i$ following a chi-square distribution with freedom degree $2/V_i$ under a randomization hypothesis, which is given as follows:

$$V_i = \frac{1}{N-1}\left(\frac{1}{h_1 W_{i1}}\right)^2 \left(h_2 - h_1^2\right)\left(NW_{i2} - W_{i1}^2\right); \tag{3.3.4}$$

$$W_{i1} = \sum_j w_{ij};\ W_{i2} = \sum_j w_{ij}^2;\ h_1 = \frac{1}{N}\sum_{i=1}^{N} |e_i^\alpha|;\ h_2 = \frac{1}{N}\sum_{i=1}^{N} |e_i^\alpha|^2$$

References

Ahrens, A., Bhattacharjee, A., 2015. Two-step Lasso estimation of the spatial weights matrix. Econometrics 3 (1), 128–155.

Aldstadt, J., Getis, A., 2006. Using AMOEBA to create a spatial weights matrix and identify spatial clusters. Geographical Analysis 38 (4), 327–343.

Anselin, L., 1988. Spatial Econometrics: Methods and Models. Kluwer Academic Publishers, Dordrecht.

Anselin, L., 1995. Local indicators of spatial association—LISA. Geographical Analysis 27 (2), 93–115.

Anselin, L., 1996. The Moran scatterplot as an ESDA tool to assess local instability in spatial association. In: Fischer, M.M., Scholten, H.J., Unwin, D. (Eds.), Spatial Analytical Perspectives on GIS. Taylor and Francis, London, pp. 111–125.
Anselin, L., 2001. Rao's score test in spatial econometrics. Journal of Statistical Planning and Inference 97 (1), 113–139.
Anselin, L., 2002. Under the food: issues in the specification and interpretation of spatial regression models. Agricultural Economics 27 (3), 247–267.
Anselin, L., 2019. A local indicator of multivariate spatial association: extending Geary's c. Geographical Analysis in print.
Anselin, L., Bera, A.K., 1998. Spatial dependence in linear regression models with an introduction to spatial econometrics. In: Ullah, A., Giles, D.E. (Eds.), Handbook of Applied Economic Statistics. Marcel Dekker, New York, pp. 237–289.
Anselin, L., Griffith, D.A., 1988. Do spatial effects really matter in regression analysis? Papers in Regional Science 65 (1), 11–34.
Anselin, L., Rey, S., 1991. Properties of tests for spatial dependence in linear regression models. Geographical Analysis 23 (2), 112–131.
Arbia, G., Ghiringhelli, C., Mira, A., 2019. Estimation of spatial econometric linear models with large datasets: how big can spatial big data be? Regional Science and Urban Economics 76, 67–73.
Boots, B., 2003. Developing local measures of spatial association for categorical data. Journal of Geographical Systems 5 (2), 139–160.
Cliff, A.D., Ord, J.K., 1981. Spatial Processes: Methods and Applications. Pion, London.
Conway, K.S., Rork, J.C., 2004. Diagnosis murder: the death of state death taxes. Economic Inquiry 42 (4), 537–559.
Corrado, L., Fingleton, B., 2012. Where is the economics in spatial econometrics? Journal of Regional Science 52 (2), 210–239.
Diggle, P.J., 2013. Statistical Analysis of Spatial and Spatio-Temporal Point Patterns. Chapman and Hall/CRC.
Fernández-Vázquez, E., Mayor-Fernández, M., Rodríguez-Vález, J., 2009. Estimating spatial autoregressive models by GME-GCE techniques. International Regional Science Review 32 (2), 148–172.
Florax, R., Folmer, H., 1992. Specification and estimation of spatial linear regression models: Monte Carlo evaluation of pre-test estimators. Regional Science and Urban Economics 22 (3), 405–432.
Geary, R.C., 1954. The contiguity ratio and statistical mapping. The Incorporated Statistician 5 (3), 115–145.
Getis, A., Ord, J.K., 1992. The analysis of spatial association by use of distance statistics. Geographical Analysis 24 (3), 189–206.
Griffith, D., 1981. Interdependence in space and time: numerical and interpretative considerations. In: Griffith, D., MacKinnon, R. (Eds.), Dynamic Spatial Models, pp. 258–287. Alphen aan den Rijn, Sijthoff and Noordhoff.
Griffith, D.A., 1996. Some guidelines for specifying the geographic weights matrix contained in spatial statistical models. In: Arlinghaus, S.L. (Ed.), Practical Handbook of Spatial Statistics. CRC Press, Boca Raton, pp. 65–82.
Haining, R., 2003. Spatial Data Analysis: Theory and Practice. Cambridge University Press, Cambridge.
Haining, R., Wise, S., Ma, J., 1998. Exploratory spatial data analysis in a geographic information system environment. The Statistician 47, 457–469.
Jacqmin-Gadda, H., Commenges, D., Nejjari, C., Dartigues, J.F., 1997. Tests of geographical correlation with adjustment for explanatory variables: an application to dyspnoea in the elderly. Statistics in Medicine 16 (11), 1283–1297.

Kelejian, H.H., 2008. A spatial J-test for model specification against a single or a set of non-nested alternatives. Letters in Spatial and Resource Sciences 1 (1), 3–11.

Kelejian, H.H., Prucha, I.R., 1998. A generalized spatial two-stage least squares procedure for estimating a spatial autoregressive model with autoregressive disturbances. The Journal of Real Estate Finance and Economics 17 (1), 99–121.

Kelejian, H.H., Robinson, D.P., 1992. Spatial autocorrelation: a new computationally simple test with an application to per capita country police expenditures. Regional Science and Urban Economics 22 (3), 317–331.

Kelejian, H.H., Piras, G., 2011. An extension of Kelejian' s J-test for non-nested spatial models. Regional Science and Urban Economics 41 (3), 281–292.

Kelejian, H.H., Prucha, I.R., 2001. On the asymptotic distribution of the Moran I test statistic with applications. Journal of Econometrics 104 (2), 219–257.

Kelejian, H.H., Prucha, I.R., 2010. Specification and estimation of spatial autoregressive models with autoregressive and heteroskedastic disturbances. Journal of Econometrics 157 (1), 53–67.

Kostov, P., 2010. Model boosting for spatial weighting matrix selection in spatial lag models. Environment and Planning B 37 (3), 533–549.

Lam, C., Souza, P.C., 2019. Estimation and selection of spatial weight matrix in a spatial lag model. Journal of Business and Economic Statistics in print. https://www.tandfonline.com/doi/full/10.1080/07350015.2019.1569526.

LeSage, J.P., 1999. The Theory and Practice of Spatial Econometrics, Online Textbook. Department of Economics, University of Toledo.

LeSage, J.P., Parent, O., 2007. Bayesian model averaging for spatial econometric models. Geographical Analysis 39 (3), 241–267.

LeSage, J.P., Pace, R.K., 2009. Introduction to Spatial Econometrics. Chapman & Hall/CRC, Boca Raton.

LeSage, J.P., Polasek, W., 2008. Incorporating transportation network structure in spatial econometric models of commodity flows. Spatial Economic Analysis 3 (2), 225–245.

Lee, J., Li, S., 2017. Extending Moran's index for measuring spatiotemporal clustering of geographic events. Geographical Analysis 49 (1), 36–57.

Lin, K.P., Long, Z.H., Ou, B., 2011. The size and power of bootstrap tests for spatial dependence in a linear regression model. Computational Economics 38 (2), 153–171.

Liu, Y., Tong, D., Liu, X., 2015. Measuring spatial autocorrelation of vectors. Geographical Analysis 47 (3), 300–319.

Luo, Q., Griffith, D.A., Wu, H., 2019. Spatial autocorrelation for massive spatial data: verification of efficiency and statistical power asymptotics. Journal of Geographical Systems in print.

Lychagin, S., Pinkse, J., Slade, M.E., Reenen, J.V., 2016. Spillovers in space: does geography matter? The Journal of Industrial Economics 64 (2), 295–335.

Magnus, J.R., De Luca, G., 2016. Weighted-average least squares (WALS): a survey. Journal of Economic Surveys 30 (1), 117–148.

Maruyama, Y., 2015. An Alternative to Moran's I for Spatial Autocorrelation arXiv preprint arXiv:1501.06260.

Moran, P.A.P., 1948. The interpretation of statistical maps. Journal of the Royal Statistical Society B 10 (2), 243–251.

Moran, P.A.P., 1950. A test for the serial dependence of residuals. Biometrika 37 (1–2), 178–181.

Moscone, F., Tosetti, E., Vinciotti, V., 2017. Sparse estimation of huge networks with a block-wise structure. The Econometrics Journal 20 (3), S61–S85.

Mur, J., Angulo, A., 2009. Model selection strategies in a spatial setting: some additional results. Journal Regional Science and Urban Economics 39 (2), 200–213.

Okabe, A., Satoh, T., Sugihara, K., 2009. A kernel density estimation method for networks, its computational method and a GIS-based tool. International Journal of Geographical Information Science 23 (1), 7–32.
Ord, J.K., Getis, A., 1995. Local spatial autocorrelation statistics: distributional issues and an application. Geographical Analysis 27 (4), 286–306.
Ord, J.K., Getis, A., 2001. Testing for local spatial autocorrelation in the presence of global autocorrelation. Journal of Regional Science 41 (3), 411–432.
Ord, J.K., Getis, A., 2012. Local spatial heteroscedasticity (LOSH). The Annals of Regional Science 48 (2), 529–539.
Qu, X., Lee, L.F., 2015. Estimating a spatial autoregressive model with an endogenous spatial weight matrix. Journal of Econometrics 184 (2), 209–232.
Rusche, K., Kies, U., Schulte, A., 2011. Measuring spatial co-agglomeration patterns by extending ESDA techniques. Jahrbuch für Regionalwissenschaft 31 (1), 11–25.
Schmoyer, R.L., 1994. Permutation tests for correlation in regression errors. Journal of the American Statistical Association 89 (428), 1507–1516.
Seya, H., Tsutsumi, M., 2014. Applied Spatial Statistics (in Japanese). Asakura Publishing Co., Ltd., Tokyo.
Seya, H., Tsutsumi, M., Yamagata, Y., 2012. Income convergence in Japan: a Bayesian spatial Durbin model approach. Economic Modelling 29 (1), 60–71.
Seya, H., Tsutsumi, M., Yamagata, Y., 2014. Weighted-average least squares applied to spatial econometric models: a Monte Carlo investigation. Geographical Analysis 46 (2), 126–147.
Seya, H., Yamagata, Y., Tsutsumi, M., 2013. Automatic selection of a spatial weight matrix in spatial econometrics: application to a spatial hedonic approach. Regional Science and Urban Economics 43 (3), 429–444.
Smith, T.E., 2009. Estimation bias in spatial models with strongly connected weight matrices. Geographical Analysis 41 (3), 307–332.
Sokal, R.R., Oden, N.L., Thomson, B.A., 1998a. Local spatial autocorrelation in a biological model. Geographical Analysis 30 (4), 331–354.
Sokal, R.R., Oden, N.L., Thomson, B.A., 1998b. Local spatial autocorrelation in biological variables. Biological Journal of the Linnean Society 65 (1), 41–62.
Stakhovych, S., Bijmolt, T.H.M., 2009. Specification of spatial models: a simulation study on weights matrices. Papers in Regional Science 88 (2), 389–408.
Tamesue, K., Tsutsumi, M., Yamagata, Y., 2013. Income disparity and correlation in Japan. Review of Urban and Regional Development Studies 25 (1), 2–15. https://doi.org/10.1111/rurd.12004.
Zhou, Y., Wang, X., Holguín-Veras, J., 2016. Discrete choice with spatial correlation: a spatial autoregressive binary probit model with endogenous weight matrix (SARBP-EWM). Transportation Research Part B 94, 440–455.

CHAPTER FOUR

Geostatistics and Gaussian process models

Daisuke Murakami[1], Yoshiki Yamagata[2], Toshihiro Hirano[3]
[1]The Institute of Statistical Mathematics, Tachikawa, Tokyo, Japan
[2]Center for Global Environmental Research, National Institute for Environmental Studies, Tsukuba, Ibaraki, Japan
[3]Kanto Gakuin University, Yokohama, Kanagawa, Japan

Contents

Spatial Analysis using Big Data
ISBN: 978-0-12-813127-5
https://doi.org/10.1016/B978-0-12-813127-5.00004-7

4.1 What is geostatistics?

According to Chilès and Delfiner (2012), the name "geostatistics" was given by Georges Matheron, who also proposed the morphology theory, to a methodology for ore reserves evaluation that he developed in 1962. As discussed in Chapter 1, geostatistics assumes a continuous spatial process $Y(\mathbf{s})$ in domain D, making it easy to define the prediction at an arbitrary point. This estimation of a random variable at an arbitrary point is called kriging. The name "kriging" was given by Matheron after D. G. Krige (1951), who conducted pioneering research on a method to estimate ore reserves in the early 1950s. Matheron developed the theory of the Kriging method in the early 1960s as a best linear unbiased predictor (BLUP) of spatial data (Matheron, 1963).[1] Today, the Kriging method can be easily implemented because of the development of many statistical packages and its integration to GIS software.

Here is a brief overview of previous publications in geostatistics. As mentioned in Chapter 1, Cressie's text book (1993) has played the role of a dictionary in this field for many years, and its importance remains the same. Among standard textbooks are Schabenberger and Gotway (2005), Webster and Oliver (2007), and Chilès and Delfiner (2012). The book by Schabenberger and Gotway (2005) has particularly comprehensive content. Kitanidis (1997), Armstrong (1998), and Leuangthong and Deutsch (2008) are more entry-level textbooks, while Stein (1999) and Gaetan and Guyon (2010)

[1] For further history of geostatistics, refer to Cressie (1990). Meanwhile, Haining (2010) is compelling research that reviews the entire method of geostatistics from the perspective of geography. It also details the history of geostatistics. Hengl et al. (2009) reviewed the role and trends of geostatistics as an academic field in detail.

are dedicated to advanced users, with a mathematically rigorous theoretical development. Wackernagel (1998) details the modeling of multivariate data and Cressie and Wikle (2011) makes an extensive approach to the modeling of space-time data. Banerjee et al. (2004) and Diggle and Ribeiro (2007) are known for using Bayesian statistics in their theoretical development. Blangiardo and Cameletti (2015) and Wikle et al. (2019) explain not just methodology but also implementation using R.

Examples of other books include Journel and Huijbregts (1978), which emphasizes the application in the mining field, especially focusing on block data. For readers with interest in nonlinear Kriging, such as indicator Kriging, Goovaerts (1997) and Olea (2009) are good references. Stein et al. (1999) summarized the application in the remote sensing field with an interesting analysis of modeling image data with different resolutions. Fortin and Dale (2005) focuses on the application in the ecology field with emphasis on spatial point processes. Oliver (2010) summarized the application of geostatistics in the agricultural field. Finally, in their handbook, Gelfand et al. (2010) explains essential concepts in omnibus form. It is a valuable source to study the most recent trends.

4.2 Geostatistical model

4.2.1 Spatial data and spatial process

The measurement of spatial data is often carried out at discrete locations. For instance, because of the cost, the boring exploration for seismic surveys can only be conducted with a limited number of locations. Geostatistical models use data from such discrete observation points to estimate the spatial processes and predict the random variables in arbitrary points. Here, the data obtained (observed values) from discrete observation points $\mathbf{s}_i$ ($i = 1, \ldots, N$) is defined as $y(s_i)$ or y_i and suppose that it can be decomposed as follows (Cressie and Wikle, 2011, p.121):

$$y(\mathbf{s}_i) = Y(\mathbf{s}_i) + \varepsilon(\mathbf{s}_i), \quad i = 1, \ldots, N, \tag{4.2.1}$$

where $\varepsilon(\mathbf{s}: \mathbf{s} \in D)$ is a white-noise process with mean zero and variance σ_ε^2. This $\varepsilon(\mathbf{s}_i)$ denotes measurement error that we (typically) would like to filter out. Now, $Y(\mathbf{s}_i)$ can further be decomposed to

$$Y(\mathbf{s}_i) = m(\mathbf{s}_i) + z(\mathbf{s}_i) + e(\mathbf{s}_i); \quad \text{with } E[e(\mathbf{s}_i)] = 0; Var[e(\mathbf{s}_i)] = \sigma_e^2, \tag{4.2.2}$$

where $m(\mathbf{s}_i)$ is a large-scale trend component, $z(\mathbf{s}_i)$ is a smooth-scale variation explained by spatial dependence (autocorrelation), and $e(\mathbf{s}_i)$ is a microscale variation. The quantity, $c_0 = \sigma_e^2 + \sigma_\varepsilon^2$ is called a nugget effect (Cressie and Wikle, 2011, p.123). In traditional geostatistics, it is implicitly assumed that measurements are made perfectly; that is, $\sigma_\varepsilon^2 = 0$, which means $y(\mathbf{s}_i) = Y(\mathbf{s}_i)$. It follows that c_0 is made up of only microscale variance. We follow such tradition in our explanation below.

Typically, the trend $m(\mathbf{s}_i)$ is specified by a regression term $\sum_{k=1}^{K} x_k(\mathbf{s}_i)\beta_k$ where $x_k(\mathbf{s}_i)$ represents the k-th explanatory variable and β_k is the corresponding regression coefficient. Alternatively, it can be specified by a constant. It is important to note that not just $m(\mathbf{s}_i)$ but also the remaining terms are misspecified if a constant is used in the presence of a strong trend (Fuglstad et al., 2015). Hence detrending using the regression term, for example, is important in practice.

The next subsection explains how to model the spatially dependent process $z(\mathbf{s}: \mathbf{s} \in D)$. Some parts of our explanations are based on Seya and Tsutsumi (2014), a textbook written in Japanese, but we reflect recent advancements. We can additionally assume that $z(\mathbf{s}: \mathbf{s} \in D)$ obeys a Gaussian process (GP). While the Gaussian assumption is not necessarily needed in classical geostatistical modeling based in variogram (see Section 4.2.2), that assumption is typically made in Bayesian geostatistical modeling that is widely accepted today because of its flexibility in modeling spatial process and its uncertainty (see Section 4.7).

4.2.2 Stationary spatial process

4.2.2.1 Assumptions

One of the key concepts in geostatistics is the stationarity in space. When the distribution function of a multivariate distribution formed by N random variables $\{z(\mathbf{s}_1), ..., z(\mathbf{s}_N)\}$ in different positions $\{\mathbf{s}_1, ..., \mathbf{s}_N\}$ remains the same with any movement $\mathbf{h} \in D \sqsubseteq \Re^d$, that is, when

$$\Pr[z(\mathbf{s}_1) < z_1, ..., z(\mathbf{s}_N) < z_N] = \Pr[z(\mathbf{s}_1 + \mathbf{h}) < z_1, ..., z(\mathbf{s}_N + \mathbf{h}) < z_N], \tag{4.2.3}$$

satisfied, the spatial process is said to be *strictly stationary*. Strict stationarity means that the multivariate distribution does not change regardless of the direction or distance of the movement of the location. However, according to this definition, to examine whether the given spatial process is stationary, it is necessary to confirm that none of the N-dimensional distributions depends on position coordinates. To generate a distribution, it is necessary to provide every moment, but it is practically impossible to define all the N-dimensional distributions and confirm that none of them depends on position coordinates. For this reason, a method that loosens the assumption of strict stationarity and assumes only the stationarity of first- and second-order moment is frequently used. This method is known to work well not only with GP, whose distribution can be fully described with the moment of first and second orders, but also with data whose histogram is not very wide at the bottom (Wackernagel, 1998).

4.2.2.2 Covariance function and semivariogram

There are two concepts of stationarity related to the moment of first and second orders. The first is the concept of *second-order* or *weak* stationarity, which directly assumes the stationarity of first- and second-order moment to the variables; the second is the concept of *intrinsic* stationarity, which assumes stationarity of first- and second-order moment to the difference (or increments) between two points.

Starting with the former, a covariance function in a spatial process with zero mean is defined by the following equation (Schabenberger and Gotway, 2005):

$$C(s,h) = Cov[z(\mathbf{s}), z(\mathbf{s}+\mathbf{h})] = E[z(\mathbf{s})z(\mathbf{s}+\mathbf{h})]; \quad \forall \mathbf{s}, \mathbf{h} \in D. \tag{4.2.4}$$

If the following relationship holds, $z(\mathbf{s})$ is considered as a spatial process of second-order stationarity.

$$E[z(\mathbf{s})] = 0; \quad \forall \mathbf{s} \in D, \tag{4.2.5}$$

$$\mathrm{Cov}[z(\mathbf{s}), z(\mathbf{s}+\mathbf{h})] = c(\mathbf{h}); \quad \forall \mathbf{s}, \mathbf{h} \in D, \tag{4.2.6}$$

$$\mathrm{Cov}[z(\mathbf{s}), z(\mathbf{s}+\mathbf{0})] = \mathrm{var}[z(\mathbf{s})] = c(\mathbf{0}); \quad \forall \mathbf{s}, \mathbf{h} \in D, \tag{4.2.7}$$

where $C(\mathbf{h})$ is called a second-order stationary covariance function or covariogram. However, since the name covariogram is not commonly used, this chapter adopts the term covariance function to conform with most of the research articles. A comparison between Eqs. (4.2.4) and (4.2.6) reveals that the second-order stationarity assumes that the covariance does not depend on position $\mathbf{s}$, and depends only on $\mathbf{h}$. When $C(\mathbf{h})$ depends only on the distance $d = ||\mathbf{h}||$ and not the direction, the spatial process is said to have isotropy ($||\cdot||$ is the Euclidean norm).

In Fig. 4.2.1, the origin of the coordinates ● is the location $\mathbf{s}_1$. Also, the circle and ellipse indicate the contour lines of the covariance between $\mathbf{s}_1$ and each location. If the spatial process is isotropic, the covariance function does

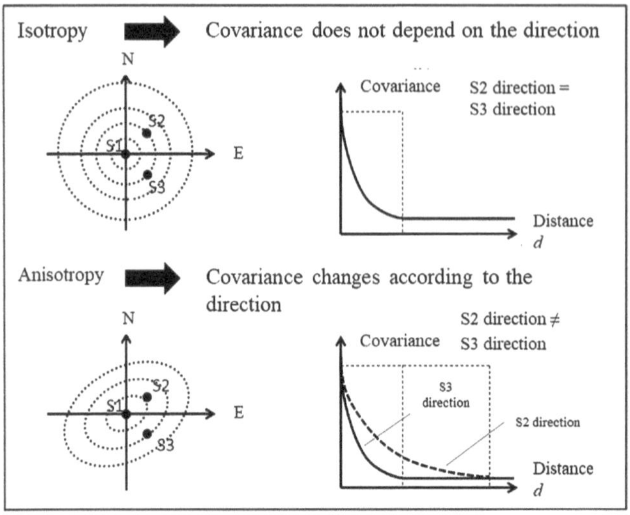

Figure 4.2.1 Isotropy and anisotropy.

not depend on the direction and maintains the same shape in all directions. Therefore, the dependency between random variables is defined only by the distance, and when $||\mathbf{s}_1 - \mathbf{s}_2|| = ||\mathbf{s}_1 - \mathbf{s}_3||$, the dependency between random variables in locations $\mathbf{s}_1$ and $\mathbf{s}_2$ becomes the same as that between locations $\mathbf{s}_1$ and $\mathbf{s}_3$. On the other hand, when there is anisotropy,[2] the dependency between the random variables in locations s_1 and s_2 and that between locations $\mathbf{s}_1$ and $\mathbf{s}_3$ are different. When there is anisotropy, it is necessary to transform it into an isotropic spatial process with an appropriate coordinate transformation, as detailed later.

If the spatial process does not satisfy second-order stationarity, it is necessary to consider the use of nonstationary covariance models, but despite their flexibility, the structure of nonstationary covariance models is relatively complex and demand a high computation load. For this reason, they are not frequently used in empirical research for now. Following are the properties of the covariance function:

It is bounded:

$$|C(\mathbf{h})| \leq C(0), \quad \forall \mathbf{s}, \mathbf{h} \in D. \tag{4.2.8}$$

And also symmetric:

$$C(-\mathbf{h}) = C(\mathbf{h}). \tag{4.2.9}$$

[2] More precisely, geometric anisotropy, which is described later.

The variance is nonnegative:

$$C(0) = Var[z(\mathbf{s})] \geq 0. \tag{4.2.10}$$

Meanwhile, with intrinsic stationarity, it is assumed that the following equations hold $\forall \mathbf{s}, \mathbf{h} \in D$:

$$E[z(\mathbf{s}+\mathbf{h}) - z(\mathbf{s})] = 0, \tag{4.2.11}$$

$$Var[z(\mathbf{s}+\mathbf{h}) - z(\mathbf{s})] = 2\gamma(\mathbf{h}), \tag{4.2.12}$$

where $2\gamma(\mathbf{h})$ and $\gamma(\mathbf{h})$ are functions called variogram and semivariogram, respectively. Unlike in the second-order stationarity, the focus here is the difference (increment). With this, it is possible to express functions with infinite variance (e.g., linear variogram, which is mentioned later).

The properties of the variogram satisfy the following:

$$\gamma(0) = 0, \tag{4.2.13}$$

$$\gamma(0) \geq 0, \tag{4.2.14}$$

$$\gamma(-\mathbf{h}) = \gamma(\mathbf{h}). \tag{4.2.15}$$

One of the characteristics of the geostatistics model, which is described in Section 4.4, is that it makes a spatial prediction of random variables at arbitrary points. The linear predictor is given by $\sum_{i=1}^{N} a_i z(\mathbf{s}_i)$, using constants $a_1, \ldots, a_N$. Since its variance,

$$Var\left[\sum_{i=1}^{N} a_i z(\mathbf{s}_i)\right] = \sum_{i=1}^{N}\sum_{j=1}^{N} a_i a_j C(\mathbf{s}_i - \mathbf{s}_j), \tag{4.2.16}$$

needs to be positive or zero (Chilès and Delfiner, 2012, p. 62), the right side has to be nonnegative (nonnegative definiteness). That is, the covariance function has to be formed to satisfy nonnegative definiteness. The necessary and sufficient conditions for $C(\cdot)$ to be a nonnegative definite are given by Bochner's theorem (e.g., Stein, 1999), and various functions that satisfy this condition have been proposed.

On the other hand, when a variogram is used, the variance of $\sum_{i=1}^{N} \tilde{a}_i z(\mathbf{s}_i)$ using the constants $\tilde{a}, \ldots, \tilde{a}_N$ can be expressed as

$$Var\left[\sum_{i=1}^{N} \tilde{a}_i z(\mathbf{s}_i)\right] = -\sum_{i=1}^{N}\sum_{j=1}^{N} \tilde{a}_i \tilde{a}_j \gamma(\mathbf{s}_i - \mathbf{s}_j). \tag{4.2.17}$$

The properties for the right side under $\sum_{i=1}^{N} \tilde{a}_i = 0$

$$\sum_{i=1}^{N} \sum_{j=1}^{N} \tilde{a}_i \tilde{a}_j \gamma(\mathbf{s}_i - \mathbf{s}_j) \leq 0, \tag{4.2.18}$$

are called conditional nonpositive definite. In practice, a theoretical function that guarantees that the variance is a nonzero positive value is used.

As for the variogram, since it can be modified as

$$2\gamma(\mathbf{h}) = Var[z(\mathbf{s}+\mathbf{h}) - z(\mathbf{s})] = Var[z(\mathbf{s}+\mathbf{h})] + Var[z(\mathbf{s})] \\ - 2Cov[z(\mathbf{s}+\mathbf{h}), z(\mathbf{s})], \tag{4.2.19}$$

if the second-order stationarity is satisfied, the following relationship holds:

$$\gamma(\mathbf{h}) = \frac{1}{2}[2C(0) - 2C(\mathbf{h})] = C(0) - C(\mathbf{h}). \tag{4.2.20}$$

On the other hand, since the variogram is not necessarily bounded, the opposite is not necessarily true. For example, the variance of the linear variogram in Fig. 4.2.2 is ∞, and it does not have a covariance function. If the variogram is interpreted as dissimilarity of the random variables, it is natural to infer that this value increases as the distance grows. If $C(\mathbf{h}) \rightarrow 0$ holds

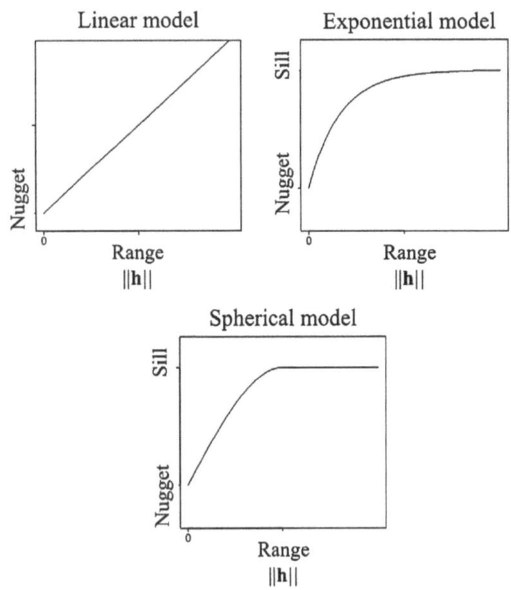

Figure 4.2.2 Examples of theoretical variogram models.

when the distance goes to infinity—that is, when $||\mathbf{h}|| \to \infty$ —the spatial process is said to have ergodicity (Arbia, 2006, p. 48). Then, if $||\mathbf{h}|| \to \infty$ holds in Eq. (4.2.19), $\lim_{||\widetilde{\mathbf{h}}|| \to \infty} \gamma(\mathbf{h}) = C(0)$ is obtained. Now, to avoid confusion, if the variable $\widetilde{\mathbf{h}}$ is used, the following equation holds:

$$C(\mathbf{h}) = C(0) - \gamma(\mathbf{h}) = \lim_{||\widetilde{\mathbf{h}}|| \to \infty} \gamma\left(\widetilde{\mathbf{h}}\right) - \gamma(\mathbf{h}). \tag{4.2.21}$$

Therefore, under constant conditions, it is possible to determine a covariance function from a variogram.

A wide range of theoretical models for variograms and corresponding covariance functions have been proposed. The shape of these models is specified basically by three parameters called nugget, sill, and range. The nugget is the value when the distance between locations is $\mathbf{0}$, which is the value of intercept. By definition, the variogram $\gamma(\mathbf{h}) = 0$ if the $\mathbf{h}$ value is exactly zero. But, as long as $\mathbf{h} > 0$, $\gamma(\mathbf{h})$ does not always approach zero even if $\mathbf{h}$ approaches zero. This is caused by local variations (and measurement errors if $\sigma_\varepsilon^2 \neq 0$) at locations shorter than the distance between observation points. Therefore, the variogram becomes discontinuous in $\mathbf{h} = \mathbf{0}$. The sill indicates the variance of the spatial process, and the value obtained by subtracting the nugget from the sill is called the partial sill. The range is the minimum $\mathbf{h}$ with which $z(\mathbf{s})$ and $z(\mathbf{s} + \mathbf{h})$ no longer have a correlation.

Tables 4.2.1 and 4.2.2, respectively, indicate the most common theoretical variograms and covariance functions. Of these, the linear, exponential, and spherical models are illustrated in Fig. 4.2.2. τ^2 is the nugget, $\tau^2+\sigma^2$ the sill ($\sigma^2$is the partial sill), and$1/\varphi$ the range. In the linear model, the nugget exists, but the sill and range are infinity. Meanwhile, in the exponential model, the sill exists, but its value can only be achieved asymptotically, and its range becomes infinity. Therefore, it can be interpreted more effectively with the concepts called effective or practical range. This value is the distance where there is almost no spatial autocorrelation (e.g., the correlation is 0.05), and is normally given as the distance where the semivariogram achieves 95% of the sill. In the case of the exponential model, the valid range is $3/\varphi$. On the other hand, in the case of the spherical model, the semivariogram can necessarily achieve 100% of the value of the sill, making the concept of effective range unnecessary. Consequently, the variance-covariance matrix becomes sparse and is often used in empirical research due to its ease of calculation.

Table 4.2.1 Examples of theoretical variogram models.

Linear	$\boldsymbol{\gamma}(\mathbf{h}) = \begin{cases} \boldsymbol{\tau}^2 + \boldsymbol{\sigma}^2 \lVert \mathbf{h} \rVert & \textbf{\textit{if}} \lVert \mathbf{h} \rVert \rangle 0 \\ 0 & \textbf{\textit{otherwise}} \end{cases}$
Spherical	$\gamma(\mathbf{h}) = \begin{cases} \tau^2 + \sigma^2 & if \lVert \boldsymbol{h} \rVert \rangle 1/\varphi \\ \tau^2 + \sigma^2 \left[\frac{3}{2} \varphi \lVert \mathbf{h} \rVert - \frac{1}{2} (\varphi \lVert \mathbf{h} \rVert)^3 \right] & if 0 < \lVert \mathbf{h} \rVert \leq 1/\varphi \\ 0 & otherwise \end{cases}$
Exponential	$\gamma(\mathbf{h}) = \begin{cases} \tau^2 + \sigma^2 [1 - \exp(-\varphi \lVert \mathbf{h} \rVert)] & if \lVert \mathbf{h} \rVert \rangle 0 \\ 0 & otherwise \end{cases}$
Gaussian	$\gamma(\mathbf{h}) = \begin{cases} \tau^2 + \sigma^2 [1 - \exp(-\varphi^2 \lVert \mathbf{h} \rVert^2)] & if \lVert \mathbf{h} \rVert \rangle 0 \\ 0 & otherwise \end{cases}$
Wave	$\gamma(\mathbf{h}) = \begin{cases} \tau^2 + \sigma^2 \left[1 - \frac{\sin(\varphi \lVert \mathbf{h} \rVert)}{\varphi \lVert \mathbf{h} \rVert} \right] & if \lVert \mathbf{h} \rVert \rangle 0 \\ 0 & otherwise \end{cases}$
Matérn	$\gamma(\mathbf{h}) = \begin{cases} \tau^2 + \sigma^2 \left[1 - \frac{(2\sqrt{\nu} \lVert \mathbf{h} \rVert \varphi)^{\nu}}{2^{\nu-1} \Gamma(\nu)} K_{\nu}(2\sqrt{\nu} \lVert \boldsymbol{h} \rVert \varphi) \right] & if \lVert \mathbf{h} \rVert \rangle 0 \\ 0 & otherwise \end{cases}$

$\Gamma(\bullet)$ is a normal gamma function and K_{ν} is a modified Bessel function of the second kind of order \nu.

Table 4.2.2 Examples of covariance functions.

Linear	**C(h) does not exist**	
Spherical	$C(\mathbf{h}) = \begin{cases} 0 \\ \sigma^2\left[1 - \frac{3}{2}\varphi\left\|\mathbf{h}\right\| + \frac{1}{2}(\varphi\|\mathbf{h}\|)^3\right] \\ \tau^2 + \sigma^2 \end{cases}$	$if\|\mathbf{h}\|\rangle 1/\varphi$ $if 0 < \|\mathbf{h}\| \leq 1/\varphi$ *otherwise*
Exponential	$C(\mathbf{h}) = \begin{cases} \sigma^2 \exp(-\varphi\|\mathbf{h}\|) \\ \tau^2 + \sigma^2 \end{cases}$	$if\|\mathbf{h}\|\rangle 0$ *otherwise*
Gaussian	$C(\mathbf{h}) = \begin{cases} \sigma^2 \exp(-\varphi^2\|\mathbf{h}\|^2) \\ \tau^2 + \sigma^2 \end{cases}$	$if\|\mathbf{h}\|\rangle 0$ *otherwise*
Wave	$C(\mathbf{h}) = \begin{cases} \sigma^2\frac{\sin(\varphi\|\mathbf{h}\|)}{\varphi\|\mathbf{h}\|} \\ \tau^2 + \sigma^2 \end{cases}$	$if\|\mathbf{h}\|\rangle 0$ *otherwise*
Matérn model	$C(\mathbf{h}) = \begin{cases} \sigma^2\frac{(2\sqrt{\nu}\|\mathbf{h}\|\varphi)^{\nu}}{2^{\nu-1}\Gamma(\nu)}K_{\nu}(2\sqrt{\nu}\|\mathbf{h}\|\varphi) \\ \tau^2 + \sigma^2 \end{cases}$	$if\|\mathbf{h}\|\rangle 0$ *otherwise*

$\Gamma(\bullet)$ is a normal gamma function and K_{ν} is a modified Bessel function of the second kind of order \nu.

The Matérn model is a family of functions proposed by the statistician Matérn (1960, 1986) and improved by Handcock and Stein (1993). Because of the smoothing parameter ν, it is a function that includes both the exponential ($\nu = 0.5$) and Gaussian models ($\nu \rightarrow \infty$), and therefore is very flexible (Hoeting et al., 2006). For more details about the Matérn model, see Stein (1999) and Guttorp and Gneiting (2006).

The selection of the theoretical variogram function to be used is also important. The most typical ones are cross-validation[3] and Akaike's information criterion (Hoeting et al., 2006); if parameter estimation is based on the Bayesian theory, the Bayes factors (Berger et al., 2001; Cowles, 2003), deviance information criterion (DIC) (Finley et al.,2007 [4]), and reversible jump Markov chain Monte Carlo (MCMC) (Johnson and Hoeting, 2011) can be used.

[3] The krige.cv function of the gstat package in R and the xvalid function of the geoR package can be used.

[4] DIC can be calculated with the spBayes of the package of R.

4.2.2.3 Anisotropy

Anisotropy is a phenomenon in which the structure of spatial autocorrelation; that is, the structure of variogram and covariance function, differs according to the direction. Taking the case of cities as an example, the cities in Japan, unlike many European cities that expanded from citadels in the past, developed around railways. For this reason, the correlation between land price data is considered strong along the railway but weak in its vertical direction (Tsutsumi and Seya, 2009). Anisotropy can be divided into two types: geometric anisotropy, in which only the range changes according to the direction and the sill remains constant regardless of the direction; and zonal anisotropy, in which both change (e.g., Zimmerman, 1993). The geometric anisotropy can be examined relatively easily with a coordinate transformation.

Suppose that $z_1(\mathbf{s})$ is a second-order stationary and isotropic spatial process with average m and covariance function $C_1(\mathbf{h})$, as with the case discussed earlier. Considering $\mathbf{B}$ a $d \times d$ matrix, the spatial process $z(\mathbf{s}) = z_1(\mathbf{Bs})$, coordinate-transformed using $\mathbf{B}$, is analyzed below. Even if there is geometric anisotropy, $E[z(\mathbf{s})] = E[z_1(\mathbf{s})]$ holds and the dimension of the sill does not change with $z(\mathbf{s})$ or $z_1(\mathbf{s})$. Hence, $Var[z(\mathbf{s})] = Var[z_1(\mathbf{s})]$ holds. Meanwhile, the covariance becomes:

$$Cov[z(\mathbf{s}), z(\mathbf{s}+\mathbf{h})] = C(\mathbf{h}) = Cov[z_1(\mathbf{Bs}), z_1(\mathbf{B}(\mathbf{s}+\mathbf{h}))] = C_1(\mathbf{Bh}). \tag{4.2.22}$$

Therefore, if $C_1(\mathbf{h})$ is isotropic, $C(\mathbf{h}) = C_1(||\mathbf{Bh}||)$ becomes a covariance function with geometric anisotropy, and $z(\mathbf{s}^*) = Y(\mathbf{B}^{-1}\mathbf{s}^*)$ acquires an isotropic covariance function. For example, the geometric anisotropy indicated in Fig. 4.2.1, in the example of $d = 2$, can be dealt with the following linear conversion that represents extension/reduction and rotation:

$$\mathbf{B}^{-1} = \begin{bmatrix} 1 & 0 \\ 0 & \delta \end{bmatrix} \begin{bmatrix} \cos(\phi) & -\sin(\phi) \\ \sin(\phi) & \cos(\phi) \end{bmatrix}. \tag{4.2.23}$$

Here, ϕ is a parameter that represents the angle of rotation of the coordinate system and δ is a parameter that represents the ratio of the range in two directions called anisotropy ratio. For examples with $d = 3$, see Chilès and Delfiner (2012), p. 99. ϕ and δ are often determined visually from the differences in empirical variograms plotted from data of different directions. But there is also an approach that sets a distribution to these parameters in advance and performs Bayesian inference (Ecker and Gelfand,

1999). Moreover, for other approaches on the process of anisotropy of the range, see Ecker and Gelfand (2003).

The zonal anisotropy can be dealt with a model that assumes a nested structure, in which the variogram is given by the sum of an isotropic variogram and another variogram related to a direction with a larger sill (Schabenberger and Gotway, 2005, p. 152). Bayesian approaches, which estimate each parameter, have been developed to estimate zonal anisotropy (e.g., Katzfuss, 2013). Furthermore, some of them estimate local anisotropy, which allows for spatially varying parameters relating anisotropy. For example, Fuglstad et al. (2015) developed a new class of nonstationarity spatial process with local anisotropy based on the stochastic partial differential equations, and implemented their approach in R-INLA, which is an R package (see Bakka et al., 2018).

4.3 Parameter estimation

This section describes the methods of parameter estimation of variograms introduced in the previous section. The most typical methods include the nonlinear ordinary least squares (NOLS) method, the method of maximum likelihood, and the restricted maximum likelihood (REML) method. Each of these methods is detailed later, but first, it is necessary to explain two important concepts of variogram cloud and empirical variogram. Following the discussion in the previous section, the spatial process can be expressed as

$$y(\mathbf{s}) = m(\mathbf{s}) + u(\mathbf{s}), \quad \forall s \in D, \tag{4.3.1}$$

without observation errors. Hence here, $u(\mathbf{s}) = z(\mathbf{s}) + e(\mathbf{s})$ is considered.

In the following analysis, it is assumed that $m(\mathbf{s})$ is already known and $u(\mathbf{s})$ has intrinsic stationarity or second-order stationarity (Hengl et al., 2007). Naturally, since $m(\mathbf{s})$ is seldom known in advance, it is necessary to structure it with some method and estimate its parameter in the same way as the variogram parameter $\theta = (\tau^2, \sigma^2, \varphi)'$. The error components in the points $\mathbf{s}_i$ and $\mathbf{s}_j = \mathbf{s}_i - \mathbf{h}$ are respectively expressed as $u(\mathbf{s}_i)$ and $u(\mathbf{s}_j)$. It can also be written as u_i and u_j, but the expression more commonly used in the geostatistics field was adopted in this analysis. The measurement γ^*, which represents the nonsimilarity between the two values, is given by the following equation (Wackernagel, 1998):

$$\gamma^*(\mathbf{h}) = [u(\mathbf{s}_i) - u(\mathbf{s}_j)]^2 / 2. \tag{4.3.2}$$

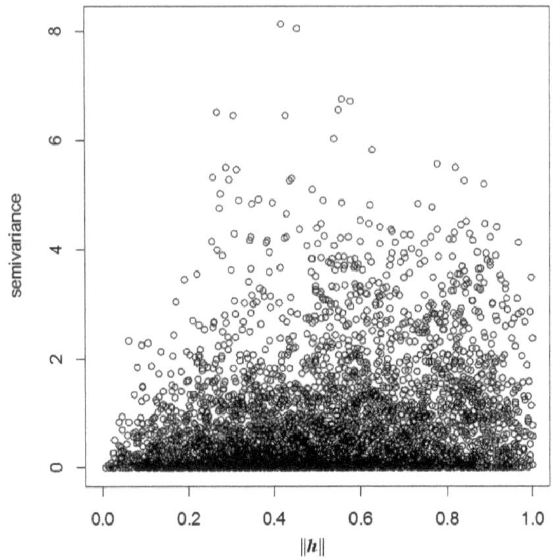

Figure 4.3.1 Example of a variogram cloud calculated from R package geoR sample data s100.

If it is plotted to $||\mathbf{h}|| = d$, assuming that the nonsimilarity γ^* depends only on the distance (the assumption of isotropy), the variogram cloud shown in Fig. 4.3.1 is obtained.

Since a variogram cloud is given only among observed data, to model a spatial autocorrelation relationship for an arbitrary point, it is necessary to replace it with one of the previously mentioned theoretical variograms (this also ensures that the variance of the prediction obtained by an arbitrary linear combination of the observed values is nonnegative). However, as shown in Fig. 4.3.1, a variogram cloud determined from actual data is commonly occupied by pairs of samples with low nonsimilarity in many distance zones (Wackernagel, 1998), and because of outliers, it is often difficult to fit a variogram cloud to a theoretical variogram.

For this reason, an operation called binning[5] needs to be performed. It consists of dividing the distance d into R units of sections $\hbar_r (r = 1, \ldots, R)$ without mutually overlapping ranges and determining the average value

[5] The data structure is often revealed by this kind of aggregation, but since binning is a difficult operation that tends to be arbitrary, other researchers point out that if the number of observation points is not too high, the theoretical variogram should be fitted to the variogram cloud directly (Glatzer and Müller, 2004).

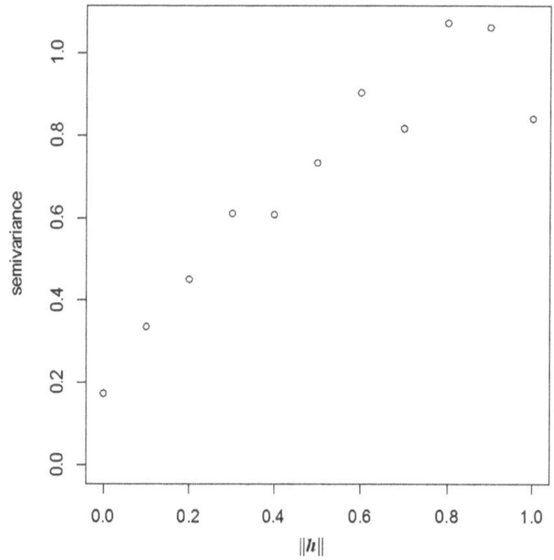

Figure 4.3.2 Example of an empirical variogram calculated from R package geoR sample data s100.

of nonsimilarity of each section (empirical variogram) (Fig. 4.3.2). The empirical variogram of a section $\hbar_r$ is given by the following equation:

$$\gamma^*(\hbar_\tau) = \frac{1}{2\#N_r} \sum_{(i,j)\in N_r} [u(\mathbf{s}_i) - u(\mathbf{s}_j)]^2, \tag{4.3.3}$$

where N_r is a set of sample pairs in which $||\mathbf{s}_i - \mathbf{s}_j|| \approx \hbar_r$ and $\#N_r$ is the number of sample pairs in which $||\mathbf{s}_i - \mathbf{s}_j|| \approx \hbar_r$. Since Eq. (4.3.3) has a $(\cdot)^2$ term, it is sensitive to outliers. For this reason, the Cressie-Hawkins's robust estimation (Cressie and Hawkins, 1980) is often used as an estimate strong against outliers.

$$\widetilde{\gamma}^*(\hbar_r) = \frac{\frac{1}{2}\left\{\frac{1}{\#N_r}\sum_{(i,j)\in N_r}\left|u(\mathbf{s}_i) - u(\mathbf{s}_j)\right|^{\frac{1}{2}}\right\}^4}{0.475 + \frac{0.494}{\#N_r}}. \tag{4.3.4}$$

where $|\cdot|$ indicates the absolute value. For the specific derivation method, see Cressie and Hawkins (1980).[6] Many other variograms robust to outliers have been proposed, including Dowd (1984)'s median estimate. The robust

[6] This function can be easily implemented with R's gstat and geoR package, for example.

estimation of the variogram was detailed by Marchant and Lark (2007). However, before applying a robust estimate, it is necessary to check for outliers very carefully. Borssoi et al. (2011) point out Cook (1986) local influence method as an effective tool to check for outliers. Other researchers have developed methods to evaluate the uncertainty of variograms by bootstrap (Ortiz and Deutsch, 2002; Wang and Wall, 2003) as well as programs that execute such tasks (Pardo-Igúzquiza and Olea, 2012). The next section describes a method to fit theoretical variograms to empirical variograms (i.e., parameter estimation of theoretical variograms).

4.3.1 Nonlinear least squares method

For this analysis, the theoretical variogram is defined as γ and the empirical variogram as γ^*. If the parameter vector of the theoretical variogram is set as $\boldsymbol{\theta}$, the NOLS method estimates the parameter $\boldsymbol{\theta}$ that minimizes the following equation:

$$\sum_{r=1}^{R}\left[\gamma^*(\hbar_r)-\gamma(\hbar_r|\boldsymbol{\theta})\right]^2. \tag{4.3.5}$$

However, in this method, neither the variation of the distribution of γ^* (the presence of heterogeneous variance) nor the covariation (serial correlation between variograms) are considered (Cressie, 1993). For this reason, in empirical research, the nonlinear weighted least squares (NWLS) method proposed by Cressie (1985) is frequently used.

$$\sum_{r=1}^{R}\left[Var\{\gamma^*(\hbar_r)\}\right]^{-1}\left[\gamma^*(\hbar_r)-\gamma(\hbar_r|\boldsymbol{\theta})\right]^2. \tag{4.3.6}$$

Generally, if d increases, the number of sample pairs decreases and the variance increases. In statistics, the reciprocal of variance is sometimes called precision, and in this case, the precision is high where d is small and vice versa. Therefore, a method that approximates the variance term in Eq. (4.3.6) with a weighting that depends on the number of sample pairs is used. More specifically,

$$Var\left[\gamma^*(\hbar_r)\right]\approx 2\gamma(\hbar_r|\boldsymbol{\theta})^2/\#N_r, \tag{4.3.7}$$

is used. Naturally, the NWLS method considers the presence only of heterogeneous variance, and the covariation of the distribution of γ^* cannot be taken into account. Although a parameter method that applies a nonlinear generalized least squares method to consider the serial correlation between variograms has been proposed, in practice, the NWLS method is more commonly used due to its convenience.

So far, it was assumed that $m(\mathbf{s})$ was already known, but naturally, such cases are rare. In many cases, a model with a trend term of linear type $m(\mathbf{s}) = \sum_{k=1}^{K} x_k(\mathbf{s})\beta_k$ is assumed. Here, since β_k is unknown, it needs to be estimated along with $\boldsymbol{\theta}$. Considering that explanatory variables were obtained at N discrete locations, with the explanatory variable matrix define as $\mathbf{X}$, many previous studies simply fitted the theoretical variogram to the empirical variogram created from the residual of the ordinary least squares (OLS)-estimated $\boldsymbol{\beta}$ (e.g., Chua, 1982; Dingman et al., 1988). However, since the OLS is a parameter estimation method that assumes that the error terms have no spatial autocorrelation, determining an empirical variogram from a residual estimated by the OLS method is logically contradictory. It is also known that variograms determined from OLS residuals and parameter estimates of covariance functions are biased (Cressie, 1993, p. 71). Therefore, the parameter estimation of trend terms has to be done through the generalized least squares (GLS) method, but with it comes a problem that the variance-covariance matrix required in GLS is unknown. To tackle this problem, a method called iteratively reweighted generalized least squares (IRWGLS), which estimates the parameters with the following iterative calculation, is used (e.g., Schabenberger and Gotway, 2005, pp. 256–259). The algorithm can be summarized as follows:

1. $\widehat{\boldsymbol{\beta}}_{ols}$, the estimated value of $\boldsymbol{\beta}$, is determined by OLS.
2. The residual vector $\mathbf{y} - \mathbf{X}\widehat{\boldsymbol{\beta}}_{ols}$ is calculated.
3. The empirical variogram related to the residual is obtained by the Cressie and Hawkins (1980) estimation.
4. The theoretical variogram is fitted to the empirical variogram by NWLS to obtain $\widehat{\boldsymbol{\theta}}_{nwls}$.
5. The covariance function is determined from the estimated theoretical variogram, and assuming that the variance-covariance matrix is known, the estimated value of the trend parameter, $\widehat{\boldsymbol{\beta}}_{gls}$, is obtained by the EGLS (estimated GLS) method.
6. Steps (3) to (5) are repeated until $\boldsymbol{\beta}$ and $\boldsymbol{\theta}$ have sufficiently converged.

The IRWGLS estimate of $\boldsymbol{\beta}$ becomes the EGLS estimate, and the result of the iterative calculation is given by the following equation:

$$\widehat{\boldsymbol{\beta}}_{\text{irwgls}} = \left[\mathbf{X}'\boldsymbol{\Sigma}\left(\widehat{\boldsymbol{\theta}}_{\text{irwgls}}\right)^{-1}\mathbf{X}\right]^{-1}\mathbf{X}'\boldsymbol{\Sigma}\left(\widehat{\boldsymbol{\theta}}_{\text{irwgls}}\right)^{-1}\mathbf{y}. \tag{4.3.8}$$

Also, its variance is given by:

$$Var\left(\widehat{\boldsymbol{\beta}}_{\text{irwgls}}\right) = \left[\mathbf{X}/\boldsymbol{\Sigma}\left(\widehat{\boldsymbol{\theta}}_{\text{irwgls}}\right)^{-1}\mathbf{X}\right]^{-1}. \tag{4.3.9}$$

where $\boldsymbol{\Sigma}$ is a variance-covariance matrix that gives its elements by a covariance function. Since the number of sample pairs decreases as d increases, it is difficult to decide the threshold for the magnitude of d that should be considered in NWLS. Cressie (1985) proposed a practical rule that the distance zones with $\#N_r > 30$ and less than half the maximum distance must be included in the estimation. However, needless to say, this is also not a general answer, and the empirical analysis requires a certain trial and error.

4.3.2 Maximum likelihood method

The parameters of geostatistical models are estimated by maximum likelihood (ML). For this analysis, let us consider the following model with no observation error:

$$\mathbf{y} \sim N(\mathbf{X}\boldsymbol{\beta}, \boldsymbol{\Sigma}(\boldsymbol{\theta})) \tag{4.3.10}$$

where $\boldsymbol{\Sigma}(\boldsymbol{\theta}) = \tau^2 \mathbf{I}_{[N]} + \sigma^2 \mathbf{H}(\varphi)$, where $\mathbf{H}$ is an $N \times N$ correlation matrix that gives its i, j elements by a correlation function. In the case of the exponential type, for example, from Table 4.2.2, it becomes $H_{ij} = \exp(-\varphi||d_{ij}||)$ (assuming isotropy). The log-likelihood function in this case is given as the following equation:

$$l(\mathbf{y}|\boldsymbol{\beta}, \boldsymbol{\theta}) = -\frac{N}{2}\ln(2\pi) - \frac{1}{2}\ln\left|\boldsymbol{\Sigma}(\boldsymbol{\theta})\right| - \frac{1}{2}(\mathbf{y} - \mathbf{X}\boldsymbol{\beta})'\boldsymbol{\Sigma}(\boldsymbol{\theta})^{-1}(\mathbf{y} - \mathbf{X}\boldsymbol{\beta}). \tag{4.3.11}$$

Then the parameters that maximize this log-likelihood function, $\boldsymbol{\beta}$ and $\boldsymbol{\theta}$, must be determined. Normally, by substituting the maximum likelihood estimator of $\boldsymbol{\beta}$,

$$\widehat{\boldsymbol{\beta}}_{ml} = \left[\mathbf{X}'\boldsymbol{\Sigma}(\boldsymbol{\theta})^{-1}\mathbf{X}\right]^{-1}\mathbf{X}'\boldsymbol{\Sigma}(\boldsymbol{\theta})^{-1}\boldsymbol{y}, \tag{4.3.12}$$

into Eq. (4.3.11), the concentrated log likelihood function related to $\boldsymbol{\theta}$ is obtained as

$$l_C(\mathbf{y}|\boldsymbol{\theta}) = const. - \frac{1}{2}\ln\left|\boldsymbol{\Sigma}(\boldsymbol{\theta})\right| - \frac{1}{2}\boldsymbol{y}'\boldsymbol{P}(\boldsymbol{\theta})\boldsymbol{y}, \tag{4.3.13}$$

where $\boldsymbol{P}(\boldsymbol{\theta}) = \boldsymbol{\Sigma}(\boldsymbol{\theta})^{-1} - \boldsymbol{\Sigma}(\boldsymbol{\theta})^{-1}\mathbf{X}\left[\mathbf{X}'\boldsymbol{\Sigma}(\boldsymbol{\theta})^{-1}\mathbf{X}\right]^{-1}\mathbf{X}'\boldsymbol{\Sigma}(\boldsymbol{\theta})^{-1}$. Since $l_C(\mathbf{y}|\boldsymbol{\theta})$ is a nonlinear function to $\boldsymbol{\theta}$, the maximum likelihood estimator $\widehat{\boldsymbol{\theta}}_{ml}$ can be obtained by nonlinear optimization. For a specific method, see Zimmerman (2010) and the references therein.

4.3.3 Restricted maximum likelihood method

With the ML method, the optional parameter $\boldsymbol{\beta}$ (the so-called nuisance parameter) is also estimated together, which ends up decreasing the estimation accuracy of $\boldsymbol{\theta}$. This problem is especially serious if the sample size is small (Harville, 1977). For this reason, the REML method, which features a linear conversion so that $\boldsymbol{\theta}$ does not depend on $\boldsymbol{\beta}$, was proposed. The REML method was introduced to geostatistical models in the 1980s (e.g., Kitanidis, 1983). With this method, the likelihood of the linear combination of observed values called error contrasts is maximized, not the likelihood of the observed value. That is, when $\mathbf{B}$ is defined as a $(N-K)\times N$ matrix that satisfies both $E[\mathbf{By}]=0$ and $rank[\mathbf{By}]=N-K$, the ML method is applied to $\mathbf{By}$, not $\mathbf{y}$. Since the term related to the average disappears with this transformation, it is also called the residual maximum method (Schabenberger and Gotway, 2005, p. 262). There are many possible ways to obtain $\mathbf{B}$, but if the idempotent matrix, $\mathbf{M_X}=\left[\mathbf{I}-\mathbf{X}(\mathbf{X}'\mathbf{X})^{-1}\mathbf{X}'\right]$ is multiplied to $\mathbf{y}$, a residual vector is generated. If this vector is used, the log-likelihood function becomes as follows:

$$l_R(\mathbf{y}|\boldsymbol{\theta})=const.-\frac{1}{2}\ln\left|\boldsymbol{\Sigma}(\boldsymbol{\theta})\right|-\frac{1}{2}\ln\left|\mathbf{X}'\boldsymbol{\Sigma}(\boldsymbol{\theta})^{-1}\mathbf{X}\right|-\frac{1}{2}\mathbf{y}'\mathbf{P}(\boldsymbol{\theta})\mathbf{y}. \tag{4.3.14}$$

Then, the covariance function parameter $\widehat{\boldsymbol{\theta}}_{reml}$ that maximizes this log-likelihood function needs to be determined. Since the estimate obtained with the maximization of $l_R(\mathbf{y}|\boldsymbol{\theta})$ estimates $\boldsymbol{\theta}$ directly, without considering the nuisance parameters, it is said to reduce the underestimation bias that the ML estimate of $\boldsymbol{\theta}$ has, especially if the sample size is small (Kitanidis, 1985). However, when Irvine et al. (2007) compared the estimates of the exponential model with the ML and REML methods, they showed that while the REML method effectively reduces the bias of covariance function parameters, in some cases, the upper skirt of the distribution of range tends to widen, making its mean squared error worse than that of the ML estimate. This problem becomes more serious as the range and the nugget/sill ratio increase. However, this result is related to $K=1$, and if there is a large number of explanatory variables, the REML method is said to generate better results than those of the ML method (Cressie, 1993, p. 93).

Unlike the nonlinear least squares approach, the ML and REML methods do not use empirical variograms, and therefore do not require binning, which averages the nonsimilarity for each distance zone (lag) as in Eq. (4.3.3). This is an important aspect because binning and the setting of the maximum distance zones are difficult operations that affect even the prediction results.

4.4 Kriging

4.4.1 Spatial prediction and Kriging

Since geostatistical models assume weak stationarity or intrinsic stationarity in spatial processes, they can be used for spatial prediction of random variables at arbitrary points in a natural way. The term "prediction," which is often used in the sense of predicting the future, can be misleading, but in this context, it designates the estimation of random variables at arbitrary points other than the observation points. In this document, "spatial prediction" and "prediction" are used without distinction.

Due to budget or technology-related constraints, or even privacy protection policies, spatial data can be measured at only limited observation points. For this reason, in many cases, it is necessary to make some kind of prediction, such as estimating the geographical distribution of the data from discrete observation data. Spatial prediction consists of spatial interpolation and extrapolation (Fig. 4.4.1). The former predicts numerical values within a geographical range containing observed values, while the latter predicts the external numerical values. As intuition suggests, it is more difficult to make highly accurate and precise predictions with extrapolation than interpolation.

Many spatial prediction methods have been proposed to date.[7] The inverse distance weighting method, a classical spatial prediction method, uses the reciprocal of distance as a weight to determine the predicted value of data at an arbitrary point deterministically as a linear sum of the observed values. This can be considered a method that attempts to make a prediction

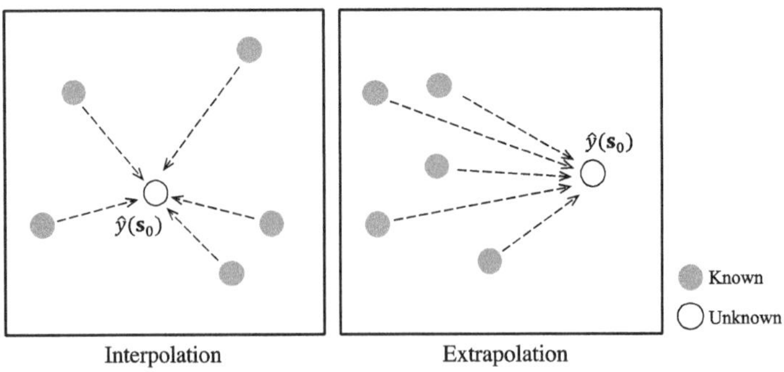

Figure 4.4.1 Spatial interpolation and extrapolation.

[7] For a review on various spatial prediction methods, see Lam (1993).

based only on spatial autocorrelation information. However, it does not consider the mutual relationship between observation points (e.g., in Fig. 4.4.1, whether the observation points are concentrated on the upper side of the diagram or well balanced between upper and lower sides).

On the other hand, in regression models, the predicted values are determined probabilistically using attribute information **X**. With this, it is possible to determine the variance of prediction errors, which in turn makes it possible to evaluate the reliability of interpolation and extrapolation values objectively. However, in predictions with the basic model, spatial autocorrelation is not taken into account.

Universal Kriging, one of the Kriging methods, considers these two aspects. Li and Heap (2011) summarized the most typical spatial prediction methods and presented 18 comparative studies about the precision and accuracy of spatial prediction. Their main conclusion was that "*in general, kriging methods perform better than non-geostatistical methods.*"

Kriging is a statistically superior method that gives the BLUP of random variables at arbitrary points.[8] The following are some of its characteristics: (1) it considers spatial autocorrelation and (2) the positional relationship between observed values, (3) it can be combined with a regression model and take various trend factors into account, (4) if there are no observation errors, the observed values match the predicted values (i.e., exact interpolator), and (5) the prediction errors can be calculated. The Kriging method is explained below based on the discussion of the previous section.

To define the *quality* of the prediction, the loss function between the prediction $\widehat{y}(\mathbf{s}_0)$ at the prediction point $\mathbf{s}_0$ and the true value $y(\mathbf{s}_0)$ is defined by

$$\text{Loss Function} = [y(\mathbf{s}_0) - \widehat{y}(\mathbf{s}_0)]^2. \tag{4.4.1}$$

However, since this amount fluctuates probabilistically, it is necessary to determine a prediction that minimizes its expected value,

$$E\left[\{y(\mathbf{s}_0) - \widehat{y}(\mathbf{s}_0)\}^2\right]. \tag{4.4.2}$$

This is called mean squared prediction error (MSPE). A Kriging prediction is a practical prediction that is determined to minimize the MSPE. Some of the most typical Kriging methods are detailed next.

[8] A few nonlinear predictions also exist.

4.4.1.1 Ordinary Kriging

In ordinary Kriging (OK), intrinsic stationarity is assumed for the variable $y(s)$, which includes a trend component $m(s)$. That is, it is important to note that there is a strong assumption that $\mathrm{E}[y(\mathbf{s})] = \mathrm{m}(\mathbf{s}) = \overline{\mathrm{m}}$ at all the points within the area. In OK, the prediction $\widehat{y}(\mathbf{s}_0)_{ok}$ at an arbitrary point s_0 is given as the linear sum of random variables at the observation points by the following equation:

$$\widehat{y}(s_0)_{ok} = \sum\nolimits_{i=1}^{N} \chi_i y(s_i) = \boldsymbol{\chi}'\mathbf{y}. \tag{4.4.3}$$

where $\boldsymbol{\chi}=(\chi_1, \ldots, \chi_N)'$. Also, the random variable vector $\mathbf{y} = [y(\mathbf{s}_1), y(\mathbf{s}_2), \ldots, y(\mathbf{s}_N)]'$ at the observation point $\boldsymbol{s}_i$ is simplified as $\mathbf{y}=(y_1, \ldots, y_N)'$. In order for the prediction to become unbiased, the expected value of prediction error has to be zero as in the following equation:

$$E\left[y(\mathbf{s}_0) - \widehat{y}(\mathbf{s}_0)_{ok}\right] = E\left[y(\mathbf{s}_0) - \sum_{i=1}^{N} \chi_i y_i\right] = \overline{m} - \sum_{i=1}^{N} \chi_i E[y_i] = 0. \tag{4.4.4}$$

In other words, $\sum_{i=1}^{N} \chi_i = 1$ (or $\overline{m} = 0$) is the condition for unbiasedness. To meet this condition, it is necessary to minimize the expected value of the loss function under this unbiased constraint, which is nothing but minimizing the Lagrange function Φ indicated in the next equation. Here, $\widetilde{\lambda}$ is a Lagrange multiplier. It is expressed as $\widetilde{\lambda}$ to distinguish it from the spatial error model parameter λ that is mentioned later. Also, the Lagrange term is multiplied by 2 to make the development of the equation easier:

$$\Phi = E\left[\left(y(\mathbf{s}_0) - \widehat{y}(\mathbf{s}_0)_{ok}\right)^2\right] - 2\widetilde{\lambda}\left(\sum_{i=1}^{N} \chi_i - 1\right), \tag{4.4.5}$$

where the expected squared prediction error, $E\left[\left(y(\mathbf{s}_0) - \widehat{y}(\mathbf{s}_0)_{ok}\right)^2\right]$, equals $Var\left[\left(y(\mathbf{s}_0) - \widehat{y}(\mathbf{s}_0)_{ok}\right)\right]$ due to the constraint of unbiasedness.

From Eq. (4.4.5), the following equation is obtained:

$$\Phi = -\sum_{i=1}^{N}\sum_{j=1}^{N} \chi_i \chi_j \gamma(\mathbf{s}_i - \mathbf{s}_j) + 2\sum_{i=1}^{N} \chi_i \gamma(\mathbf{s}_0 - \mathbf{s}_i) - 2\widetilde{\lambda}\left(\sum_{i=1}^{N} \chi_i - 1\right). \tag{4.4.6}$$

To define the parameters $\chi_1, \ldots, \chi_N$ that minimize this equation and $\widetilde{\lambda}$, it is necessary to partially differentiate Φ with these parameters and set it to 0, which generates the following normal equation (Cressie, 1993, p. 121):

$$\begin{pmatrix} \gamma(\mathbf{s}_1-\mathbf{s}_1) & \cdots & \gamma(\mathbf{s}_1-\mathbf{s}_N) & 1 \\ \vdots & \gamma(\mathbf{s}_i-\mathbf{s}_j) & \vdots & \vdots \\ \gamma(\mathbf{s}_N-\mathbf{s}_1) & \cdots & \gamma(\mathbf{s}_N-\mathbf{s}_N) & 1 \\ 1 & \cdots & 1 & 0 \end{pmatrix} \begin{pmatrix} \chi_1 \\ \vdots \\ \chi_N \\ \widetilde{\lambda} \end{pmatrix} = \begin{pmatrix} \gamma(\mathbf{s}_0-\mathbf{s}_1) \\ \vdots \\ \gamma(\mathbf{s}_0-\mathbf{s}_N) \\ 1 \end{pmatrix}, \tag{4.4.7}$$

or $\boldsymbol{\Gamma}_0\boldsymbol{\chi}_0 = \boldsymbol{\gamma}_0$.

When this equation is solved, the weight parameter vector $\boldsymbol{\chi} = (\chi_1, \ldots, \chi_N)'$ and the Lagrange multiplier $\widetilde{\lambda}$ are defined as follows:

$$\boldsymbol{\chi}' = \left[\boldsymbol{\gamma} + 1\frac{(1-1'\boldsymbol{\Gamma}^{-1}\boldsymbol{\gamma})}{1'\boldsymbol{\Gamma}^{-1}1}\right]'\boldsymbol{\Gamma}^{-1}, \tag{4.4.8}$$

$$\widetilde{\lambda} = -\frac{1-1'\boldsymbol{\Gamma}^{-1}\boldsymbol{\gamma}}{1'\boldsymbol{\Gamma}^{-1}1}, \tag{4.4.9}$$

where $\boldsymbol{\gamma} \equiv [\gamma(\mathbf{s}_0-\mathbf{s}_1), \ldots, \gamma(\mathbf{s}_0-\mathbf{s}_N)]'$ and $\boldsymbol{\Gamma}$ is an $N \times N$ matrix whose (i, j) element is given by $\gamma(\mathbf{s}_i-\mathbf{s}_j)$.

From this, the OK prediction at point $\mathbf{s}_0$ is given by

$$\widehat{y}(\mathbf{s}_0)_{ok} = \boldsymbol{\chi}'\mathbf{y}. \tag{4.4.10}$$

The variance of the minimized prediction error $\widehat{\sigma}^2(\mathbf{s}_0)_{ok} \equiv Var\left[y(\mathbf{s}_0) - \widehat{y}(\mathbf{s}_0)_{ok}\right]$ (or expected square prediction error) is called Kriging variance, and the OK variance is given by

$$\widehat{\sigma}^2(\mathbf{s}_0)_{ok} = \boldsymbol{\chi}'\boldsymbol{\gamma} + \widetilde{\lambda}, \tag{4.4.11}$$

or

$$\widehat{\sigma}^2(\mathbf{s}_0)_{ok} = 2\sum_{i=1}^{N}\chi_i\gamma(\mathbf{s}_0-\mathbf{s}_i) - \sum_{i=1}^{N}\sum_{j=1}^{N}\chi_i\chi_j\gamma(\mathbf{s}_i-\mathbf{s}_j). \tag{4.4.12}$$

Note that Kriging variance does not designate variance of the prediction. In Section 4.2, it was said that a variogram needs to satisfy the condition of conditional nonpositive definite?, but all this says is that the variance of the prediction has to have a nonnegative value.

Based on the assumption that the spatial process $y(s)$ follows a GP, the 95% confidence interval of the predicted value can be formed as (Chilès and Delfiner, 2012, p. 175):

$$\left[\widehat{y}(\mathbf{s}_0)_{ok} - 1.96\widehat{\sigma}(\mathbf{s}_0)_{ok}, \widehat{y}(\mathbf{s}_0)_{ok} + 1.96\widehat{\sigma}(\mathbf{s}_0)_{ok}\right]. \tag{4.4.13}$$

Then, assuming that $y(s)$ is second-order stationary, if a covariance function is used, Eq. (4.4.6) can be rewritten as the following equation:

$$\begin{aligned}\Phi = C(0) + \sum_{i=1}^{N}\sum_{j=1}^{N}\chi_i\chi_j C(\mathbf{s}_i - \mathbf{s}_j) - 2\sum_{i=1}^{N}\chi_i C(\mathbf{s}_0 - \mathbf{s}_i) \\ - 2\widetilde{\lambda}\left(\sum_{i=1}^{N}\chi_i - 1\right).\end{aligned} \tag{4.4.14}$$

If this equation minimized for $\{\chi_1, \ldots, \chi_N\}$ and, $\widetilde{\lambda}$

$$\chi' = \left[\mathbf{c} + 1\frac{\left(1 - 1'\boldsymbol{\Sigma}^{-1}\mathbf{c}\right)}{1'\boldsymbol{\Sigma}^{-1}1}\right]'\boldsymbol{\Sigma}^{-1}, \tag{4.4.15}$$

$$\widetilde{\lambda} = \frac{1 - 1'\boldsymbol{\Sigma}^{-1}\mathbf{c}}{1'\boldsymbol{\Sigma}^{-1}1}, \tag{4.4.16}$$

is obtained. Also, the OK variance becomes

$$\widehat{\sigma}^2(\mathbf{s}_0)_{ok} = C(0) - \chi'\mathbf{c} + \widetilde{\lambda}. \tag{4.4.17}$$

Warnes (1986) conducted a sensitivity analysis on how the parameters of a covariance function affect the Kriging prediction. They demonstrated that the exponential type is relatively robust against changes in the range, but the Gaussian type is sensitive. Bardossy (1988) also obtained a result that a prediction using the Gaussian type is more sensitive to parameter changes than the spherical and exponential types. Moreover, many functional forms of theoretical variograms have been proposed other than those described in this document.

It has been long known that if a variogram does not satisfy the non-positive definite condition, the Kriging variance may become negative (Armstrong and Jabin, 1981), and this is also one of the reasons parametric functions are frequently used. However, Shapiro and Botha (1991) and Huang and cressie. (2011) proposed clever nonparametric functions that do not satisfy the conditional negative definiteness.[9] For example, image textures often have similar patterns repeated (e.g., apartment houses in aerial photography), displaying complex shapes that cannot be approximated with theoretical variograms. In such cases, a nonparametric approach may be useful. For nonparametric functions, see Schabenberger and Gotway (2005) and the references therein.

4.5 Universal Kriging

In OK, it was assumed that the variable $y(\mathbf{s})$, including the trend component $m(\mathbf{s})$, are second-order stationary, and $\mathrm{E}[y(\mathbf{s})] = \mathrm{m}(\mathbf{s}) = \overline{\mathrm{m}}$ holds at all points within the area. Meanwhile, in universal Kriging (UK), $y(\mathbf{s})$ can be expressed as follows:

$$y(\mathbf{s}) = \mathbf{x}(\mathbf{s})\boldsymbol{\beta} + u(\mathbf{s}), \tag{4.4.18}$$

where $\mathbf{x}(\mathbf{s})$ is a $1 \times K$ explanatory variable vector. Therefore, UK is a Kriging method when the trend components can be expressed by a linear combination of the known variables. According to Hengl et al. (2007), UK is originally a method used when the trend component $\mathbf{x}(s)$ is expressed by a function of position coordinates (e.g., geographic coordinates). To clarify their point, they use the name of regression Kriging (RK) to designate the introduction of explanatory variables other than position coordinates. However, since this term RK is not yet widely used, this document employs the designation UK regardless of whether $\mathbf{x}(s)$ is only position coordinates. Naturally, when performing a UK that includes variables other than position coordinates, it is necessary to determine the explanatory variables at the points to be predicted, which often makes it more difficult than when only position coordinates are involved. If the explanatory variable matrix at N observation points is set as $\mathbf{X}$, the prediction in UK is given by

$$\widehat{y}(\mathbf{s}_0)_{uk} = \sum_{i=1}^{N} \chi_i y_i, \quad \mathbf{x}(s_0) = \boldsymbol{\chi}'\mathbf{X}, \tag{4.4.19}$$

Here, the conditions of the latter are unbiased ($E[y(s_0)] = E[\boldsymbol{\chi}'\mathbf{y}]$); that is, they are determined by

$$\mathbf{x}(s_0)\boldsymbol{\beta} = \boldsymbol{\chi}'\mathbf{X}\boldsymbol{\beta}, \tag{4.4.20}$$

[9] There is also an approach that analyzes the periodicity with a triangular function. See Webster and Oliver (2007) for examples.

where $\mathbf{x}(\mathbf{s}_0)$ is a $1 \times K$ explanatory variable vector at the prediction point. The Lagrange function is given by

$$\Phi = -\boldsymbol{\chi}'\boldsymbol{\Gamma}\boldsymbol{\chi} + 2\boldsymbol{\chi}'\boldsymbol{\gamma} - 2\widetilde{\lambda}(\mathbf{X}'(\mathbf{s}_0) - \boldsymbol{\chi}'\mathbf{X}). \tag{4.4.21}$$

Here, $\widetilde{\lambda}$ is a $K \times 1$ vector of Lagrange multipliers. If Φ is partially differentiated with $\boldsymbol{\chi}$ and $\widetilde{\lambda}$ and set as 0, the following normal equation is obtained:

$$\begin{pmatrix} \gamma(s_1 - s_1) & \cdots & \gamma(s_1 - s_N) & x_1(s_1) & \cdots & x_k(s_1) \\ \vdots & \gamma(s_i - s_j) & \vdots & \vdots & \cdots & \vdots \\ \gamma(s_N - s_1) & \cdots & \gamma(s_N - s_N) & x_1(s_N) & \cdots & x_k(s_N) \\ x_1(s_1) & \cdots & x_1(s_N) & 0 & \cdots & 0 \\ \vdots & \cdots & \vdots & \vdots & \cdots & \vdots \\ x_k(s_1) & \cdots & x_k(s_N) & 0 & \cdots & 0 \end{pmatrix} \begin{pmatrix} \chi_1 \\ \vdots \\ \chi_N \\ \widetilde{\lambda}_1 \\ \vdots \\ \widetilde{\lambda}_k \end{pmatrix} = \begin{pmatrix} \gamma(s_0 - s_1) \\ \vdots \\ \gamma(s_0 - s_N) \\ x_1(s_0) \\ \vdots \\ x_k(s_0) \end{pmatrix}. \tag{4.4.22}$$

When this equation is solved,

$$\boldsymbol{\chi}' = \left[\boldsymbol{\gamma} + \mathbf{X}\frac{(\mathbf{x}'(\mathbf{s}_0) - \mathbf{X}'\boldsymbol{\Gamma}^{-1}\boldsymbol{\gamma})}{\mathbf{X}'\boldsymbol{\Gamma}^{-1}\mathbf{X}}\right]'\boldsymbol{\Gamma}^{-1}, \tag{4.4.23}$$

$$\widetilde{\boldsymbol{\lambda}}' = -\frac{(\mathbf{x}'(\mathbf{s}_0) - \mathbf{X}'\boldsymbol{\Gamma}^{-1}\boldsymbol{\gamma})'}{\mathbf{X}'\boldsymbol{\Gamma}^{-1}\mathbf{X}}, \tag{4.4.24}$$

are obtained. The same calculation can be made with a covariance function, generating

$$\boldsymbol{\chi}' = \left[\mathbf{c} + \mathbf{X}\frac{(\mathbf{x}'(\mathbf{s}_0) - \mathbf{X}'\boldsymbol{\Sigma}^{-1}\mathbf{c})}{\mathbf{X}'\boldsymbol{\Sigma}^{-1}\mathbf{X}}\right]'\boldsymbol{\Sigma}^{-1}, \tag{4.4.25}$$

$$\widetilde{\boldsymbol{\lambda}}' = \frac{(\mathbf{x}'(\mathbf{s}_0) - \mathbf{X}'\boldsymbol{\Sigma}^{-1}\mathbf{c})'}{\mathbf{X}'\boldsymbol{\Sigma}^{-1}\mathbf{X}}. \tag{4.4.26}$$

Here, considering that the GLS estimate is given by $\widehat{\boldsymbol{\beta}}_{gls} = \left(\mathbf{X}'\boldsymbol{\Sigma}^{-1}\mathbf{X}\right)^{-1}\mathbf{X}'\boldsymbol{\Sigma}^{-1}\mathbf{y}$, the UK prediction is given by

$$\widehat{y}(\mathbf{s}_0)_{uk} = \mathbf{x}(s_0)\widehat{\boldsymbol{\beta}}_{gls} + \mathbf{c}'\boldsymbol{\Sigma}^{-1}\left(\mathbf{y} - \mathbf{X}\widehat{\boldsymbol{\beta}}_{gls}\right). \tag{4.4.27}$$

Also, the UK variance, using a variogram, is given by

$$\widehat{\sigma}^2(\mathbf{s}_0)_{uk} = \boldsymbol{\gamma}'\boldsymbol{\Gamma}^{-1}\boldsymbol{\gamma} - \left(\mathbf{x}(\mathbf{s}_0) - \mathbf{X}'\boldsymbol{\Gamma}^{-1}\boldsymbol{\gamma}\right)'\left(\mathbf{X}'\boldsymbol{\Gamma}^{-1}\mathbf{X}\right)^{-1}\left(\mathbf{x}(\mathbf{s}_0) - \mathbf{X}'\boldsymbol{\Gamma}^{-1}\boldsymbol{\gamma}\right). \tag{4.4.28}$$

If a covariance function is used, it is given by

$$\begin{aligned}\widehat{\sigma}^2(\mathbf{s}_0)_{uk} &= C(0) - \mathbf{c}'\boldsymbol{\Sigma}^{-1}\mathbf{c}\\ &+ \left(\mathbf{x}(\mathbf{s}_0) - \mathbf{X}'\boldsymbol{\Sigma}^{-1}\mathbf{c}\right)'\left(\mathbf{X}'\boldsymbol{\Sigma}^{-1}\mathbf{X}\right)^{-1}\left(\mathbf{x}(\mathbf{s}_0) - \mathbf{X}'\boldsymbol{\Sigma}^{-1}\mathbf{c}\right).\end{aligned} \tag{4.4.29}$$

The 95% confidence interval can be defined as

$$\left[\widehat{y}(\mathbf{s}_0)_{uk} - 1.96\widehat{\sigma}(\mathbf{s}_0)_{uk}, \widehat{y}(\mathbf{s}_0)_{uk} + 1.96\widehat{\sigma}(\mathbf{s}_0)_{uk}\right], \tag{4.4.30}$$

as with the case of OK. UK can also be interpreted as a two-step operation, in which intrinsic/second-order stationarity is assumed to the part of the error term from which the trend component is removed, then the prediction of the error term at an arbitrary point s_0 is added to the trend component at the same point. The result obtained this way is the same as the UK prediction earlier (Cressie, 1993, p. 173).

The maps below are an expansion of the work by Tsutsumi et al. (2011). They were created with UK[10] to indicate the land price distribution of the Tokyo metropolitan area in Japan. The price data used was taken from the official land prices (Land Market Price Publication) and the Prefectural Land Price Survey (expressed as survey land price below) of 2006 of land whose purpose was set as residential land, prospective residential land, and residential land in the urbanization adjustment area. However, since there is a gap of 6 months between the evaluation dates (the official land prices and survey land prices are respectively published on January 1st and July 1st every year), the survey land price was corrected with a simple average between 2005 and 2006. Also, the data of locations that overlap with the standard locations of assessed land prices and locations that were newly added in 2006 as indicators of the prefectural land price survey were excluded. Fig. 4.4.2 shows the spatial distribution of land price data.

[10] The likfit function (parameter estimation) and krige.cov function (calculation of estimated land price) of the geoR package in R were used in the estimation.

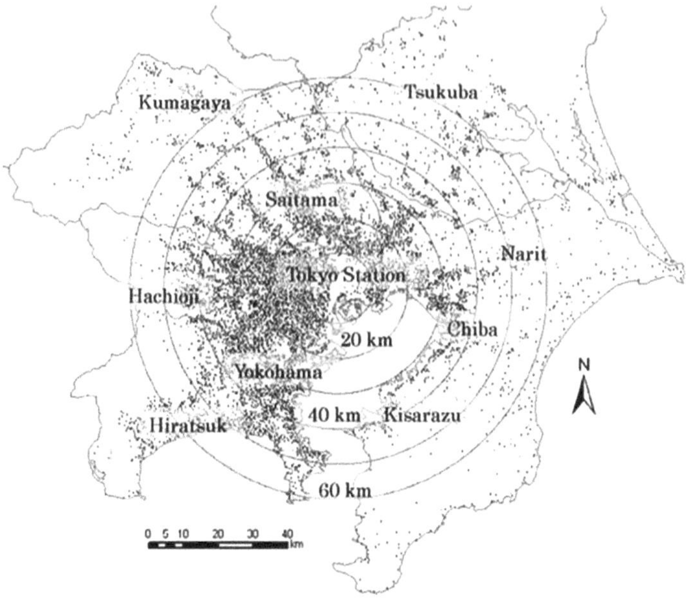

Figure 4.4.2 Spatial distribution of land price data of the three major metropolitan areas.

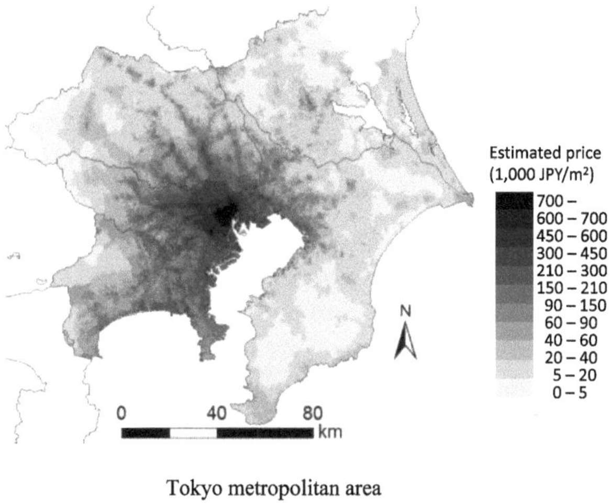

Tokyo metropolitan area

Figure 4.4.3 Land price distribution map created with UK.

Fig. 4.4.3 is a residential land price distribution map created with UK. For the colored version and details of the explanatory variables, see Tsutsumi et al. (2011). It reveals that the highest price range is over 700,000 yen/m^2 in the Tokyo metropolitan area, 200,000–300,000 yen/m.^{2} This kind of visual approach is an effective tool to understand a phenomenon intuitively.

4.5.1 Nonlinear Kriging

4.5.1.1 Lognormal Kriging

All the Kriging methods are based on linear Kriging prediction. If a spatial process follows a GP, the best linear unbiased prediction becomes the best unbiased prediction, and therefore it is appropriate to use linear prediction. Also, even in cases where the data clearly shows nonlinearity, it is often possible to make it follow a GP with adequate transformation.

If the natural logarithmic transformation of the spatial process $y(\mathbf{s})$, $y_{(ln)}(\mathbf{s}) = ln[y(\mathbf{s})]$ follows an intrinsic stationary GP, the model for $y_{(\mathrm{ln})}(\mathbf{s})$ is built, and the OK prediction $\widehat{y}_{(ln)}(\mathbf{s}_0)_{ok}$ is obtained. However, its inverse transformation, $\widetilde{y}\left(\mathbf{s}_0\right) = \exp\left[\widehat{y}_{(ln)}(\mathbf{s}_0)_{ok}\right]$, is a prediction of bias about $y(\mathbf{s})$. In his work, Cressie (1993, pp. 135–136) introduced lognormal Kriging (LK) prediction with bias correction. However, LK has a problem regarding the uncertainty of the prediction after logarithmic transformation; that is, while the prediction before logarithmic transformation gives the BLUP, there is no guarantee that the prediction after logarithmic transformation gives the smallest variance among the linear unbiased predictions of $y(\mathbf{s}_0)$. An LK prediction is also sensitive to the violation of the assumption of lognormal distribution and, since the correction is made with Kriging variance, it is easily influenced by outliers. Meanwhile, since $\widetilde{y}(\mathbf{s}_0) = \exp\left[\widehat{y}_{(ln)}(\mathbf{s}_0)_{ok}\right]$, a simple inverse exponential transformation, can be considered an unbiased prediction on the median, Chilès and Delfiner (2012, pp. 194–195) claims that unbiasedness concerning the average is not necessary. Tolosana-Delgado and Pawlowsky-Glahn (2007) also emphasized the usefulness of this inverse transformation and stated that its prediction result is roughly the same as that by LK.

4.5.1.2 Trans-Gaussian Kriging

Trans-Gaussian Kriging (TGK) is a method for more general nonlinear transformations than logarithmic. With TGK, the inverse transformation to obtain an unbiased prediction of original scale becomes even more complex than LK, but its function is included in the gstat package in R, which makes its application relatively easy. In their analysis of cases that use Box–Cox transformation as nonlinear transformation, De Oliveira et al. (1997) proposed a method to apply Bayesian inference to transformation parameters. The TGK is outlined below with an equation development proposed by Schabenberger and Gotway (2005, pp. 270–271).

Assuming that $z(\mathbf{s})$ follows a GP with an average m_Z and the variogram $\gamma_z(\mathbf{h})$, if the function $\phi(\cdot)$ is used, $y(\mathbf{s}) = \phi(z(\mathbf{s}))$ holds. Then, if the OK prediction $\widehat{z}(\mathbf{s}_0)$ of point $\mathbf{s}_0$ is obtained from $z_i, i = 1, \ldots, N$, the natural prediction of $y(\mathbf{s}_0)$ is obtained as $\widehat{y}(\mathbf{s}_0) = \phi(\widehat{z}(\mathbf{s}_0))$. However, since this prediction has bias, it needs to be corrected as with the case of logarithm. Taylor expansion is applied to $\phi(\widehat{z}(\mathbf{s}_0))$ until the second-order term around m_Z,

$$\phi(\widehat{z}(\mathbf{s}_0)) \approx \phi(m_z) + \phi'(m_z)(\widehat{z}(\mathbf{s}_0) - m_z) + \frac{\phi''(m_z)}{2}(\widehat{z}(\mathbf{s}_0) - m_z)^2, \tag{4.4.31}$$

is obtained. But ($'$) here is an operator that expresses differentiation, not transposition. If the expected value of both sides of this equation are determined, the term of first-order differentiation disappears, generating

$$E[\phi(\widehat{z}(\mathbf{s}_0))] \approx \phi(m_z) + \frac{\phi''(m_z)}{2} E\left[(\widehat{z}(\mathbf{s}_0) - m_z)^2\right]. \tag{4.4.32}$$

To satisfy the constraint of unbiasedness, this equation has to be equal to $E[y(\mathbf{s}_0)]$. Therefore, to obtain $E[y(s_0)]$, the same Taylor expansion can be applied to $\phi(z(\mathbf{s}_0))$ to determine the expected value, generating

$$E[\phi(y(\mathbf{s}_0))] \approx \phi(m_z) + \frac{\phi''(m_z)}{2} E\left[(y(\mathbf{s}_0) - m_z)^2\right]. \tag{4.4.33}$$

Therefore, the bias correction term is given by the following equation:

$$\frac{\phi''(m_z)}{2} E\left[(\widehat{y}(\mathbf{s}_0) - m_z)^2\right] - \frac{\phi''(m_z)}{2} E\left[(y(\mathbf{s}_0) - m_z)^2\right] \tag{4.4.34}$$

$$= \frac{\phi''(m_z)}{2}\left[\widehat{\sigma}^2(\mathbf{s}_0; \mathbf{z})_{OK} - 2\widetilde{\lambda}_z\right]. \tag{4.4.35}$$

Here, $\widetilde{\lambda}_z$ is a Lagrange multiplier and $\widehat{\sigma}^2(\mathbf{s}_0; \mathbf{Z})_{ok}$ is the OK variance. From these, the TGK prediction is obtained as the following equation:

$$\widehat{y}(\mathbf{s}_0)_{tgk} = \phi(\widehat{z}(\mathbf{s}_0)) + \frac{\phi''(m_z)}{2}\left[\widehat{\sigma}^2(\mathbf{s}_0; \mathbf{z})_{OK} - 2\widetilde{\lambda}_z\right]. \tag{4.4.36}$$

Based on the Taylor expansion until the first-order term, the TGK variance can be determined as

$$\widehat{\sigma}^2(\mathbf{s}_0)_{tgk} \approx [\phi'(m_z)]^2 \widehat{\sigma}^2(\mathbf{s}_0; \mathbf{z})_{ok}. \tag{4.4.37}$$

TGK can flexibly model nonlinearity through the inverse function of $\varphi(\cdot)$, $\varphi^{-1}(\cdot)$. For example, the Box–Cox transformation indicated in the following equation is one of the transformations frequently used in TGK:

$$\mathbf{z}(\mathbf{s}_i) = \begin{cases} \dfrac{y(\mathbf{s}_i)^K - 1}{\kappa} & if \quad \kappa \neq 0 \\ \ln(y(\mathbf{s}_i)) & if \quad \kappa = 0 \end{cases}. \tag{4.4.38}$$

κ is a parameter that defines the function form. With a linear $\mathbf{X\beta}$ as the trend term, it can be formulated as $z(\kappa) \sim N(\mathbf{X\beta}, \mathbf{\Sigma}(\mathbf{\theta}))$. Here, $z(\kappa)$ is an $N \times 1$ vector with transformed GP. Assuming that data $\mathbf{y} = (y(\mathbf{s}_1), \ldots, y(\mathbf{s}_N))'$ was obtained, the log-likelihood function of TGK can be obtained by the following equation:

$$l(\mathbf{y}|\mathbf{\beta}, \mathbf{\theta}) = -\frac{N}{2}\ln(2\pi) - \frac{1}{2}\ln|\mathbf{\Sigma}(\mathbf{\theta})|$$
$$-\frac{1}{2}\{z(\lambda) - \mathbf{X\beta}\}'\mathbf{\Sigma}(\mathbf{\theta})^{-1}\{\mathbf{z}(\lambda) - \mathbf{X\beta}\} + (\kappa - 1)\sum_{i=1}^{N} \ln y(\mathbf{s}_i). \tag{4.4.39}$$

It is necessary to determine the parameters that maximize this likelihood function.

4.5.1.3 Indicator Kriging

The previous Kriging methods dealt with the prediction of random variables themselves. In applied research, however, the focus is often the probability of a random variable at an arbitrary point of being lower or higher than a certain threshold y_a, such as $Pr[y(\mathbf{s}_0) \leq y_a | y(\mathbf{s})]$ and $Pr[y(\mathbf{s}_0) > y_a | y(\mathbf{s})]$. This method is called indicator Kriging (IK) (Journel, 1983). IK is defined as a method of estimating not the property value itself, but the range at which the property value exists at the intended place, as well as its probability. IK is used, for example, to estimate health risks due to groundwater contamination with arsenic (Lee et al., 2007, 2008), to assess the hazard of soil pollution (Goovaerts, 1997), and to classify remote sensing images (Van Der Meer, 1996).

If y(s) is transformed into a 1,0 indicator, the following equation is obtained:

$$I(\mathbf{s}, y_a) = \begin{cases} 1 & if \;\; y(\mathbf{s}) \leq y_a \\ 0 & otherwise \end{cases}. \tag{4.4.40}$$

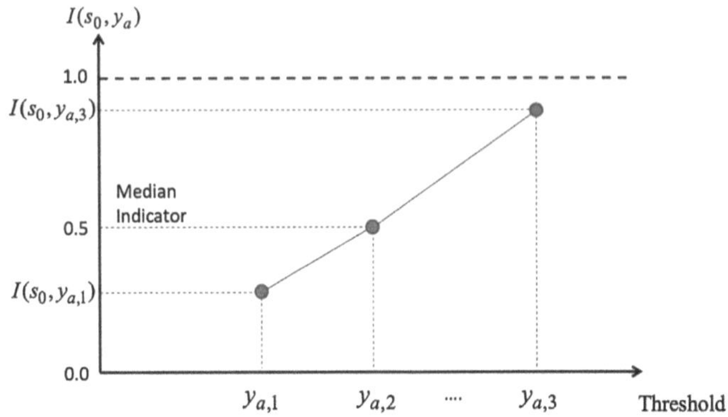

Figure 4.4.4 Threshold and indicator variable. Created by the authors of this paper based on Otsu et al. (2004).

Since $E[I(\mathbf{s}_0, y_a)] = Pr[y(\mathbf{s}_0) \leq y_a] = F[y(\mathbf{s}_0), y_a]$ is unknown, Kriging can be applied to the indicator transformation $\boldsymbol{I}(\mathbf{s}, y_a) = [I(\mathbf{s}_1, y_a), \ldots, I(\mathbf{s}_N, y_a)]'$ of the observed values. All it takes is to use its indicator transformation $\{1,0\}$ instead of the observed values, following the same calculation process as in OK. Hence,

$$E[I(\mathbf{s}_0, y_a)|\boldsymbol{I}(\mathbf{s}, y_a)] = \Pr[y(\mathbf{s}_0) \leq y_a|\boldsymbol{I}(\mathbf{s}, y_a)], \tag{4.4.41}$$

is obtained. Naturally, this value is not the actual $Pr[y(\mathbf{s}_0) \leq y_a|y(\mathbf{s})]$ of our interest, but its approximation. By preparing multiple units of threshold y_a, as in $y_{a,j}$ $(j = 1, \ldots, J)$ and applying them as shown in Fig. 4.4.4, it is possible to obtain the estimated value of $F[y(\mathbf{s}_0), y_{a,j}]$, $\widehat{F}\left[y(\mathbf{s}_0), y_{a,j}\right]$. However, since $\widehat{F}\left[y(\mathbf{s}_0), y_{a,j}\right]$ is estimated separately for $y_{a,j}$, $\widehat{F}\left[y(\mathbf{s}_0), y_{a,j}\right]$ does not increase monotonously, and there is no guarantee that the probability stays between 0 and 1. Therefore, in order to consider $\widehat{F}\left[y(\mathbf{s}_0), y_{a,j}\right]$ a cumulative distribution function, it is necessary to correct these two aspects. For more about this specific method, see Goovaerts (1997) and Olea (2009). Also, if a threshold corresponding to $Pr[y(\mathbf{s}_0) \leq y_a] = 0.5$ is used, the IK is called median IK (Journel, 1983).

IK is a nonparametric method that does not require a specific distribution to be assigned to a spatial process, which is useful in cases where it is difficult to consider a parametric distribution for the spatial process.

4.5.2 Block Kriging

The previous Kriging methods are designed to predict point data, but Kriging, developed in the mining field, was originally a method to

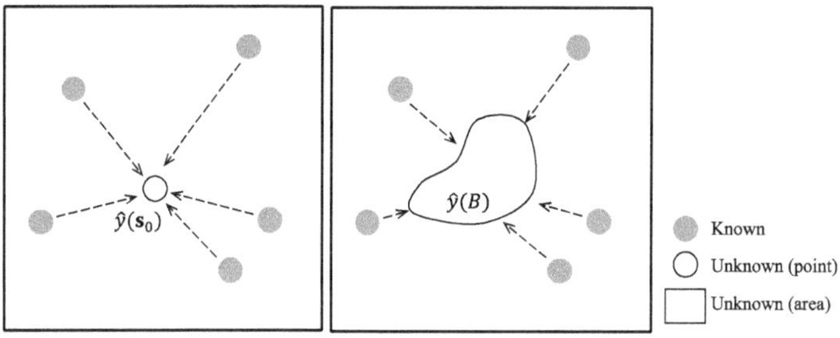

Figure 4.4.5 Concept of block Kriging.

determine the average value in a block, as shown in Fig. 4.4.5. This method is called block Kriging (BK).

BK is an essential modeling technique when dealing with area instead of points, such as pixels of image data (Collins and Woodcock, 1999; Atkinson and Tate, 2000). Following is a simple description of BK.

In BK, the prediction $\widehat{y}(B)_{bk}$ is given as the linear sum of random variables at the observation points by the following equation, in the same way as in OK:

$$\widehat{y}(B)_{bk} = \sum_{i=1}^{N} \chi_i y_i = \boldsymbol{\chi}'\mathbf{y}. \tag{4.4.42}$$

The loss function that must be minimized is given by the following equation:

$$E\left[y(B) - \widehat{y}(B)_{bk}\right] = -\sum_{i=1}^{N}\sum_{j=1}^{N} \chi_i\chi_j\gamma(\mathbf{s}_i - \mathbf{s}_j) + 2\sum_{i=1}^{N} \chi_i\overline{\gamma}(B, \mathbf{s}_i) - \overline{\gamma}(B, B). \tag{4.4.43}$$

Here,

$$\overline{\gamma}(B, \mathbf{s}_i) = \frac{1}{|B|}\int_B \gamma(\mathbf{s}_i - \mathbf{s})d\mathbf{s}, \tag{4.4.44}$$

$$\overline{\gamma}(B, B) = \frac{1}{|B|^2}\int_B\int_B \gamma(\mathbf{t} - \mathbf{s})d\mathbf{s}d\mathbf{t}, \tag{4.4.45}$$

where $|B|$ indicates the volume (area) of B. Unlike in OK, it contains the term $\overline{\gamma}(B, B)$, but this is because in the case of point modeling (OK), this term is equal to 0. The normal equation of BK is given by

$$\begin{pmatrix} \gamma(\mathbf{s}_1 - \mathbf{s}_1) & \cdots & \gamma(\mathbf{s}_1 - \mathbf{s}_N) & 1 \\ \vdots & \gamma(\mathbf{s}_i - \mathbf{s}_j) & \vdots & \vdots \\ \gamma(\mathbf{s}_N - \mathbf{s}_1) & \cdots & \gamma(\mathbf{s}_N - \mathbf{s}_N) & 1 \\ 1 & \cdots & 1 & 0 \end{pmatrix} \begin{pmatrix} \chi_1 \\ \vdots \\ \chi_N \\ \widetilde{\lambda} \end{pmatrix} = \begin{pmatrix} \overline{\gamma}(B - \mathbf{s}_1) \\ \vdots \\ \overline{\gamma}(B - \mathbf{s}_N) \\ 1 \end{pmatrix}, \tag{4.4.46}$$

$$\mathbf{\Gamma}_0 \boldsymbol{\chi}_0 = \boldsymbol{\gamma}_B.$$

If this equation is solved, the weight and BK variance are respectively given by $\boldsymbol{\chi}_0 = \mathbf{\Gamma}_0^{-1} \boldsymbol{\gamma}_B$ and $\widehat{\sigma}^2(B)_{bk} = \boldsymbol{\chi}_0' \boldsymbol{\gamma}_B - \overline{\gamma}(B, B)$.

Kyriakidis (2004) proposed area-to-point Kriging as a natural application of BK. This method, one of the techniques called areal interpolation, is designed to make precise proportional divisions of data, as in municipalities to meshes, considering spatial autocorrelation and volume conservation law (consistency of an area before and after form conversion). This problem, when the space units of interest and the available space units are different, is called change of support problem, one of the hot? issues in the field of spatial statistics in recent years. For more details, see Gotway and Young (2002) or Murakami and Tsutsumi (2012).

4.6 Extended model

In this section, as extended models, we explain two models: spatial generalized linear model (spatial GLM) and geo-additive model.

4.6.1 Spatial generalized linear model

In Chapter 2, we introduced GLM in the following way.

$$E[y(\mathbf{s}_i)] = m(\mathbf{s}_i), \quad y(\mathbf{s}_i) \sim N\left(m(\mathbf{s}_i), \sigma_\varepsilon^2\right), \tag{4.5.1}$$

$$f(\mathbf{m}) = f(E[\mathbf{y}]) = \mathbf{X}\boldsymbol{\beta}, \tag{4.5.2}$$

$$\mathbf{\Sigma} = Var[\mathbf{y}] = \psi \mathbf{V}_{\mathbf{m}}, \tag{4.5.3}$$

where $\mathbf{m}=(m(\mathbf{s}_1),\ldots, m(\mathbf{s}_N))'$ and $\psi\mathbf{V}_\mathbf{m} = \psi diag[V(m(\mathbf{s}_i))]$ is the variance function that describes how the variance, $Var[\mathbf{y}]$ depends on the mean. Let us generalize the variance-covariance matrix of Eq. (4.5.3) to the case in which there is spatial autocorrelation, following Schabenberger and Gotway (2005). In the presence of spatial autocorrelation, if we rewrite as $\psi = \sigma_\varepsilon^2$, the variance-covariance matrix of $\mathbf{y}$ is given by the following (Gotway and Stroup, 1997; Waller and Gotway, 2004, p. 382),

$$Var[\mathbf{y}] = \mathbf{\Sigma}(\mathbf{m}, \boldsymbol{\theta}) = \sigma^2 \mathbf{V}_\mathbf{m}^{1/2} \mathbf{R}(\varphi) \mathbf{V}_\mathbf{m}^{1/2}. \tag{4.5.4}$$

Here, $\mathbf{R}(\varphi)$ is an $N \times N$ matrix whose elements are given by the correlation function $\rho(\mathbf{s}_i - \mathbf{s}_j;\varphi)$. If we allow the existence of nugget terms, we can do the following,

$$Var[\mathbf{y}] = \mathbf{\Sigma}(\mathbf{m}, \boldsymbol{\theta}) = \tau^2 \mathbf{V}_\mathbf{m} + \sigma^2 \mathbf{V}_\mathbf{m}^{1/2} \mathbf{R}(\varphi) \mathbf{V}_\mathbf{m}^{1/2}, \tag{4.5.5}$$

Parameter estimation methods include the Bayesian estimation (Diggle and Ribeiro, 2007) and the quasi likelihood (QL) method (Gotway and Stroup, 1997). Here, we briefly explain the latter. In GLM, distribution information is not necessarily required because models can be created if there are link and dispersion functions. However, in the case of not assuming distribution, to conduct a maximum likelihood estimation of the parameters, information for substituting the likelihood is needed. The QL method uses the concept of QL for substituting the log likelihood. First, let us briefly explain the concept of QL. Now, if we define variables as

$$U_i = \frac{y(\mathbf{s}_i) - m(\mathbf{s}_i)}{\psi V(m(\mathbf{s}_i))}, \tag{4.5.6}$$

it becomes $Var[U_i] = 1/(\psi V(m(\mathbf{s}_i)))$. Here, we can obtain the following when considering the expected value of differentiating U_i by $m(\mathbf{s}_i)$.

$$\frac{dU_i}{dm(\mathbf{s}_i)} = \frac{1}{\psi V(m(\mathbf{s}_i))}, \tag{4.5.7}$$

That is, U_i has the same property as a score, in which the expected value is 0, and the result of differentiation and sign change is equal to the variance. Therefore, it is the integral of U_i, that is,

$$Q_i = \int_{y(\mathbf{s}_i)}^{m(\mathbf{s}_i)} \left(\frac{y(\mathbf{s}_i) - m(\mathbf{s}_i)}{\psi V(r)} \right) dr, \tag{4.5.8}$$

$Q = \sum_{i=1}^{N} Q_i$ is considered to behave similarly to log likelihood and is known as the quasi likelihood (QL).[11] In addition, $U = \sum_{i=1}^{N} U_i$ is known as the quasi score. In the QL method, parameters are found by setting $\boldsymbol{U}$ equal to 0.

The parameter estimation procedure of space GLM by the QL method shown in Gotway and Stroup (1997) is described below. Since $m(\mathbf{s}_i)$ depends on β_k ($k = 1, \ldots, K$), the quasi score can be defined as

$$U_h = \sum_{i=1}^{N} \frac{y(\mathbf{s}_i) - m(\mathbf{s}_i)}{\psi V(m(\mathbf{s}_i))} \cdot \frac{\partial m(\mathbf{s}_i)}{\partial \beta_k} = 0, \tag{4.5.9}$$

We generalized this to a global statistical model, and obtained the following:

$$\frac{\partial Q(\mathbf{m}; \mathbf{y})}{\partial \mathbf{m}} = \boldsymbol{\Sigma}^{-1}[\mathbf{y} - \mathbf{m}(\boldsymbol{\beta})], \tag{4.5.10}$$

where $\mathbf{m}(\boldsymbol{\beta})$ is an expression to emphasize that the mean $\mathbf{m} = [m(\mathbf{s}_1), \ldots, m(\mathbf{s}_N)]'$ depends on $\boldsymbol{\beta}$. If the QL function $\mathbf{Q}$ is differentiated by the elements of $\boldsymbol{\beta}$, the quasi score vector can be obtained as

$$\mathbf{U} = \boldsymbol{\Delta}'\boldsymbol{\Sigma}^{-1}[\mathbf{y} - \boldsymbol{\mu}(\boldsymbol{\beta})] = 0 \tag{4.5.11}$$

However, it is $[\boldsymbol{\Delta}]_{ih} = \frac{\partial m(\mathbf{s}_i)}{\partial \beta_k}$, $k = 1, \cdots, K$. In this way, when $\mathbf{V}$ depends on a function other than $\boldsymbol{\beta}$, the quasi score is referred to as a generalized estimation equation. Now, if we set $\boldsymbol{\delta} = f(\mathbf{m}) = \mathbf{X}\boldsymbol{\beta}$ and substitute $\boldsymbol{\Delta} = \boldsymbol{\Psi}\mathbf{X}$, $\boldsymbol{\Psi} = diag[\partial m(\mathbf{s}_i)/\partial \delta_i]$, $\mathbf{A}(\boldsymbol{\theta}) = \boldsymbol{\Psi}'\boldsymbol{\Sigma}(\mathbf{m}, \boldsymbol{\theta})^{-1}\boldsymbol{\Psi}$ for Eq. (4.5.11), we obtain the following equation (Gotway and Stroup, 1997):

$$\mathbf{X}'\mathbf{A}(\boldsymbol{\theta})\mathbf{X}\boldsymbol{\beta} = \mathbf{X}'\mathbf{A}(\boldsymbol{\theta})\mathbf{y}^*, \tag{4.5.12}$$

where $\mathbf{y}^* = \mathbf{X}\boldsymbol{\beta} + \boldsymbol{\Psi}^{-1}(\mathbf{y} - \mathbf{m})$. Assuming that $\boldsymbol{\theta}$ is known, we obtain the following:

$$\boldsymbol{\beta} = (\mathbf{X}'\mathbf{A}(\boldsymbol{\theta})\mathbf{X})^{-1}\mathbf{X}'\mathbf{A}(\boldsymbol{\theta})\mathbf{y}^*, \tag{4.5.13}$$

However, since $\boldsymbol{\theta}$ is unknown, it is necessary to obtain a variogram from the residual and estimate it using the NWLS method. Therefore, the estimations of $\boldsymbol{\beta}$ and $\boldsymbol{\theta}$ are obtained by repeated calculations (Schabenberger and Gotway, 2005, p. 362).

[11] Strictly speaking, it is a quasi log likelihood, but conventionally it is referred to as a quasi likelihood.

4.6.2 Geo-additive model

The geo-additive model (Kammann and Wand, 2003) considers both spatial autocorrelation and nonlinearity. In addition, it attains fast computation compared to Kriging. In the additive model, $g_1(\cdot)$ and $g_2(\cdot)$ are smoothing functions for scalar variables. Here, we introduce the multivariable smoothing function $S(\cdot)$, which depends on the coordinate $\mathbf{s}$. The geo-additive model is expressed as

$$y_i = \beta_0 + x_{1i}\beta_1 + x_{2i}\beta_2 + g_1(x_{1i}) + g_2(x_{2i}) + S(\mathbf{s}_i) + e_i, \qquad (4.5.13a)$$

where, for simplicity, we denote $y(\mathbf{s}_i)$ as y_i and $x_k(\mathbf{s}_i)$ as x_{ki} in this section.

We now define it as a matrix representation.

$$\mathbf{y} = \mathbf{X}\ddot{\boldsymbol{\beta}} + \mathbf{G}\mathbf{u} + \mathbf{e}. \qquad (4.5.14)$$

Each variable and parameter are given by

$$\mathbf{X} = \begin{bmatrix} 1 & x_{11} & x_{21} \\ \vdots & \vdots & \vdots \\ 1 & x_{1n} & x_{2N} \end{bmatrix}, \quad \ddot{\boldsymbol{\beta}} = [\beta_0, \beta_1, \beta_2]',$$

$$\mathbf{u} = \left[\mathbf{u}_1', \mathbf{u}_2', \widetilde{\mathbf{u}}_S'\right]' = \left[u_{11}, \ldots, u_{1Q_1}, u_{21}, \ldots, u_{2Q_2}, \widetilde{u}_{S,1}, \ldots, \widetilde{u}_{S,N}\right], \mathbf{G}$$
$$= \left[\mathbf{g}_1, \mathbf{g}_2, \widetilde{\mathbf{g}}_S\right]'.$$

where

$$\mathbf{g}_1 = \begin{bmatrix} (x_{11} - \kappa_{11})_+ & \cdots & (x_{11} - \kappa_{1Q_1})_+ \\ \vdots & \ddots & \vdots \\ (x_{1N} - \kappa_{11})_+ & \cdots & (x_{1N} - \kappa_{1Q_1})_+ \end{bmatrix},$$

$$\mathbf{g}_2 = \begin{bmatrix} (x_{21} - \kappa_{21})_+ & \cdots & (x_{21} - \kappa_{2Q_2})_+ \\ \vdots & \ddots & \vdots \\ (x_{2N} - \kappa_{21})_+ & \cdots & (x_{2N} - \kappa_{2Q_2})_+ \end{bmatrix},$$

$$\widetilde{\mathbf{g}}_S = \begin{bmatrix} \rho(\mathbf{s}_1 - \mathbf{s}_1) & \cdots & \rho(\mathbf{s}_1 - \mathbf{s}_N) \\ \vdots & \ddots & \vdots \\ \rho(\mathbf{s}_N - \mathbf{s}_1) & \cdots & \rho(\mathbf{s}_N - \mathbf{s}_N) \end{bmatrix},$$

where $(x - \kappa)_+$ is an operator that is 0 when $x < \kappa$ and $x - \kappa$ when $x \geq \kappa$, and κ represents a knot. In addition, the following is satisfied.

$$\mathrm{Cov}(\widetilde{\mathbf{u}}_S) = \sigma_{Su}^2 \left(\widetilde{\mathbf{g}}_S^{-1/2}\right)\left(\widetilde{\mathbf{g}}_S^{-1/2}\right)' \qquad (4.5.15)$$

In this way, if $\mathrm{Cov}(\widetilde{\mathbf{u}}_S)$ is specified to satisfy positive definiteness, in the case of $g_1(x_{1i}) = g_1(x_{2i}) = 0$, it becomes identical to OK in terms of being applied to observed values (Ruppert et al., 2003, p. 252). However, when using this expression, there is the advantage of being able to use statistical packages for mixed models. The relationship between Kriging and spline is described in Nychka (2000). If N is large, calculating the inverse of an $N \times N$ variance-covariance matrix becomes a very large load. In the geo-additive model, we define lattice points and some positions of observation points as knots κ ($\kappa = 1, \ldots, Q_S$) ($Q_S \leq N$) and attempt to model the spatial autocorrelation in the knots. That is, we use $\mathbf{u} = \left[\mathbf{u}_1', \mathbf{u}_2', \widetilde{\mathbf{u}}_S'\right]' = \left[u_{11}, \ldots, u_{1Q_1}, u_{21}, \ldots, u_{2Q_2}, \widetilde{u}_{S,1}, \ldots, \widetilde{u}_{S,N}\right]'$, and replace $\widetilde{\mathbf{g}}_S$ with $\widetilde{\mathbf{g}}_\kappa$ as follows:

$$\widetilde{\mathbf{g}}_\kappa = \begin{bmatrix} \rho(\mathbf{s}_1 - \boldsymbol{\kappa}_1) & \cdots & \rho\left(\mathbf{s}_1 - \boldsymbol{\kappa}_{Q_S}\right) \\ \vdots & \ddots & \vdots \\ \rho(\mathbf{s}_N - \boldsymbol{\kappa}_1) & \cdots & \rho\left(\mathbf{s}_N - \boldsymbol{\kappa}_{Q_S}\right) \end{bmatrix}, \tag{4.5.16}$$

$$\Omega_\kappa = \begin{bmatrix} \rho(\boldsymbol{\kappa}_1 - \boldsymbol{\kappa}_1) & \cdots & \rho\left(\boldsymbol{\kappa}_1 - \boldsymbol{\kappa}_{Q_S}\right) \\ \vdots & \ddots & \vdots \\ \rho\left(\boldsymbol{\kappa}_{Q_S} - \boldsymbol{\kappa}_1\right) & \cdots & \rho\left(\boldsymbol{\kappa}_{Q_S} - \boldsymbol{\kappa}_{Q_S}\right) \end{bmatrix}, \tag{4.5.17}$$

$$\mathrm{Cov}(\widetilde{\mathbf{u}}_{\boldsymbol{\kappa}}) = \sigma_{\boldsymbol{\kappa}u}^2\left(\Omega_{\boldsymbol{\kappa}}^{-1/2}\right)\left(\Omega_{\boldsymbol{\kappa}}^{-1/2}\right)'. \tag{4.5.18}$$

In the actual calculation, we set it as $\mathbf{u} = \left[\mathbf{u}_1', \mathbf{u}_2', \widetilde{\mathbf{u}}_{\boldsymbol{\kappa}}'\right]' = \left[u_{11}, \ldots, u_{1Q_1}, u_{21}, \ldots, u_{2Q_2}, \widetilde{u}_{\boldsymbol{\kappa},1}, \ldots, \widetilde{u}_{\boldsymbol{\kappa},N}\right]'$, and since we want to ascertain the covariance, it becomes

$$\mathrm{Cov}\begin{bmatrix} \mathbf{u} \\ \mathbf{e} \end{bmatrix} = \begin{bmatrix} \sigma_{1u}^2\mathbf{I}_{[Q_1]} & \mathbf{O} & \mathbf{O} & \mathbf{O} \\ \mathbf{O} & \sigma_{2u}^2\mathbf{I}_{[Q_2]} & \mathbf{O} & \mathbf{O} \\ \mathbf{O} \quad \mathbf{O} & & \sigma_{\kappa u}^2\mathbf{I}_{[Q_S]} & \mathbf{O} \\ \mathbf{O} \quad \mathbf{O} & & \mathbf{O} & \sigma_e^2\mathbf{I}_{[N]} \end{bmatrix}, \tag{4.5.19}$$

We rewrite $\mathbf{G} = [\mathbf{G}_1, \mathbf{G}_2, \mathbf{G}_\kappa]$ and $\mathbf{G}_\kappa = \widetilde{\mathbf{G}}_\kappa \Omega_\kappa^{-1/2}$ and estimate the parameters using the REML method. The predicted quantity is given by $\widehat{y}(\mathbf{s}_0) = \mathbf{X}'(\mathbf{s}_0)\widehat{\boldsymbol{\beta}} + \mathbf{G}_{S_0}\widehat{\mathbf{u}}$ using $\mathbf{G}_{S_0}$ ($1 \times Q$) ($Q = Q_1 + Q_2 + Q_S$) in the predicted point. Seya et al. (2011) compared the prediction accuracy of the geo-additive model with the UK method and suggested that a geo-additive model that is able to account for nonlinearity of explanatory variables can show high prediction accuracy. Here, in the application of such a model, the spatial arrangement of the two-dimensional knot κ

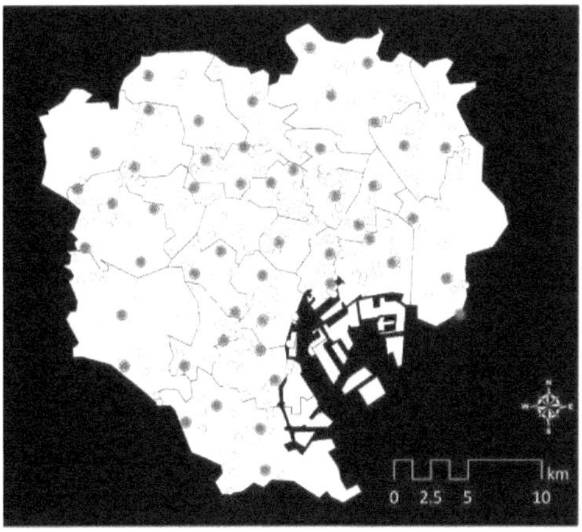

Figure 4.5.1 Arrangement of knots.

becomes a problem. The Clara algorithm of Kaufman and Rousseeuw (1990) is often used as a way to place an appropriate number of knots Q_s in a balanced manner in a space. The number of knots in the Clara algorithm is given by the following equation.

$$Q_S = \max\{10,\ \min(50,\ \text{round}(n/4))\}. \tag{4.5.20}$$

Fig. 4.5.1 shows the results of knot extraction from apartment data using the Clara algorithm according to Seya et al. (2011). It can be seen that these are arranged in a well-balanced manner in the space. In the geo-additive model, this correlation among knots replaces the correlation among observed values.

In addition, thin plate splines are often used as the correlation function $\rho(\cdot)$. Please refer to Ruppert et al. (2003) and so on for details of these and an extended model.[12]

4.7 Hierarchical Bayesian model

4.7.1 Data model, process model, and parameter model

Modeling uncertainty in data ($\mathbf{y}$), process ($\mathbf{z}$), and parameters ($\boldsymbol{\theta}$) is crucially important. Models identify spatial and temporal processes hidden

[12] The geo-additive model can be easily implemented using, for example, the SemiPar package of R (Wand, 2009). In the SemiPar package, the degree of nonlinearity of each variable can be estimated endogenously using the REML method as the degree of freedom.

behind noisy data. Given this background, the following factorization of $[\mathbf{y},\mathbf{z},\boldsymbol{\theta}] = [\mathbf{y}|\mathbf{z}, \boldsymbol{\theta}][\mathbf{z}|\boldsymbol{\theta}][\boldsymbol{\theta}]$ is becoming popular because of its flexibility in modeling uncertainty in each element (Berliner, 1996; Cressie and Wikle, 2011):

$$\text{Data model}: [\mathbf{y}|\mathbf{z}, \boldsymbol{\theta}], \tag{4.6.1}$$

$$\text{Process model}: [\mathbf{z}|\boldsymbol{\theta}], \tag{4.6.2}$$

$$\text{Parameter model}: [\boldsymbol{\theta}]. \tag{4.6.3}$$

Extension of the classical geostatistical model can be complicated in many cases because of the need to model data, process, and parameters simultaneously. By contrast, this specification allows us to model data, process, and parameters not simultaneously but in a conditionally independent manner. This hierarchical specification enables us to extend geostatistical approaches to a wider range of problems, including non-Gaussian data modeling, data fusion, spatiotemporal modeling, and fast computation, which we will explain later, by modifying each submodel (e.g., Eqs. (4.6.7), (4.6.8), (4.6.9)) to fit in specific problems.

The data model expresses the data distribution given the process $\mathbf{z}$. This model deals with normality or nonnormality of data distribution, measurement error, change of support, and a combination of multiple data sources. The process model expresses the process given the parameters. It is typically given by a GP. The full GP can be replaced with a rank reduced or sparse GP for fast computation. Boundary conditions and/or prior knowledge can be considered. The parameter model specifies priors for each parameter.

Similar to other hierarchical Bayesian models, Eqs. (4.6.7), (4.6.8), (4.6.9) are suitable for Bayesian modeling. Given the three models by parametric models, the posterior for $\{\mathbf{z},\boldsymbol{\theta}\}$ is derived using the Bayes' theorem as follows:

$$p(\mathbf{z}, \boldsymbol{\theta}|\mathbf{y}) = \frac{p(\mathbf{y}|\mathbf{z}, \boldsymbol{\theta})p(\mathbf{z}|\boldsymbol{\theta})p(\boldsymbol{\theta})}{p(\mathbf{y})} \propto p(\mathbf{y}|\mathbf{z}, \boldsymbol{\theta})p(\mathbf{z}|\boldsymbol{\theta})p(\boldsymbol{\theta}), \tag{4.6.4}$$

where $\propto$ represents proportion. Because the normalizing constant $p(\mathbf{y})$, which does not include unknown quantity, is difficult to evaluate, we cannot obtain $p(\mathbf{z},\boldsymbol{\theta}|\mathbf{y})$ but only $p(\mathbf{y}|\mathbf{z},\boldsymbol{\theta})p(\mathbf{z}|\boldsymbol{\theta})p(\boldsymbol{\theta})$. The marginal posterior distribution for $\mathbf{z}$ is obtained by integrating out $\boldsymbol{\theta}$ from Eq. (4.6.4) as

$$p(\mathbf{z}|\mathbf{y}) \propto \int p(\mathbf{y}|\mathbf{z}, \boldsymbol{\theta})p(\mathbf{z}|\boldsymbol{\theta})p(\boldsymbol{\theta})d\boldsymbol{\theta}, \tag{4.6.5}$$

whereas the posterior distribution for the l-th parameter θ_l in $\boldsymbol{\theta} \in \{\boldsymbol{\theta}_{-l}, \theta_l\}$ as

$$p(\theta_l|\mathbf{y}) \propto \int\int p(\mathbf{y}|\mathbf{z},\boldsymbol{\theta})p(\mathbf{z}|\boldsymbol{\theta})p(\boldsymbol{\theta})d\mathbf{z}d\boldsymbol{\theta}_{-l}. \tag{4.6.6}$$

Because the normalizing constant is underivable (i.e., we can evaluate only a quantity that is proportional to the posterior), we need to rely on an approximation, for example, using the MCMC method.

The next section explains the hierarchical representation of the classical geostatistical model as an example.

4.7.2 Bayesian geostatistical model

Following Eqs. (4.6.1), (4.6.2), (4.6.3), the classical geostatistical model may be rewritten as follows:

$$\text{Data model: } \mathbf{y}|\boldsymbol{\beta},\mathbf{z},\tau^2 \sim N(\mathbf{X}\boldsymbol{\beta}+\mathbf{z},\tau^2\mathbf{I}), \tag{4.6.7}$$

$$\text{Process model: } \mathbf{z}|\sigma^2,\varphi \sim N(0,\sigma^2\mathbf{H}(\varphi)), \tag{4.6.8}$$

$$\text{Parameter model: } p(\boldsymbol{\beta})p(\tau^2)p(\sigma^2)p(\varphi), \tag{4.6.9}$$

which implies $\boldsymbol{\theta} \in \{\boldsymbol{\beta},\tau^2,\sigma^2,\varphi\}$. The priors for the four parameters can be specified as $\boldsymbol{\beta} \sim \mathrm{N}(\dot{\boldsymbol{\beta}},\dot{\mathbf{E}})$, $\tau^2 \sim IG(a_\tau/2,b_\tau/2)$, $\sigma^2 \sim IG(a_\sigma/2,b_\sigma/2)$, and $\varphi \sim Ga(a_\varphi,b_\varphi)$, where $Ga(a_\varphi,b_\varphi)$ indicates a gamma distribution whose average is $a_\varphi \cdot b_\varphi$. $\{\dot{\boldsymbol{\beta}}, \dot{\mathbf{E}}, a_\tau, b_\tau, a_\sigma, b_\sigma.a_\varphi,b_\varphi\}$ are parameters, which we consider as known.

The joint posterior distribution is specified following Eq. (4.6.4) as follows:

$$p(\mathbf{z},\boldsymbol{\beta},\tau^2,\sigma^2,\varphi|\mathbf{y}) \propto p(\mathbf{y}|\mathbf{z},\boldsymbol{\beta},\eta,\tau^2)p(\mathbf{z}|\sigma^2,\varphi)p(\boldsymbol{\beta})p(\tau^2)p(\sigma^2)p(\varphi) \tag{4.6.10}$$

Based on Eqs. (4.6.5) and (4.6.6), and using the conjugacy of the normal and inverse Gamma distributions for a normal distribution, the posterior distribution for the parameters $\{\boldsymbol{\beta},\mathbf{z},\tau^2,\sigma^2\}$ are derived in the following closed forms:

$$\boldsymbol{\beta}|\mathbf{z},\tau^2,\mathbf{y},\mathbf{X} \sim N(\ddot{\boldsymbol{\beta}},\ddot{\mathbf{E}}), \tag{4.6.11}$$

$$\mathbf{z}|\boldsymbol{\beta},\tau^2,\sigma^2,\varphi,\mathbf{y} \sim N(\ddot{\mathbf{z}},\ddot{\mathbf{F}}), \tag{4.6.12}$$

$$\tau^2|\boldsymbol{\beta},\mathbf{z},\mathbf{y} \sim IG(a_\tau+n, b_\tau+(\mathbf{y}-\mathbf{X}\boldsymbol{\beta}-\mathbf{z})'(\mathbf{y}-\mathbf{X}\boldsymbol{\beta}-\mathbf{z})) \tag{4.6.13}$$

$$\sigma^2|\mathbf{z},\varphi \sim IG(a_\sigma+n, b_\sigma+\mathbf{z}'\mathbf{H}^{-1}(\varphi)\mathbf{z}), \tag{4.6.14}$$

where

$$\ddot{\boldsymbol{\beta}} = \left(\frac{1}{\tau^2}\mathbf{X}'\mathbf{X} + \dot{\mathbf{E}}^{-1}\right)^{-1}\left(\frac{1}{\tau^2}\mathbf{X}'(\mathbf{y}-\mathbf{z}) + \mathbf{E}^{-1}\dot{\boldsymbol{\beta}}\right),$$
$$\ddot{\mathbf{E}} = \frac{1}{\tau^2}\mathbf{X}'(\mathbf{y}-\mathbf{z}) + \mathbf{E}^{-1}\dot{\boldsymbol{\beta}}, \tag{4.6.15}$$

$$\ddot{\boldsymbol{\eta}} = \left(\frac{1}{\tau^2}\mathbf{I} + \frac{1}{\sigma^2}\mathbf{H}^{-1}(\varphi)\right)^{-1}\left(\frac{1}{\tau^2}(\mathbf{y}-\mathbf{X}\boldsymbol{\beta})\right),\ \ddot{\mathbf{F}} = \frac{1}{\tau^2}(\mathbf{y}-\mathbf{X}\boldsymbol{\beta}). \tag{4.6.16}$$

On the other hand, the φ parameter, which does not have a closed form expression, yields the following form:

$$p(\varphi|\mathbf{z},\sigma^2) \propto p(\varphi) \times \exp\left(-\frac{1}{2\sigma^2}\mathbf{z}'\mathbf{H}^{-1}(\varphi)\mathbf{z}\right), \tag{4.6.17}$$

The parameters are estimated with the MCMC method. Except for the parameter φ, the conditional posterior distribution is a standard distribution, and random numbers can be generated more easily because of Gibbs sampler. However, the posterior distribution related to φ does not have a closed form, and therefore it is necessary to use, for example, the Metropolis–Hastings (MH) algorithm.

4.7.3 Bayesian spatial prediction

In this Bayesian framework, the spatial prediction is to obtain a predictive distribution. It is implemented by modifying the data model (Eq. 4.6.7) and the process model (Eq. 4.6.8) as follows:

$$\left[\begin{matrix}\mathbf{y}\\ y(\mathbf{s}_0)\end{matrix}\right]\left|\left[\begin{matrix}\mathbf{z}\\ z(\mathbf{s}_0)\end{matrix}\right],\boldsymbol{\beta},\tau^2 \sim N\left[\left(\begin{matrix}\mathbf{X}\\ \mathbf{x}(\mathbf{s}_0)\end{matrix}\right)\boldsymbol{\beta} + \left(\begin{matrix}\mathbf{z}\\ z(\mathbf{s}_0)\end{matrix}\right),\tau^2\left(\begin{matrix}\mathbf{I} & \mathbf{O}\\ \mathbf{O} & 1\end{matrix}\right)\right],\right. \tag{4.6.18}$$

$$\left[\begin{matrix}\mathbf{z}\\ z(\mathbf{s}_0)\end{matrix}\right]\left|\sigma^2,\varphi \sim N\left[\left(\begin{matrix}0\\ 0\end{matrix}\right),\sigma^2\left(\begin{matrix}\mathbf{H}(\varphi) & \mathbf{c}\\ \mathbf{c}' & 1\end{matrix}\right)\right],\right. \tag{4.6.19}$$

where $y(\mathbf{s}_0)$ is the unknown explained variable, $z(\mathbf{s}_0)$ is an unknown latent variable, $\mathbf{x}(\mathbf{s}_0)$ is a $1 \times K$ explanatory variable vector at the prediction point, $\mathbf{O}$ is a matrix of zeros, and $\mathbf{c}$ is an $N \times 1$ vector formed by the covariance function of the predicted value and observed value. Using the Gaussianity of the data model (Eq. 4.6.18) and the process model (Eq. 4.6.19), the conditional distribution of $y(\mathbf{s}_0)$ is derived as follows:

$$y(\mathbf{s}_0)|\mathbf{y},\boldsymbol{\theta} \sim N\left[\mathbf{x}(\mathbf{s}_0)\boldsymbol{\beta} + c'\boldsymbol{\Sigma}^{-1}(\mathbf{y}-\mathbf{X}\boldsymbol{\beta}),\ \tau^2 + \sigma^2 - \mathbf{c}'\boldsymbol{\Sigma}^{-1}\mathbf{c}\right] \tag{4.6.20}$$

Thus the marginal posterior distribution is derived as follows:

$$p(y(\mathbf{s}_0)|\mathbf{y}) = \int p(y(\mathbf{s}_0)|\mathbf{y}, \boldsymbol{\theta})p(\boldsymbol{\theta}|\mathbf{y})d\boldsymbol{\theta} \quad (4.6.21)$$

If the frequency or likelihood-based methods are used for parameter estimation (square error maximization approach and ML method), these apply a method that substitutes (plugs in) the estimated parameter in the equation that determines the Kriging prediction, and therefore the uncertainty of the parameter is not reflected on the spatial prediction. Meanwhile, with the Bayesian approach, it is possible to predict the uncertainty of the parameter as a distribution using Eq. (4.6.18).

In the calculation of MCMC, the two variance parameters may also be logarithmically transformed to remove the high correlation between the MCMC samples (Johnson and Hoeting, 2011). Research in this area includes studies to develop a more sophisticated MH algorithm (Minasny et al., 2011; Neal, 2011), algorithm optimization through slice sampling (Agarwal and Gelfand, 2005), variational Bayes (see Bishop, 2006), the Integrated Nested Laplace approximation (Rue et al., 2009), as well as enhanced ways to generate preliminary distribution (Kazianka and Pilz, 2012).

4.8 Spatiotemporal model

4.8.1 Outline

Geostatistics has traditionally developed targeting space with two (x, y) or three dimensions (x, y, z), but studies on spatiotemporal geostatistics considering the time axis have been actively conducted (Cressie and Wikle, 2011; Wikle et al., 2019). Assuming continuity in space, these studies have been roughly classified into approaches that view the time axis as continuous and approaches that view the time axis as discrete.

4.8.2 Approaches that view time axis as continuous

Now, we consider the spatiotemporal process $\{y(\mathbf{s},t): \mathbf{s} \in D,\ t \in T\}$ (see Chapter 1 about the definition). Here, let us assume that the spatiotemporal process is composed of the trend component $m(\mathbf{s},t)$ and the error component $u(\mathbf{s},t)$ whose mean equals zero as follows.

$$y(\mathbf{s}, t) = m(\mathbf{s}, t) + u(\mathbf{s}, t). \quad (4.7.1)$$

Here, as in Eq. (4.3.1), we assume $u(\mathbf{s},t) = z(\mathbf{s},t) + e(\mathbf{s},t)$ and $z(\mathbf{s},t)$ follows second-order stationarity GP, which follows

$$\mathrm{Cov}[y(\mathbf{s}, t), y(\mathbf{s} + \mathbf{h_s}, t + h_t)] = C^0(\mathbf{h_s}, h_t). \tag{4.7.2}$$

where $C^0(\mathbf{h_s},h_t)$ is known as the spatiotemporal covariance function.

In spatiotemporal modeling, the point is how to construct a spatiotemporal covariance function that satisfies positive definiteness. There are separable and nonseparable covariance functions for $C^0(\mathbf{h_s}, h_t)$; the former can be decomposed into spatial and temporal covariance functions while the latter cannot. The representative separable covariance functions are as follows:

(1) Linear model

$$C^0(\mathbf{h_s}, \mathrm{h_t}|\boldsymbol{\theta}) = C^1(\mathbf{h_s}|\boldsymbol{\theta}_1) + C^2(\mathbf{h_s}|\boldsymbol{\theta}_2), \tag{4.7.3}$$

(2) Product model

$$C^0(\mathbf{h_s}, \mathrm{h_t}|\boldsymbol{\theta}) = C^1(\mathbf{h_s}|\boldsymbol{\theta}_1) \cdot C^2(\mathbf{h_s}|\boldsymbol{\theta}_2). \tag{4.7.4}$$

where $\boldsymbol{\theta} \in \{\boldsymbol{\theta}_1,\boldsymbol{\theta}_2\}$ and $C^1(\mathbf{h_s}|\boldsymbol{\theta}_1)$ is a spatial covariance function satisfying positive definiteness, and $C^2(\mathrm{h_t}|\boldsymbol{\theta}_2)$ is a temporal covariance function. In this way, the linear and product models define covariance functions separately in spatial and temporal directions. Unfortunately, both these functions ignore the interaction between time and space. In other words, the pattern of spatial dependence is assumed as constant over time. The opposite is also true (i.e., the temporal dependence pattern is assumed as constant over space). However, spatial dependence pattern can change over time interaction. To model space-time interaction effects, a more flexible specification is required.

Representative nonseparable covariance functions, which consider space—time interaction, are as follows.

(1) Product-sum model

$$C^0(\mathbf{h_s}, h_t|\boldsymbol{\theta}) = k_1 C^1(\mathbf{h_s}|\boldsymbol{\theta}_1) + k_2 C^2(\mathbf{h_s}|\boldsymbol{\theta}_2) + k_3 C^1(\mathbf{h_s}|\boldsymbol{\theta}_1) \cdot C^2(\mathbf{h_s}|\boldsymbol{\theta}_2), \tag{4.7.5}$$

where k_1, k_2, k_3 are parameters.

(2) Cressie-Huang model

$$C^0(\mathbf{h_s}, h_t|\boldsymbol{\theta}) = \frac{\sigma^2}{\theta_1^2|h_t|^2+1} exp\left\{-\frac{\theta_2^2|\mathbf{h_s}|^2}{\theta_1^2|h_t|^2+1}\right\}. \quad (4.7.6)$$

where $\boldsymbol{\theta} \in \{\theta_1,\theta_2,\sigma^2\}$ with $\theta_1 \geq 0$ is the scaling parameter of time, $\theta_2 \geq 0$ is the scaling parameter of space, and $\sigma^2 = C^0(\mathbf{0},0)$.

The product-sum model (De Cesare et al., 2001) is a combination of the linear and product models that can take the interaction between time and space into consideration depending on the value of the parameters. Cressie and Huang (1999) derived Eq. (4.7.6) based on a necessary and sufficient condition for the covariance function to be a nonnegative definite function with a spectral representation under regular conditions. For other non-separable covariances, there is the monotone function approach of Gneiting (2002) and the mixture approach of Ma (2002). For details, refer to the review by Mateu et al. (2008).

In the same way as spatial Kriging, the BLUP for the spatiotemporal UK at an arbitrary location/time point is obtained as follows.

$$y(\mathbf{s}_0, t_0) = \mathbf{X}'(\mathbf{s}_0, t_0)\boldsymbol{\beta} + \mathbf{c}'\boldsymbol{\Sigma}^{-1}(\mathbf{y} - \mathbf{X}\boldsymbol{\beta}). \quad (4.7.7)$$

where $\mathbf{X}(\mathbf{s}_0,t_0)$ is the explanatory variable vector in the prediction point of $k \times 1$, $\mathbf{c}$ is the covariance vector among the random variables in the observation point of $NT \times 1$ and the random variables at the prediction point, and $\boldsymbol{\Sigma}$ is the variance-covariance matrix of $NT \times NT$.

In spatiotemporal modeling, the computational complexity rapidly increases as N and/or T increase because an inversion of the $NT \times NT$ variance-covariance matrix is needed. Exceptionally, separable covariance functions allow for calculating the inverse from the inverse of the $N \times N$ spatial covariance matrix and the inverse of the $T \times T$ temporal covariance matrix. Therefore, statistical tests for separability become important. Such methods include the spectrum method of Fuentes (2006) and the likelihood ratio test of Mitchell et al. (2006).

4.8.3 Approaches that view time axis as discrete

As previously mentioned, the space-continuous/time-continuous model has a very large calculation load, because it handles $NT \times NT$ variance-covariance matrices. On the contrary, since the dynamic spatiotemporal model (Gelfand et al., 2005; Sahu et al., 2006; Paez et al., 2008; Lee and

Ghosh, 2008), which is briefly explained in this section, handles only a variance-covariance matrix in each period; that is, $N \times N$ matrix T; the calculation load is relatively small. For details, refer to Gamerman (2010). The following is an outline of the model of Gelfand et al. (2005). The dynamic spatiotemporal model is formulated as follows.

$$y(\mathbf{s}, t) = \mathbf{X}'(\mathbf{s}, t)\widetilde{\boldsymbol{\beta}}(\mathbf{s}, t) + e(\mathbf{s}, t), \quad e(\mathbf{s}, t) \sim N(0, \sigma_\varepsilon^2) \tag{4.7.8}$$

$$\widetilde{\boldsymbol{\beta}}(\mathbf{s}, t) = \boldsymbol{\beta}_t + \boldsymbol{\beta}(\mathbf{s}, t),$$

$$\boldsymbol{\beta}_t = \boldsymbol{\beta}_{t-1} + \boldsymbol{\eta}_t, \quad \boldsymbol{\eta}_t \sim N(0, \boldsymbol{\Sigma}_\eta),$$

$$\boldsymbol{\beta}(\mathbf{s}, t) = \boldsymbol{\beta}(\mathbf{s}, t-1) + \mathbf{Au}(\mathbf{s}, t).$$

where $\mathbf{A}$ is a $k \times k$ matrix, $\mathbf{u}(\mathbf{s},t) = [u_1(\mathbf{s},t), \ldots, u_k(\mathbf{s},t)]'$ where $u_l(\mathbf{s},t)$ follows a second-order stationary spatial process with mean 0, variance 1, and correlation function $\rho_l(\varphi_l)$ for $l = 1, \ldots, k$. Eq. (4.7.8) models dynamic change of spatial process behind the regression coeffiients $\boldsymbol{\beta}(\mathbf{s},t)$. If prior distribution is set for each parameter, parameter estimation can be performed relatively easily using a Gibbs sampler or random walk process.

On the other hand, Cressie et al. (2010) and Katzfuss and Cressie (2012) proposed a hierarchical model of two levels known as a spatiotemporal random effect model, which is a data and a process model. This model is similar to the dynamic spatial model, but rather than regression coefficients, it is assumed that potential spatial autocorrelation factors evolve over time according to vector autoregression.

4.9 Methods for large data

4.9.1 Outline

Numerous studies have been conducted on large-scale geostatistical data modeling. Most existing approaches are classified into either low-rank or sparse approximation. Low-rank approximation applies a rank reduction to a GP to model global spatial patterns behind data computationally efficiently. On the other hand, the sparse approximation replaces the typically dense covariance matrix or its inverse (i.e., precision matrix) with a sparse matrix considering neighboring sites. Thus low-rank approximation attempts to estimate large-scale spatial variations while the sparse approximation attempts to estimate small-scale spatial variations. This section introduces representative approaches in these two approximations. See Sun et al. (2012),

Heaton et al. (2018), and Liu et al. (2018) for literature review for GP-based large data modeling.

4.9.2 Low-rank approximation

Typical low-rank approximation methods include the fixed rank Kriging of Cressie and Johannesson (2008) and the predictive process model of Banerjee et al. (2008).[13] Fixed rank Kriging is an approach similar to the geo-additive model in which the spatial effect $z(\mathbf{s})$ in a point $\mathbf{s}$ is represented by the random effect generated by knots and the basis function that is a function of distance from knots. However, this method is characterized by the fact that it models heterogeneity due to differences in data resolution, such as remote sensing data.

In the predictive process model, the second-order stationary spatial process $\boldsymbol{z}^* = [z(\mathbf{s}_1^*), \ldots, z(\mathbf{s}_m^*)]'$ is defined on the knot set $\{\mathbf{s}_1^*, \ldots, \mathbf{s}_m^*\}$, where $m \ll N$. The knots, which are often called inducing points, may or may not be included in the observation point. Suppose that $\mathbf{z}^* \sim N(0, \boldsymbol{\Sigma}^*(\boldsymbol{\theta}))$ and $\boldsymbol{\Sigma}_{i,j}^*(\boldsymbol{\theta}) = [C(\mathbf{s}_i^*, \mathbf{s}_j^*; \boldsymbol{\theta})]$. Then the predictive process at point $\mathbf{s}$ can be written in the form of a Kriging prediction equation as follows.

$$\tilde{z}(\mathbf{s}) = E\left[z(\mathbf{s})|\mathbf{z}^*\right] = \mathbf{c}'(\mathbf{s}; \boldsymbol{\theta})\boldsymbol{\Sigma}^{*-1}(\boldsymbol{\theta})\mathbf{z}^*, \tag{4.8.1}$$

where $\mathbf{c}'(\mathbf{s}; \boldsymbol{\theta}) = \left[c\left(\mathbf{s}, \mathbf{s}_1^*; \boldsymbol{\theta}\right), \ldots, c\left(\mathbf{s}, \mathbf{s}_m^*; \boldsymbol{\theta}\right)\right]$. $\tilde{z}(\mathbf{s})$ follows GP with mean 0 and covariance given by

$$C(\mathbf{s}_i, \mathbf{s}_j; \boldsymbol{\theta}) = \mathbf{c}'(\mathbf{s}_i; \boldsymbol{\theta})\boldsymbol{\Sigma}^{*-1}(\boldsymbol{\theta})\mathbf{c}(\mathbf{s}_j; \boldsymbol{\theta}), \tag{4.8.2}$$

The predictive process model is a model that replaces the spatial effect $z(\mathbf{s})$ of a normal global statistical model with $\tilde{z}(\mathbf{s})$. However, it needs to be corrected, because the variance of the predictive process $\tilde{z}(\mathbf{s})$ is systematically smaller than the variance of the parent process $z(\mathbf{s})$. Eq. (4.8.2) suggests that the bias is quantified by $\boldsymbol{\Sigma}_{i,j}(\boldsymbol{\theta}) - \boldsymbol{\Sigma}_{i,j}^*(\boldsymbol{\theta}) = C(\mathbf{s}_i, \mathbf{s}_j; \boldsymbol{\theta}) - \mathbf{c}'(\mathbf{s}_i; \boldsymbol{\theta})\boldsymbol{\Sigma}^{*-1}(\boldsymbol{\theta})\mathbf{c}(\mathbf{s}_j; \boldsymbol{\theta})$. Using this relationship, Finley et al. (2009) proposed a bias-adjusted predictive process whose realization at location $\mathbf{s}_i$ is formulated as follows:

$$\tilde{\tilde{z}}(\mathbf{s}_i) = \tilde{z}(\mathbf{s}_i) + \tilde{e}(\mathbf{s}_i), \quad \tilde{e}(\mathbf{s}_i) \sim N\left(0, \delta^2(\mathbf{s}_i)\right), \tag{4.8.3}$$

[13] Regarding the former, the code for MATLAB is available from the proposer's website (http://www.stat.osu.edu/~sses/collab_co2.html), and there is also an R package called LatticeKrig. Furthermore, for the latter, functions are provided in the R package called spBayes.

where $\delta^2(\mathbf{s}_i) = C(\mathbf{s}_i,\mathbf{s}_i;\boldsymbol{\theta}) - \mathbf{c}'(\mathbf{s}_i;\boldsymbol{\theta})\boldsymbol{\Sigma}^{*-1}(\boldsymbol{\theta})\mathbf{c}(\mathbf{s}_i;\boldsymbol{\theta})$. They showed that this adjustment effectively reduces the bias in variance.

While they adjust only variance, further refinement is needed in practice to capture small-scape spatial variations. Actually, as studied in Stein (2014), the low-rank approach cannot capture small-scale spatial variations, and the resulting spatial pattern becomes over-smooth. To address this problem, multiresolution basis functions have been used. Nychka et al. (2015) proposed a multiresolution GP, which is an extension of the fixed-rank Kriging, whereas Katzfuss (2017) proposed another multiresolution approximation extending the predictive process approach. Both these approaches specify an approximate GP as follows:

$$z(\mathbf{s}_i) = \sum_{r=1}^{R} \mathbf{b}_r(\mathbf{s}_i)'\mathbf{v}_r, \tag{4.8.4}$$

where $r \in \{1, \ldots, R\}$ represents resolution, $\mathbf{b}_r(\mathbf{s}_i)$ is a vector of basis functions at r-th resolution, and $\mathbf{v}_r$ is the corresponding random coefficient. The predictive process model is a special case of Eq. (4.8.4) where $R = 1$, $\mathbf{b}_1(\mathbf{s}_i)' = \mathbf{c}'(\mathbf{s};\boldsymbol{\theta})\boldsymbol{\Sigma}^{*-1}(\boldsymbol{\theta})$, $\mathbf{v}_1 = \mathbf{z}^*$. While the approaches of Nychka et al. (2015) and Katzfuss (2017) are similar, Nychka et al. (2015) used radial basis functions to model spatial process in each resolution while Katzfuss (2017) used the predictive process approach to estimate the process in each resolution.

4.9.3 Sparse approximation

This section lists representative sparse approximation methods.

4.9.3.1 Covariance tapering method

The covariance tapering method (Furrer et al., 2006; Kaufman et al., 2008) is relatively simple in its line of thinking, and it replaces the covariance beyond a certain distance with 0. Specifically, it is a method that replaces the covariance function $C(\mathbf{h};\boldsymbol{\theta})$, which depends on the parameter vector $\boldsymbol{\theta}$, with $\tilde{C}\left(\mathbf{h};\boldsymbol{\theta};\overline{h}\right) = C(\mathbf{h};\boldsymbol{\theta})C_{tap}\left(\mathbf{h};\overline{h}\right)$. Here, the tapering function $C_{tap}\left(\mathbf{h};\overline{h}\right)$ is an isotropic autocorrelation function, and with regard to a certain threshold value $\overline{h} > 0$, it is 0 if it is $\mathbf{h} \geq \overline{\mathbf{h}}$. This simplifies the calculation because the variance-covariance matrix given by $\tilde{C}\left(\mathbf{h};\boldsymbol{\theta};\overline{h}\right)$ is a sparse matrix whose elements are mostly 0. According to Kaufman et al. (2008), since the variance-covariance matrix can be expressed as $\sum(\theta)^{\circ}\mathbf{T}\left(\bar{h}\right)$ as an element product of $C(\mathbf{h};\boldsymbol{\theta})C_{tap}\left(\mathbf{h};\bar{h}\right)$, the log likelihood function can be expressed as follows:

$$l_{1tap}(\boldsymbol{\beta};\boldsymbol{\theta};\mathbf{y}) = -\frac{N}{2}\ln(2\pi) - \frac{1}{2}\ln\left|\boldsymbol{\Sigma}(\boldsymbol{\theta})^{\circ}\mathbf{T}\left(\bar{h}\right)\right| - \frac{1}{2}(\mathbf{y}-\mathbf{X}\boldsymbol{\beta})'\left[\boldsymbol{\Sigma}(\boldsymbol{\theta})^{\circ}\mathbf{T}\left(\bar{h}\right)\right]^{-1}(\mathbf{y}-\mathbf{X}\boldsymbol{\beta}), \tag{4.8.5}$$

The derivative (score function) of the log likelihood function becomes $E[(\partial/\partial\boldsymbol{\theta})\cdot l_{1tap}(\boldsymbol{\theta})]\neq 0$, and the asymptotic unbiasedness of the parameter estimator is not satisfied. Therefore, the log likelihood function of the following equation is also proposed, in which the third term is modified to satisfy this point.

$$l_{2tap}(\boldsymbol{\beta};\boldsymbol{\theta};\mathbf{y}) = -\frac{N}{2}\ln(2\pi) - \frac{1}{2}\ln\left|\boldsymbol{\Sigma}(\boldsymbol{\theta})^{\circ}\mathbf{T}\left(\bar{h}\right)\right| - \frac{1}{2}(\mathbf{y}-\mathbf{X}\boldsymbol{\beta})'\left\{\left[\boldsymbol{\Sigma}(\boldsymbol{\theta})^{\circ}\mathbf{T}\left(\bar{h}\right)\right]^{-1\circ}\mathbf{T}\left(\bar{h}\right)\right\}(\mathbf{y}-\mathbf{X}\boldsymbol{\beta}). \tag{4.8.6}$$

Please refer to Kaufman et al. (2008) for more details, including development of the equation.

4.9.3.2 Composite likelihood approach

Now, let us express the likelihood function using a conditional distribution as follows.

$$L(\mathbf{y}|\boldsymbol{\beta},\boldsymbol{\theta}) = p(y(\mathbf{s}_1)|\boldsymbol{\beta},\boldsymbol{\theta})\prod_{j=2}^{N} p\left(y(\mathbf{s}_j)\middle|\mathbf{y}_{-j},\boldsymbol{\beta},\boldsymbol{\theta}\right). \tag{4.8.7}$$

Vecchia (1988) focused on the fact that $\mathbf{y}_{-j}$ contains a lot of extra information and proposed replacing $\mathbf{y}_{-j}$ with the subvector $\mathbf{y}_{-j}\in S_j$. As a method of configuring $\mathbf{y}_{-j}\in S_j$, he presented a convenient method using either latitude or longitude of coordinates and using 10 units from the nearest side. Stein et al. (2004) extended Vecchia (1988) to cases where the length of $y(\mathbf{s}_j)$ is not 1 and proposed a parameter estimation method using the REML method. As a similar approach, Curriero and Lele (1999) proposed a parameter estimation method using the composite likelihood method, which is easier to calculate than the ML method. Varin et al. (2011) reviewed recent studies on the composite likelihood method.

4.9.3.3 Nearest-neighbor Gaussian process

Let us apply Vecchia (1988)'s expression to the GP as follows:

$$p(\mathbf{z}|\boldsymbol{\theta}) = p(z_1|\boldsymbol{\theta})\prod_{j=2}^{N} p(z_j|\mathbf{z}_{-j}, \boldsymbol{\theta}). \tag{4.8.8}$$

where $\mathbf{z}_{-j} = \{z_1, \ldots, z_{j-1}\}$ is defined on j-1 distinct locations called reference set. The nearest-neighbor GP (NNGP) (Datta et al., 2016) is constructed by approximating Eq. (4.8.8) as follows:

$$p(\widetilde{\mathbf{z}}|\boldsymbol{\theta}) = p(\widetilde{z}_1|\boldsymbol{\theta})\prod_{j=2}^{N} p\left(\widetilde{z}_j \middle| \widetilde{\mathbf{z}}_{nn(j)}, \boldsymbol{\theta}\right). \tag{4.8.9}$$

where $\widetilde{\mathbf{z}}_{nn(j)}$ is defined on the k-nearest nearest neighbors from the j-th sample site. Thus NNGP approximates the full GP expressed as a joint distribution using the nearest neighbors. While the realization depends on the ordering of the samples (i.e., how to determine j for each sample), Datta et al. (2016) showed that NNGP is insensitive to the ordering. They proposed fully Bayesian NNGP, which applied MCMC for the estimation, and the conjugate NNGP, which estimates parameters based on a cross validation. While the latter is theoretically more sophisticated, the former is MCMC-free and, of course, faster. They showed both these specifications approximate the full GP computationally quite accurately.

4.9.3.4 Approximation by Gaussian Markov random field

In the typical lattice process of Gaussian Markov random field (GMRF), the focus is on the precision matrix, which is the inverse of the variance-covariance matrix, and the reduction of the calculation load is carried out (Rue and Held, 2005). Unlike the variance-covariance matrix, the precision matrix is often sparse. A variety of studies have been accumulated that approximate the Gaussian process using GMRF (Rue et al., 2009; Blangiardo and Cameletti, 2015). The GMRF approach is used together with the integrated nested Laplace approximation (INLA) that performs a Bayesian inference not relying on simulations but through an optimization. Thus INLA allows for estimating the GMRF-based geostatistical model computationally efficiently. Besides, INLA is a general routine for a latent Gaussian model that assumes that the data have an exponential family of distributions (e.g., Gaussian, Poisson, Cox, etc.), and one or more latent variables describing spatial dependence, temporal dependence, group effects, and so on. Owing to this property, the INLA + GMRF approach is easily extended for a wide variety of spatial and temporal modeling.

References

Agarwal, D.K., Gelfand, A.E., 2005. Slice sampling for simulation based fitting of spatial data models. Statistics and Computing 15 (1), 61–69.

Arbia, G., 2006. Spatial Econometrics: Statistical Foundations and Applications to Regional Convergence. Springer Science & Business Media, New York.

Armstrong, M., 1998. Basic Linear Geostatistics. Springer Science & Business Media, Berlin.

Armstrong, M., Jabin, R., 1981. Variogram models must be positive-definite. Mathematical Geology 13 (5), 455–459.

Atkinson, P.M., Tate, N.J., 2000. Spatial scale problems and geostatistical solutions: a review. The Professional Geographer 52 (4), 607–623.

Bakka, H., Rue, H., Fuglstad, G.A., Riebler, A., Bolin, D., Illian, J., Krainski, E., Simpson, D., Lindgren, F., 2018. Spatial modeling with R-INLA: a review. Wiley Interdisciplinary Reviews: Computational Statistics 10 (6), e1443.

Banerjee, S., Gelfand, A.E., Finley, A.O., Sang, H., 2008. Gaussian predictive process models for large spatial data sets. Journal of the Royal Statistical Society: Series B 70 (4), 825–848.

Banerjee, S., Carlin, B.P., Gelfand, A.E., 2004. Hierarchical Modeling and Analysis for Spatial Data. Chapman & Hall/CRC, Boca Raton.

Bardossy, A., 1988. Notes on the robustness of the kriging system. Mathematical Geology 20 (3), 189–203.

Berger, J.O., De Oliveira, V., Sanso, B., 2001. Objective Bayesian analysis of spatially correlated data. Journal of the American Statistical Association 96 (456), 1361–1374.

Berliner, L.M., 1996. Hierarchical Bayesian time series models. In: Hanson, K.M., Silver, R.N. (Eds.), Maximum entropy and Bayesian methods. Dordrecht. Springer, pp. 15–22.

Bishop, C.M., 2006. Pattern Recognition and Machine Learning. Springer, New York.

Blangiardo, M., Cameletti, M., 2015. Spatial and Spatio-Temporal Bayesian Models with R-INLA. John Wiley & Sons, West Sussex, UK.

Borssoi, J.A., De Bastiani, F., Uribe-Opazo, M.A., Galea, M., 2011. Local influence of explanatory variables in Gaussian spatial linear models. The Chilean Journal of Statistics 2 (2), 29–38.

Chilès, J.P., Delfiner, P., 2012. Geostatistics: Modeling Spatial Uncertainty. Wiley series in probability and statistics, pp. 705–714.

Chua, S.H., 1982. Optimal estimators of mean areal precipitation in regions of orographic Influence. Journal of Hydrology 57 (1–2), 713–728.

Cook, R.D., 1986. Assessment of local influence. Journal of the Royal Statistical Society: Series B(Methodological) 48 (2), 133–155.

Collins, J.B., Woodcock, C.E., 1999. Geostatistical estimation of resolution-dependent variance in remotely sensed images. Photogrammetric Engineering and Remote Sensing 65 (1), 41–50.

Cowles, M.K., 2003. Efficient model-fitting and model-comparison for high-dimensional Bayesian geostatistical models. Journal of Statistical Planning and Inference 112 (1–2), 221–239.

Cressie, N., 1985. Fitting variogram models by weighted least squares. Mathematical Geology 17 (5), 563–586.

Cressie, N., 1990. The origins of kriging. Mathematical Geology 22 (3), 239–252.

Cressie, N., 1993. Statistics for Spatial Data. Wiley, New York.

Cressie, N., Hawkins, D.M., 1980. Robust estimation of the variogram: I. Journal of the International Association for Mathematical Geology 12 (2), 115–125.

Cressie, N., Huang, H.C., 1999. Classes of nonseparable, spatio-temporal stationary covariance functions. Journal of the American Statistical Association 94 (448), 1330–1340.

Cressie, N., Johannesson, G., 2008. Fixed rank kriging for very large spatial data sets. Journal of the Royal Statistical Society: Series B 70 (1), 209–226.
Cressie, N., Shi, T., Kang, E.L., 2010. Fixed rank filtering for spatio-temporal data. Journal of Computational and Graphical Statistics 19 (3), 724–745.
Cressie, N., Wikle, C.K., 2011. Statistics for Spatio-Temporal Data. Wiley, Hoboken, New Jersey.
Curriero, F.C., Lele, S., 1999. A composite likelihood approach to semivariogram estimation. Journal of Agricultural, Biological, and Environmental Statistics 4 (1), 9–28.
Datta, A., Banerjee, S., Finley, A.O., Gelfand, A.E., 2016. Hierarchical nearest-neighbor Gaussian process models for large geostatistical datasets. Journal of the American Statistical Association 111 (514), 800–812.
De Cesare, L., Myers, D.E., Posa, D., 2001. Product-sum covariance for space-time modeling: an environmental application. Environmetrics 12 (1), 11–23.
De Oliveira, V., Kedem, B., Short, D.A., 1997. Bayesian prediction of transformed Gaussian random fields. Journal of the American Statistical Association 92 (440), 1422–1433.
Diggle, P.J., Ribeiro, P.J., 2007. Model-based Geostatistics. Springer, New York.
Dingman, S.L., Seely-Reynolds, D.M., Reynolds III, R.C., 1988. Application of kriging to estimating mean annual precipitation in a region of orographic influence 1. JAWRA Journal of the American Water Resources Association 24 (2), 329–339.
Dowd, P.A., 1984. The variogram and kriging: robust and resistant estimators. Geostatistics for Natural Resources Characterization. Springer, Dordrecht, pp. 91–106.
Ecker, M.D., Gelfand, A.E., 1999. Bayesian modeling and inference for geometrically anisotropic spatial data. Mathematical Geology 31 (1), 67–83.
Ecker, M.D., Gelfand, A.E., 2003. Spatial modeling and prediction under stationary non-geometric range anisotropy. Environmental and Ecological Statistics 10 (2), 165–178.
Finley, A.O., Banerjee, S., Carlin, B.P., 2007. spBayes: an R package for univariate and multivariate hierarchical point-referenced spatial models. Journal of Statistical Software 19 (4), 1.
Finley, A.O., Sang, H., Banerjee, S., Gelfand, A.E., 2009. Improving the performance of predictive process modeling for large datasets. Computational Statistics and Data Analysis 53 (8), 2873–2884.
Fortin, M.J., Dale, M.R., 2005. Spatial Analysis: A Guide for Ecologists. Cambridge University Press.
Fuentes, M., 2006. Testing for separability of spatial–temporal covariance functions. Journal of Statistical Planning and Inference 136 (2–1), 447–466.
Fuentes, M., 2007. Approximate likelihood for large irregularly spaced spatial data. Journal of the American Statistical Association 102 (477), 321–331.
Fuglstad, G.A., Simpson, D., Lindgren, F., Rue, H., 2015. Does non-stationary spatial data always require non-stationary random fields? Spatial Statistics 14, 505–531.
Furrer, R., Genton, M. G., Nychka, D. (2006) Covariance tapering for interpolation of large spatial datasets, Journal of Computational and Graphical Statistics, 15 (3), 502–523. (2012. Erratum and Addendum: Journal of Computational and Graphical Statistics 21 (3), 823–824.)
Gaetan, C., Guyon, X., 2010. Spatial Statistics and Modeling. Springer, New York.
Gamerman, D., 2010. Dynamic spatial models including spatial time series. In: Gelfand, A.E., Diggle, P.J., Fuentes, M., Guttorp, P. (Eds.), Handbook of Spatial Statistics. Chapman & Hall/CRC, Boca Raton, pp. 437–448.
Gelfand, A.E., Banerjee, S., Gamerman, D., 2005. Spatial process modelling for univariate and multivariate dynamic spatial data. Environmetrics 16 (5), 465–479.
Gelfand, A.E., Diggle, P., Guttorp, P., Fuentes, M. (Eds.), 2010. Handbook of Spatial Statistics. CRC press.

Glatzer, E., Müller, W.G., 2004. Residual diagnostics for variogram fitting. Computers and Geosciences 30 (8), 859–866.
Gneiting, T., 2002. Nonseparable, stationary covariance functions for space-time data. Journal of the American Statistical Association 97 (458), 590–600.
Goovaerts, P., 1997. Geostatistics for Natural Resources Evaluation. Oxford University Press on Demand.
Gotway, C.A., Stroup, W.W., 1997. A generalized linear model approach to spatial data analysis and prediction. Journal of Agricultural, Biological, and Environmental Statistics 2 (2), 157–178.
Gotway, C.A., Young, L.J., 2002. Combining incompatible spatial data. Journal of the American Statistical Association 97 (458), 632–648.
Guttorp, P., Gneiting, T., 2006. Studies in the history of probability and statistics XLIX on the Matern correlation family. Biometrika 93 (4), 989–995.
Haining, R.P., 2010. The nature of georeferenced data. In: Fischer, M.M., Getis, A. (Eds.), Handbook of Applied Spatial Analysis. Springer, Berlin, Heidelberg, pp. 197–217.
Handcock, M.S., Stein, M.L., 1993. A Bayesian analysis of kriging. Technometrics 35 (4), 403–410.
Hengl, T., Minasny, B., Gould, M., 2009. A geostatistical analysis of geostatistics. Scientometrics 80 (2), 491–514.
Huang, H.C., Cressie, N., 2011. Nonparametric estimation of the variogram and its spectrum. Biometrika 98 (4), 775–789.
Harville, D.A., 1977. Maximum likelihood approaches to variance component estimation and to related problems. Journal of the American Statistical Association 72 (358), 320–338.
Heaton, M.J., Datta, A., Finley, A.O., Furrer, R., Guinness, J., Guhaniyogi, R., Gerber, F., Gramacy, R.B., Hammerling, D., Katzfuss, M., Lindgren, F., Nychka, D.W., Sun, F., Zammit-Mangion, A., 2018. A case study competition among methods for analyzing large spatial data. Journal of Agricultural, Biological, and Environmental Statistics 1–28.
Hengl, T., Heuvelink, G.B., Rossiter, D.G., 2007. About regression-kriging: from equations to case studies. Computers and Geosciences 33 (10), 1301–1315.
Hoeting, J.A., Davis, R.A., Merton, A.A., Thompson, S.E., 2006. Model selection for geostatistical models. Ecological Applications 16 (1), 87–98.
Irvine, K.M., Gitelman, A.I., Hoeting, J.A., 2007. Spatial design and properties of spatial correlation: effects on covariance estimation. Journal of Agricultural, Biological, and Environmental Statistics 12 (4), 1–20.
Johnson, D.S., Hoeting, J.A., 2011. Bayesian multimodel inference for geostatistical regression models. PLoS One 6 (11), e25677.
Journel, A.G., 1983. Nonparametric estimation of spatial distributions. Journal of the International Association for Mathematical Geology 15 (3), 445–468.
Journel, A.G., Huijbregts, C.J., 1978. Mining Geostatistics. Academic press, London.
Kammann, E.E., Wand, M.P., 2003. Geoadditive models. Journal of the Royal Statistical Society C 52 (1), 1–18.
Kaufman, L., Rousseeuw, P.J., 1990. Finding Groups in Data: An Introduction to Cluster Analysis. Wiley, New York.
Kaufman, C., Schervish, M., Nychka, D., 2008. Covariance tapering for likelihood-based estimation in large spatial datasets. Journal of the American Statistical Association 103 (484), 1556–1569.
Katzfuss, M., 2013. Bayesian nonstationary spatial modeling for very large datasets. Environmetrics 24 (3), 189–200.
Katzfuss, M., 2017. A multi-resolution approximation for massive spatial datasets. Journal of the American Statistical Association 112 (517), 201–214.

Katzfuss, M., Cressie, N., 2012. Bayesian hierarchical spatio-temporal smoothing for very large datasets. Environmetrics 23 (1), 94–107.
Kazianka, H., Pilz, J., 2012. Objective Bayesian analysis of spatial data with uncertain nugget and range parameters. Canadian Journal of Statistics 40 (2), 304–327.
Kitanidis, P.K., 1983. Statistical estimation of polynomial generalized covariance functions and hydrological applications. Water Resources Research 19 (4), 909–921.
Kitanidis, P.K., 1985. Maximum likelihood parameter estimation of hydrologic spatial processes by the Gauss-Newton method. Journal of Hydrology 79 (1–2), 53–71.
Kitanidis, P.K., 1997. Introduction to Geostatistics: Applications in Hydrogeology. Cambridge University Press.
Kyriakidis, P.C., 2004. A geostatistical framework for area-to-point spatial interpolation. Geographical Analysis 36 (3), 259–289.
Krige, D.G., 1951. A statistical approach to some basic mine valuation problems on the Witwatersrand. Journal of the South African Institute of Mining and Metallurgy 52 (6), 119–139.
Lam, N., 1993. Spatial interpolation methods: a review. The American Cartographer 10 (2), 129–149.
Lee, H., Ghosh, S.K., 2008. A reparametrization approach for dynamic space-time models. Journal of Statistical Theory and Practice 2 (1), 1–14.
Lee, J.J., Jang, C.S., Wang, S.W., Liu, C.W., 2007. Evaluation of potential health risk of arsenic-affected groundwater using indicator kriging and dose response model. The Science of the Total Environment 384 (1–3), 151–162.
Lee, J.J., Liu, C.W., Jang, C.S., Liang, C.P., 2008. Zonal management of multi-purpose use of water from arsenic-affected aquifers by using a multi-variable indicator kriging approach. Journal of Hydrology 359 (3–4), 260–273.
Leuangthong, O., Deutsch, C.V. (Eds.), 2008. Geostatistics Banff 2004, vol. 14. Springer Science & Business Media, Netherlands.
Li, J., Heap, A.D., 2011. A review of comparative studies of spatial interpolation methods in environmental sciences: performance and impact factors. Ecological Informatics 6 (3–4), 228–241.
Liu, H., Ong, Y.S., Shen, X., Cai, J., 2018. When Gaussian Process Meets Big Data: A Review of Scalable GPs. ArXiv, 1807.01065.
Ma, C., 2002. Spatio-temporal covariance functions generated by mixtures. Mathematical Geology 34 (8), 965–975.
Marchant, B.P., Lark, R.M., 2007. Optimized sample schemes for geostatistical surveys. Mathematical Geology 39 (1), 113–134.
Matérn, B., 1960. Spatial variation. Meddelanden Fran Statens Skogsforskningsinstitut 49 (5). Stockholm.
Matérn, B., 1986. Spatial Variation, second ed. Springer, New York.
Mateu, J., Porcu, E., Gregori, P., 2008. Recent advances to model anisotropic space–time data. Statistical Methods and Applications 17 (2), 209–223.
Matheron, G., 1963. Principles of geostatistics. Economic Geology 58 (8), 1246–1266.
Minasny, B., Vrugt, J.A., McBratney, A.B., 2011. Confronting uncertainty in model-based geostatistics using Markov chain Monte Carlo simulation. Geoderma 163 (3–4), 150–162.
Mitchell, M.W., Genton, M.G., Gumpertz, M.L., 2006. A likelihood ratio test for separability of covariances. Journal of Multivariate Analysis 97 (5), 1025–1043.
Murakami, D., Tsutsumi, M., 2012. Practical spatial statisics for areal interpolation. Environment and Planning B 39 (6), 1016–1033.
Neal, R.M., 2011. MCMC using Hamiltonian dynamics. In: Brooks, S., Gelman, A., Jones, G.L., Meng, X. (Eds.), Handbook of Markov Chain Monte Carlo, vol. 2. Chapman & Hall/CRC, pp. 113–162 (11).

Nychka, D., 2000. Spatial process estimates as smoothers. In: Schimek, M.G. (Ed.), Smoothing and Regression. Approaches, Computation and Application. Wiley, New York, pp. 393–424.
Nychka, D., Bandyopadhyay, S., Hammerling, D., Lindgren, F., Sain, S., 2015. A multiresolution Gaussian process model for the analysis of large spatial datasets. Journal of Computational and Graphical Statistics 24 (2), 579–599.
Olea, R.A., 2009. Geostatistics for Engineers and Earth Scientists. Springer Science & Business Media.
Oliver, M.A., 2010. An overview of geostatistics and precision agriculture. In: Oliver, M.A. (Ed.), Geostatistical Applications for Precision Agriculture. Springer, Dordrecht, pp. 1–34.
Ortiz, J., Deutsch, C.V., 2002. Calculation of uncertainty in the variogram. Mathematical Geology 34 (2), 169–183.
Paez, M.S., Gamerman, D., Landim, F.M.P., Salazar, E., 2008. Spatially-varying dynamic coefficient models. Journal of Statistical Planning and Inference 138 (4), 1038–1058.
Pardo-Igúzquiza, E., Olea, R.A., 2012. VARBOOT: a spatial bootstrap program for semivariogram uncertainty assessment. Computers and Geosciences 41, 188–198.
Rue, H., Held, L., 2005. Gaussian Markov Random Fields: Theory and Applications. Chapman and Hall/CRC, London.
Rue, H., Martino, S., Chopin, N., 2009. Approximate Bayesian inference for latent Gaussian models by using integrated nested Laplace approximations. Journal of the Royal Statistical Society: Series B (Statistical Methodology) 71 (2), 319–392.
Ruppert, D., Wand, M.P., Carroll, R.J., 2003. Semiparametric Regression (Cambridge Series in Statistical and Probabilistic Mathematics). Cambridge University Press, Cambridge.
Sahu, S.K., Gelfand, A.E., Holland, D.M., 2006. Spatio-temporal modeling of fine particulate matter. Journal of Agricultural, Biological, and Environmental Statistics 11 (1), 61–86.
Schabenberger, O., Gotway, C.A., 2005. Statistical Methods for Spatial Data Analysis. Chapman Hall/CRC, Boca Raton.
Seya, H., Tsutsumi, M., 2014. Applied Spatial Statistics (In Japanese). Asakura Publishing, Tokyo.
Seya, H., Tsutsumi, M., Yoshida, Y., Kawaguchi, Y., 2011. Empirical comparison of the various spatial prediction models: in spatial econometrics, spatial statistics, and semiparametric statistics. Procedia-Social and Behavioral Sciences 21, 120–129.
Shapiro, A., Botha, J.D., 1991. Variogram fitting with a general class of conditionally nonnegative definite functions. Computational Statistics and Data Analysis 11 (1), 87–96.
Stein, M.L., 1999. Interpolation of Spatial Aata: Some Theory for Kriging. Springer Science & Business Media, New York.
Stein, M.L., 2014. Limitations on low rank approximations for covariance matrices of spatial data. Spatial Statistics 8, 1–19.
Stein, M.L., Chi, Z., Welty, L.J., 2004. Approximating likelihoods for large spatial data sets. Journal of the Royal Statistical Society: Series B 66 (2), 275–296.
Sun, Y., Li, B., Genton, M.G., 2012. Geostatistics for large datasets. In: Montero, J.M., Porcu, E., Schlather, M. (Eds.), Advances and Challenges in Space-Time Modelling of Natural Events. Springer, Berlin, pp. 55–77.
Tolosana-Delgado, R., Pawlowsky-Glahn, V., 2007. Kriging regionalized positive variables revised: sample space and scale considerations. Mathematical Geology 39 (6), 529–558.
Tsutsumi, M., Seya, H., 2009. Hedonic approaches based on spatial econometrics and spatial statistics: application to evaluation of project benefits. Journal of Geographical Systems 11 (4), 357–380.

Tsutsumi, M., Shimada, A., Murakami, D., 2011. Land price maps of Tokyo metropolitan area. Procedia Social and Behavioral Sciences 21, 193–202.

Van Der Meer, F., 1996. Classification of remotely-sensed imagery using an indicator kriging approach: application to the problem of calcite-dolomite mineral mapping. International Journal of Remote Sensing 17 (6), 1233–1249.

Varin, C., Reid, N., Firth, D., 2011. An overview of composite likelihood methods. Statistica Sinica 21 (1), 5–42.

Vecchia, A.V., 1988. Estimation and model identification for continuous spatial processes. Journal of the Royal Statistical Society: Series B (Methodological) 50 (2), 297–312.

Wackernagel, H., 1998. Multivariate Geostatistics: An Introduction with Applications. Springer Science & Business Media, Berlin.

Waller, L.A., Gotway, C.A., 2004. Applied spatial statistics for public health data, Vol. 368. John Wiley & Sons.

Wang, F., Wall, M.M., 2003. Incorporating parameter uncertainty into prediction intervals for spatial data modeled via a parametric variogram. Journal of Agricultural, Biological, and Environmental Statistics 8 (3), 296–309.

Wand, M.P., 2009. SemiPar—An R Package for Semiparametric Regression, (The SemiPar 1.0 Users' Manual). https://cran.r-project.org/web/packages/SemiPar/index.html.

Warnes, J.J., 1986. A sensitivity analysis for universal kriging. Mathematical Geology 18 (7), 653–676.

Webster, R., Oliver, M.A., 2007. Geostatistics for Environmental Scientists. John Wiley & Sons.

Wikle, C.K., Zammit-Mangion, A., Cressie, N., 2019. Spatio-temporal Statistics with R. CRC Press, Boca Raton.

Zimmerman, D.L., 1993. Another look at anisotropy in geostatistics. Mathematical Geology 25 (4), 453–470.

Zimmerman, D.L., 2010. Likelihood-based methods. In: Gelfand, A.E., Diggle, P.J., Fuentes, M., Guttorp, P. (Eds.), Handbook of Spatial Statistics. Chapman & Hall/CRC, Boca Raton.

CHAPTER FIVE

Spatial econometric models

Hajime Seya[1], Takahiro Yoshida[2], Yoshiki Yamagata[2]
[1]Departments of Civil Engineering, Kobe University, Kobe, Hyogo, Japan
[2]Center for Global Environmental Research, National Institute for Environmental Studies, Tsukuba, Ibaraki, Japan

Contents

Spatial Analysis using Big Data
ISBN: 978-0-12-813127-5
https://doi.org/10.1016/B978-0-12-813127-5.00005-9

5.1 What is spatial econometrics?

The modeling of lattice data can be broadly classified into methods based on the conditional distribution of Besag (1974) and methods based on the joint distribution of Anselin (1988). In terms of models, the former often use the conditional autoregressive model, which forms the basis for Gaussian Markov random fields (Rue and Held, 2005), and the latter often use the simultaneous autoregressive model. It is convenient to use the former in a hierarchical Bayesian modeling framework (Congdon, 2010), and it is often used as a prior distribution (Lee, 2013). However, the former approach is rarely used in spatial econometrics except for some studies (Parent and LeSage, 2008). Since this chapter focuses on spatial econometrics in particular, the explanations are focused on the latter. For the former, please refer to Cressie (1993) and Rue and Held (2005).

According to Anselin and Bera (1998), the term *spatial econometrics* was first used by the Belgian economist Jean Paelinck in the early 1970s, and Paelinck and Klaassen (1979) provide the first textbook on spatial econometrics. The spatial aspect of the data has long been ignored in mainstream economics and econometrics (Fujita et al., 1999), but the situation has changed dramatically in the present, and spatial econometrics is fast becoming one of the major fields of econometrics, including the fact that its special issues are being published in many academic journals of econometrics (Arbia, 2011). The memoir of Anselin (2010) of the past 30 years is an accurate account of the development of spatial econometrics as an academic field until the year 2010.[1] Beyond regional science and geography, in which spatial econometrics was originated, now spatial econometric techniques are used in numerous other fields including environment science (Yamgata et al., 2017) and others as explained in Arbia (2014).

Here, we would like to simply enumerate the books related to spatial econometrics. Since there is an ambiguous delineation between spatial statistics (or geostatistics) and spatial econometrics, it is difficult to clearly classify books, but the most influential book for spatial econometrics may be Anselin (1988), which played a major role in the development of spatial econometrics in the 1990s. However, conversely, Anselin (1988) does not contain the vast knowledge accumulated in the 1990s and after

[1] Also, Anselin and Rey (2012) reviewed the development of software in spatial econometrics.

(see Pinkse and Slade, 2010). LeSage and Pace (2009) is one of the representative books that covers many important topics related to spatial econometrics. However, LeSage and Pace (2009) emphasize Bayesian estimation, and there is little mention of generalized method of moments (GMM)-based approaches à la Kelejian-Prucha (Kelejian and Prucha, 1998) as well as local indicators of spatial association. Both Bivand et al. (2013b) and Arbia (2014) provide a good introduction to spatial econometrics, and also include R codes for implementation. Arbia (2014), especially, includes some explanations about the modeling for spatial big data. Comprehensive books on spatial econometrics was published by Anselin and Rey (2014) and by Kelejian and Piras (2017). The former is an introductory and a practical guide to spatial econometrics (with software GeoDa, GeoDaSpace, and PySAL), whereas the latter is written in a theoretically rigorous manner. The book by Elhorst (2014a) is also useful, especially when we are interested in spatial panel models.

Moreover, Cliff and Ord (1973, 1981), Griffith (1988), and Haining (1990, 2003) are recognized textbooks written by geography researchers. Griffith (2003) and Griffith and Paelinck (2010) are books specialized on the spatial filtering approach, which is described in Chapter 6. Fotheringham et al. (2002) summarizes studies related to the geographically weighted regression (GWR) model, which is a representative modeling technique for spatial heterogeneity, though there is some important progress recently, which is also explored in Chapter 6.

5.2 Spatial econometric models

5.2.1 Spatial lag model and spatial error model

In spatial econometrics, there are two representative models that are used to consider spatial autocorrelation (or dependence) among data—spatial lag model (SLM), which considers it as autocorrelation among observed variables, and spatial error model (SEM), which considers it as autocorrelation of error terms.

The SLM models the equilibrium outcome resulting from spatial and/or social interactions (Anselin, 2002; Brueckner, 2003).[2] Although we cannot observe the actual process of such interactions from cross-sectional spatial

[2] Xu and Lee (2019) indicate that we can regard this equilibrium as a Nash equilibrium of static complete information game when specific function form on utility of each agent is imposed.

data, it is possible to model the correlation structure in the equilibrium resulting from the interactions. Hence in contrast to geostatistical (spatial statistical) models that focus on spatial process underlying observations (see Cressie and Wikle, 2011), the SLM rather focuses on the interaction among observations (or samples) themselves. We think this is one of the interesting differences between geostatistics and spatial econometrics.

In regression model framework, such modeling of the SLM is achieved by introducing a function of observed values of the surrounding areas into the classical linear regression (CLR) model (see Chapter 2).

$$y_i = g\left(y_{j\in S_i}, \boldsymbol{\theta}\right) + \sum_{k=1}^{K} x_{k,i}\beta_k + \varepsilon_i \tag{5.2.1}$$

where the function g with parameter vector $\boldsymbol{\theta}$ can take a fairly general function form, including a nonlinear form, but it is typically simplified using a spatial weighting matrix. The SLM is formulated as follows using w_{ij} (Anselin, 1988; LeSage and Pace, 2009).

$$y_i = \rho \sum_{j=1}^{N} w_{ij} y_j + \sum_{k=1}^{K} x_{k,i}\beta_k + \varepsilon_i \tag{5.2.2}$$

where, ρ is a spatial parameter and takes a value in the range of $(1/\omega_{\min}, 1)$, with the smallest (real) eigenvalue $\omega_{\min}$ of $\mathbf{W}$, when the weight matrix is row-standardized as described in Chapter 3.[3] It is suggested that a negative spatial autocorrelation may exist when $\rho < 0$, whereas a positive spatial autocorrelation may exist when $\rho > 0$. In matrix form, Eq. (5.2.2) can be rewritten as

$$\mathbf{y} = \rho\mathbf{W}\mathbf{y} + \mathbf{X}\boldsymbol{\beta} + \boldsymbol{\varepsilon}. \tag{5.2.3}$$

The SLM is similar to the autoregressive model in the field of time series analysis in that it includes the (spatial) lag of the observed variables (i.e., autoregressive term) on the right side. However, spatial autocorrelation is different from unidirectional time series correlation, in the sense that space provides no *order* to the data. Thus, when there is a dependence relationship between observed values at the spatial points i and j, y_j goes on the right side of the equation of y_i (Eq. 5.2.2)), and y_i also goes on the right side of the

[3] In this case the singular point is outside of $(-1,1)$, and therefore the singular point can be avoided by the assumption $(-1 < \rho < 1)$ (Lee, 2004), thus standardization is important to ensure continuous parameter space. This may be one of the reasons why typically $|\rho| < 1$ is assumed on ρ.

equation of y_j, and this relationship complicates the estimation. In SLM, the spatial lag variable $\mathbf{Wy}$ has a correlation with the error term, and because of this, it must be treated as an endogenous variable. Therefore, the estimation of model parameters by ordinary least squares (OLS), which does not consider endogeneity, may result in inconsistent estimates, and also the OLS estimate does not satisfy unbiasedness unless $\rho = 0$ (Anselin, 1988).

In contrast, the SEM attempts to model spatial autocorrelation in the error term, and it is often used for the purpose of addressing data problems, such as when measurement errors systematically exist in a spatial sense, rather than for economic theoretical reasons (Anselin, 2009). Dubin (1988) points out, in terms of hedonic analysis, that *houses which are near each other will tend to have a similar value on the omitted variables causing the error term to be spatially autocorrelated.* A representative SEM is a model having error term of a spatial autoregressive (SAR) type as follows (hereinafter referred to as SAR error model).

$$\mathbf{y} = \mathbf{X}\boldsymbol{\beta} + \mathbf{u}, \ \mathbf{u} = \lambda\mathbf{Wu} + \boldsymbol{\varepsilon} \tag{5.2.4}$$

where, λ is a spatial parameter, which also takes a value in between $(1/\omega_{\min}, 1)$ when the $\mathbf{W}$ is row-standardized. In previous studies, Eq. (5.2.4) itself is often referred to as SEM.

By the way, it should be noted that the names SLM and SEM are not necessarily commonly used terms. To give an example, there are various names for SLM in the representative literature on spatial econometrics, including spatial lag model (Anselin and Bera, 1998), mixed regressive spatial autoregressive model (Anselin, 1988), spatial autoregressive model (LeSage and Pace, 2009) (Arbia, 2006, p.110), and spatial autoregressive response model (Griffith, 2003). Also, in spatial statistics textbooks (for example, Cressie, 1993), SEM (spatial error model) is called simultaneous autoregressive model, and it is introduced in comparison with the conditional autoregressive model (see Section 5.6.1). Hence whether SAR represents SLM or SEM depends on the background of the author and context.

According to Eq. (5.2.4), the variance-covariance matrix of $\mathbf{u}$ in the SAR error model is given by $E[\mathbf{uu}'] = \sigma_\varepsilon^2(\mathbf{I} - \lambda\mathbf{W})^{-1}(\mathbf{I} - \lambda\mathbf{W}')^{-1}$. Assuming that $\mathbf{W}$ is a row-standardized contiguity matrix, if $|\lambda| < 1$, then $(\mathbf{I} - \lambda\mathbf{W})^{-1} = \mathbf{I} + \lambda\mathbf{W} + \lambda^2\mathbf{W}^2 + \lambda^3\mathbf{W}^3 + \ldots.$, is obtained by Leontief expansion, and hence the product of the inverse matrix in the variance-covariance matrix may become $\mathbf{I} + \lambda(\mathbf{W} + \mathbf{W}') + \lambda^2(\mathbf{WW} + \mathbf{WW}' + W'\mathbf{W}) + \ldots.$. thereby, the SAR error model leads to a modeling of *global* (i.e., large-scale) effect where a shock at a certain point spreads to all other points, and the term $(\mathbf{I} - \lambda\mathbf{W})^{-1}$ is called a spatial multiplier, just like a Leontief multiplier in input-output analysis. On the other hand, assuming that the error term obeys a spatial moving average (SMA) process (hereinafter referred to as SMA error model) $\mathbf{u} = \gamma\mathbf{W}\boldsymbol{\varepsilon} + \boldsymbol{\varepsilon}$, then the variance-covariance matrix of $\mathbf{u}$ is given by $E[\mathbf{uu}'] = \sigma_\varepsilon^2(\mathbf{I} + \gamma\mathbf{W})(\mathbf{I} + \gamma\mathbf{W})' = \sigma_\varepsilon^2\left[\left(\mathbf{I} + \gamma(\mathbf{W} + \mathbf{W}'\right) + \gamma^2\mathbf{WW}'\right]$. Obviously, it has only a first-order effect through $\mathbf{W}$ and a second-order effect through $\mathbf{WW}'$, and it can be seen that it is a model of *local* (i.e., small-scale) effect (Anselin, 2001; Fingleton, 2008a). In the SAR and SMA error models, when the number of neighborhood $j \in S_i$ of $\mathbf{s}_i$ changes from point to point, even if the element of $\boldsymbol{\varepsilon}$ is independent and identically distributed (i.i.d.), the variance of $\mathbf{u}$ inevitably becomes heteroskedastic, so the stationarity of the covariance is not satisfied. Stationarity is satisfied only in exceptional cases where observation points are obtained on lattice points (Anselin, 2001). Actually, this *induced heteroskedasticity* makes it difficult to estimate discrete choice models considering spatial autocorrelation (McMillen, 1992).

Kelejian and Robinson (1993, 1995) adopted the spatial error component (SEC) model (hereinafter SEC error model), which is often used in panel data analysis, and structured the error term as $\mathbf{u} = \mathbf{W}\boldsymbol{\psi} + \boldsymbol{\varepsilon}$. In the SEC error model, it is assumed that the error term is composed of two elements, which are indicated in the first term and the second term on the right side. The first term represents a spillover element and is given as a linear combination of spillover shocks occurring in other areas. The second term represents the effect peculiar to the area (local error element), and it is the same as $\boldsymbol{\varepsilon}$ in SAR or SMA. Each $N \times 1$ error vector $\boldsymbol{\psi}$, $\boldsymbol{\varepsilon}$ is assumed to be a vector whose elements are i.i.d., and there is no correlation between the two elements; that is, $\mathrm{E}[\boldsymbol{\psi}\boldsymbol{\varepsilon}'] = \mathbf{O}$ (where $\mathbf{O}$ is a matrix of $N \times N$ consisting of 0). As a result, the variance-covariance matrix of the error term of SEC is obtained as $E[\mathbf{uu}'] = \sigma_\psi^2\mathbf{WW}' + \sigma_\varepsilon^2\mathbf{I}$. The SEC error model was originally proposed as a solution to the issue that $(\mathbf{I} - \lambda\mathbf{W})$ must be nonsingular in SAR, in other words, as an alternative model of SAR (Kelejian and Robinson, 1995). However, the structure of the variance-covariance matrix is rather similar to SMA and is a model that takes local correlation into consideration (Anselin and Bera, 1998; Anselin and Moreno, 2003).

In addition, Kelejian and Prucha (2007) presented a method for nonparametric estimation of the variance-covariance matrix using the spatial heteroskedastic and autocorrelation (HAC) robust estimator. In this method, heteroskedasticity of variance can also be considered. This approach will be explained in Section 5.3.2.

5.2.2 Spatial Durbin model and generalized spatial model

Various types of specifications can be considered as SEM, such as SAR, SMA, and SEC, but SAR is the most common one in spatial econometrics. Therefore, the following discussion is based on SAR type error and we simply term it as SEM. Let us consider the following general model, termed spatial Durbin error model, including SLM and SEM as a special case.

$$\mathbf{y} = \rho\mathbf{W}\mathbf{y} + \mathbf{X}\boldsymbol{\beta} + \mathbf{W}\mathbf{x}\boldsymbol{\delta} + \mathbf{u}, \ \mathbf{u} = \lambda\mathbf{W}\mathbf{u} + \boldsymbol{\varepsilon}. \tag{5.2.5}$$

Here, it should be noted that $\mathbf{x}$ does not include a constant term. The combination of SLM and SEM, which dropped the term of $\mathbf{Wx}$ from Eq. (5.2.5), is called the spatial autoregressive combined (SAC) model or the spatial autoregressive model with spatial autoregressive disturbances. On the other hand, the model that drops the $\mathbf{Wu}$ term with $\lambda = 0$, and introduces the spatial lag of the observed variables and the explanatory variables in addition to the usual explanatory variables, is called the spatial Durbin model (SDM) as an analogy with the Durbin model in time series analysis (Durbin, 1960). Since the SAC model and SDM are not nested, it is, generally speaking, difficult to decide which model is desirable by conducting a statistical test. However, a method for testing nonnested models, such as spatial *J* test (Kelejian, 2008; Kelejian and Piras, 2011), has also been developed.[4] Another model, which can be obtained with putting the restriction of $\rho = \lambda = 0$ (i.e., introduces the spatial lag of the explanatory variables in addition to the usual explanatory variables), is termed spatial lag of $\mathbf{X}$ (SLX) model. Because of the identification reason, Gibbons and Overman (2012) advocated this specification rather than much complex SLM or SDM, and Vega and Elhorst (2015) further elaborated the SLX model.

Interestingly enough, SDM can be derived from the SEM. That is, in the SEM, since the error term is given by $\mathbf{u} = (\mathbf{I} - \lambda\mathbf{W})^{-1}\boldsymbol{\varepsilon}$, it can be transformed into $\mathbf{y} = \lambda\mathbf{W}\mathbf{y} + \mathbf{X}\boldsymbol{\beta} - \lambda\mathbf{W}\mathbf{X}\boldsymbol{\beta} + \boldsymbol{\varepsilon}$. If $-\lambda\boldsymbol{\beta} = \boldsymbol{\delta}$ is satisfied, then we have SDM (note however, that we do not consider the spatial lag of the constant term). The test of the null hypothesis of $\lambda\boldsymbol{\beta} + \boldsymbol{\delta} = 0$ is called a common factor test, which examines whether SDM is the desired

[4] kpjtest function of sphet package in R is available.

modeling approach compared to SEM by using the likelihood ratio (LR) (e.g., Mur and Angulo, 2006).

5.2.3 Impact measures

In the spatial econometric model, attention must be paid to the interpretation of the regression coefficient estimates if spatial lag of a dependent variable is introduced. That is, it is not possible to directly compare the coefficient estimates of the CLR model with those of the SLM or SDM. Here, let us explain the possible interpretation with the example of SDM. When the k-th attribute changes, the marginal change of expected value of $\mathbf{Y}$ is obtained by

$$\left[\frac{\partial E[\mathbf{y}]}{\partial x_{k,1}} \cdots \frac{\partial E[\mathbf{y}]}{\partial x_{k,N}}\right] = \begin{bmatrix} \frac{\partial E[y_1]}{\partial x_{k,1}} & \cdots & \frac{\partial E[y_1]}{\partial x_{k,N}} \\ \vdots & \ddots & \vdots \\ \frac{\partial E[y_N]}{\partial x_{k,1}} & \cdots & \frac{\partial E[y_N]}{\partial x_{k,N}} \end{bmatrix} \tag{5.2.6}$$

$$= (\mathbf{I} - \rho\mathbf{W})^{-1} \begin{bmatrix} \beta_k & w_{12}\delta_k & \cdots & w_{1N}\delta_k \\ w_{21}\delta_k & \beta_k & \cdots & w_{2N}\delta_k \\ \vdots & \vdots & \ddots & \vdots \\ w_{N1}\delta_k & w_{N2}\delta_k & \cdots & \beta_k \end{bmatrix}$$

For further illustration, we adopt the simple example by Elhorst (2010a). Let us consider the three areas of 1, 2, and 3, which are arranged in a linear fashion. When areas are adjacent, if we define that there is a dependency, the following spatial weighting matrix can be obtained.

$$\mathbf{W} = \begin{bmatrix} 0 & 1 & 0 \\ w_{21} & 0 & w_{23} \\ 0 & 1 & 0 \end{bmatrix} \tag{5.2.7}$$

And we have

$$(\mathbf{I} - \rho\mathbf{W})^{-1} = \frac{1}{1-\rho^2} \begin{bmatrix} 1 - w_{23}\rho^2 & \rho & \rho^2 w_{23} \\ \rho w_{21} & 1 & \rho w_{23} \\ \rho^2 w_{21} & \rho & 1 - w_{21}\rho^2 \end{bmatrix}, \tag{5.2.8}$$

Therefore

$$\left[\frac{\partial E[\mathbf{y}]}{\partial x_{k,1}}\ \frac{\partial E[\mathbf{y}]}{\partial x_{k,2}}\ \frac{\partial E[\mathbf{y}]}{\partial x_{k,3}}\right] =$$

$$\frac{1}{1-\rho^2}\begin{bmatrix} \left(1-w_{23}\rho^2\right)\beta_k+(w_{21}\rho)\gamma_k & \rho\beta_k+\gamma_k & \left(w_{23}\rho^2\right)\beta_k+(w_{23}\rho)\gamma_k \\ (w_{21}\rho)\beta_k+w_{21}\gamma_k & \beta_k+\rho\gamma_k & (w_{23}\rho)\beta_k+w_{23}\gamma_k \\ \left(w_{21}\rho^2\right)\beta_k+(w_{21}\rho)\gamma_k & \rho\beta_k+\gamma_k & \left(1-w_{21}\rho^2\right)\beta_k+(w_{23}\rho)\gamma_k \end{bmatrix} \tag{5.2.9}$$

Note that changes in explanatory variables in a certain area affect not only the outcome of the area itself but also the outcomes of the neighboring areas. Here, the effect on the own area is called a direct impact (DI),[5] and the effect on other areas is called an indirect impact (IDI).[6] Needless to say, DI is a diagonal term on the right side of Eq. (5.2.9), and IDI is a nondiagonal term. Another point is that DI and IDI differ depending on the area, as suggested by Eq. (5.2.9). Hence LeSage and Pace (2009) propose summary statistics for DI and IDI, and Seya et al. (2012) apply them to income disparity analysis in Japan. The summary statistics of the DI is given by the average of the diagonal elements of Eq. (5.2.9) (average direct impact—ADI), whereas that of the IDI is given by the average of column sums of the off diagonals (average indirect impact—AII) (or average of row sums when we are interested in the effect *from* other areas). The sum of ADI and the AII is termed average total impact.[7]

When we use the Bayesian Markov chain Monte Carlo (MCMC) for a parameter estimation, it is straightforward to calculate the distribution of ADI and AII from MCMC samples. But when impacts (or effects) estimates are calculated by using the ML method for example, an additional step is needed for the calculation of standard errors of impact measures. Typically, standard errors are created by the Monte Carlo sampling with the ML estimates and its covariance matrix (LeSage and Pace, 2009).[8]

[5] Or direct effect (LeSage and Pace, 2009).

[6] Or indirect effect (LeSage and Pace, 2009).

[7] These term came from Arbia et al. (2019a).

[8] Arbia et al. (2019a) show the possibility of the estimating equation approach and the classical delta method, which require a smaller computational burden, as an alternative or a complement to such a simulation-based approach.

5.2.4 Models for spatial heterogeneity: varying coefficient models in space

Regarding the consideration of spatial heterogeneity, the expansion method proposed by Casetti (1972), which gives a regression coefficient for each point as a function of location, could be mentioned as a seminal work. In the latter half of the 1990s, the GWR model that naturally extends the expansion method using kernel functions was proposed (Brunsdon et al., 1996; McMillen, 1996; Fotheringham et al., 1998), and numerous empirical studies are continuing to pile up. Geniaux and Martinetti (2018) proposed a combined model of the SLM with the GWR. The details with regard to the GWR model will be described in Chapter 6. For the related approach, the spatially varying coefficient model (SVCM) of Gelfand et al. (2003) exists as a way of considering spatial heterogeneity in the field of spatial statistics (geostatistics). This model assumes a weak stationary spatial process of regression coefficients, not of an error term. A faster version of the SVCM is proposed, with transfer learning (Bussas et al., 2017) or with integrated nested Laplace approximation (INLA) (Franco-Villoria et al., 2018).[9]

5.3 Parameter estimation of the spatial econometric models

5.3.1 Ordinary least squares method

The most widely used parameter estimation method in the CLR model is OLS. However, it is well known that the OLS estimator is not the best linear unbiased estimator if spatial autocorrelation exists. In the following, after briefly discussing this, we explain a representative parameter estimation method of the spatial econometric models.

First, let us consider the following simple equation where spatial autocorrelation exists among observations. This model, for example in Anselin (1988), is called the first-order spatial autoregressive model.

$$\mathbf{y} = \rho \mathbf{W} \mathbf{y} + \boldsymbol{\varepsilon} \tag{5.3.1}$$

The OLS estimator of ρ, say $\widehat{\rho}$, is obtained

$$\widehat{\rho} = (\mathbf{y}'_L \mathbf{y}_L)^{-1} \mathbf{y}'_L \mathbf{y} \tag{5.3.2}$$

[9] The SVCM can be estimated with the spBayes package in R (Finley and Banerjee, 2019) or the R-INLA.

with $\mathbf{y}_L \equiv \mathbf{W}\mathbf{y}$. By plugging Eq. (5.3.1) into $\mathbf{y}$ of Eq. (5.3.2) and taking the expected values of both sides, we have

$$\begin{aligned} E(\widehat{\rho}) &= E\left[(\mathbf{y}'_L\mathbf{y}_L)^{-1}(\mathbf{y}'_L\mathbf{y}_L)\rho\right] + E\left[(\mathbf{y}'_L\mathbf{y}_L)^{-1}\mathbf{y}'_L\boldsymbol{\varepsilon}\right] \\ &= \rho + E\left[(\mathbf{y}'_L\mathbf{y}_L)^{-1}\mathbf{y}'_L\boldsymbol{\varepsilon}\right] \end{aligned} \tag{5.3.3}$$

Here, since $E(\mathbf{y}'_L\boldsymbol{\varepsilon})$ does not equal zero, the OLS estimator is biased. Also, because probability limit: plim $N^{-1}(\mathbf{y}'_L\boldsymbol{\varepsilon}) = \text{plim } N^{-1}\boldsymbol{\varepsilon}'\mathbf{W}(\mathbf{I}-\rho\mathbf{W})^{-1}\boldsymbol{\varepsilon} \neq 0$ (because of the presence of the $\mathbf{W}$) except in the case of $\rho = 0$, the OLS estimator is inconsistent (Anselin, 1988).

Next, let us examine the case where there is spatial autocorrelation among error terms using the SAR error model. As described previously, the variance-covariance matrix of the SAR error term is expressed as $E[\mathbf{u}\mathbf{u}'] = \sigma_\varepsilon^2(\mathbf{I}-\lambda\mathbf{W})^{-1}(\mathbf{I}-\lambda\mathbf{W}')^{-1}$ or as follows:

$$E[\mathbf{u}\mathbf{u}'] = \sigma_\varepsilon^2\left[(\mathbf{I}-\lambda\mathbf{W})'(\mathbf{I}-\lambda\mathbf{W})\right]^{-1}. \tag{5.3.4}$$

Then the OLS estimator of $\boldsymbol{\beta}$ in the SAR error model is given by

$$\widehat{\boldsymbol{\beta}} = (\mathbf{X}'\mathbf{X})^{-1}\mathbf{X}'\mathbf{y}. \tag{5.3.5}$$

The following equation can be obtained when plugging $\mathbf{y} = \mathbf{X}\boldsymbol{\beta}+\mathbf{u}$ in $\mathbf{y}$ of Eq. (5.3.5) and taking the expected value.

$$\begin{aligned} E\left(\widehat{\boldsymbol{\beta}}\right) &= E\left[(\mathbf{X}'\mathbf{X})^{-1}(\mathbf{X}'\mathbf{X})\boldsymbol{\beta}\right] + E\left[(\mathbf{X}'\mathbf{X})^{-1}\mathbf{X}'\mathbf{u}\right] \\ &= \boldsymbol{\beta} + E\left[(\mathbf{X}'\mathbf{X})^{-1}\mathbf{X}'\mathbf{u}\right] \end{aligned} \tag{5.3.6}$$

Therefore, if there is no correlation between the explanatory variables and the error term, the OLS estimator is unbiased regardless of the existence of spatial autocorrelation in the error term. However, the variance of $\widehat{\boldsymbol{\beta}}$ is given as follows:

$$\begin{aligned} E\left[\left(\widehat{\boldsymbol{\beta}}-\boldsymbol{\beta}\right)\left(\widehat{\boldsymbol{\beta}}-\boldsymbol{\beta}\right)'\right] &= E\left[(\mathbf{X}'\mathbf{X})^{-1}\mathbf{X}'\mathbf{u}\mathbf{u}'\mathbf{X}(\mathbf{X}'\mathbf{X})^{-1}\right] \\ &= \sigma_\varepsilon^2(\mathbf{X}'\mathbf{X})^{-1}\mathbf{X}'\left[(\mathbf{I}-\lambda\mathbf{W})'(\mathbf{I}-\lambda\mathbf{W})\right]^{-1}\mathbf{X}(\mathbf{X}'\mathbf{X})^{-1} \end{aligned} \tag{5.3.7}$$

Thus the OLS estimate of the regression coefficient variance may be lower than the actual variance to be, except when $\lambda = 0$. Since the variance of the error term is underestimated, the t-value and F-value are overestimated when conducting the significance test of the regression coefficient. Needless to say, this is problematic for empirical studies.

As aforementioned, the parameters of SLM and SEM should not be estimated using OLS. Several alternative parameter estimation methods have been proposed, and representative ones include the ML method, GMM, and Bayesian method. We explain GMM, which requires a smaller computational burden, in Section 5.7; here we explain the remaining two methods.

5.3.2 Maximum likelihood method

In this section, let us first consider the SDM shown in the following equation.

$$\mathbf{y} = \rho\mathbf{W}\mathbf{y} + \beta_1\mathbf{1} + \mathbf{x}\boldsymbol{\beta}_2 + \mathbf{W}\mathbf{x}\boldsymbol{\delta} + \boldsymbol{\varepsilon} = \rho\mathbf{W}\mathbf{y} + \mathbf{X}\boldsymbol{\beta} + \mathbf{W}\mathbf{x}\boldsymbol{\delta} + \boldsymbol{\varepsilon}. \tag{5.3.8}$$

If we define $\widetilde{\mathbf{X}} = [\mathbf{1}; \mathbf{x}; \mathbf{W}\mathbf{x}]$ and $\widetilde{\boldsymbol{\beta}} = [\beta_1; \boldsymbol{\beta}_2'; \boldsymbol{\delta}']'$, SDM can be expressed as

$$\mathbf{y} = \rho\mathbf{W}\mathbf{y} + \widetilde{\mathbf{X}}\widetilde{\boldsymbol{\beta}} + \boldsymbol{\varepsilon} \tag{5.3.9}$$

or

$$\mathbf{y} - \rho\mathbf{W}\mathbf{y} = (\mathbf{I} - \rho\mathbf{W})\mathbf{y} = \widetilde{\mathbf{X}}\widetilde{\boldsymbol{\beta}} + \boldsymbol{\varepsilon}. \tag{5.3.10}$$

If we assume $\boldsymbol{\varepsilon} \sim N(\mathbf{0}, \sigma_\varepsilon^2\mathbf{I})$ for estimating parameters with the maximum likelihood method, the log-likelihood function of $\boldsymbol{\varepsilon}$ is given as

$$\begin{aligned} \ln l(\boldsymbol{\varepsilon}) &= \ln p(\varepsilon_1) + \cdots + \ln p(\varepsilon_N) = \sum_{i=1}^{N} \ln p(\varepsilon_i) \\ &= \ln\left[\left(\frac{1}{\sqrt{2\pi\sigma_\varepsilon^2}}\right)^N \exp\left\{-\frac{\sum_{i=1}^{N}\varepsilon_i^2}{2\sigma_\varepsilon^2}\right\}\right] \\ &= -\frac{N}{2}\ln\left(2\pi\sigma_\varepsilon^2\right) - \frac{1}{2\sigma_\varepsilon^2}\sum_{i=1}^{N}\varepsilon_i^2 = -\frac{N}{2}\ln\left(2\pi\sigma_\varepsilon^2\right) - \frac{\boldsymbol{\varepsilon}'\boldsymbol{\varepsilon}}{2\sigma_\varepsilon^2} \end{aligned} \tag{5.3.11}$$

where $p(\varepsilon_i)$is the probability density function of ε_i and $\boldsymbol{\varepsilon} = (\mathbf{I} - \rho\mathbf{W})\mathbf{y} - \widetilde{\mathbf{X}}\widetilde{\boldsymbol{\beta}}$. Since

$$l(\mathbf{y}) = l(\boldsymbol{\varepsilon})\left|\frac{\partial\boldsymbol{\varepsilon}}{\partial\mathbf{y}}\right| = l(\boldsymbol{\varepsilon})\left|\mathbf{I} - \rho\mathbf{W}\right| \tag{5.3.12}$$

the log-likelihood function of $\mathbf{y}$ is then given as

$$\ln l(\mathbf{y}) = -\frac{N}{2}\ln\left(2\pi\sigma_\varepsilon^2\right) + \ln\left|\mathbf{I} - \rho\mathbf{W}\right| - \frac{\left(\mathbf{y} - \rho\mathbf{W}\mathbf{y} - \widetilde{\mathbf{X}}\widetilde{\boldsymbol{\beta}}\right)'\left(\mathbf{y} - \rho\mathbf{W}\mathbf{y} - \widetilde{\mathbf{X}}\widetilde{\boldsymbol{\beta}}\right)}{2\sigma_\varepsilon^2} \tag{5.3.13}$$

$$\rho \in \left(\omega_{\min}^{-1}, \omega_{\max}^{-1}\right)$$

In the parameter estimation, instead of simultaneously obtaining the ML estimates for $\widetilde{\boldsymbol{\beta}}$, σ_ε^2 and ρ, it is convenient to find the estimate of ρ by maximizing the concentrated log-likelihood (or profile log-likelihood) function obtained by substituting the analytically derived ML estimates of $\widetilde{\boldsymbol{\beta}}$ and σ_ε^2. It is known that the log-likelihood function and the concentrated log-likelihood function differ in their theoretical properties (Arbia, 2006, p.114), but the same maximum likelihood estimates for $\widetilde{\boldsymbol{\beta}}$, σ_ε^2 and ρ can be obtained (LeSage and Pace, 2009, p. 47). The ML estimate $\widehat{\widetilde{\boldsymbol{\beta}}}$ of $\widetilde{\boldsymbol{\beta}}$ is given by:

$$\widehat{\widetilde{\boldsymbol{\beta}}} = \left(\widetilde{\mathbf{X}}'\widetilde{\mathbf{X}}\right)^{-1}\widetilde{\mathbf{X}}'(\mathbf{I} - \rho\mathbf{W})\mathbf{y} = \widehat{\widetilde{\boldsymbol{\beta}}}_o - \rho\widehat{\widetilde{\boldsymbol{\beta}}}_d \tag{5.3.14}$$

with

$$\widehat{\widetilde{\boldsymbol{\beta}}}_o = \left(\widetilde{\mathbf{X}}'\widetilde{\mathbf{X}}\right)^{-1}\widetilde{\mathbf{X}}'\mathbf{y},\ \widehat{\widetilde{\boldsymbol{\beta}}}_d = \left(\widetilde{\mathbf{X}}'\widetilde{\mathbf{X}}\right)^{-1}\widetilde{\mathbf{X}}'\mathbf{W}\mathbf{y}. \tag{5.3.15}$$

Also, by defining the residual:

$$\widehat{\boldsymbol{\varepsilon}}_o = \mathbf{y} - \widetilde{\mathbf{X}}\widehat{\widetilde{\boldsymbol{\beta}}}_o,\ \widehat{\boldsymbol{\varepsilon}}_d = \mathbf{W}\mathbf{y} - \widetilde{\mathbf{X}}\widehat{\widetilde{\boldsymbol{\beta}}}_d,\ \widehat{\boldsymbol{\varepsilon}} = \widehat{\boldsymbol{\varepsilon}}_o - \rho\widehat{\boldsymbol{\varepsilon}}_d \tag{5.3.16}$$

the estimate of the error variance σ_ε^2 is obtained by:

$$\widehat{\sigma}_\varepsilon^2 = \frac{(\widehat{\boldsymbol{\varepsilon}}_o - \rho\widehat{\boldsymbol{\varepsilon}}_d)'(\widehat{\boldsymbol{\varepsilon}}_o - \rho\widehat{\boldsymbol{\varepsilon}}_d)}{N}. \tag{5.3.17}$$

Using the estimates of $\widetilde{\boldsymbol{\beta}}$ and σ_ε^2, the concentrated log-likelihood function is given as:

$$l_C = const. + \ln\left|\mathbf{I} - \rho\mathbf{W}\right| - \frac{N}{2}\ln\left(\frac{(\widehat{\boldsymbol{\varepsilon}}_o - \rho\widehat{\boldsymbol{\varepsilon}}_d)'(\widehat{\boldsymbol{\varepsilon}}_o - \rho\widehat{\boldsymbol{\varepsilon}}_d)}{N}\right). \tag{5.3.18}$$

Maximizing this function for ρ gives the maximum likelihood estimate of $\widehat{\rho}$. The calculation procedure can be summarized as follows (Anselin, 1988).

1. Regressing $\mathbf{y}$ to $\widetilde{\mathbf{X}}$ and obtaining the OLS estimate $\widehat{\widetilde{\boldsymbol{\beta}}}_o$.
2. Regressing $\mathbf{Wy}$ to $\widetilde{\mathbf{X}}$ and obtaining the OLS estimate $\widehat{\widetilde{\boldsymbol{\beta}}}_d$.
3. Calculating the residuals $\widehat{\boldsymbol{\varepsilon}}_o$ and $\widehat{\boldsymbol{\varepsilon}}_d$.
4. Obtaining the estimate $\widehat{\rho}$ that maximizes the concentrated log-likelihood function.
5. Obtaining $\widehat{\widetilde{\boldsymbol{\beta}}}$ and $\widehat{\sigma}_\varepsilon^2$ by Eqs. (5.3.14) and (5.3.17) using $\widehat{\rho}$.

Note that the parameters of the SLM can be estimated in the same framework as SDM. Next, we describe the ML estimation of SEM parameters. Here, we take the example of the SAR error model, given as

$$\mathbf{y} = \mathbf{X}\boldsymbol{\beta} + \mathbf{u}, \quad \mathbf{u} = \lambda\mathbf{Wu} + \boldsymbol{\varepsilon}, \quad \boldsymbol{\varepsilon} \sim N\left(0, \sigma_\varepsilon^2 \boldsymbol{I}\right) \tag{5.3.19}$$

Here, with assuming that $(\mathbf{I}-\lambda\mathbf{W})$ is nonsingular, we can rewrite as

$$\mathbf{y} = \mathbf{X}\boldsymbol{\beta} + (\mathbf{I} - \lambda\mathbf{W})^{-1}\boldsymbol{\varepsilon} \tag{5.3.20}$$

and the log-likelihood function can be obtained as follows

$$l(\mathbf{y}) = -\frac{N}{2}\ln\left(2\pi\sigma_\varepsilon^2\right) + \ln\left|\mathbf{I} - \lambda\mathbf{W}\right| - \frac{[(\mathbf{I} - \lambda\mathbf{W})(\mathbf{y} - \mathbf{X}\boldsymbol{\beta})]'[(\mathbf{I} - \lambda\mathbf{W})(\mathbf{y} - \mathbf{X}\boldsymbol{\beta})]}{2\sigma_\varepsilon^2} \tag{5.3.21}$$

$$\lambda \in \left(\omega_{\min}^{-1}, \omega_{\max}^{-1}\right)$$

Here, if the variance-covariance matrix is defined as

$$E[\mathbf{uu}'] = \sigma_\varepsilon^2\Omega = \sigma_\varepsilon^2\left[(\mathbf{I} - \lambda\mathbf{W})'(\mathbf{I} - \lambda\mathbf{W})\right]^{-1} \tag{5.3.22}$$

the maximum likelihood estimate $\widehat{\widetilde{\boldsymbol{\beta}}}$ of $\widetilde{\boldsymbol{\beta}}$ is given by:

$$\widehat{\boldsymbol{\beta}} = \left(\mathbf{X}'\Omega^{-1}\mathbf{X}\right)^{-1}\mathbf{X}'\Omega^{-1}\mathbf{y} \tag{5.3.23}$$

where $\boldsymbol{\Omega}^{-1} = (\mathbf{I} - \lambda\mathbf{W})'(\mathbf{I} - \lambda\mathbf{W})$. With defining $\mathbf{y}_d = \mathbf{y} - \lambda\mathbf{Wy}$ and $\mathbf{X}_d = \mathbf{X} - \lambda\mathbf{WX}$, it can be rewritten as

$$\widehat{\boldsymbol{\beta}} = (\mathbf{X}'_d\mathbf{X}_d)^{-1}\mathbf{X}'_d\mathbf{y}_d \tag{5.3.24}$$

and thus OLS expression. Also, if the estimate of $\mathbf{u}$ is given as

$$\widehat{\mathbf{u}} = \mathbf{y} - \mathbf{X}\widehat{\boldsymbol{\beta}}, \tag{5.3.25}$$

the maximum likelihood estimate of variance is obtained as

$$\widehat{\sigma}_{\varepsilon}^{2}=\frac{\widehat{\mathbf{u}}'\Omega^{-1}\widehat{\mathbf{u}}}{N}. \tag{5.3.26}$$

Using the estimates of $\boldsymbol{\beta}$ and σ_{ε}^{2}, the concentrated log-likelihood function is given by

$$l_C = const. - \frac{N}{2}\ln\left(\frac{\widehat{\mathbf{u}}'\Omega^{-1}\widehat{\mathbf{u}}}{N}\right) + \ln\left|\mathbf{I}-\lambda\mathbf{W}\right|. \tag{5.3.27}$$

Unlike the case of SDM, it is not possible to obtain an efficient ML estimate with one-step optimization, because the estimator of $\boldsymbol{\beta}$ depends on the spatial parameter (Anselin, 1988, p. 182). Therefore, the following repetitive calculation is required.

1. Regressing $\mathbf{y}$ to $\mathbf{X}$ and obtaining the OLS estimate $\widehat{\boldsymbol{\beta}}_o$.
2. Obtaining the initial value, $\widehat{\mathbf{u}}_o = \mathbf{y} - \mathbf{X}\widehat{\boldsymbol{\beta}}_o$.
3. Obtaining an estimate $\widehat{\lambda}$ that maximizes the concentrated log-likelihood function.
4. Implementing estimated generalized least squares (EGLS) and obtaining $\widehat{\boldsymbol{\beta}}$.
5. Updating $\widehat{\mathbf{u}}$ by using $\widehat{\mathbf{u}} = \mathbf{y} - \mathbf{X}\widehat{\boldsymbol{\beta}}$.
6. If the convergence criterion is satisfied, moving forward to step 7, otherwise returning to step 3.
7. $\widehat{\sigma}_{\varepsilon}^{2} = \frac{\widehat{\mathbf{u}}'\Omega^{-1}\widehat{\mathbf{u}}}{N}$ is calculated.

Subsequently, let us consider the SAC model:

$$\mathbf{y}=\rho\mathbf{W}_1\mathbf{y}+\mathbf{X}\boldsymbol{\beta}+\mathbf{u}, \mathbf{u}=\lambda\mathbf{W}_2\mathbf{u}+\boldsymbol{\varepsilon}, \boldsymbol{\varepsilon}\sim N\left(\mathbf{0},\sigma_{\varepsilon}^{2}\mathbf{I}\right). \tag{5.3.28}$$

The log-likelihood function of the SAC model is given by the following equation.

$$l(\mathbf{y}) = -\frac{N}{2}\ln\left(2\pi\sigma_{\varepsilon}^{2}\right)+\ln\left|\mathbf{A}\right|+\ln\left|\mathbf{B}\right|-\frac{[\mathbf{B}(\mathbf{A}\mathbf{y}-\mathbf{X}\boldsymbol{\beta})]'[\mathbf{B}(\mathbf{A}\mathbf{y}-\mathbf{X}\boldsymbol{\beta})]'}{2\sigma_{\varepsilon}^{2}} \tag{5.3.29}$$

$$\mathbf{A}=\mathbf{I}-\rho\mathbf{W}_1 \tag{5.3.30}$$

$$\mathbf{B}=\mathbf{I}-\lambda\mathbf{W}_2. \tag{5.3.31}$$

Kelejian and Prucha (2007) argued that if $\boldsymbol{\beta} \neq \mathbf{0}$, in other words, if $\mathbf{X}\boldsymbol{\beta}$ contributes to the explanation of $\mathbf{y}$, two spatial parameters can be identified even when $\mathbf{W}_1$=$\mathbf{W}_2$.

Meanwhile, Lacombe (2004) used the following model.

$$\mathbf{y} = \rho_1 \mathbf{W}_1 \mathbf{y} + \rho_2 \mathbf{W}_2 \mathbf{y} + \mathbf{X}\boldsymbol{\beta} + \mathbf{W}_1 \mathbf{x}\boldsymbol{\chi} + \mathbf{W}_2 \mathbf{x}\boldsymbol{\delta} + \boldsymbol{\varepsilon}, \boldsymbol{\varepsilon} \sim N\left(\mathbf{0}, \sigma_\varepsilon^2 \mathbf{I}\right). \tag{5.3.32}$$

In this case, the log of Jacobian term in the log-likelihood function may be given by $\ln|\mathbf{I} - \rho_1 \mathbf{W}_1 - \rho_2 \mathbf{W}_2|$. In such a model, which has multiple spatial lag terms, after plugging in analytically derived estimates of the variance parameter and regression coefficients other than spatial parameters, the concentrated log-likelihood function is maximized using, for example, lattice point search[10]. Elhorst et al. (2012) proposed a practical method to obtain the possible range of spatial parameters.

After the estimate of the spatial parameter is obtained, our interest moves to inference, for which Hessian matrix is used. In SDM, the Hessian matrix is given by the following equation.

$$\mathbf{H} = \begin{bmatrix} \dfrac{\partial^2 l}{\partial \rho^2} & \dfrac{\partial^2 l}{\partial \rho \partial \widetilde{\boldsymbol{\beta}}'} & \dfrac{\partial^2 l}{\partial \rho \partial \sigma_\varepsilon^2} \\ \dfrac{\partial^2 l}{\partial \widetilde{\boldsymbol{\beta}} \partial \rho} & \dfrac{\partial^2 l}{\partial \widetilde{\boldsymbol{\beta}} \partial \widetilde{\boldsymbol{\beta}}'} & \dfrac{\partial^2 l}{\partial \widetilde{\boldsymbol{\beta}} \partial \sigma_\varepsilon^2} \\ \dfrac{\partial^2 l}{\partial \sigma_\varepsilon^2 \partial \rho} & \dfrac{\partial^2 l}{\partial \sigma_\varepsilon^2 \widetilde{\boldsymbol{\beta}}'} & \dfrac{\partial^2 l}{\partial \left(\sigma_\varepsilon^2\right)^2} \end{bmatrix}. \tag{5.3.33}$$

In SEM, we should replace $\widetilde{\boldsymbol{\beta}}$ with $\boldsymbol{\beta}$ and ρ with λ. In case of SDM, analytical Hessian can be given as (LeSage and Pace, 2009, p. 57)

$$\mathbf{H}^{(a)} = \begin{bmatrix} -tr(\mathbf{WAWA}) - \dfrac{\kappa_3}{\sigma_\varepsilon^2} & -\dfrac{\mathbf{y}'\mathbf{W}'\widetilde{\mathbf{X}}}{\sigma_\varepsilon^2} & \dfrac{2\kappa_3 - \kappa_2 + 2\mathbf{y}'\mathbf{W}'\widetilde{\mathbf{X}}\widetilde{\boldsymbol{\beta}}}{2\sigma_\varepsilon^4} \\ \cdot & -\dfrac{\widetilde{\mathbf{X}}'\widetilde{\mathbf{X}}}{\sigma_\varepsilon^4} & \mathbf{0} \\ \cdot & \cdot & \dfrac{-N}{2\sigma_\varepsilon^4} \end{bmatrix} \tag{5.3.34}$$

[10] The log of Jacobian term here is computationally demanding to evaluate for higher-order model, and therefore researchers typically rely on IV/GMM (see e.g., Lee and Liu, 2010).

where $\mathbf{A} = (\mathbf{I} - \rho\mathbf{W})^{-1}$, $\kappa_2 = \mathbf{y}'(\mathbf{W} + \mathbf{W}')\mathbf{y}$ and $\kappa_3 = \mathbf{y}'(\mathbf{W}'\mathbf{W})\mathbf{y}$. Here, the computational load of the analytical Hessian is large, because the tr(**WAWA**) term requires $O(N^3)$ operations. Hence instead of directly calculating analytical Hessian, LeSage and Pace (2009) proposed the use of the *mixed analytical numerical Hessian*, which utilizes the Hessian from concentrated log-likelihood to approximate Eq. (5.3.34). They suggested that a key point is that ML estimation already yields a vector of the concentrated log-likelihood values as a function of the parameter ρ, and therefore $\partial^2 l_C/\partial\rho^2$ costs almost nothing. They further demonstrated that quite similar *t*-statistics can be obtained with comparison to the case of analytical Hessian.

5.3.3 Bayesian method

LeSage (1997) proposed a method to estimate SLM parameters with the MCMC method. This method has a merit in that it explicitly accounts for the heteroscedasticity of the error term as shown in Eq. (5.3.35). Although the explanations here use SLM as an example, estimation can also be done using other models with the same manner. Now, it is assumed that SLM error terms follow the multivariate normal distribution as follows:

$$\boldsymbol{\varepsilon} \sim N\left(\mathbf{0}, \sigma_\varepsilon^2\mathbf{V}\right), \mathbf{V} = diag(v_1, \ldots, v_n) \tag{5.3.35}$$

Here, because of the lack of the degree of freedom, it is impossible to use the ML method to estimate the $2 + K + N$ parameters σ_ε^2, ρ, $\boldsymbol{\beta}$, v_1, …, v_N from N observations. However, this estimation becomes possible when using a Bayesian method in which the prior distributions, assigned to each parameter, are updated. Here, we assume the independent priors: $p\left(\sigma_\varepsilon^2, \boldsymbol{\beta}, \mathbf{V}, \rho\right) = p\left(\sigma_\varepsilon^2\right)p(\boldsymbol{\beta})p(\mathbf{V})p(\rho)$. Additionally, $p\left(v_i^{-1}\right)$, $(i = 1, \ldots, N)$ is assumed to follow the distribution $\chi^2(q)/q$ (q is the degree of freedom) independently. On top of these, the following priors are assumed

$$p(\boldsymbol{\beta}) \sim N\left(\dot{\boldsymbol{\beta}}, \dot{\mathbf{E}}\right), \tag{5.3.36}$$

$$p\left(\sigma_\varepsilon^2\right) \sim IG\left(\dot{a}/2, \dot{b}/2\right), \tag{5.3.37}$$

$$p\left(v_i^{-1}|q\right) \sim i.i.d.\chi^2(q)/q, \tag{5.3.38}$$

$$p(\rho) \sim Unif(-1, 1), \tag{5.3.39}$$

where $Unif(-1,1)$ represents a uniform distribution among open sets. When the value of the hyperparameter q takes large value, $\mathbf{V}=\mathbf{I}$ becomes closer to being true (LeSage, 1997). However, the goal of setting a value for v_i is to ensure the robustness of outliers, and it is better to assign it a relatively small value. For instance, because the prior for v_i leads to the mean 1, and variance $2/q$; using a small value of about 2−7 enables an estimation based on the presence of heteroscedasticity.[11] One advantage of this method to account for heteroscedasticity is that there is no need to identify the function form. Combining the prior distribution with the likelihood function yields a conditional posterior distribution like the following:

1. Conditional posterior distribution of $\boldsymbol{\beta}$:

$$p(\boldsymbol{\beta}|\rho,\sigma_\varepsilon^2,\mathbf{V}) \sim N(\dot{\boldsymbol{\beta}},\dot{\mathbf{E}}) \tag{5.3.40}$$

$$\ddot{\boldsymbol{\beta}} = \left(\sigma_\varepsilon^{-2}\mathbf{X}'\mathbf{V}^{-1}\mathbf{X}+\dot{\mathbf{E}}^{-1}\right)^{-1}\left(\sigma_\varepsilon^{-2}\mathbf{X}'\mathbf{V}^{-1}(\mathbf{I}-\rho\mathbf{W})\mathbf{y}+\dot{\mathbf{E}}^{-1}\dot{\boldsymbol{\beta}}\right)$$

$$\ddot{\mathbf{E}} = \left(\sigma_\varepsilon^{-2}\mathbf{X}'\mathbf{V}^{-1}\mathbf{X}+\dot{\mathbf{E}}^{-1}\right)^{-1}.$$

2. Conditional posterior distribution of σ_ε^2:

$$p(\sigma_\varepsilon^2|\boldsymbol{\beta},\rho,\mathbf{V}) \sim IG\left(\frac{N+\dot{a}}{2},\frac{\mathbf{e}'\mathbf{V}^{-1}\mathbf{e}+\dot{b}}{2}\right) \tag{5.3.41}$$

$$\mathbf{e}=\mathbf{y}-\rho\mathbf{W}\mathbf{y}-\mathbf{X}\boldsymbol{\beta}.$$

3. Conditional posterior distribution of v_i:

$$P\left(\left(\sigma_\varepsilon^{-2}e_i^2+q\right)/v_i|\boldsymbol{\beta},\rho,\sigma_\varepsilon^2,\mathbf{v}_{-i},q\right) \sim i.i.d.\chi^2(q+1) \tag{5.3.42}$$

where e_i is the i-th component of $\mathbf{e}$.

[11] Of course it is possible to estimate hierarchical models in which a prior is further assumed for q (Seya et al., 2012).

4. Conditional posterior distribution of ρ:

$$p(\rho|\boldsymbol{\beta}, \sigma_\varepsilon^2, \mathbf{V}) \propto |\mathbf{I} - \rho\mathbf{W}|\exp\left(-\frac{1}{2\sigma_\varepsilon^2}(\mathbf{e}'\mathbf{V}^{-1}\mathbf{e})\right) \tag{5.3.43}$$

However, because the conditional posterior distribution of parameter ρ is not a standard form (such as normal), Gibbs sampling cannot be used. To address this problem, Kakamu (2009), for example, used the random walk Metropolis algorithm (random walk process) for the MCMC sampling. In the random walk process, ρ is generated from

$$\rho^* = \rho^{t-1} + v_t, v_t \sim N(0, \xi^2), \tag{5.3.44}$$

where ρ^{t-1} is the value of ρ in step $t-1$. ξ^2 is determined by making adjustments as explained in Chapter 2. The acceptance probability is given by

$$\alpha(\rho^{t-1}, \rho^*) = \min\left(\frac{p(\rho^*|rest)}{p(\rho^{(t-1)}|rest)}, 1\right), \tag{5.3.45}$$

Specifically, with probability $\alpha(\rho^{t-1},\rho^*)$ set $\rho^t = \rho^*$ otherwise set $\rho^t = \rho^{t-1}$ (here, *rest* is a vector consisting of the parameters other than ρ). Although the random walk Metropolis algorithm is typically used, other samplers for ρ, which might be more efficient, are the slice sampler (Wolf et al., 2018) and the gridded-gibbs sampler (Otsuka and Kakamu, 2015).

5.4 Testing spatial autocorrelation based on the spatial econometric models

As discussed in Chapter 4, because it is difficult to specify the correct model from Global Moran's I alone, it is common to concurrently use test statistics based on a maximum-likelihood method that assumes a certain spatial autocorrelation structure as an alternative hypothesis. This section describes the Wald test, LR test, and Lagrangean multiplier (LM) test when an SLM or SAR error model is alternative hypothesis H_1 and a CLR model is the null hypothesis H_0,[12] based on Anselin (1988).

First, in the discussion of spatial autocorrelation in error terms, we focus on the SAR error model $\mathbf{u} = \lambda\mathbf{W}\mathbf{u} + \boldsymbol{\varepsilon}$. Null and alternative hypothesis are given by:

$$H_0: \lambda = 0$$

[12] spdep package of R can be used.

$$H_1 : \lambda \neq 0$$

5.4.1 Wald test

The Wald test statistic with the ML estimate $\widehat{\lambda}$ is given by

$$W_\lambda = \frac{\widehat{\lambda}^2}{AsyVar\left(\widehat{\lambda}\right)}. \quad (5.4.1)$$

Here, the asymptotic variance is derived as in the following equation.

$$AsyVar\left[\widehat{\lambda}\right] = \left[tr[\mathbf{W}_B]^2 + tr[\mathbf{W}'_B \mathbf{W}_B] - \frac{\{tr(\mathbf{W}_B)\}^2}{N}\right]^{-1} \quad (5.4.2)$$

where $\mathbf{W}_B = \mathbf{W}(\mathbf{I} - \lambda \mathbf{W})^{-1}$. The hypotheses can be tested using the standard asymptotic t test.

5.4.2 Likelihood ratio test

Eq. (5.4.3) provides the definition of the LR test statistic:

$$LR_\lambda = 2\left[\widehat{l}_C - \widetilde{l}_C\right] \quad (5.4.3)$$

where $\widetilde{l}_C$ is a concentrated log-likelihood under the restriction of $\lambda = 0$, whereas $\widehat{l}_C$ is that without the restriction. Hypothesis testing uses the fact that LR_λ asymptotically follows the χ^2 distribution with degree of freedom equal to 1.

5.4.3 Lagrangean multiplier test

Eq. (5.4.4) provides definition of the LM test statistic:

$$LM_\lambda = \frac{\left[\mathbf{e}'\mathbf{W}\mathbf{e}/\widetilde{\sigma}^2\right]^2}{T} \quad (5.4.4)$$

where $T = tr[(\mathbf{W}' + \mathbf{W})\mathbf{W}]$. Also, $\mathbf{e}$, and $\widetilde{\sigma}^2$ are the residuals and residual variance of the ML estimate (i.e., $\mathbf{e}'\mathbf{e}/N$) under the restriction $\lambda = 0$, and they can be estimated with OLS.[13] Hypothesis testing uses the fact that LM_λ asymptotically follows the χ^2 distribution with a degree of freedom equal to 1. The LM test is convenient in that it can be performed using only OLS

[13] Because the residual variance estimated with OLS is $\mathrm{e}'\mathbf{e}/(N - K)$, it can be used with correction.

results. However, note that it cannot determine whether an error term is autoregressive or a moving-average type.

Similarly, in hypothesis testing with SLM, null and alternative hypothesis are given by:

$$\mathrm{H}_0 : \rho = 0$$

$$\mathrm{H}_1 : \rho \neq 0$$

The descriptions in this chapter focus particularly on LM test statistic. For Wald test statistics and LR test statistics, refer to Anselin (1988).

The following equation provides the definition of LM test statistic.

$$LM_\rho = \frac{\left[\mathrm{e}\prime\mathbf{Wy}/\tilde{\sigma}^2\right]^2}{\left(R\tilde{J}_{\rho-\beta}\right)} \tag{5.4.5}$$

where $\mathbf{e}$, $\tilde{\sigma}^2$, and $\tilde{\boldsymbol{\beta}}$ are residuals, residual variance, and the ML estimate under the restriction $\rho = 0$, respectively, and again, they can be obtained with OLS. The denominator is given by $R\tilde{J}_{\rho-\beta} = T + \left(\mathbf{WX}\tilde{\boldsymbol{\beta}}\right)' \left[\mathbf{I} - \mathbf{X}(\mathbf{X}'\mathbf{X})^{-1}\mathbf{X}'\right]\left(\mathbf{WX}\tilde{\boldsymbol{\beta}}\right)/\tilde{\sigma}^2$, and hypothesis testing can be carried out with the fact that LM_ρ follows the distribution χ^2 with a degree of freedom equal to 1.

When neither the null hypothesis $\rho = 0$ (spatial lag autocorrelation) nor the null hypothesis $\lambda = 0$ (spatial error autocorrelation) are rejected, a CLR model can be used. When only one is rejected, the specification of that hypothesis can be followed, but when both are rejected, the robust LM test proposed by Anselin et al. (1996) can be used. When (an SAR type) spatial error autocorrelation exists, even if $\rho = 0$ is true, the hypothesis of $\rho = 0$ tends to be rejected. Similarly, when a spatial lag autocorrelation exists, even if $\lambda = 0$ is true, the hypothesis of $\lambda = 0$ tends to be rejected. The test statistics proposed in Anselin et al. (1996) is robust in the presence of such other types of spatial autocorrelations.

When the local presence of spatial lag autocorrelation is permitted, a new null hypothesis on the SAR error autocorrelation is provided by

$$\mathrm{H}_0 : \lambda = 0, \left(\rho = \delta/\sqrt{N}, \delta < \infty\right)$$

and the following equation provides the LM test statistic when the local presence of spatial lag is permitted.

$$LM_{\lambda\_Robust} = \frac{\left[\mathbf{e}'\mathbf{We}/\widetilde{\sigma}^2 - T\left(R\widetilde{J}_{\rho-\beta}\right)^{-1}\left(\mathbf{e}'\mathbf{Wy}/\widetilde{\sigma}^2\right)\right]^2}{\left[T - T^2\left(R\widetilde{J}_{\rho-\beta}\right)^{-1}\right]} \tag{5.4.6}$$

where $\widetilde{\boldsymbol{\beta}}$ is the ML (OLS) estimate. LM_{λ_Robust} also follows the χ^2 distribution with a degree of freedom equal to 1. Similarly, when local presence of an SAR error autocorrelation is permitted, a new null hypothesis on the spatial lag autocorrelation is provided by

$$\mathrm{H}_0: \rho = 0, \left(\lambda = \tau/\sqrt{N}, \tau < \infty\right),$$

and the following equation provides the LM test statistic.

$$LM_{\rho\_Robust} = \frac{\left[\mathbf{e}'\mathbf{Wy}/\widetilde{\sigma}^2 - \mathbf{e}'\mathbf{We}/\widetilde{\sigma}^2\right]^2}{\left[R\widetilde{J}_{\rho-\beta} - T\right]}. \tag{5.4.7}$$

LM_{ρ_Robust} also follows the χ^2 distribution with a degree of freedom equal to 1.

This description uses an SAR error model. On situations when an SMA error or SEC error model is used, refer to Anselin et al. (1996) and Anselin and Moreno (2003). Saavedra (2003) proposed Wald, LR, and LM test statistics for GMM estimate values. Egger et al. (2009) used Monte Carlo experiments to demonstrate that the Wald test performs well with a small sample. Although several test statistics for the spatial panel model were also proposed, they are essentially an extension of the above (see Debarsy and Ertur, 2010; Baltagi and Bresson, 2011).

The method of specification for the models introduced here could be referred to as a specific-to-general (StG) approach that builds on a basic model. Some research used Monte Carlo experiments to compare whether the best approach when specifying a true model is the general-to-specific approach, which starts with a general model such as the spatial Durbin error model and simplifies it, or the StG approach. However, prior research did not reach a clear conclusion (Mur and Angulo, 2009). Further research on this point will be needed in the future. Needless to say, for model specifications, not only these statistical considerations but also econometric theoretical considerations (e.g., Pinkse et al., 2002; Behrens et al., 2012; Small and Steimetz, 2012) are also important.

5.5 Testing spatial heterogeneity based on the spatial econometric models

This section describes the spatially adjusted Breusch-Pagan (SABP) test statistic for heteroscedasticity, and the spatial Chow (SC) test for structural instability, from Anselin (1988).

5.5.1 Spatially adjusted Breusch-Pagan test

Suppose that the error term variance in an SAR error model is in a heteroscedastic state.

$$\mathbf{u} = \lambda \mathbf{W}\mathbf{u} + \boldsymbol{\varepsilon},$$

$$\boldsymbol{\varepsilon} \sim N(\mathbf{0}, \mathbf{V}), \tag{5.5.1}$$

where the diagonal element of $\mathbf{V}$ is provided by the following formula.

$$\mathbf{V}_{ii} = h_i(\mathbf{Z}_i\boldsymbol{\alpha}), \quad h_i > 0, \tag{5.5.2}$$

where $\mathbf{Z}_i$ is the i-th line of the $N \times p$ variable matrix $\mathbf{Z}$, which is thought to explain heteroscedasticity. Additionally, $\boldsymbol{\alpha}$ is the corresponding parameter vector. Now let $\mathbf{v}$ denotes the $N \times 1$ vector comprising i.i.d. errors and fulfills the following equation.

$$\boldsymbol{\varepsilon} = \mathbf{V}^{1/2}\mathbf{v}. \tag{5.5.3}$$

Eqs. (5.5.1) and (5.5.3) yield the following:

$$\mathbf{V}^{-1/2}(\mathbf{I} - \lambda\mathbf{W})(\mathbf{y} - \mathbf{X}\boldsymbol{\beta}) = \mathbf{v}. \tag{5.5.4}$$

When $\boldsymbol{\alpha} = \mathbf{0}$, we obtain a standard SAR error model with homogenous variance. Hence the null hypothesis to test is

$$\mathrm{H}_0\text{:}\ \ \boldsymbol{\alpha} = \mathbf{0},$$

where the following equation provides the SABP test statistic

$$SABP = \frac{1}{2}\mathbf{f}'\mathbf{Z}[\mathbf{Z}'\mathbf{D}\mathbf{Z}]^{-1}\mathbf{Z}'\mathbf{f}, \tag{5.5.5}$$

where $\mathbf{f}$ is the $N \times 1$ vector with $f_i = \left(\widetilde{\sigma}_\nu^{-1} e_i\right)^2 - 1$ as an element. e_i is the OLS residual and $\widetilde{\sigma}_\nu^2$ is the ML variance estimate based on OLS residuals.

Here, the presence of **D** in the following equation is a divergence from the standard Breusch-Pagan test statistic (which assumes no spatial autocorrelation).

$$\mathbf{D} = \mathbf{I} - \left(1/2\tilde{\sigma}_\nu^4\right)\mathbf{dMd}' \tag{5.5.6}$$

where $\mathbf{d} = \left[\mathbf{1}; 2\tilde{\sigma}_\nu^2\mathbf{w}\right]$, with **w** as a vector consisting of the diagonal element of $\mathbf{W}\left(\mathbf{I} - \hat{\lambda}\mathbf{W}\right)^{-1}$, and **M** is the estimated covariance between σ_ν^2 and λ. Because LM_α follows theχ^2 distribution with a degree of freedom equal to K, hypothesis testing is straightforward.[14]

5.5.2 Spatial chow test

The Chow is a representative method for testing hypotheses on whether a regression model structure differs by group. A null hypothesis and an alternative hypothesis are given as

$$\mathrm{H}_0 : \mathbf{y} = \mathbf{X}\boldsymbol{\beta} + \mathbf{u},$$

$$\mathrm{H}_1 : \mathbf{y} = \begin{bmatrix} \mathbf{X}_i & \mathbf{O} \\ \mathbf{O} & \mathbf{X}_j \end{bmatrix} \begin{bmatrix} \boldsymbol{\beta}_i \\ \boldsymbol{\beta}_j \end{bmatrix} + \mathbf{u}.$$

Note that grouping is needed beforehand.

Because the power of the standard Chow test statistic drops when there is spatial autocorrelation in **u**. Hence the error term **u** is specified as SAR errors. Then the SC test statistic is given as

$$SC = \left\{\mathbf{e}'_R\left(\mathbf{I} - \hat{\lambda}\mathbf{W}\right)'\left(\mathbf{I} - \hat{\lambda}\mathbf{W}\right)\mathbf{e}_R - \mathbf{e}'_U\left(\mathbf{I} - \hat{\lambda}\mathbf{W}\right)'\left(\mathbf{I} - \hat{\lambda}\mathbf{W}\right)\mathbf{e}_U\right\}/\hat{\sigma}_\varepsilon^2, \tag{5.5.7}$$

where $\mathbf{e}_R$ and $\mathbf{e}_U$ are residuals under H_0 (restricted) and H_1 (unrestricted), respectively, while $\hat{\lambda}$ and $\hat{\sigma}_\varepsilon^2$ are derived under H_0.[15] This statistic follows the χ^2 distribution with a degree of freedom equal to K, and therefore hypothesis testing is possible.

[14] bptest.sarlm function in spdep package for R can be used. Note that the function is not exactly the same as that of Anselin (1988).

[15] spchow function in an spregime package for R can be used.

5.6 Related methods

5.6.1 Conditional autoregressive model

Since the SAR error model is modeled as a simultaneous (joint) distribution of random vector $\mathbf{u}$, it is called simultaneous AR in the field of spatial statistics, and it is often introduced in contrast to conditional AR (CAR error model), which models as a conditional distribution of neighbor sets. Let us assume that u_i is the random variable given by

$$u_i|\mathbf{u}_{-i} \sim N\left(\frac{\eta \sum_{j=1}^{N} w_{ij}u_j}{\sum_{j=1}^{N} w_{ij}}, \sigma_i^2\right) \quad \text{with } \sigma_i^2 = \frac{\sigma^2}{\sum_{j=1}^{N} w_{ij}}, \tag{5.6.1}$$

where η is a spatial parameter and σ^2 is the variance parameter. Note that the conditional expectation is the average of the random effects in neighboring areas, whereas the conditional variance is inversely proportional to the number of neighbors. Let us define the $\mathbf{S} = \text{diag}(\sigma_1, \ldots, \sigma_N)$, then the variance-covariance matrix of the error term is given by $\text{E}[\mathbf{uu}'] = \sigma^2(\mathbf{I} - \eta\widetilde{\mathbf{W}})^{-1}\mathbf{S}^2$ where i, j th element of $\widetilde{\mathbf{W}}$ is given by $\widetilde{w}_{ij} = w_{ij} \Big/ \sum_{j=1}^{N} w_{ij}$.

Because of the difference of the variance-covariance matrix between SAR and CAR, the CAR model shows a spatial autocorrelation pattern different from the SAR model (Wall, 2004; Ver Hoef et al., 2018).

For the CAR model, the $\mathbf{W}$ should be symmetric (Cressie, 1993), and therefore different from the SAR model; we cannot perform row-standardization for the CAR model. With setting $\eta = 0$, we have the intrinsic conditional autoregressive (ICAR) model, originated by Besag et al. (1991). ICAR is typically used as the prior distribution for the random effects. For information on CAR/ICAR, see Congdon (2010), Haining and Law (2011), and Lee (2013).

5.6.2 Spatial discrete choice models

A standard approach for modeling categorical (nominal or ordinal) data is either logit or probit model. For illustration, let's take an example of an incumbent shop's exit/continue behavior from a market. Let's denote the latent profit of i th shop for continue as π_{1i} and the latent profit for exit as π_{2i} $(i = 1, \ldots, N)$, where N denotes the sample size (i.e., number of the shops). Then, the latent profit difference between continue and exit state can be written as $\pi_i = \pi_{1i} - \pi_{0i}$, and the probit model can be given as

$$y_i = 1, \quad if \quad \pi_i = \mathbf{x}'_i\boldsymbol{\beta} + \varepsilon_i > 0$$

$$y_i = 0, \quad if \quad \pi_i = \mathbf{x}'_i\boldsymbol{\beta} + \varepsilon_i \leq 0 \tag{5.6.2}$$

where y_i denotes the observed dichromatic choice variable on continue ($y_i = 1$) or exit ($y_i = 0$), $\mathbf{x}_i$ denotes the $K \times 1$ vector of explanatory variables, $\boldsymbol{\beta}$ denotes the $K \times 1$ vector of corresponding coefficients, and ε_i is the error term, which is assumed to be $N(0, \sigma_i^2)$. If the probability of y_i being 1 is given as $\Phi(\mathbf{X}_i\boldsymbol{\beta}/\sigma_i)$, where $\Phi(\bullet)$ is the cumulative distribution function of the normal distribution, then the log-likelihood function of the probit model (for i th shop) is given by

$$y_i \ln[\Phi(\mathbf{X}_i\boldsymbol{\beta}/\sigma_i)] + (1 - y_i)\ln[1 - \Phi(\mathbf{X}_i\boldsymbol{\beta}/\sigma_i)] \tag{5.6.3}$$

Here, if the error term is homoscedastic, meaning that it fulfills $\sigma_i = \sigma$, then the ML estimator of the ratio $\boldsymbol{\beta}/\sigma$ is consistent. However, because variance is not homoscedastic in spatial econometric models *by construction* due to induced heteroscedasticity (see Section 5.2.1), this assumption is usually not fulfilled.

Unfortunately, this specification is too simple because in reality, exit/continue behavior of a shop may be affected not only by $\mathbf{x}_i$, but also by the exit/continue behaviors of the other shops. That is, if an existing shop's neighboring shops exit, then the shop may try to make a further effort to continue because its profit is expected be improved in a certain degree. Naturally, such kind of competition can be spatial because markets are localized due to the restriction of travel costs.[16]

One of the simplest ways to consider such spatial competition is to use autologistic model from Besag (1974). It is simply a CAR model derived from a Markov random field using an approach in which the observed values y_i:{1, 0} of neighboring shops are directly introduced. Such approach is often used in the ecology field, but also in the sociology field to analyze international relations (Yamagata et al., 2013). Caragea and Kaiser (2009) proposed a centered autologistic model that excludes the average component of the spatial lag terms from an autologistic model, and Hughes et al. (2011) used simulation experiments to demonstrate that

[16] In the transportation field, methods that consider spatial autocorrelation among *alternatives* rather than among *individuals* have also been developed (Bhat and Guo, 2004).

the centered autologistic model is superior to the autologistic model in terms of parameter bias.[17]

Other approaches include spatial econometric approach (spatial lag model) and social interaction approach. In the former, an existing shop's latent profit difference is affected by the neighboring shop's latent profit differences as $\sum_j w_{ij}\pi_j$. Instead, in the social interaction approach, a shop's latent profit difference is affected by the subjective expectation on the other shop's continue behavior; that is to say, $\sum_j w_{ij}\mathbb{E}(y_j)$. If we can conduct a survey to obtain subjective expectation of exit behavior, we can specify expected probability $\mathbb{E}(y_j)$ directly with the observed subjective expectation like the work of Li and Lee (2009). However, when it is difficult, it is reasonable to assume that expected probability is unobservable to the researcher and to accept the rational expectations hypothesis; that is, subjective expectation can be replaced by the objective probability generated by the model (Brock and Durlauf, 2001). While Brock and Durlauf (2001) assume that the expected probability is constant across groups, Lee et al. (2014) assume that because $\mathbf{x}$ values may in general be different across individuals, the expected probabilities p_j for individuals would be heterogeneous; that is, $\mathbb{E}(y_j) = p_j = p(y_j = 1)$ for all j. In rational expectation equilibrium, the following relation may hold (Lee et al., 2014).

$$p_i = \Phi\left(\rho \sum_{j=1}^{N} w_{ij} p_j + \mathbf{x}'_i \boldsymbol{\beta}\right) \tag{5.6.4}$$

The difficulty of such a social interaction approach is in that possibility of multiple equilibria. Lee and Lin (2014) proved that when a dichromatic variable takes one or zero, then a sufficient condition for a unique rational expectation equilibrium is $|\rho| < 2\pi \approx 2.5$ in probit case. In other words,

[17] Estimating the parameters in the centered autologistic model is possible with the ngspatial package of R. Here, let us turn our attention to discrete data, particularly count data. The Poisson regression model requires special attention when accounting for spatial autocorrelation. The following auto model in the style of Besag (1974) that introduces dependent variable from surrounding areas cannot express positive spatial autocorrelation: $\mu_i = \exp(\mathbf{X}_i\boldsymbol{\beta} + \eta\sum_j w_{ij} y_j)$. This stems from the fact that the dependent variable in the Poisson regression model can take infinite values, as expressed by 0, 1, ..., ∞. To improve this issue, Kaiser and Cressie (1997) proposed the Winsorizing method (Haining et al., 2009) in which the dependent variable is censored at an appropriate cut-off point. Also, Lambert et al. (2010) modeled this as the spatial autocorrelation between mean terms, as in $\mu_i = \exp(\mathbf{X}_i\boldsymbol{\beta} + \eta\sum_j w_{ij}\mu_j)$, and presented two types of ML methods.

multiple equilibria may exist if $|\rho| > 2.5$. The parameter estimation of discrete choice model with social interactions may be performed using structural estimation techniques (see Ellickson and Misra, 2011; Su and Judd, 2012).

Now we turn to the spatial econometric approach. The spatial lag (or autoregressive) probit model can be formulated in the following manner (e.g., LeSage and Pace, 2009):

$$y_i = 1, \quad \text{if} \quad \pi_i = \rho \sum_{j=1}^{N} w_{ij}\pi_j + \mathbf{x}'_i\boldsymbol{\beta} + \varepsilon_i > 0$$

$$y_i = 0, \quad \text{if} \quad \pi_i = \rho \sum_{j=1}^{N} w_{ij}\pi_j + \mathbf{x}'_i\boldsymbol{\beta} + \varepsilon_i \leq 0 \tag{5.6.5}$$

where ρ denotes a scalar parameter indicating the degree of spatial autocorrelation, and w_{ij} denotes a spatial weight. $\rho > 0$ suggests strategic complement (positive spatial autocorrelation among latent profit differences) and $\rho < 0$ suggests strategic substitute (negative spatial autocorrelation among latent profit differences). As such, thought behind the spatial lag probit model is that spatial autocorrelation among latent profit differences. Let's rewrite the profit difference in Eq. (5.6.5) in matrix form as:

$$\boldsymbol{\Pi} = (\mathbf{I} - \rho\mathbf{W})^{-1}\mathbf{X}\boldsymbol{\beta} + (\mathbf{I} - \rho\mathbf{W})^{-1}\boldsymbol{\varepsilon} \tag{5.6.6}$$

where $\boldsymbol{\Pi}$ denotes an $N \times 1$ vector whose i th element is given by π_i. When $\mathbf{W}$ is row-standardized, then spatial lag variable $w_{ij}\pi_j$ represents the average effect from the neighbors and when it does not, $w_{ij}\pi_j$ represents an aggregate effect from the neighbors (Liu et al., 2014). The spatial econometric approach can attain unique equilibrium and not suffer from multiple equilibria (see Kim and Parent, 2016).

Now let's term the i th diagonal element of $(\mathbf{I} - \rho\mathbf{W})^{-1}\boldsymbol{\varepsilon}$ as v_i, and define $\mathbf{x}_i^* = \mathbf{x}_i / v_i$ and $\mathbf{H} = (\mathbf{I} - \rho\mathbf{W})^{-1}\mathbf{X}^*$, where $\mathbf{X}^*$ denotes an $N \times K$ matrix constructed by stacking $\mathbf{x}_i'^*$. Then the probability of continue may be given in the following manner:

$$\mathbf{p} = \Phi(\mathbf{H}\boldsymbol{\beta}) \tag{5.6.7}$$

where $\Phi(.)$ denotes the cumulative distribution function of standard normal distribution.

It is important to note that $(\mathbf{I} - \rho\mathbf{W})^{-1}\boldsymbol{\varepsilon}$ induce heteroskedastic variance even if $\boldsymbol{\varepsilon}$ has unit homoscedastic variance (see Section 5.2.1). Hence the standard maximum likelihood procedure cannot be applied because it leads to an inconsistent estimate for $\boldsymbol{\beta}$. Possible alternatives include expectation-maximization (EM) algorithm (McMillen, 1992); Bayesian MCMC (LeSage, 2000); GMM (Pinkse and Slade, 1998); linearized GMM (Klier and McMillen, 2008); and partial (composite marginal) maximum likelihood (Bhat, 2011; Wang et al., 2013) among others.[18]

The developments of spatial econometric discrete choice models have begun for binary data, by McMillen (1992) (lag/error). He employed EM algorithm for estimation. Faster version of the ML-based approach was developed by Bhat (2011), Wang et al. (2013), and Martinetti and Geniaux (2017). In the former two, the partial (composite marginal) ML estimators are introduced by dividing observations into pairwise groups and bivariate normal distributions are specified; in the last one, a univariate conditioning procedure was introduced to approximate the likelihood function. Smirnov (2010) presented a pseudo-ML estimation method for a spatial-lag-type multinomial logit model.

Meanwhile, LeSage (2000) proposed a method to estimate the parameters of a binary spatial probit model (lag/error) using the Bayesian MCMC method. As a normal distribution case, the merit of this approach is that it can address heteroscedasticity in $\boldsymbol{\varepsilon}$ in addition to spatial autocorrelation. The Bayesian method was expanded into a spatial multinomial probit model by Chakir and Parent (2009) and Wang and Kockelman (2009), spatial bivariate probit model by Brasington and Parent (2017), and sample selection model by Doğan and Taşpinar (2018).

Pinkse and Slade (1998) proposed a GMM approach for a spatial error probit model, followed by Klier and McMillen (2008), where a linearized logit version of Pinkse and Slade's spatial GMM estimator has been proposed (lag/error). They showed that linearization produces a model that can be estimated using large datasets, and they showed that method performs well overall if the spatial autocorrelation is mild (spatial parameter equals 0.5 or less). The variants of this approach include that of Carrión-Flores et al. (2018), which generalized Pinkse and Slade's spatial GMM estimator to multinomial choice models with spatial lag dependence, and Flores-Lagunes and Schnier (2012) for sample selection models.

[18] Calabrese and Elkink (2014) compared estimators by some of these methods and others using Monte Carlo experiments. R package for estimating spatial lag probit model includes McSpatial, ProbitSpatial, and spatialprobit.

Readers of this subsection can refer to Fleming (2004), Smirnov (2010), and Billé and Arbia (2013) for reviews by that date. Also, consult Lacombe and LeSage (2018) with respect to the impact (effect) estimates (see Section 5.2.3) for spatial-lag type probit models.

5.6.3 Spatial panel models

While the discipline of spatial econometrics has a long interest in cross-sectional data, modeling techniques for panel data are also developing (Elhorst, 2014a). Let us look at a few leading:

$$y_{i,t} = \beta_1 + \rho \sum_{j=1}^{N} w_{ij} y_{j,t} + \sum_{k=2}^{K} \beta_k x_{k,i,t} + \mu_i + \varphi_t + \varepsilon_{i,t} \tag{5.6.8}$$

$$y_{i,t} = \beta_1 + \sum_{k=2}^{K} \beta_k x_{k,i,t} + \mu_i + \varphi_t + u_{i,t}, \quad u_{i,t} = \lambda \sum_{j=1}^{N} w_{ij} u_{j,t} + \varepsilon_{i,t} \tag{5.6.9}$$

where μ_i represents individual-specific effect and φ_t represents the time-specific effect. Note that if μ_i and/or φ_t are fixed effects, the intercept term β_1 can be identified under $\sum_{i=1}^{N} \mu_i = 0$ and/or $\sum_{i=1}^{N} \phi_i = 0$. In spatial econometrics, its common cross-sectional dimension (N) vastly exceeds the time dimension ($N \gg T$), thereby the time-specific effect is simply considered with dummy variables. Hence in the following explanation, we take this position and set $\varphi_t = 0$.

$$y_{i,t} = \beta_1 + \rho \sum_{j=1}^{N} w_{ij} y_{j,t} + \sum_{k=2}^{K} \beta_k x_{k,i,t} + \mu_i + \varepsilon_{i,t} \tag{5.6.10}$$

$$y_{i,t} = \beta_1 + \sum_{k=2}^{K} \beta_k x_{k,i,t} + \mu_i + u_{i,t}, \quad u_{i,t} = \lambda \sum_{j=1}^{N} w_{ij} u_{j,t} + \varepsilon_{i,t} \tag{5.6.11}$$

This type of model is sometimes called the Anselin type after Anselin et al. (2008).

Meanwhile, Kapoor et al. (2007) specified the error correlation as follows:

$$y_{i,t} = \beta_1 + \sum_{k=2}^{K} \beta_k x_{k,i,t} + u_{i,t}, \quad u_{i,t} = \lambda \sum_{j=1}^{N} w_{ij} u_{j,t} + \xi_{i,t}, \xi_{i,t} = \mu_i + \varepsilon_{i,t} \tag{5.6.12}$$

Here, Eqs. (5.6.11) and (5.6.12) differ based on whether they place μ_i inside or outside the formula for the spatial error correlation. This is not a question of which is better; it is important to choose the option that is most appropriate for the research purpose. The latter is sometimes called the Kapoor (KKP) type. The Hausman test, which determines whether μ_i is a fixed effect or a random effect, is just as important as regular panel data analysis. For the KKP type model, Mutl and Pfaffermayr (2011) proposed the Hausman test for spatial panels.

Parameter estimation in these models is essentially an expansion of the cross-sectional spatial econometrics model and can be performed using the ML method (Elhorst, 2010b, 2011; Lee and Yu, 2010b) and spatial two-stage least squares (S2SLS)/GMM (Kapoor et al., 2007; Fingleton, 2008b; Baltagi and Liu, 2011; Mutl and Pfaffermayr, 2011). Additionally, LM test statistics for model specification were also proposed, and Anselin et al. (2008) organized them in a way that is easy to understand. For reviews of spatial panel models, please see Anselin et al. (2008), Elhorst (2014a), and Lee and Yu (2010a).[19] Additionally, research on dynamic spatial panel models has also been flourishing in recent years. In dynamic spatial panels, there are issues with how initial points in time or the steadiness of time-space are handled. Interested readers should refer to Parent and LeSage (2010) or Elhorst (2014a), for example.

5.7 Methods for large data

5.7.1 Outline

In recent years, spatially indexed large or even massive data are becoming available. Researchers try to refine spatial econometrics models to be applicable to such data. The following subsections briefly overview such an attempt.

Before that, we would like to mention Arbia et al. (2019b), who reported the results of a systematic simulation study on the limits of the current methodologies when estimating spatial models with large datasets. They simulate an SLM, and estimated it using two-stage least squares (2SLS) (see the next subsection), ML, and Bayesian estimator. They found that for the last two methods, it is not possible to estimate models with

[19] For spatial panel model estimation and testing, the splm package for R can be used, as well as the MATLAB routine from Elhorst (2014b). Also, stata uses can rely on Belotti et al. (2017).

more than 10,000 units when matrices are characterized by a high density, due to the prohibitive amount of time required, while with 2SLS a sample of dimension 70,000 could be easily accommodated. They further showed that very dense **W** negatively affects both the computing time and the accuracy of the estimates. These findings are a good starting point for this section.

5.7.2 Generalized spatial two stage least squares method

In Section 5.3, we explained the ML method as the representative parameter estimation methods of spatial econometric models. However, as discussed in outline, it suffers from its computational cost. Hence here, we introduce the faster alternative: the generalized spatial two stage least squares (GS2SLS) approach.

The 2SLS method is a representative econometrics technique for dealing with the endogeneity problem, which was described in Chapter 2. Kelejian and Robinson (1993) proposed an SLM parameter estimation method by using the S2SLS method. The S2SLS estimator has both consistency and asymptotic normality, but when error terms follow a normal distribution, it is relatively inefficient when compared to the estimator by the ML method. However, the S2SLS method is advantageous in that it has a small computational load and is robust to the divergence from the normality. Attention is required regarding the estimation of the SAR error model, because the S2SLS estimator of spatial parameter is not consistent (Kelejian and Prucha, 1997). Instead, Kelejian and Prucha (1999) developed a parameter estimation method by using the GMM. The GMM estimator is consistent, and computationally simple. Kelejian and Prucha (1998) proposed a method to estimate the parameters of the SAC model (SLM +SEM) by combining aforementioned S2SLS with GMM—GS2SLS. This GS2SLS method has the advantage that the computational load is very small compared to the ML method.

Here, we introduce the GS2SLS method. Kelejian and Robinson (1993) proposed a parameter estimation method of the SLM using the S2SLS method. First, for simplicity, let us assume $|\rho| < 1$ and that $(\mathbf{I}-\rho\mathbf{W})$ is a nonsingular matrix for $|\rho| < 1$. Then, the SLM can be transformed as follows:

$$\mathbf{y} = (\mathbf{I} - \rho\mathbf{W})^{-1}\mathbf{X}\boldsymbol{\beta} + (\mathbf{I} - \rho\mathbf{W})^{-1}\boldsymbol{\varepsilon} \tag{5.7.1}$$

Because $E[\mathbf{y}] = (\mathbf{I} - \rho\mathbf{W})^{-1}\mathbf{X}\boldsymbol{\beta}$, we have $E[\mathbf{W}\mathbf{y}] = \mathbf{W}(\mathbf{I} - \rho\mathbf{W})^{-1}\mathbf{X}\boldsymbol{\beta} = \mathbf{W}\left[\sum_{p=0}^{\infty} \rho^p \mathbf{W}^p\right]\mathbf{X}\boldsymbol{\beta}$ with $\mathbf{W}^0 = \mathbf{I}$. Hence the instrumental variables

(IVs) $\mathbf{Z}_{[N\times q]}$ with $q \geq K+1$, can be constructed using linearly independent column vectors in $(\mathbf{X},\mathbf{WX},\mathbf{W}^2\mathbf{X}, \ldots,\mathbf{W}^p\mathbf{X})$. In the (spatial) 2SLS method, an *exclusion restriction* must be satisfied. Hence we cannot use this approach if $\mathbf{WX}$, ..., $\mathbf{W}^p\mathbf{X}$ directly affects $\mathbf{y}$. The S2SLS method can be readily expanded even when there are additional endogenous explanatory variables $\dot{\mathbf{X}}_{[N\times L]}$ in the following way (Fingleton and Le Gallo, 2008; Drukker et al., 2013):

$$\mathbf{y} = \rho\mathbf{Wy} + \mathbf{X\beta} + \dot{\mathbf{X}}\dot{\boldsymbol{\beta}} + \boldsymbol{\varepsilon} \tag{5.7.2}$$

Drukker et al. (2013) proposed constructing IVs $\mathbf{Z}_{[N\times q]}$ with $q \geq K+L+1$ by replacing $\mathbf{X}$ of $(\mathbf{X},\mathbf{WX},\mathbf{W}^2\mathbf{X}, \ldots,\mathbf{W}^p\mathbf{X})$ with $\mathbf{X}_f$, where $\mathbf{X}_f$ includes the IV for $\dot{\mathbf{X}}$, say $\mathbf{X}_e$. That is, $\mathbf{Z}$ can be constructed using linearly independent column vectors as $\mathbf{Z} = (\mathbf{X}_f,\mathbf{WX}_f,\mathbf{W}^2\mathbf{X}_f, \ldots,\mathbf{W}^p\mathbf{X}_f)$. Anselin and Lozano-Gracia (2008) used latitude and longitude as $\mathbf{X}_e$.

If an appropriate $\mathbf{Z}$ can be selected, parameter estimation can be easily performed using the S2SLS method. Let us rewrite SLM as follows:

$$\mathbf{y} = \mathbf{R}\boldsymbol{\xi} + \boldsymbol{\varepsilon} \tag{5.7.3}$$

where $\mathbf{R} = \left(\mathbf{Wy};\mathbf{X};\dot{\mathbf{X}}\right)$ and $\boldsymbol{\xi} = (\rho;\boldsymbol{\beta}';\dot{\boldsymbol{\beta}}')'$. The S2SLS estimator of $\boldsymbol{\xi}$ and its variance are given by:

$$\widehat{\boldsymbol{\xi}} = \left(\widehat{\mathbf{R}}'\widehat{\mathbf{R}}\right)^{-1}\widehat{\mathbf{R}}'\mathbf{y} \tag{5.7.4}$$

$$Var\left(\widehat{\boldsymbol{\xi}}\right) = \widehat{\sigma}_{\varepsilon}^2\left(\widehat{\mathbf{R}}'\widehat{\mathbf{R}}\right)^{-1} = \widehat{\sigma}_{\varepsilon}^2\left[\mathbf{R}'\mathbf{Z}(\mathbf{Z}'\mathbf{Z})^{-1}\mathbf{Z}'\mathbf{R}\right]^{-1} \tag{5.7.5}$$

where $\widehat{\mathbf{R}} = \mathbf{PR}$, and $\mathbf{P}$ is a projection matrix satisfying $\mathbf{P} = \mathbf{Z}(\mathbf{Z}'\mathbf{Z})^{-1}\mathbf{Z}'$[20]. Also, $\widehat{\sigma}_{\varepsilon}^2 = N^{-1}\sum_{i=1}^{N}\widehat{\varepsilon}_i^2$ is the S2SLS residual, and it is calculated using $\widehat{\boldsymbol{\varepsilon}} = \mathbf{y} - \mathbf{R}\widehat{\boldsymbol{\xi}}$. If the variance matrix $\boldsymbol{\Omega} = \mathrm{E}[\boldsymbol{\varepsilon}\boldsymbol{\varepsilon}']$ may be heteroskedastic, heteroscedasticity-robust asymptotic variance of White (1980) can be used:

$$Var\left(\widehat{\boldsymbol{\xi}}\right) = \left[\mathbf{R}'\mathbf{Z}\left(\mathbf{Z}'\widehat{\Omega}\mathbf{Z}\right)^{-1}\mathbf{Z}'\mathbf{R}\right]^{-1} \tag{5.7.6}$$

where $\left(\mathbf{Z}'\widehat{\Omega}\mathbf{Z}\right)^{-1} \equiv (\mathbf{Z}'\mathbf{SZ})^{-1}$ and $\mathbf{S}$ is a diagonal matrix containing the squared S2SLS residuals.

[20] Note that $\mathbf{P} = \mathbf{P}' = \mathbf{P}^2$ holds for a projection matrix.

Now we can consider not only heteroscedasticity, but also remaining spatial error autocorrelation of unspecified form by the HAC robust approach of Kelejian and Prucha (2007). The spatial HAC technique is a nonparametric estimator for the spatial covariance, using weighted averages of cross-products of residuals, the range of which is determined by a kernel function K. The r, s element of $\mathbf{\Omega}$ may be given as

$$\psi_{rs} = (1/N)\sum_i \sum_j q_{ir} q_{js} \widehat{u}_i \widehat{u}_j K(d_{ij}/d) \tag{5.7.7}$$

where d is the bandwidth. See Kelejian and Prucha (2007) with respect to the type of kernel function.

Since the S2SLS estimator of the spatial parameter of the SAR error model is not consistent (Kelejian and Prucha, 1997), it is recommended to use, for example, the ML method or the GMM. Because the GMM does not require an assumption of normality and the calculation of the log of the Jacobian term is not needed, it has the advantage of a small calculation load. In the following, we describe the GMM for the SAR error model as an example:

$$\mathbf{y} = \mathbf{X}\boldsymbol{\beta} + \mathbf{u},$$

$$\mathbf{u} = \lambda \mathbf{W}\mathbf{u} + \boldsymbol{\varepsilon},\ Var(\boldsymbol{\varepsilon}) = \sigma_\varepsilon^2 \mathbf{I} \tag{5.7.8}$$

Since $\mathbf{u} - \lambda\mathbf{W}\mathbf{u} = \boldsymbol{\varepsilon}$, if we multiply both sides by $\mathbf{W}$, the following equation is obtained ($\mathbf{W}^2 = \mathbf{W}\mathbf{W}$):

$$\mathbf{W}\mathbf{u} - \lambda\mathbf{W}^2\mathbf{u} = \mathbf{W}\boldsymbol{\varepsilon} \tag{5.7.9}$$

In Eqs. (5.7.8) and (5.7.9), if the elements $\mathbf{u}$, $\mathbf{W}\mathbf{u}$, $\mathbf{W}^2\mathbf{u}$, $\boldsymbol{\varepsilon}$, $\mathbf{W}\boldsymbol{\varepsilon}$ of the i-th line are assumed as $u_i, \dot{u}_i, \ddot{u}_i, \varepsilon_i, \dot{\varepsilon}_i$ respectively, $u_i - \lambda\dot{u}_i = \varepsilon_i$, $\dot{u}_i - \lambda\ddot{u}_i = \dot{\varepsilon}_i$ can be obtained. When taking the squared sum and dividing by N, we have

$$\frac{1}{N}\sum_i u_i^2 + \lambda^2\frac{1}{N}\sum_i \dot{u}_i^2 - 2\lambda\frac{1}{N}\sum_i u_i\dot{u}_i = \frac{1}{N}\sum_i \varepsilon_i^2 \tag{5.7.10}$$

$$\frac{1}{N}\sum_i \dot{u}_i^2 + \lambda^2\frac{1}{N}\sum_i \ddot{u}_i^2 - 2\lambda\frac{1}{N}\sum_i \dot{u}_i\ddot{u}_i = \frac{1}{N}\sum_i \dot{\varepsilon}_i^2 \tag{5.7.11}$$

Also, when multiplying the left side and right side of $u_i - \lambda\dot{u}_i = \varepsilon_i$, $\dot{u}_i - \lambda\ddot{u}_i = \dot{\varepsilon}_i$, summing and dividing by N, the following is obtained:

$$\frac{1}{N}\sum_i u_i\dot{u}_i + \lambda^2\frac{1}{N}\sum_i \dot{u}_i\ddot{u}_i - \lambda\left(\frac{1}{N}\sum_i u_i\ddot{u}_i + \frac{1}{N}\sum_i \dot{u}_i^2\right) = \frac{1}{N}\sum_i \varepsilon_i\dot{\varepsilon}_i \tag{5.7.12}$$

Through these, the following three moment conditions hold:

$$E\left[\frac{\boldsymbol{\varepsilon}'\boldsymbol{\varepsilon}}{N}\right] = \sigma_\varepsilon^2, \tag{5.7.13}$$

$$E\left[\frac{\boldsymbol{\varepsilon}'\mathbf{W}'\mathbf{W}\boldsymbol{\varepsilon}}{N}\right] = \sigma_\varepsilon^2 N^{-1} tr(\mathbf{W}'\mathbf{W}), \tag{5.7.14}$$

$$E\left[\frac{\boldsymbol{\varepsilon}'\mathbf{W}'\boldsymbol{\varepsilon}}{N}\right] = 0. \tag{5.7.15}$$

The third condition depends on the diagonal element of $\mathbf{W}$ being 0. If we rewrite these equations as equations related to $\mathbf{u}$, we obtain the following:

$$E\left[\frac{\mathbf{u}'(\mathbf{I}-\lambda\mathbf{W})'(\mathbf{I}-\lambda\mathbf{W})\mathbf{u}}{N}\right] = \sigma_\varepsilon^2, \tag{5.7.16}$$

$$E\left[\frac{\mathbf{u}'(\mathbf{I}-\lambda\mathbf{W})'\mathbf{W}'\mathbf{W}(\mathbf{I}-\lambda\mathbf{W})\mathbf{u}}{N}\right] = \sigma_\varepsilon^2 N^{-1} tr(\mathbf{W}'\mathbf{W}), \tag{5.7.17}$$

$$E\left[\frac{\mathbf{u}'(\mathbf{I}-\lambda\mathbf{W})'\mathbf{W}'(\mathbf{I}-\lambda\mathbf{W})\mathbf{u}}{N}\right] = 0. \tag{5.7.18}$$

When we define $\dot{\mathbf{u}} \equiv \mathbf{W}\mathbf{u}$, $\ddot{\mathbf{u}} \equiv \mathbf{W}\mathbf{W}\mathbf{u}$, moment conditions are expressed as a matrix as follows:

$$\boldsymbol{\Gamma}\left[\lambda, \lambda^2, \sigma_\varepsilon^2\right]' - \boldsymbol{\gamma} = \mathbf{0} \tag{5.7.19}$$

with

$$\boldsymbol{\Gamma} = \begin{bmatrix} \frac{-2}{N}E(\mathbf{u}'\dot{\mathbf{u}}) & \frac{1}{N}E(\dot{\mathbf{u}}'\dot{\mathbf{u}}) & -1 \\ \frac{-2}{N}E(\ddot{\mathbf{u}}'\dot{\mathbf{u}}) & \frac{1}{N}E(\ddot{\mathbf{u}}'\ddot{\mathbf{u}}) & \frac{-1}{N}tr(\mathbf{W}'\mathbf{W}) \\ \frac{1}{N}E(\mathbf{u}'\ddot{\mathbf{u}}+\dot{\mathbf{u}}'\dot{\mathbf{u}}) & \frac{1}{N}E(\dot{\mathbf{u}}'\ddot{\mathbf{u}}) & 0 \end{bmatrix}, \boldsymbol{\gamma} = \begin{bmatrix} \frac{1}{N}E(\mathbf{u}'\mathbf{u}) \\ \frac{1}{N}E(\dot{\mathbf{u}}'\dot{\mathbf{u}}), \\ \frac{1}{N}E(\mathbf{u}'\dot{\mathbf{u}}) \end{bmatrix}$$

Here, let us assume that the estimator $\widehat{\boldsymbol{\varepsilon}}$ of $\boldsymbol{\varepsilon}$ is obtained by using OLS, and also let $\dot{\boldsymbol{\varepsilon}} \equiv \mathbf{W}\widehat{\boldsymbol{\varepsilon}}$, $\ddot{\boldsymbol{\varepsilon}} \equiv \mathbf{W}\mathbf{W}\widehat{\boldsymbol{\varepsilon}}$. Then, sample analogues of Eq. (5.7.19) can be written as follows:

$$\mathbf{G}\left[\lambda, \lambda^2, \sigma_\varepsilon^2\right]' - \mathbf{g} = \boldsymbol{\mu}\left(\lambda, \sigma_\varepsilon^2\right) \tag{5.7.20}$$

where

$$\mathbf{G}=\begin{bmatrix} \dfrac{-2}{N}\widehat{\mathbf{u}}'\dot{\widehat{\mathbf{u}}} & \dfrac{1}{N}\dot{\widehat{\mathbf{u}}}'\dot{\widehat{\mathbf{u}}} & -1 \\ \dfrac{-2}{N}\ddot{\widehat{\mathbf{u}}}'\dot{\widehat{\mathbf{u}}} & \dfrac{1}{N}\ddot{\widehat{\mathbf{u}}}'\ddot{\widehat{\mathbf{u}}} & \dfrac{-1}{N}tr(\mathbf{W}'\mathbf{W}) \\ \dfrac{1}{N}\left(\widehat{\mathbf{u}}'\ddot{\widehat{\mathbf{u}}}+\dot{\widehat{\mathbf{u}}}'\dot{\widehat{\mathbf{u}}}\right) & \dfrac{1}{N}\dot{\widehat{\mathbf{u}}}'\ddot{\widehat{\mathbf{u}}} & 0 \end{bmatrix}, \mathbf{g}=\begin{bmatrix} \dfrac{1}{N}\widehat{\mathbf{u}}'\widehat{\mathbf{u}} \\ \dfrac{1}{N}\dot{\widehat{\mathbf{u}}}'\dot{\widehat{\mathbf{u}}} \\ \dfrac{1}{N}\widehat{\widehat{\mathbf{u}}}'\dot{\mathbf{u}} \end{bmatrix}.$$

$\boldsymbol{\mu}\left(\lambda, \sigma_{\varepsilon}^{2}\right)$ can be regarded as the residual vector of 3×1. Therefore, if $\boldsymbol{\mu}\left(\lambda, \sigma_{\varepsilon}^{2}\right)'\boldsymbol{\mu}\left(\lambda, \sigma_{\varepsilon}^{2}\right)$ is minimized, the GMM estimator $\widehat{\lambda}, \widehat{\sigma}_{\varepsilon}^{2}$ is obtained, and $\boldsymbol{\beta}$ can be estimated by the EGLS method based on these.

Kelejian and Prucha (1998) proposed the GS2SLS method to estimate the parameters of the SAC model $\mathbf{y}=\mathbf{R}\boldsymbol{\xi}+(\mathbf{I}-\lambda\mathbf{W})^{-1}\boldsymbol{\varepsilon}$ by combining the GMM for error terms and the S2SLS method for trend terms. Specifically, it is calculated by the following three steps:

1. Obtaining the initial parameter estimate $\widehat{\boldsymbol{\xi}}$ by the S2SLS method.
2. Obtaining $\widehat{\lambda}, \widehat{\sigma}_{\varepsilon}^{2}$ by GMM.
3. Removing spatial error correlation from the model using $\widehat{\lambda}$; in other words, using $\mathbf{y}^{*}=\left(\mathbf{I}-\widehat{\lambda}\mathbf{W}\right)\mathbf{y}$, $\mathbf{R}^{*}=\left(\mathbf{I}-\widehat{\lambda}\mathbf{W}\right)\mathbf{R}$. After that, performing the S2SLS method again in $\mathbf{y}^{*}=\mathbf{R}^{*}\xi+\varepsilon$.

Note that the estimates for λ obtained from the nonlinear least squares are consistent, but not efficient. Optimal estimates are found from a weighted nonlinear least squares procedure. Hence a few more steps are needed for its actual use (see Bivand and Piras, 2015).

5.7.3 Maximum likelihood–based methods

5.7.3.1 Approximation of log of Jacobian

In applying the ML method, the computational burden of the Jacobian term (or its logarithm) becomes a problem. The approximation method of Ord (1975) is a popular countermeasure:

$$\left|\mathbf{I}-\lambda\mathbf{W}\right|=\prod_{i=1}^{N}(1-\lambda\omega_{i}) \tag{5.7.21}$$

where an example of the SAR error model is shown. In this equation, if the eigenvalue is calculated beforehand, the repetitive evaluation of $ln|\mathbf{I}-\lambda\mathbf{W}|$ becomes unnecessary, and the computational cost is greatly reduced.

However, it is known that the accurate calculation of the eigenvalue of $\mathbf{W}$ becomes difficult when the sample size is large. Smirnov and Anselin (2001) point out that eigenvalue calculations are numerically unstable in data sets such as $N > 1000$.[21]

On the other hand, there have been various alternative proposals to date, including approximation by characteristic polynomial (Smirnov and Anselin, 2001), Cholesky decomposition (Smirnov and Anselin, 2001; Suesse, 2018), Chebyshev decomposition (Pace and LeSage, 2004), and Monte Carlo estimation (Barry and Pace, 1999). For regular square tessellations, where analytical eigenvalues can be used, Griffith (2015) shows the simple approximation and suggests that SLM for cases as large as $N = 37{,}214{,}101$ could be estimated.

Bivand et al. (2013a) conducted comparison of available methods, and concluded that if data set is large, "*sparse, symmetric spatial weights matrices, an analyst can choose between the Cholesky and updating Cholesky methods, the characteristic polynomial approximation, the lower-order moments approximation, the Chebyshev approximation, or the Monte Carlo approximation. If the data take the form of a regular grid and binary spatial weights with the rook or queen neighbor criterion are appropriate, analytical eigenvalues may be used. Finally, for larger, sparse, asymmetric spatial weights matrices, the choice is between the LU method and the Monte Carlo approximation.*"

5.7.3.2 Matrix exponential spatial specification method

Let us consider the following SLM.

$$(\mathbf{I} - \rho \mathbf{W})\mathbf{y} = \mathbf{S}\mathbf{y} = \mathbf{X}\boldsymbol{\beta} + \boldsymbol{\varepsilon} \tag{5.7.22}$$

Instead, LeSage and Pace (2007) specified $\mathbf{S} = e^{\alpha \mathbf{W}} = \sum_{t=0}^{\infty} \frac{\alpha^t \mathbf{W}^t}{t!}$ with α denoting a scalar parameter. This model is called matrix exponential spatial specification (MESS). The relation between α and ρ values suggests a correspondence, $\rho = 1 - \exp(\alpha)$. Thus values for α correspond to positive spatial dependence ($\rho > 0$), with positive values indicating negative dependence ($\rho < 0$) (see LeSage and Pace, 2007).

The concentrated likelihood function of MESS is given as

$$l_C = const. - \frac{N}{2}\ln(\mathbf{y}'\mathbf{S}'\mathbf{M}\mathbf{S}\mathbf{y}) + \ln|\mathbf{S}| \tag{5.7.24}$$

[21] Or even $N > 400$ as shown in Kelejian and Prucha (1998).

where $\mathbf{M} = \mathbf{I} - \mathbf{P}$ and $\mathbf{P} = \mathbf{X}(\mathbf{X}'\mathbf{X})^{-1}\mathbf{X}'$. Now it is important to note that $|\mathbf{S}| = |e^{\alpha\mathbf{W}}| = e^{trace(\alpha\mathbf{W})}$. Because trace($\mathbf{W}$) $= 0$, we have $|\mathbf{S}| = 1$. It follows that log of the Jacobian term is zero. Hence we can just minimize $(\mathbf{Sy} - \mathbf{X\beta})'(\mathbf{Sy} - \mathbf{X\beta})$ for parameter estimation. The MESS model was expanded to MESS (1,1) by Debarsy et al. (2015), for the general model that has MESS in both the dependent variable and disturbances.

5.7.3.3 Spatiotemporal autoregressive model

Although the spatial panel model essentially assumes that data has a fixed observation point, actual data contain many instances in which the observation point varies at different points in time, as in real estate transactions, for example, and observation times do not follow regular intervals. If there is little replacement data, the values are considered missing values, and parameter estimation can be used with supplementation with the EM algorithm (Pfaffermayr, 2009). However, when there is an extremely large number of replacement points or when the placement of observation points is entirely different in each timeframe, it is difficult to consider the data as panel data. In that case, the spatiotemporal autoregressive model (STAR) from Pace et al. (1998) can be used.[22] This model will be explained in the following section.

$$\mathbf{y} = \mathbf{X\beta} + \mathbf{Sx\beta}_S + \mathbf{Tx\beta}_T + \mathbf{STx\beta}_{ST} + \mathbf{TSx\beta}_{TS} + \varphi_S\mathbf{Sy} + \varphi_T\mathbf{Ty} + \varphi_{ST}\mathbf{STy} + \varphi_{TS}\mathbf{TSy} \tag{5.7.25}$$

where $\mathbf{S}$ is a matrix representing spatial autocorrelation and is essentially the $\mathbf{W}$ included in the spatial econometric model. However, the STAR model uses a few techniques to simplify calculations. Specifically, it reorders all data in order of the oldest observation and models only unidirectional effects from old data → new data. Accordingly, $\mathbf{S}$ is given as a lower triangular matrix. Thus the log of the likelihood function's Jacobian term becomes zero and the parameter estimation is simplified significantly just like the MESS model. Meanwhile, $\mathbf{T}$ is a matrix representing temporal correlation and one method, for example, applies a weight to point k in order of the most recent point in time (Fig. 5.7.1). $\mathbf{ST}$ and $\mathbf{TS}$ are matrixes representing the interaction between time and space. Because these elements are usually

[22] STAR model estimation can be performed using the MATLAB codes from Professor Kelley Pace's Spatial Statistics Toolbox (http://www.spatial-statistics.com/).

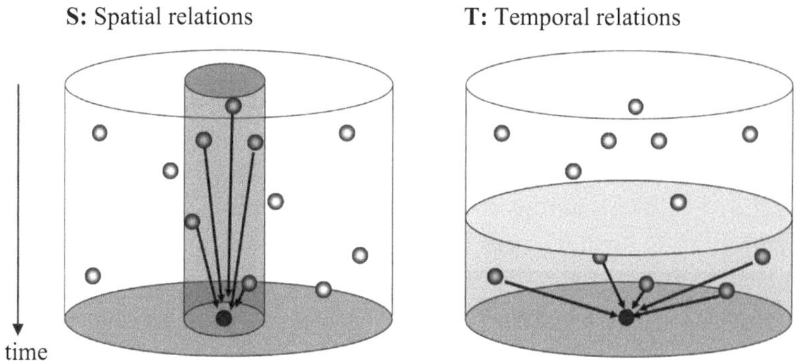

Figure 5.7.1 Example of S and T.

different, it is common to introduce both (Pace et al., 1998). Because STAR is a method proposed by researchers in the field of real estate, most examples of its application are in that field. However, it seems that the method could be applied in a broader range of cases. The STAR suggests when some logical *ordering* or data is possible, then we can reduce the computational cost because log of Jacobian term becomes zero.

5.7.4 Bayesian method

Spatial econometric works with Bayesian approach typically uses the MCMC method. However, the limitation of the MCMC method, which uses simulation to infer the joint posterior distribution, is its computational burden. Variational Bayes methods, which try to *approximate* the joint posterior distribution, has risen to be a faster alternative to MCMC.

Wu (2018) proposes two variational Bayes methods that are more scalable and computationally faster in estimating an SAC model: the hybrid mean-field variational Bayes method and the integrated nonfactorized variational Bayes (INFVB) method. Wu (2018) showed that INFVB method can yield very accurate estimates for posterior means of model parameters with faster computation time compared to MCMC method. Currently very few studies employed variational Bayes methods for spatial econometric models, but Wu (2018) showed that this method may be promising.

5.7.5 Sampling-based method

In Chapter 4, we explained the approaches for low rank approximation of the Gaussian process. In spatial econometrics, low-rank approximation can be achieved by *sampling* from data. When sample size is large, it is typical in statistical science to conduct sampling to make the analysis feasible. But in case of spatial or network data, caution is needed for sampling because the network topology may change due to sampling (e.g., Liu et al., 2017; Tsutsumi and Seya, 2009). Chen et al. (2018) recognized this, and proposed a sequential sampling method, combined with a composite likelihood approach, to reduce computation cost. Such sampling-based methods are worth developing further in the area of big data when we note the following comments by Arbia et al. (2019b): "*With the state-of-the-art spatial econometric methodologies, it is easy to forecast that in the near future we will find ourselves in the practical impossibility to analyze data in a timely and accurate way. Hence the studies related to time-efficient and statistically-accurate procedures represent an area that requires urgent solutions and a discontinuity step with respect to the recent evolution of the methodology.*"

References

Anselin, L., 1988. Spatial Econometrics: Methods and Models. Kluwer Academic Publishers, Dordrecht.

Anselin, L., 2001. Spatial econometrics. In: Baltagi, B. (Ed.), A Companion to Theoretical Econometrics. Blackwell, Oxford, pp. 310–330.

Anselin, L., 2002. Under the food: issues in the specification and interpretation of spatial regression models. Agricultural Economics 27 (3), 247–267.

Anselin, L., 2009. Spatial regression. In: Fotheringham, A.S., Rogerson, P.A. (Eds.), The SAGE Handbook of Spatial Analysis. SAGE Publications, Los Angeles, pp. 255–275.

Anselin, L., 2010. Thirty years of spatial econometrics. Papers in Regional Science 89 (1), 3–25.

Anselin, L., Bera, A.K., 1998. Spatial dependence in linear regression models with an introduction to spatial econometrics. In: Ullah, A., Giles, D.E. (Eds.), Handbook of Applied Economic Statistics. Marcel Dekker, New York, pp. 237–289.

Anselin, L., Lozano-Gracia, N., 2008. Errors in variables and spatial effects in hedonic house price models of ambient air quality. Empirical Economics 34 (1), 5–34.

Anselin, L., Moreno, R., 2003. Properties of tests for spatial error components. Regional Science and Urban Economics 33 (5), 595–618.

Anselin, L., Rey, S.J., 2012. Spatial econometrics in an age of CyberGIScience. International Journal of Geographical Information Science 26 (12), 2211–2226.

Anselin, L., Rey, S.J., 2014. Modern Spatial Econometrics in Practice: A Guide to Geoda, Geodaspace and Pysal. Geoda Press LLC, Chicago.

Anselin, L., Bera, A.K., Florax, R.J.G.M., Yoon, M.J., 1996. Simple diagnostic tests for spatial dependence. Regional Science and Urban Economics 26 (1), 77–104.

Anselin, L., Le Gallo, J., Jayet, H., 2008. Spatial panel econometrics. In: Matyas, L., Sevestre, P. (Eds.), The Econometrics of Panel Data, Fundamentals and Recent Developments in Theory and Practice, third ed. Kluwer, Dordrecht, pp. 627–662.

Arbia, G., 2006. Spatial Econometrics: Statistical Foundations and Applications to Regional Growth Convergence. Springer, New York.

Arbia, G., 2011. A lustrum of SEA: recent research trends following the creation of the Spatial Econometrics Association (2007–2011). Spatial Economic Analysis 6 (4), 377–395.

Arbia, G., 2014. A Primer for Spatial Econometrics: With Applications in R (Palgrave Texts in Econometrics). Palgrave Macmillan, Basingstoke.

Arbia, G., Bera, A.K., Doğan, O., Taşpınar, S., 2019a. Testing impact measures in spatial autoregressive models. International Regional Science Review in print.

Arbia, G., Ghiringhelli, C., Mira, A., 2019b. Estimation of spatial econometric linear models with large datasets: how big can spatial Big Data be? Regional Science and Urban Economics in print.

Baltagi, B.H., Bresson, G., 2011. Maximum likelihood estimation and Lagrange Multiplier tests for panel seemingly unrelated regressions with spatial lag and spatial errors: an application to hedonic housing prices in Paris. Journal of Urban Economics 69 (1), 24–42.

Baltagi, B.H., Liu, L., 2011. Instrumental variable estimation of a spatial autoregressive panel model with random effects. Economics Letters 111 (2), 135–137.

Barry, R.P., Pace, R.K., 1999. Monte Carlo estimates of the log determinant of large sparse matrices. Linear Algebra and Its Applications 289 (1–3), 41–54.

Behrens, K., Ertur, C., Koch, W., 2012. 'Dual'gravity: using spatial econometrics to control for multilateral resistance. Journal of Applied Econometrics 27 (5), 773–794.

Belotti, F., Hughes, G., Mortari, A.P., 2017. Spatial panel-data models using Stata. STATA Journal 17 (1), 139–180.

Besag, J., 1974. Spatial interaction and the statistical analysis of lattice systems (with discussion). Journal of the Royal Statistical Society B 36 (2), 192–236.

Besag, J., York, J., Mollié, A., 1991. Bayesian image restoration, with two applications in spatial statistics. Annals of the Institute of Statistical Mathematics 43 (1), 1–20.

Bhat, C.R., 2011. The maximum approximate composite marginal likelihood (MACML) estimation of multinomial probit-based unordered response choice models. Transportation Research Part B: Methodological 45 (7), 923–939.

Bhat, C.R., Guo, J., 2004. A mixed spatially correlated logit model: formulation and application to residential choice modeling. Transportation Research Part B: Methodological 38 (2), 147–168.

Billé, A.G., Arbia, G., 2013. Spatial Discrete Choice and Spatial Limited Dependent Variable Models: A Review with an Emphasis on the Use in Regional Health Economics. Cornell University library working paper.

Bivand, R., Piras, G., 2015. Comparing implementations of estimation methods for spatial econometrics. Journal of Statistical Software 63, 1–36.

Bivand, R., Hauke, J., Kossowski, T., 2013a. Computing the Jacobian in Gaussian spatial autoregressive models: an illustrated comparison of available methods. Geographical Analysis 45 (2), 150–179.

Bivand, R.S., Pebesma, E.J., Gomez-Rubio, V., 2013b. Applied Spatial Data Analysis with R, second ed. Springer, New York.

Brasington, D.M., Parent, O., 2017. Public school consolidation: a partial observability spatial bivariate probit approach. Journal of the Royal Statistical Society: Series A 180 (2), 633–656.

Brock, W., Durlauf, S., 2001. Discrete choice with social interactions. The Review of Economic Studies 68 (2), 235–260, 2001.

Brueckner, J.K., 2003. Strategic interaction among governments: an overview of empirical studies. International Regional Science Review 26 (2), 175–188.

Brunsdon, C., Fotheringham, A.S., Charlton, M.E., 1996. Geographically weighted regression: a method for exploring spatial nonstationarity. Geographical Analysis 28 (4), 281–298.

Bussas, M., Sawade, C., Kuhn, N., Scheffer, T., Landwehr, N., 2017. Varying-coefficient models for geospatial transfer learning. Machine Learning 106 (9–10), 1419–1440.

Calabrese, R., Elkink, J.A., 2014. Estimators of binary spatial autoregressive models: a Monte Carlo study. Journal of Regional Science 54 (4), 664–687.

Caragea, P.C., Kaiser, M.S., 2009. Autologistic models with interpretable parameters. Journal of Agricultural, Biological, and Environmental Statistics 14 (3), 281–300.

Carrion-Flores, C.E., Flores-Lagunes, A., Guci, L., 2018. An estimator for discrete-choice models with spatial lag dependence using large samples, with an application to land-use conversions. Regional Science and Urban Economics 69, 77–93.

Casetti, E., 1972. Generating models by the expansion method: applications to geographic research. Geographical Analysis 4 (1), 81–91.

Chakir, R., Parent, O., 2009. Determinants of land use changes: a spatial multinomial probit approach. Papers in Regional Science 88 (2), 327–344.

Chen, Y., Qi, Y., Liu, Q., Chien, P., 2018. Sequential sampling enhanced composite likelihood approach to estimation of social intercorrelations in large-scale networks. Quantitative Marketing and Economics 16 (4), 409–440.

Cliff, A.D., Ord, J.K., 1973. Spatial Autocorrelation. Pion, London.

Cliff, A.D., Ord, J.K., 1981. Spatial Processes: Methods and Applications. Pion, London.

Congdon, P., 2010. Applied Bayesian Hierarchical Methods. Chapman & Hall/CRC, Boca Raton.

Cressie, N.A.C., 1993. Statistics for Spatial Data, Revised Edition. Wiley, New York.

Cressie, N.A.C., Wikle, C.K., 2011. Statistics for Spatio-Temporal Data. Wiley, New York.

Debarsy, N., Ertur, C., 2010. Testing for spatial autocorrelation in a fixed effects panel data model. Regional Science and Urban Economics 40 (6), 453–470.

Debarsy, N., Jin, F., Lee, L.-F., 2015. Large sample properties of the matrix exponential spatial specification with an application to FDI. Journal of Econometrics 188 (1), 1–21.

Doğan, O., Taşpinar, S., 2018. Bayesian inference in spatial sample selection models. Oxford Bulletin of Economics & Statistics 80 (1), 90–121.

Drukker, D.M., Prucha, I.R., Raciborski, R., 2013. A command for estimating spatial-autoregressive models with spatial-autoregressive disturbances and additional endogenous variables. The Stata Journal 13 (2), 287–301.

Dubin, R.A., 1988. Estimation of regression coefficient in the presence of spatially autocorrelated error terms. The Review of Economics and Statistics 70 (3), 466–474.

Durbin, J., 1960. The fitting of time-series models. Revue de l'Institut International de Statistique 28 (3), 233–244.

Egger, P., Larch, M., Pfaffermayr, M., Walde, J., 2009. Small sample properties of maximum likelihood versus generalized method of moments based tests for spatially autocorrelated errors. Regional Science and Urban Economics 39 (6), 670–678.

Elhorst, J.P., 2010a. Applied spatial econometrics: raising the bar. Spatial Economic Analysis 5 (1), 9–28.

Elhorst, J.P., 2010b. Spatial panel data models. In: Fischer, M.M., Getis, A. (Eds.), Handbook of Applied Spatial Analysis. Springer, Berlin Heidelberg New York, pp. 377–407.

Elhorst, J.P., 2014a. Spatial Econometrics: From Cross-Sectional Data to Spatial Panels. Springer, New York.

Elhorst, J.P., 2014b. Matlab software for spatial panels. International Regional Science Review 37 (3), 389–405.

Elhorst, J.P., Lacombe, D.J., Piras, G., 2012. On model specification and parameter space definitions in higher order spatial econometric models. Regional Science and Urban Economics 42 (1–2), 211–220.

Ellickson, P.B., Misra, S., 2011. Estimating discrete games. Marketing Science 30 (6), 997–1010.

Fingleton, B., 2008a. A generalized method of moments estimator for a spatial model with moving average errors, with application to real estate prices. Empirical Economics 34 (1), 35–57.

Fingleton, B., 2008b. A generalized method of moments estimator for a spatial panel model with an endogenous spatial lag and spatial moving average errors. Spatial Economic Analysis 3 (1), 27–44.

Fingleton, B., Le Gallo, J., 2008. Estimating spatial models with endogenous variables, a spatial lag and spatially dependent disturbances: finite sample properties. Papers in Regional Science 87 (3), 319–339.

Finley, A.O., Banerjee, S., 2019. Bayesian Spatially Varying Coefficient Models in the spBayes R Package arXiv:1903.03028.

Fleming, M., 2004. Techniques for estimating spatially dependent discrete choice models. In: Anselin, L., Florax, R., Rey, S. (Eds.), Advances in Spatial Econometrics. Springer, Amsterdam, pp. 145–167.

Flores-Lagunes, A., Schnier, K.E., 2012. Estimation of sample selection models with spatial dependence. Journal of Applied Econometrics 27 (2), 173–204.

Fotheringham, A.S., Charlton, M.E., Brunsdon, C., 1998. Geographically weighted regression: a natural evolution of the expansion method for spatial data analysis. Environment and Planning 30 (11), 1905–1927.

Fotheringham, A.S., Brunsdon, C., Charlton, M.E., 2002. Geographically Weighted Regression: The Analysis of Spatially Varying Relationships. Wiley, Chichester.

Franco-Villoria, M., Ventrucci, M., Rue, H., 2018. Bayesian Varying Coefficient Models Using PC Priors arXiv:1806.02084.

Fujita, M., Krugman, P., Venables, A.J., 1999. The Spatial Economy: Cities, Regions and International Trade. MIT Press, Cambridge.

Gelfand, A.E., Kim, H.-J., Sirmans, C.F., Banerjee, S., 2003. Spatial modeling with spatially varying coefficient processes. Journal of the American Statistical Association 98 (462), 387–396.

Geniaux, G., Martinetti, D., 2018. A new method for dealing simultaneously with spatial autocorrelation and spatial heterogeneity in regression models. Regional Science and Urban Economics 72, 74–85.

Gibbons, S., Overman, H.G., 2012. Mostly pointless spatial econometrics? Journal of Regional Science 52 (2), 172–191.

Griffith, D.A., 1988. Advanced Spatial Statistics. Kluwer Academic Publishers, Dordrecht.

Griffith, D.A., 2003. Spatial Autocorrelation and Spatial Filtering: Gaining Understanding through Theory and Scientific Visualization. Springer, Berlin.

Griffith, D.A., 2015. Approximation of Gaussian spatial autoregressive models for massive regular square tessellation data. International Journal of Geographical Information Science 29 (12), 2143–2173.

Griffith, D.A., Paelinck, J.H.P., 2010. Non-standard Spatial Statistics and Spatial Econometrics. Springer, Berlin.

Haining, R., 1990. Spatial Data Analysis in the Social and Environmental Sciences. Cambridge University Press, Cambridge.

Haining, R., 2003. Spatial Data Analysis: Theory and Practice. Cambridge University Press, Cambridge.

Haining, R., Law, J., 2011. Geographical information systems models and spatial data analysis. In: Batabyal, A., Nijkamp, P. (Eds.), Research Tools in Natural Resource and Environmental Economics. World Scientific Publishing, Singapore, pp. 377–401.

Haining, R., Law, J., Griffith, D.A., 2009. Modelling small area counts in the presence of overdispersion and spatial autocorrelation. Computational Statistics & Data Analysis 53 (8), 2923–2937.

Hughes, J., Haran, M., Caragea, P.C., 2011. Autologistic models for binary data on a lattice. Environmetrics 22 (7), 857–871.

Kaiser, M.S., Cressie, N.A.C., 1997. Modeling Poisson variables with positive spatial dependence. Statistics & Probability Letters 35 (4), 423–432.

Kakamu, K., 2009. Small sample properties and model choice in spatial models: a Bayesian approach. Far East Journal of Applied Mathematics 34 (1), 31–56.

Kapoor, M., Kelejian, H.H., Prucha, I.R., 2007. Panel data models with spatially correlated error components. Journal of Econometrics 140 (1), 97–130.
Kelejian, H.H., 2008. A spatial J-test for model specification against a single or a set of non-nested alternatives. Letters in Spatial and Resource Sciences 1 (1), 3–11.
Kelejian, H.H., Piras, G., 2011. An extension of Kelejian's J-test for non-nested spatial models. Regional Science and Urban Economics 41 (3), 281–292.
Kelejian, H.H., Piras, G., 2017. Spatial Econometrics. Academic Press, Cambridge.
Kelejian, H.H., Prucha, I.R., 1997. Estimation of spatial regression models with autoregressive errors by two–stage least squares procedures: a serious problem. International Regional Science Review 20 (1–2), 103–111.
Kelejian, H.H., Prucha, I.R., 1998. A generalized spatial two?stage least squares procedure for estimating a spatial autoregressive model with autoregressive disturbances. The Journal of Real Estate Finance and Economics 17 (1), 99–121.
Kelejian, H.H., Prucha, I.R., 1999. A generalized moments estimator for the autoregressive parameter in a spatial model. International Economic Review 40 (2), 509–533.
Kelejian, H.H., Prucha, I.R., 2007. HAC estimation in a spatial framework. Journal of Econometrics 140 (1), 131–154.
Kelejian, H.H., Robinson, D.P., 1993. A suggested method of estimation for spatial interdependent models with autocorrelated errors, and an application to a country expenditure model. Papers in Regional Science 72 (3), 297–312.
Kelejian, H.H., Robinson, D.P., 1995. Spatial correlation: a Suggested alternative to the autoregressive model. In: Anselin, L., Florax, R.J.G.M. (Eds.), New Directions in Spatial Econometrics. Spriger, Berlin, pp. 75–95.
Kim, C., Parent, O., 2016. Modeling individual travel behaviors based on intra-household interactions. Regional Science and Urban Economics 57, 1–11.
Klier, T., McMillen, D.P., 2008. Clustering of auto supplier plants in the United States: generalized method of moments spatial logit for large samples. Journal of Business & Economic Statistics 26 (4), 460–471.
Lacombe, D.J., 2004. Does econometric methodology matter? An analysis of public policy using spatial econometric techniques. Geographical Analysis 36 (2), 105–118.
Lacombe, D.J., LeSage, J.P., 2018. Use and interpretation of spatial autoregressive probit models. The Annals of Regional Science (in press), 2016.
Lambert, D.M., Brown, J.P., Florax, R.J.G.M., 2010. A two-step estimator for a spatial lag model of counts: theory, small sample performance and an application. Regional Science and Urban Economics 40 (4), 241–252.
Lee, L.-F., 2004. Asymptotic distributions of quasi-maximum likelihood estimators for spatial autoregressive models. Econometrica 72 (6), 1899–1925.
Lee, D., 2013. CARBayes: an R package for Bayesian spatial modeling with conditional autoregressive priors. Journal of Statistical Software 55 (13), 1–24.
Lee, L.-F., Liu, X., 2010a. Efficient GMM estimation of high order spatial autoregressive models with autoregressive disturbances. Econometric Theory 26, 187–230.
Lee, L.-F., Yu, J., 2010b. Estimation of spatial autoregressive panel data models with fixed effects. Journal of Econometrics 154 (2), 165–185.
Lee, L.-F., Yu, J., 2010a. Some recent developments in spatial panel data models. Regional Science and Urban Economics 40 (5), 255–271.
Lee, L.-F., Li, J., Lin, X., 2014. Binary choice models with social network under heterogeneous rational expectations. The Review of Economics and Statistics 96 (3), 402–417.
LeSage, J.P., 1997. Bayesian estimation of spatial autoregressive models. International Regional Science Review 20 (1), 113–129.
LeSage, J.P., 2000. Bayesian estimation of limited dependent variable spatial autoregressive models. Geographical Analysis 32 (1), 19–35.

LeSage, J.P., Pace, R.K., 2007. A matrix exponential spatial specification. Journal of Econometrics 140 (1), 190–214.
LeSage, J.P., Pace, R.K., 2009. Introduction to Spatial Econometrics. Chapman & Hall/CRC, Boca Raton.
Li, J., Lee, L.-F., 2009. Binary choice under social interactions: an empirical study with and without subjective data on expectations. Journal of Applied Econometrics 24 (2), 257–281.
Liu, X., Patacchini, E., Zenou, Y., 2014. Endogenous peer effects: local aggregate or local average ? Journal of Economic Behavior & Organization 103, 39–59.
Liu, X., Patacchini, E., Rainone, E., 2017. Peer effects in bedtime decisions among adolescents: a social network model with sampled data. The Econometrics Journal 20 (3), S103–S125.
Martinetti, D., Geniaux, G., 2017. Approximate likelihood estimation of spatial probit models. Regional Science and Urban Economics 64, 30–45.
McMillen, D.P., 1992. Probit with spatial autocorrelation. Journal of Regional Science 32 (3), 335–348.
McMillen, D.P., 1996. One hundred fifty years of land values in Chicago: a nonparametric approach. Journal of Urban Economics 40 (1), 100–124.
Mur, J., Angulo, A., 2006. The spatial Durbin model and the common factor tests. Spatial Economic Analysis 1 (2), 207–226.
Mur, J., Angulo, A., 2009. Model selection strategies in a spatial setting: some additional results. Regional Science and Urban Economics 39 (2), 200–213.
Mutl, J., Pfaffermayr, M., 2011. The Hausman test in a Cliff and Ord panel model. The Econometrics Journal 14 (1), 48–76.
Ohtsuka, Y., Kakamu, K., 2015. Comparison of the sampling efficiency in spatial autoregressive model. Open Journal of Statistics 5, 10–20.
Ord, J.K., 1975. Estimation methods for models of spatial interaction. Journal of the American Statistical Association 79 (349), 120–126.
Pace, R.K., LeSage, J.P., 2004. Chebyshev approximation of log-determinants of spatial weight matrices. Computational Statistics & Data Analysis 45 (2), 179–196.
Pace, R.K., Barry, R., Clapp, J.M., Rodriguez, M., 1998. Spatiotemporal autoregressive models of neighborhood effects. The Journal of Real Estate Finance and Economics 17 (1), 15–33.
Paelinck, J.H.P., Klaassen, L., 1979. Spatial Econometrics. Saxon House, Farnborough.
Parent, O., LeSage, J.P., 2008. Using the variance structure of the conditional autoregressive spatial specification to model knowledge spillovers. Journal of Applied Econometrics 23 (2), 235–256.
Parent, O., LeSage, J.P., 2010. A spatial dynamic panel model with random effects applied to commuting times. Transportation Research Part B 44 (5), 633–645.
Pinkse, J., Slade, M.E., 1998. Contracting in space: an application of spatial statistics to discrete-choice models. Journal of Econometrics 85 (1), 125–154.
Pfaffermayr, M., 2009. Maximum likelihood estimation of a general unbalanced spatial random effects model: A Monte Carlo study. Spatial Economic Analysis 4 (4), 467–483.
Pinkse, J., Slade, M.E., 2010. The future of spatial econometrics. Journal of Regional Science 50 (1), 103–117.
Pinkse, J., Slade, M.E., Brett, C., 2002. Spatial price competition: a semiparametric approach. Econometrica 70 (3), 1111–1153.
Rue, H., Held, L., 2005. Gaussian Markov Random Fields: Theory and Applications. Chapman and Hall/CRC, London.
Saavedra, L.A., 2003. Tests for spatial lag dependence based on method of moments estimation. Regional Science and Urban Economics 33 (1), 27–58.

Seya, H., Tsutsumi, M., Yamagata, Y., 2012. Income convergence in Japan: a Bayesian spatial Durbin model approach. Economic Modelling 29 (1), 60–71.
Small, K.A., Steimetz, S.S., 2012. Spatial hedonics and the willingness to pay for residential amenities. Journal of Regional Science 52 (4), 635–647.
Smirnov, O.A., 2010. Modeling spatial discrete choice. Regional Science and Urban Economics 40 (5), 292–298.
Smirnov, O.A., Anselin, L., 2001. Fast maximum likelihood estimation of very large spatial autoregressive models: a characteristic polynomial approach. Computational Statistics & Data Analysis 35 (3), 301–319.
Su, C.L., Judd, K.L., 2012. Constrained optimization approaches to estimation of structural models. Econometrica 80 (5), 2213–2230.
Suesse, T., 2018. Estimation of spatial autoregressive models with measurement error for large data sets. Computational Statistics 33 (4), 1627–1648.
Tsutsumi, M., Seya, H., 2009. Hedonic approaches based on spatial econometrics and spatial statistics: application to evaluation of project benefits. Journal of Geographical Systems 11 (4), 357–380.
Vega, G.S., Elhorst, J.P., 2015. The SLX model. Journal of Regional Science 55 (3), 339–363.
Ver Hoef, J.M., Hanks, E.M., Hooten, M.B., 2018. On the relationship between conditional (CAR) and simultaneous (SAR) autoregressive models. Spatial statistics 25, 68–85.
Wall, M.M., 2004. A close look at the spatial structure implied by the CAR and SAR models. Journal of Statistical Planning and Inference 121 (2), 311–324.
Wang, X., Kockelman, K.M., 2009. Baysian inference for ordered response data with a dynamic spatial-ordered probit model. Journal of Regional Science 49 (5), 877–913.
Wang, H., Iglesias, E.M., Wooldridge, J.M., 2013. Partial maximum likelihood estimation of spatial probit models. Journal of Econometrics 172, 77–89.
White, H., 1980. A heteroskedastic-covariance matrix estimator and a direct test for heteroskedasticity. Econometrica 48 (4), 817–838.
Wolf, L.J., Anselin, L., Arribas-Bel, D., 2018. Stochastic efficiency of Bayesian Markov chain Monte Carlo in spatial econometric models: an empirical comparison of exact sampling methods. Geographical Analysis 50 (1), 97–119.
Wu, G., 2018. Fast and scalable variational Bayes estimation of spatial econometric models for Gaussian data. Spatial Statistics 24, 32–53.
Xu, X., Lee, L.F., 2019. Theoretical Foundations for Spatial Econometric Research. Regional Science and Urban Economics in print.
Yamagata, Y., Yang, J., Galaskiewicz, J., 2013. A contingency theory of policy innovation: how different theories explain the ratification of the UNFCCC and Kyoto Protocol. International Environmental Agreements: Politics, Law and Economics 13 (3), 251–270.
Yamagata, Y., Yang, J., Galaskiewicz, J., 2017. State power and diffusion processes in the ratification of global environmental treaties, 1981–2008. International Environmental Agreements: Politics, Law and Economics 17 (4), 501–529.

CHAPTER SIX

Models in quantitative geography

Daisuke Murakami[1], Yoshiki Yamagata[2]
[1]The Institute of Statistical Mathematics, Tachikawa, Tokyo, Japan
[2]Center for Global Environmental Research, National Institute for Environmental Studies, Tsukuba, Ibaraki, Japan

Contents

6.1 Introduction

Beyond geo-(spatial) statistics and spatial econometrics, research on spatial autocorrelation and spatial heterogeneity has been conducted in (quantitative) geography (Getis, 2008). Important and original contributions of geographers that we focus on in this chapter are the development of the spatially varying coefficient model termed geographically weighted regression (GWR) (Brunsdon et al., 1998; Fotheringham et al., 2002) and the eigenvector spatial filtering approach (ESF) (Griffith, 2003). These two methods have widely been applied in fields other than geography, including

Spatial Analysis using Big Data
ISBN: 978-0-12-813127-5
https://doi.org/10.1016/B978-0-12-813127-5.00006-0

regional science, urban studies, economics, ecology, and epidemiology, among others.

Both GWR and ESF aim to detect hidden map patterns behind noisy spatial data; GWR estimates spatial patterns behind regression coefficients while ESF (typically) detects patterns in residuals. The objective of this chapter is introducing the theories of the GWR model and ESF approach. We then discuss that *caution* is needed when these approaches are empirically applied, and how we can avoid an erroneous use.

6.2 Geographically weighted regression models

6.2.1 Concept of the geographically weighted regression models

GWR is an extension of the linear regression model that allows the regression coefficients to vary across geographical space. The basic model for a site $\mathbf{s}_i$ in a two-dimensional domain $D \subset \Re^2$ is specified as

$$y(\mathbf{s}_i) = \sum_{k=1}^{K} x_k(\mathbf{s}_i)\beta_k(\mathbf{s}_i) + \varepsilon(\mathbf{s}_i), \quad \varepsilon(\mathbf{s}_i) \sim N(0, \sigma^2), \tag{6.2.1}$$

where $y(\mathbf{s}_i)$ denotes a dependent variable, $x_k(\mathbf{s}_i)$ denotes a k-th explanatory variable, $\varepsilon(\mathbf{s}_i)$ denotes an error term (independent and identically distributed normal), and σ^2 is an error variance. The first row of the explanatory variable, $x_1(\mathbf{s}_i)$, is considered an intercept (i.e., $x_1(\mathbf{s}_i) = 1$). GWR aims to estimate the regression coefficient $\beta_k(\mathbf{s}_i)$, which varies over space (i.e., depending on i).

To estimates the coefficients vector $\boldsymbol{\beta}(\mathbf{s}_i) = [\beta_1(\mathbf{s}_i)\ldots\beta_K(\mathbf{s}_i)]'$ at i-th site, the samples are geographically weighted, as explained later. The resulting GWR estimator yields

$$\widehat{\boldsymbol{\beta}}(\mathbf{s}_i) = [\mathbf{X}'\mathbf{G}_i(b)\mathbf{X}]^{-1}\mathbf{X}'\mathbf{G}_i(b)\mathbf{y}, \tag{6.2.2}$$

where $\mathbf{y}$ is a vector of dependent variables and $\mathbf{X}$ is a matrix of covariates. $\mathbf{G}_i(b)$ is a diagonal matrix whose j-th element is given by the geographical weight $g(\mathbf{s}_i,\mathbf{s}_i;b)$ for the j-th sample. The weight is specified by a distance-decay kernel function. Representative kernel functions are

$$\text{Gaussian kernel} \ : g(\mathbf{s}_i, \mathbf{s}_j; b) = exp\left(-\frac{d(\mathbf{s}_i, \mathbf{s}_j)^2}{b^2}\right) \tag{6.2.3}$$

$$\text{Exponential kernel}: g(\mathbf{s}_i, \mathbf{s}_j; b) = exp\left(-\frac{d(\mathbf{s}_i, \mathbf{s}_j)}{b} \right) \quad (6.2.4)$$

$$\text{Bisquare kernel} \ : \ g(\mathbf{s}_i, \mathbf{s}_j; b) = \begin{cases} \left[1 - \left(\frac{d(\mathbf{s}_i, \mathbf{s}_j)}{b}\right)^2\right]^2 & \text{if } d(\mathbf{s}_i, \mathbf{s}_j) < b \\ 0 & \text{Otherwise} \end{cases} \quad (6.2.5)$$

$$\text{Tricube kernel} \ : \ g(\mathbf{s}_i, \mathbf{s}_j; b) = \begin{cases} \left[1 - \left(\frac{d(\mathbf{s}_i, \mathbf{s}_j)}{b}\right)^3\right]^3 & \text{if } d(\mathbf{s}_i, \mathbf{s}_j) < b \\ 0 & \text{Otherwise} \end{cases} \quad (6.2.6)$$

where $d(\mathbf{s}_i,\mathbf{s}_j)$ is the (typically Euclidean) distance between $\mathbf{s}_i$ and $\mathbf{s}_j$. b is a bandwidth parameter determining the speed of decay of each kernel. If b is small, weights are assigned only on nearby samples, and the resulting varying coefficients have a small-scale (i.e., local) map pattern. As b increases, greater weights are assigned on distant samples, and the resulting coefficients have a larger-scale (i.e., global) map pattern. The coefficient estimates converge to that of the ordinary least squares (OLS) as $b \rightarrow \infty$.

Fig. 6.2.1 plots the kernel functions with $b = 40$. As shown in this figure, the bisquare and tricube kernels assign nonzero weights only to samples within the bandwidth distance. By contrast, the Gaussian kernels assume nonzero weights even for samples farther than b. Note also, the exponential kernel emphasized more distant samples than the Gaussian kernel. Thus the

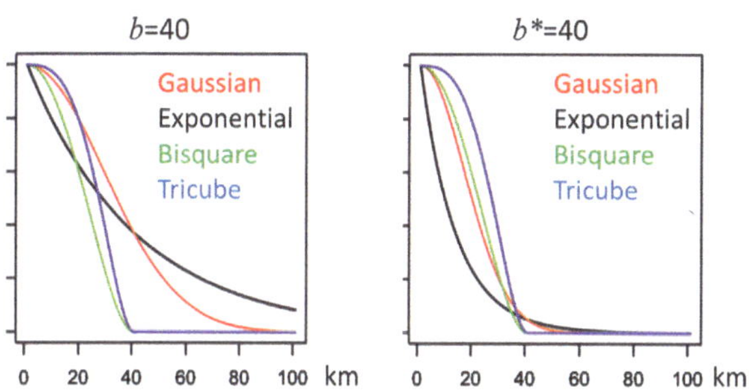

Figure 6.2.1 Kernel functions.

bandwidth value does not have a clear interpretation as a *range* when the exponential or Gaussian kernel is used. For the interpretation, effective bandwidth b^*, which is defined by the distance that achieves the 95% of the influence that vanishes, is useful. For the exponential kernel, b^* equals $3b$ whereas $b^* = 3b$ for the Gaussian kernel. The right-hand side of Fig. 6.2.1 represents the kernels with $b^* = 40$, suggesting that weights are nearly zero around the distance of 40 km.

6.2.2 Parameter estimation of the geographically weighted regression model

The regression coefficients of the GWR model is estimated in the following steps: (1) the bandwidth b is optimized; (2) the regression coefficients $\boldsymbol{\beta}(\mathbf{s}_i)$ for each site are estimated by substituting the estimated bandwidth into Eq. (6.2.2). In step (1), the bandwidth can be estimated by the leave-one-out cross-validation (LOOCV) minimizing the cross-validation (CV) score, which is formulated as follows:

$$\text{CV score} = \sum_{i=1}^{N}\left(y(\mathbf{s}_i) - \sum_{k=1}^{K} x_k(\mathbf{s}_i)\widehat{\beta}_k(\mathbf{s}_{-i})\right)^2 \tag{6.2.7}$$

The coefficient $\widehat{\beta}_k(\mathbf{s}_{-i})$ is estimated using the $N-1$ samples other than the i-th sample. Specifically, $\widehat{\boldsymbol{\beta}}(\mathbf{s}_{-i}) = \left[\widehat{\beta}_1(\mathbf{s}_{-i}), \ldots, \widehat{\beta}_K(\mathbf{s}_{-i})\right]'$ is estimated using Eq. (6.2.8):

$$\widehat{\boldsymbol{\beta}}(\mathbf{s}_{-i}) = [\mathbf{X}'\mathbf{G}_{-i}(b)\mathbf{X}]^{-1}\mathbf{X}'\mathbf{G}_{-i}(b)\mathbf{y}, \tag{6.2.8}$$

where $\mathbf{G}_{-i}(b)$ equals $\mathbf{G}_i(b)$ with its i-th element being replaced with zero. The LOOCV identifies the optimal bandwidth minimizing the CV score.

Alternatively, b can be optimized by minimizing the corrected Akaike's information criterion (AIC_c; Eq. 6.2.9), which is a measure of generalization error:

$$\text{AIC}_\text{C} = Nlog\left(\widehat{\sigma}^2\right) + Nlog(2\pi) + N\left(\frac{N + tr(\mathbf{Q})}{N - 2 - tr(\mathbf{Q})}\right), \tag{6.2.9}$$

where $tr(\mathbf{Q})$ is the trace of the hat matrix $\mathbf{Q} = [\mathbf{q}(\mathbf{s}_1)', \ldots, \mathbf{q}(\mathbf{s}_N)']'$, in which $\mathbf{q}(\mathbf{s}_i)' = \mathbf{x}(\mathbf{s}_i)[\mathbf{X}'\mathbf{G}_i(b)\mathbf{X}]^{-1}\mathbf{X}'\mathbf{G}_i(b)$ and $\mathbf{x}(\mathbf{s}_i)$ is the i-th row of $\mathbf{X}$.

$\widehat{\sigma}^2$ is the estimated error variance that becomes

$$\widehat{\sigma}^2 = \frac{\sum_{i=1}^{N}\left[y(\mathbf{s}_i) - \sum_{k=1}^{K} x_k(\mathbf{s}_i)\widehat{\beta}_k(\mathbf{s}_i)\right]^2}{N - (2tr[\mathbf{Q}] - tr[\mathbf{Q}'\mathbf{Q}])}, \tag{6.2.10}$$

where $N-(2tr[\mathbf{Q}]-tr[\mathbf{Q}'\mathbf{Q}])$ is the effective sample size. The accuracy of the estimated GWR model may be evaluated by the CV score, AIC_c, or the error variance.

The variance of the estimated coefficient $\widehat{\beta}_k(\mathbf{s}_i)$, which is useful to evaluate the statistical significance, is analytically obtained as

$$Var\left[\widehat{\boldsymbol{\beta}}(\mathbf{s}_i)\right] = \widehat{\sigma}^2[\mathbf{X}'\mathbf{G}_i(b)\mathbf{X}]^{-1}\mathbf{X}'\mathbf{G}_i(b)^2\mathbf{X}[\mathbf{X}'\mathbf{G}_i(b)\mathbf{X}]^{-1}. \quad (6.2.11)$$

Eq. (6.2.11) lets us test the statistical significance of the regression coefficient for each location. However, such a testing procedure suffers from the multiple testing problem that overestimates the statistical significance. For example, if the statistical significance of GWR coefficients are tested at 1000 locations, coefficients at 50 locations are expected to be statistically significant at the 5% level even if the coefficients are insignificant. da Silva and Fotheringham (2016) have developed a correction to evaluate statistical significance without suffering the problem.

6.2.3 Example: application of the geographically weighted regression model

This section applies the GWR model with the Gaussian kernel to an empirical analysis of residential land price[1] in the year 2010 in Tachikawa area, Japan (see Fig. 6.2.2). The sample size is 128. The area comprises four municipalities with two central areas including the *Tachikawa* and *Tama center*. Dependent variables are the logged land prices [JPY/m^2], and explanatory variables include logged Euclidean distance [km] to the nearest railway station (*Station*) and logged railway distance [km] between the nearest stations to Tokyo station (*Tokyo*).

Figs. 6.2.3 and 6.2.4 represent the estimated coefficients and their statistical significance in terms of p-values, respectively. The bandwidth value was estimated at 0.94 km, implying local-scale variations in the regression coefficients. The estimated intercept suggests that (logged) land prices tend to be higher near the two central areas. Tokyo access is statistically significant around the two centers. The estimated coefficients on Station access are negatively significant in the south part of the study area. In this area, the Keio line, which is a principal rail line, is in the south area. The result suggests the strong impact of the railway. Although the analysis result is

[1] The official land prices (Land Market Price Publication) in Japan, published by the Ministry of Land, Infrastructure, Transport and Tourism.

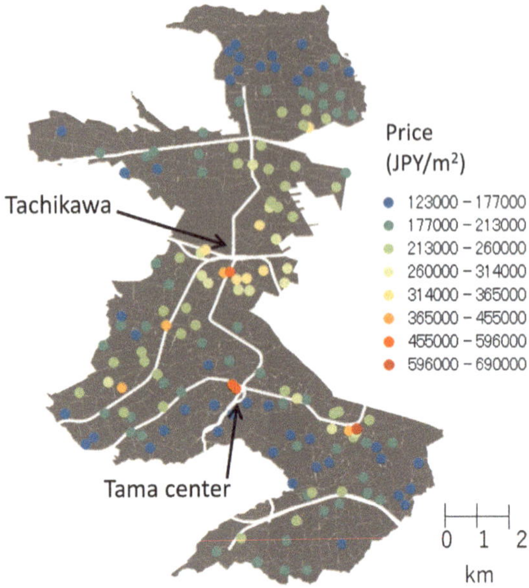

Figure 6.2.2 Residential land price (2010) in Tachikawa Japan.

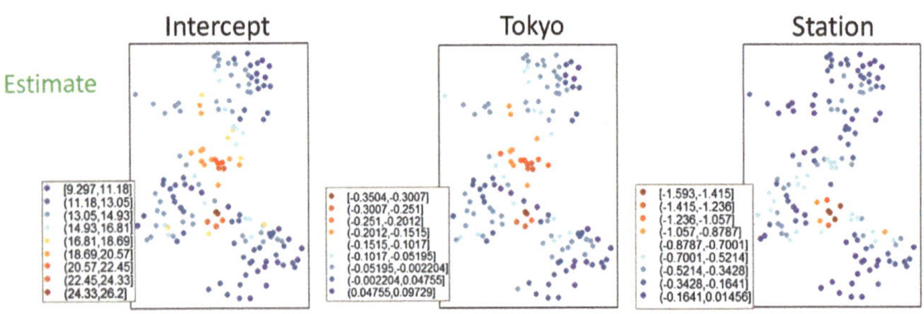

Figure 6.2.3 Estimated spatially varying coefficients.

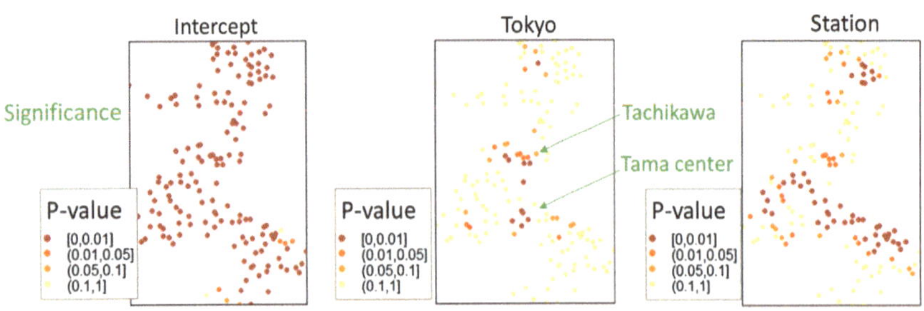

Figure 6.2.4 Statistical significance of the coefficients.

reasonable here, generally speaking, result of the GWR must be interpreted with caution because of the instability. The next section will go into the details about this problem.

6.2.4 Geographically weighted regression and collinearity

Although the GWR model is a very useful empirical tool, sometimes the map pattern of the parameters becomes unstable. It is attributable to the following reasons:

1. Only nearby samples are considered.
2. Geographical weight makes explanatory variables collinear even if the explanatory variables themselves are uncorrelated (Wheeler and Tiefelsdorf, 2005). Specifically, the GWR estimator (Eq. 6.2.2) is the least squares estimator of the following model:

$$g(\mathbf{s}_i, \mathbf{s}_j; b)^{1/2} y(\mathbf{s}_i) = \sum_{k=1}^{K} g(\mathbf{s}_i, \mathbf{s}_j; b)^{1/2} x_k(\mathbf{s}_i)\beta_k(\mathbf{s}_i) + \varepsilon(\mathbf{s}_i), \quad \varepsilon(\mathbf{s}_i) \sim N\left(0, \sigma^2\right), \tag{6.2.12}$$

The weighted explanatory variables $g(\mathbf{s}_i, \mathbf{s}_j; b)^{1/2} x_k(\mathbf{s}_i)$ are collinear because they share the same weight $g(\mathbf{s}_i, \mathbf{s}_j; b)^{1/2}$. Thus, problem (1) reduces the effective sample size and (2) introduces multicollinearity. It is crucially important to use GWR while paying attention to these problems.

The seriousness of problem (1) depends on two factors: (1a) the scale of the kernel and (1b) the scale of explanatory variables (Murakami et al., 2019). (1a) simply means that the number of samples being considered increases as the kernel window expands. Remember that the bisquare and tricube kernels ignore samples distant more than b whereas the exponential and Gaussian kernels consider these samples; in terms of the local sample size, the latter kernels are better. The latter kernels tend to be more stable than the kernels with hard thresholding.

Still, the local sample size can be very small in areas with sparsely sampled locations. To address this problem, adaptive bandwidth, which defines the bandwidth by the distance to the k-th nearest neighbor (see Chapter 3 in terms of the spatial weight matrix), has often been used (e.g., Nakaya et al., 2005). The k value minimizing the CV value is estimated through the LOOCV. The resulting bandwidth becomes wide in sparsely sampled areas while narrow in densely sampled areas. Thus use of the adaptive kernels can avoid small local samples in sparse areas. Instead, the adaptive kernel is more difficult to interpret than the fixed distance kernel.

Multicollinearity is also attributable to (1b) the spatial scale of $x_k(\mathbf{s}_i)$s. Of course, the explanatory variables must not be collinear as in the usual regression analysis. In addition to that, in the case of GWR analysis, multicollinearity can emerge when explanatory variables have small or no variation in a kernel window. For example, a dummy variable indicating 0 at most sample sites and 1 at only some sites is an example of such explanatory variables; in this case, the dummy variable can take zero value at all/most sites within the window; the GWR model is unidentifiable. Explanatory variables that have a large-scale spatial pattern (e.g., distance to the city center) is another example. Let $x_{i,2}$ be a large-scale variable; then it is known to be difficult to identify with the spatially varying intercept $g(\mathbf{s}_i, \mathbf{s}_j; b)^{1/2} x_{i,1} = g(\mathbf{s}_i, \mathbf{s}_j; b)^{1/2}$. (Note: intercept is interpretable as an explanatory variable with an extremely large-scale or global spatial pattern.)

One way to check multicollinearity is to draw a correlation plot between estimated regression coefficients. Fig. 6.2.5 displays the correlation plots in the case of land price analysis. This figure shows a strong correlation between spatially varying intercept ($x_1(\mathbf{s}_i)$) and the spatially varying coefficients on

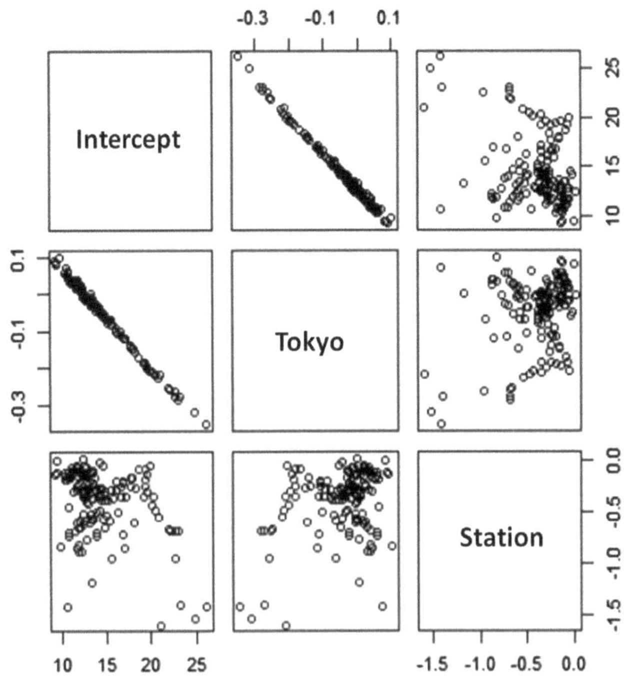

Figure 6.2.5 Correlation plot between regression coefficients.

Tokyo access ($x_{i,\text{Tokyo}}$); it is attributable to the global map pattern of the Tokyo access leading the multicollinearity between $g(\mathbf{s}_i, \mathbf{s}_j; b)^{1/2} x_1(\mathbf{s}_i)$ and $g(\mathbf{s}_i, \mathbf{s}_j; b)^{1/2} x_{\text{Tokyo}}(\mathbf{s}_i)$. In this case, it is unclear if the estimated coefficients describe the true (i.e., meaningful) map pattern or a spurious pattern due to the collinearity. Note that the local variance inflation factor and local condition number have also been proposed to infer the multicollinearity in GWR coefficients (Brunsdon et al., 2012).

6.2.5 Extended geographically weighted regression models

If multicollinearity is found among GWR coefficients, spatially varying coefficients can be replaced with a constant (i.e., usual spatially fixed) coefficient. Such a GWR, with spatially varying and fixed coefficients, is called the mixed (semiparametric) GWR (Mei et al., 2004). The model is formulated as

$$y(\mathbf{s}_i) = \sum_{k=1}^{K} x_k(\mathbf{s}_i)\beta_k(\mathbf{s}_i) + \sum_{k'=1}^{K'} z_{k'}(\mathbf{s}_i)\alpha_{k'} + \varepsilon(\mathbf{s}_i) \quad \varepsilon(\mathbf{s}_i) \sim N\left(0, \sigma^2\right), \tag{6.2.13}$$

where $z_{k'}(\mathbf{s}_i)$ is the k'-th explanatory variable whose coefficient $\alpha_{k'}$ is constant across space. The model is a mix of the GWR model and a standard linear regression model. The model is estimated using a back-fitting algorithm that is summarized as follows:

1. Initialize $\widehat{\beta}_k(\mathbf{s}_i)$ and $\widehat{\alpha}_{k'}$.
2. Given $\widehat{\alpha}_{k'}$, the bandwidth parameter behind $\beta_k(\mathbf{s}_i)$ is optimized by the LOOCV or the AIC_c minimization. Then $\widehat{\beta}_k(\mathbf{s}_i)$ is updated.
3. Given $\widehat{\beta}_k(\mathbf{s}_i)$, $\widehat{\alpha}_{k'}$ is estimated by regressing $y(\mathbf{s}_i) - \sum_{k=1}^{K} x_k(\mathbf{s}_i)\widehat{\beta}_k(\mathbf{s}_i)$ on $\sum_{k'=1}^{K'} z_{k'}(\mathbf{s}_i)\alpha_{k'}$.
4. Steps (2) and (3) are alternated until the CV score or the AIC_c value converges.

The mixed GWR model can be implemented using gwr.mixed function in the GWmodel package of R[2] or GWR 4.0 software.[3]

More and more studies use a back-fitting algorithm to estimate extended GWR models. Fotheringham et al. (2017) employed this algorithm to

[2] https://cran.r-project.org/web/packages/GWmodel/index.html
[3] https://gwrtools.github.io/gwr4-downloads.html

estimate a multiscale GWR (MGWR), which is also called flexible bandwidth GWR (Yang, 2014) or conditional GWR (Leong and Yue, 2017). MGWR estimates bandwidth parameter for each coefficient to consider difference of spatial scale in these coefficients (e.g., some coefficients might have large-scale spatial variations while others might have small-scale variations). MGWR contributes not only to an estimated scale of each coefficient accurately but also mitigates the problem of multicollinearity. Intuitively, this is because each explanatory variable is weighted using different kernel functions, respectively. Other than MGWR, Lu et al. (2017) proposed GWR with parameter-specific distance metrics (GWR-PSDM) that optimizes not only bandwidth but also distance metric among candidates for individual coefficients. They demonstrated a significant improvement of the GWR-PSDM model accuracy compared to the standard GWR.

The MGWR and GWR-PSDM models can be written as

$$y(\mathbf{s}_i) = \sum_{k=1}^{K} x_k(\mathbf{s}_i)\beta_k(\mathbf{s}_i; \boldsymbol{\theta}_k) + \varepsilon(\mathbf{s}_i) \quad \varepsilon(\mathbf{s}_i) \sim N\left(0, \sigma^2\right), \tag{6.2.14}$$

where $\boldsymbol{\theta}_k$ is the set of parameters characterizing the k-th coefficient. It is the coefficient-specific bandwidth in the case of the MGWR whereas $\boldsymbol{\theta}_k$ is the coefficient-specific bandwidth and distance metric in case of GWR-PSDM. The back-fitting procedure yields:

1. Initialize $\widehat{\beta}_k\left(\mathbf{s}_i; \widehat{\boldsymbol{\theta}}_k\right)$ for all k.
2. Given $\left\{\widehat{\beta}_1\left(\mathbf{s}_i; \widehat{\boldsymbol{\theta}}_1\right), \cdots, \widehat{\beta}_{k-1}\left(\mathbf{s}_i; \widehat{\boldsymbol{\theta}}_{k-1}\right), \widehat{\beta}_{k+1}\left(\mathbf{s}_i; \widehat{\boldsymbol{\theta}}_{k+1}\right), \cdots, \widehat{\beta}_K\left(\mathbf{s}_i; \widehat{\boldsymbol{\theta}}_K\right)\right\}$, $\widehat{\boldsymbol{\theta}}_k$ is optimized by the LOOCV or the $\mathrm{AIC_c}$ minimization. Then $\widehat{\beta}_k\left(\mathbf{s}_i; \widehat{\boldsymbol{\theta}}_k\right)$ is updated.

Step (2) is repeated for each k until the CV score or the $\mathrm{AIC_c}$ value converges.

Both the MGWR and GWR-PSDM are implemented using the aforementioned GWmodel package. Yet, this approach requires applying the CV repeatedly to estimate $\{\boldsymbol{\theta}_1, \ldots, \boldsymbol{\theta}_K\}$. So, both MGWR and GWR-PSDM approaches are computationally expensive. For example, while GWR takes 2.44 s on average for 400 samples, MGWR with three explanatory variables takes 93.52 s for the same sample (Murakami et al., 2019). Unfortunately, even for the basic GWR, its computational cost rapidly increases; at most 15,000 samples are upper limits of GWR modeling using the GWmodel package. Section 6.4 introduces some approaches to break this bottleneck and accelerate GWR and MGWR modeling.

6.3 Spatial filtering approach

6.3.1 Types of spatial filtering

The spatial filtering approach literally applies a spatial filter to capture spatial dependence behind data. The popular approaches include the ESF approach and the Getis approach (see Getis and Griffith, 2002). The former constructs the spatial filters using the Moran I statistic (see Chapter 3), whereas the latter constricts the filters using the Getis G statistic (see also Chapter 3). Thus, simply saying, spatial filtering is an approach to model spatial dependence using spatial filters—map pattern variables that are interpretable in terms of these diagnostic statistics.

This chapter focuses on the ESF. The ESF has merits in its simplicity and expandability. Furthermore, ESF is deeply related to the Gaussian process as we will explain later.

6.3.2 Moran eigenvectors

ESF, which is also called principal coordinates of neighborhood matrices (Dray et al., 2006) or Moran eigenvector mapping in ecology, is based on the Moran coefficient (MC), a popular diagnostic statistics for spatial dependence. MC of Eq. (3.2.1) can be rewritten as

$$MC[\mathbf{y}] = \frac{N}{\mathbf{1}'\mathbf{C}\mathbf{1}} \frac{\mathbf{y}'\mathbf{MCMy}}{\mathbf{y}/\mathbf{My}}, \tag{6.3.1}$$

where $\mathbf{C}$ is an $N \times N$ symmetric connectivity matrix with zero diagonals, and $\mathbf{1}$ is a vector of ones. Intuitively speaking, $MC[\mathbf{y}]$ evaluates the correlation coefficient between $\mathbf{y}$ and $\mathbf{Cy}$. Just like the usual correlation coefficient, $\mathbf{y}$ is centered by multiplying it with the centering matrix $\mathbf{M} = \mathbf{I} - \mathbf{11}'/N$. MC takes a positive value in the presence of positive spatial dependence (i.e., positive correlation coefficient between $\mathbf{y}$ and $\mathbf{Cy}$) but takes a negative value in the presence of negative dependence.

Let eigen-decompose of $\mathbf{MCM}$ to $\mathbf{E}^*\mathbf{\Lambda}^*\mathbf{E}^{*\prime}$, where $\mathbf{E}^* = [\mathbf{e}_1,...,\mathbf{e}_N]$ is a matrix of the eigenvectors. $\mathbf{\Lambda}^* = diag[\lambda_1,...,\lambda_N]$ is a diagonal matrix whose entries are given by the eigenvalues $\{\lambda_1,...,\lambda_N\}$. Fig. 6.3.1 displays spatial plot of the eigenvectors. As shown in this figure, eigenvectors corresponding to large eigenvalues portray positively dependent spatial patterns while those corresponding to negative eigenvalues portray negatively dependent patterns.

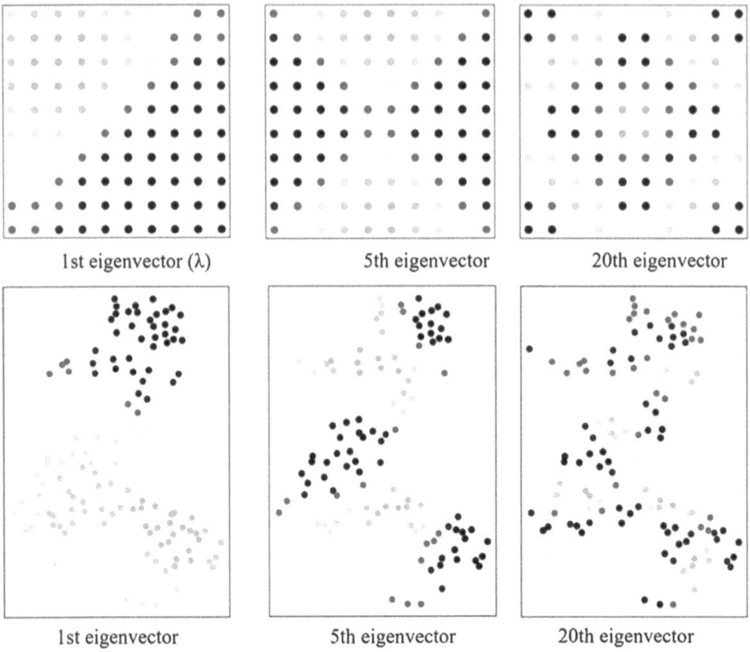

Figure 6.3.1 Two examples of Moran eigenvectors (e_1, e_5, e_{20}).

Interestingly, such patterns are directly linked to the MC value. To see this, let us evaluate the MC value of the l-th eigenvector as

$$MC[\mathbf{e}_l]=\frac{N}{\mathbf{1'C1}}\frac{\mathbf{e'}_l\mathbf{MCMe}_l}{\mathbf{e'}_l\boldsymbol{M}\mathbf{e}_l}=\frac{N}{\mathbf{1'C1}}\frac{\mathbf{e}_l'\mathbf{E}^*\boldsymbol{\Lambda}^*\mathbf{E}^{*\prime}\mathbf{e}_l}{\mathbf{e}_l'\boldsymbol{M}\mathbf{e}_l}=\frac{N}{\mathbf{1'C1}}\frac{\lambda_l}{\mathbf{e}_l'\mathbf{e}_l}=\frac{N}{\mathbf{1'C1}}\lambda_l \tag{6.3.2}$$

Eq. (6.3.2) shows that MC values for the eigenvectors are proportional to their corresponding eigenvalues. In other words, the eigenvectors furnish orthogonal map pattern descriptions of latent spatial dependence, with each level being indexed by an MC that is proportional to its corresponding eigenvalue (Griffith, 2003). Specifically, the first eigenvector, $\mathbf{e}_1$, is the set of numerical values that has the largest positive MC (maximum positive spatial dependence) achievable by any set of real numbers for the spatial arrangement defined by $\mathbf{C}$; the second eigenvector, $\mathbf{e}_2$, is the set of values that has the largest positive MC that is uncorrelated with and orthogonal to $\mathbf{e}_1$; and $\mathbf{e}_N$ is the set of numerical values that has the largest negative MC (maximum negative spatial dependence) achievable that is uncorrelated with and orthogonal to $\mathbf{e}_1, \ldots \mathbf{e}_l, \ldots \mathbf{e}_{N-1}$.

6.3.3 Eigenvector spatial filtering approach

Linear combination of the eigenvalues is still interpretable in terms of the MC. Suppose that $\mathbf{E} = [\mathbf{e}_1,...,\mathbf{e}_L]$ is a matrix that consists of $L(<N)$ eigenvectors in $\mathbf{E}^*$, and $\boldsymbol{\gamma} = [\gamma_1,...,\gamma_L]'$ is a coefficient vector; the MC value for the linear combination $\mathbf{E}\boldsymbol{\gamma}$ is derived using Eq.(6.3.2) as follows:

$$MC[\mathbf{E}\boldsymbol{\gamma}] = MC\left[\sum_{l=1}^{L} \mathbf{e}_l \gamma_l\right] = \frac{N}{\mathbf{1'C1}} \sum_{l=1}^{L} \lambda_l \gamma_l \quad (6.3.3)$$

Thus by simply estimating the regression coefficients $\boldsymbol{\gamma}$, we can model a spatial dependent process $\mathbf{E}\boldsymbol{\gamma}$ behind data.

ESF models spatial dependence behind explanatory variables by fitting the spatial filtering term $\mathbf{E}\boldsymbol{\gamma}$. The basic ESF model is formulated as

$$y = \mathbf{X}\boldsymbol{\beta} + \mathbf{E}\boldsymbol{\gamma} + \boldsymbol{\varepsilon}, \quad \boldsymbol{\varepsilon} \sim N\left(0, \sigma^2\mathbf{I}\right). \quad (6.3.4)$$

The model is identical to the standard linear regression model. The L eigenvectors in $\mathbf{E}$ can be selected as follows:

1. Eigenvectors representing inconsequential levels of spatial dependence are removed a priori.
2. Significant eigenvectors are chosen based on any criterion.

In addition to geography, the ESF approach is especially popular in regional science and ecology fields.

In regional science, ESF has been used to eliminate residual spatial dependence to estimate regression coefficients and their standard errors appropriately. Similar to spatial econometrics, a binary connectivity matrix is typically assumed for $\mathbf{C}$, though it is not row-standardized. In step (1), only eigenvectors satisfying $\frac{MC[\mathbf{e}_l]}{MC[\mathbf{e}_1]} = \frac{\lambda_l}{\lambda_1} > 0.25$ are typically retained to eliminate positive spatial dependence while assuring model parsimony. Griffith (2003) and Chun et al. (2016) among others have suggested that this criterion effectively eliminates residual spatial dependence while assuring model parsimony. $\left|\frac{MC[\mathbf{e}_l]}{MC[\mathbf{e}_1]}\right| = \left|\frac{\lambda_l}{\lambda_1}\right| > 0.25$ is an another criterion to eliminate both positive and negative spatial dependence from the residuals (see Tiefelsdorf and Griffith, 2007). In step (2) significant eigenvectors are selected by maximizing model accuracy (e.g., adjusted R^2 and Akaike information criterion) or minimizing residual MC value. Because Eq. (6.3.4) is identical to the standard linear regression model, this step can be conducted by using OLS estimation-based stepwise methods.

On the other hand, in ecology, the ESF approach has typically been used to identify map patterns behind ecological processes. Unlike regional science, a distance-decay function is assumed in $\mathbf{C}$ to model spatial dependence, and all the eigenvectors corresponding to positive eigenvalues are retained in step (1). Partly because of the consideration of small-scale spatial variations, which are explained by eigenvectors with relatively small eigenvalues, it is important to appropriately estimate hidden map patterns (see Dray et al., 2006).

While ESF is conceptually simple and easy to understand, the ESF has often been criticized because of its ignorance of uncertainty in spatial process. Because ESF just fits a deterministic function $\mathbf{E}\boldsymbol{\gamma}$, it cannot distinguish hidden spatially processes and other spurious signals (including noise). In other words, it can depict noise together with spatial signals. Also, just like Gaussian process (GP) models in geostatistics, it is required to consider uncertainty in the spatial process $\mathbf{E}\boldsymbol{\gamma}$ to correctly model the spatial process behind data. Fortunately, the ESF model can be viewed as a rank-reduced GP model when the fixed coefficients in $\mathbf{E}\boldsymbol{\gamma}$ are replaced with random coefficients. This specification, which is called random effects ESF (RE-ESF; Murakami and Griffith, 2015), is formulated as

$$\boldsymbol{\gamma} \sim N\left(\mathbf{0}, \tau^2 \boldsymbol{\Lambda}^{\alpha}\right), \tag{6.3.5}$$

where τ^2 represents the variance of the spatial process while α is a parameter controlling the decay of the eigenvalues. The resulting spatial filtering term yields $\mathbf{E}\boldsymbol{\gamma} \sim N(0, \tau^2 \mathbf{E}\boldsymbol{\Lambda}^{\alpha}\mathbf{E}')$, which is a rank-reduced and centered GP. If α is large, coefficients on eigenvectors corresponding to large $MC[\mathbf{e}_l]$ values are emphasized, and the resulting process has a large-scale spatial pattern. The opposite is true for small α. Thus, just like the bandwidth parameter in GWR, α estimates the scale of the residual spatial process. Murakami and Griffith (2015) showed through simulation studies that Eq.(6.3.5) improves estimation accuracy of the coefficients and their statistical significance.

In this specification, the data uncertainty/noise and the spatial process uncertainty are balanced by estimating σ^2 and τ^2, respectively; thus the spatial process can correctly be identified. This property considerably improves the estimation accuracy of extended ESF models including a spatially varying coefficient (SVC) model (Murakami et al., 2017) and a spatial unconditional quantile regression model (Murakmai and Seya, 2019). These models are implemented in an R package spmoran,[4] developed by the first author of this chapter.

6.3.4 Example: application of the eigenvector spatial filtering approach

This section applies the standard linear regression model (LM), the ESF model, and the RE-ESF model to the land price data with sample size of 128. The dependent variables are again logged residential land prices, and the explanatory variables are the logged distance [km] to the nearest railway station (Station), and the logged railway distance [km] from the station to the Tokyo station (Tokyo). Following Dray et al. (2006), the (i, j)-th element of the $\mathbf{C}$ matrix is defined by $\exp(-d(\mathbf{s}_i, \mathbf{s}_j)/r)$ where r is the maximum distance in the minimum spanning tree connecting sample sites.

The estimation results are summarized in Table 6.3.1. LM indicates the statistical significance of Tokyo but the insignificance of Station. Unfortunately, the residual MC value becomes statistically significant, implying existence of residual spatial dependence. LM is found to be misspecified, and the estimation results are unreliable. By contrast, residual MC values for both ESF and RE-ESF are statistically insignificant. It is verified that they effectively filter residual spatial dependence. Furthermore, RE-ESF

Table 6.3.1 Estimation result; *** and ** represent statistical significance at the 1% and 5% levels, respectively.

	LM		ESF		RE-ESF	
	Estimates	**t-value**	**Estimates**	**t-value**	**Estimates**	**t-value**
Constant	11.34	32.5 ***	10.81	18.5 ***	10.51	20.9 ***
Tokyo	−0.181	−3.95 ***	−0.130	−7.10 ***	−0.135	−8.30 ***
Station	−0.138	−0.69	−0.730	−1.34	−0.993	−2.09 **
SE of residuals (σ)	0.201		0.073		0.066	
SE of spatial process (τ)					0.258	
α					0.659	
Residual MC	0.342 (***)		−0.060		−0.058	

[4] https://cran.r-project.org/web/packages/spmoran/index.html

successfully identifies residual standard error (SE), which equals 0.066, and the SE of the spatial process, which equals 0.258. In other words, 79.6 (=0.258/(0.258 + 0.066)) % of residual variations are explained by the spatial process. The RE-ESF coefficient estimates suggest that Tokyo and Station are negatively significant. These results are intuitively consistent.

6.4 Methods for large data

6.4.1 Fast geographically weighted regression modeling

There are some GWR approaches for large samples. One approach is using samples for the CV-based bandwidth optimization, which is the heaviest part in the GWR. For example, Yu (2007) used randomly selected 3437 samples among 68,606 samples where the sample size is determined so that the estimation error is in the ±2% range. Feuillet et al. (2018) split their study area into smaller units and apply GWR in each of these units.

Another popular approach is parallel computation. Harris et al. (2010), Tran et al. (2016) and Li et al. (2019) studied parallelized GWR making use of, for example, Spark (http://www.sparkpc.ca/) and message passing interface, which are platforms for parallel processing. Besides, Li et al. (2019) improved linear algebra and showed that even without penalization, GWR is applicable to millions of samples. They published mgwr, which is a Python package for GWR and MGWR modeling with and without parallel computation. Based on Li et al. (2019), this package enables us to estimate the basic GWR from millions of samples, whereas the MGWR can be time consuming. Lu et al. (2018) proposed a fast MGWR calibration routine based on an early stopping. Their approach, which was implemented in the GWmodel package, might be useful to estimate MGWR and GWR-PSDM computationally efficiently.

6.4.2 Fast eigenvector spatial filtering modeling

The original ESF has two computational bottlenecks: (1) the eigen-decomposition and (2) the stepwise eigenvector selection. The computational complexity for (1) is the order of n^3. The eigen-decomposition is available roughly only when $n < 10{,}000$ in a standard computing environment. Fortunately, approximate eigen-decompositions have been proposed in machine-learning literature. One popular approach, called the Nystrom extension, is available for the Moran eigenvector approximation. Following

Murakami and Griffith (2019), the first L approximate eigen-pairs are formulated as follows:

$$\widehat{\mathbf{E}} = \left[\mathbf{C}_{NL} - \mathbf{1} \otimes \left(\mathbf{1}'_L(\mathbf{C}_L + \mathbf{I}_L)/L\right)\right]\mathbf{E}_L(\mathbf{\Lambda}_L + \mathbf{I}_L), \tag{6.4.1}$$

$$\widehat{\mathbf{\Lambda}}_L = \frac{L+N}{L}(\mathbf{\Lambda}_L + \mathbf{I}_L) - \mathbf{I}_L, \tag{6.4.2}$$

where $\mathbf{C}_L$ is an $L \times L$ matrix of spatial connectivity matrix among L anchor points. The anchor points are defined by k-mean centers (geometric centers of the clusters defined by the k-mean method). Greater L yields better approximation but slower computation. Murakami and Griffith (2019) suggest $L = 200$ to balance the accuracy and the computational efficiency. Fig. 6.4.1 shows an example of the 1st, 10th, and 100th exact and approximate eigenvectors extracted from the **MCM** matrix. This figure illustrates that the approximate eigenvectors successfully preserve the spatial scale information.

Another approach for the eigen-decomposition is the cascading approach proposed by Griffith and Chun (2019), which divides a study

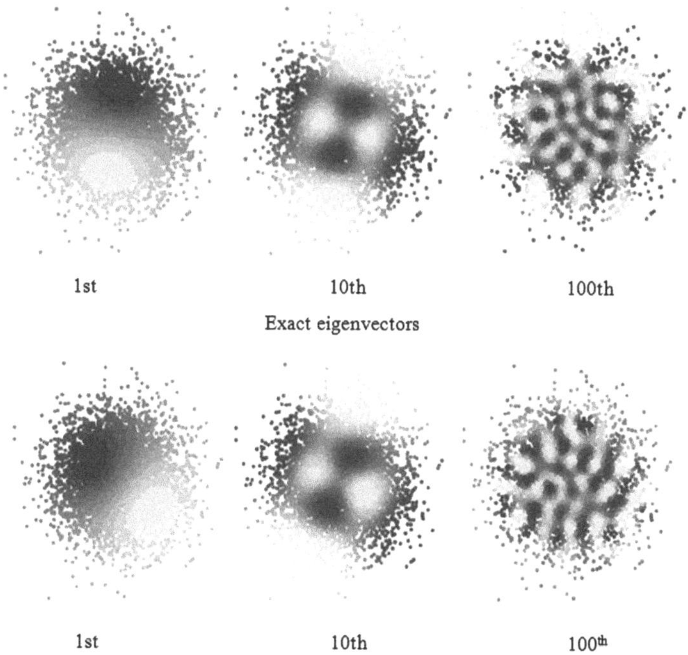

Figure 6.4.1 Exact and approximate Moran eigenvectors ($\mathbf{e}_1$, $\mathbf{e}_{10}$, $\mathbf{e}_{100}$).

area into small subsets and performs the ESF in each small subset. While the Nystrom extension-based approach, which is a low-rank approach, is suitable to approximate large-scale spatial structure just like the principal component analysis, the subset-based approach is more suitable to capture small-scale spatial variations.

The Nystrom extension-based approximation is implemented in the spmoran packages together with extended spatial regression models including the SVC model. The SVC model is formulated as

$$y(\mathbf{s}_i) = \sum_{k=1}^{K} x_k(\mathbf{s}_i)\beta_k(\mathbf{s}_i;\boldsymbol{\theta}_k) + \varepsilon(\mathbf{s}_i) \quad \varepsilon(\mathbf{s}_i) \sim N\left(0,\sigma^2\right), \tag{6.4.3}$$

Suppose that $\boldsymbol{\beta}_k = [\beta_k(\mathbf{s}_1;\boldsymbol{\theta}_k),\beta_k(\mathbf{s}_N;\boldsymbol{\theta}_k)]'$, then $\boldsymbol{\beta}_k = \mathbf{E}\boldsymbol{\gamma}_k$ where $\boldsymbol{\gamma}_k \sim N\left(\mathbf{0}, \tau_k^2\boldsymbol{\Lambda}^{\alpha_k}\right)$. τ_k^2 and α_k are parameters determining the variance and scale of the k-th spatially varying coefficients. In other words, the Moran eigenvectors are used to model spatial variations behind regression coefficients. Although the random coefficients $\boldsymbol{\gamma}_k$ can be replaced with fixed coefficients, the fixed-effects specification tends to fail the coefficients accurately (see Murakami et al., 2019). Murakami and Griffith (2019) developed a computationally efficient restricted likelihood estimation method for the SVC model.

References

Brunsdon, C., Fotheringham, S., Charlton, M., 1998. Geographically weighted regression. Journal of the Royal Statistical Society: Series D (The Statistician) 47 (3), 431–443.

Brunsdon, C., Charlton, M., Harris, P., 2012. Living with collinearity in local regression models. In: 10th International Symposium on Spatial Accuracy Assessment in Natural Resources and Environmental Sciences, Florianopolis, Brazil.

Chun, Y., Griffith, D.A., Lee, M., Sinha, P., 2016. Eigenvector selection with stepwise regression techniques to construct eigenvector spatial filters. Journal of Geographical Systems 18 (1), 67–85.

da Silva, A.R., Fotheringham, A.S., 2016. The multiple testing issue in geographically weighted regression. Geographical Analysis 48 (3), 233–247.

Dray, S., Legendre, P., Peres-Neto, P.R., 2006. Spatial modelling: a comprehensive framework for principal coordinate analysis of neighbour matrices (PCNM). Ecological Modelling 196 (3–4), 483–493.

Feuillet, T., Commenges, H., Menai, M., Salze, P., Perchoux, C., Reuillon, R., Kesse-Guyot, E., Enaux, C., Nazare, J.-A., Hercberg, S., Simon, C., Charreire, H., Oppert, J.M., 2018. A massive geographically weighted regression model of walking-environment relationships. Journal of transport geography 68, 118–129.

Fotheringham, A.S., Brunsdon, C., Charlton, M., 2002. Geographically Weighted Regression: The Analysis of Spatially Varying Relationships. Wiley, New York.

Fotheringham, A.S., Yang, W., Kang, W., 2017. Multiscale geographically weighted regression (mgwr). Annals of the Association of American Geographers 107 (6), 1247–1265.

Getis, A., 2008. A history of the concept of spatial autocorrelation: A geographer's perspective. Geographical Analysis 40 (3), 297–309.

Getis, A., Griffith, D.A., 2002. Comparative spatial filtering in regression analysis. Geographical Analysis 34 (2), 130–140.

Griffith, D.A., 2003. Spatial Autocorrelation and Spatial Filtering: Gaining Understanding through Theory and Scientific Visualization. Springer Science & Business Media.

Griffith, D.A., Chun, Y., 2019. Implementing Moran eigenvector spatial filtering for massively large georeferenced datasets. International Journal of Geographical Information Science 1–15.

Harris, R., Singleton, A., Grose, D., Brunsdon, C., Longley, P., 2010. Grid-enabling geographically weighted regression: a case study of participation in higher education in England. Transactions in GIS 14 (1), 43–61.

Leong, Y.Y., Yue, J.C., 2017. A modification to geographically weighted regression. International Journal of Health Geographics 16 (1), 11.

Li, Z., Fotheringham, A.S., Li, W., Oshan, T., 2019. Fast Geographically Weighted Regression (FastGWR): a scalable algorithm to investigate spatial process heterogeneity in millions of observations. International Journal of Geographical. Information Science 33 (1), 155–175.

Lu, B., Brunsdon, C., Charlton, M., Harris, P., 2017. Geographically weighted regression with parameter-specific distance metrics. International Journal of Geographical Information Science 31 (5), 982–998.

Lu, B., Yang, W., Ge, Y., Harris, P., 2018. Improvements to the calibration of a geographically weighted regression with parameter-specific distance metrics and bandwidths. Computers, Environment and Urban Systems 71, 41–57.

Mei, C.L., He, S.Y., Fang, K.T., 2004. A note on the mixed geographically weighted regression model. Journal of Regional Science 44 (1), 143–157.

Murakami, D., Griffith, D.A., 2015. Random effects specifications in eigenvector spatial filtering: a simulation study. Journal of Geographical Systems 17 (4), 311–331.

Murakami, D., Griffith, D.A., 2019. Spatially varying coefficient modeling for large datasets: eliminating N from spatial regressions. Spatial Statistics 30, 39–64.

Murakami, D., Lu, B., Harris, P., Brunsdon, C., Charlton, M., Nakaya, T., Griffith, D.A., 2019. The importance of scale in spatially varying coefficient modeling. Annals of the Association of American Geographers 109 (1), 50–70.

Murakami, D., Seya, H., 2019. Spatially filtered unconditional quantile regression: application to a hedonic analysis. Environmetrics 30 (5), e2556.

Murakami, D., Yoshida, T., Seya, H., Griffith, D.A., Yamagata, Y., 2017. A Moran coefficient-based mixed effects approach to investigate spatially varying relationships. Spatial Statistics 19, 68–89.

Nakaya, T., Fotheringham, A.S., Brunsdon, C., Charlton, M., 2005. Geographically weighted Poisson regression for disease association mapping. Statistics in Medicine 24 (17), 2695–2717.

Tiefelsdorf, M., Griffith, D.A., 2007. Semiparametric filtering of spatial autocorrelation: the eigenvector approach. Environment and Planning A:Economy and space 39 (5), 1193–1221.

Tran, H.T., Nguyen, H.T., Tran, V.T., 2016, October. Large-scale geographically weighted regression on Spark. In: 2016 Eighth International Conference on Knowledge and Systems Engineering (KSE), pp. 127–132. IEEE.

Wheeler, D., Tiefelsdorf, M., 2005. Multicollinearity and correlation among local regression coefficients in geographically weighted regression. Journal of Geographical Systems 7 (2), 161–187.

Yang, W., 2014. An Extension of Geographically Weighted Regression with Flexible Bandwidths. Doctoral dissertation. University of St Andrews.

Yu, D., 2007. Modeling owner-occupied single-family house values in the city of Milwaukee: a geographically weighted regression approach. GIScience & Remote Sensing 44 (3), 267–282.

PART TWO

Implementations

CHAPTER SEVEN

Implementation with R language

Takahiro Yoshida[1], Daisuke Murakami[2]
[1]Center for Global Environmental Research, National Institute for Environmental Studies, Tsukuba, Ibaraki, Japan
[2]The Institute of Statistical Mathematics, Tachikawa, Tokyo, Japan

Contents

Spatial Analysis using Big Data
ISBN: 978-0-12-813127-5
https://doi.org/10.1016/B978-0-12-813127-5.00007-2

7.1 Implementation of spatial (geo-)statistical and spatial econometric methods with R

This chapter provides implementations of spatial (geo-)statistical and spatial econometric methods with R.[1] In fact, because spatial statisticians and spatial econometricians often use R, now there are many excellent and well-maintained (as you know, this is very important!) packages that enable us to implement almost all standard methods. For the latest information, readers can check "CRAN Task View: Analysis of Spatial Data."[2]

7.2 Housing price data in Lucas County (Ohio, USA)

In this chapter, we demonstrate implementations with R for spatial data analysis methods described in Chapters 3–6. First of all, we introduce ***Lucas County Ohio housing data***, which consist of 25,357 single-family homes sold in Lucas County, Ohio, from 1993 to 1998 as testbed data. The data are originally provided by the Spatial Econometrics Toolbox for Matlab (https://www.spatial-econometrics.com/) maintained by Professor James P. LeSage, Texas State University. Currently, the data is also available at **spData** package[3] in R (Bivand et al., 2013). Although sample size of this dataset is medium, rather than large, this number is enough as an example in the sense that a traditional full-rank model is difficult to implement.

[1] Filzmoser et al. (2018) briefly summarizes R history and the current situation: "R (http://cran.r-project.org) was founded in 1995 and based on S, a programming language developed by Bell Laboratories, USA. Since 1997, it is internationally developed and distributed over the Comprehensive R Archive Network (CRAN). R nowadays belongs to the most popular and most used software environments in the statistics world. In addition, R is free and open-source (under the GPL2). R is not only a software for doing statistics, it is an environment for interactive computing with data supporting facilities to produce high-quality graphics. R is an object-oriented programming language and has interfaces to many other software products such as C, C++, Java, and interfaces to databases. The basic installation of R is extendable with approximately 10,000 add-on packages."

[2] https://cran.r-project.org/web/views/Spatial.html, currently maintained by Professor Roger Bivand.

[3] In the context of *spatial big data*, currently, **spDataLarge** package for large spatial datasets is under development (https://github.com/Nowosad/spDataLarge). See Lovelace et al. (2019) for more details.

We can use and check the data in R with the following command:

```
install.packages("spData", dep=T)
library(spData)
data(house, package="spData")
summary(house)

Object of class SpatialPointsDataFrame
Coordinates:
            min         max
long        484574.5    538364.2
lat         195270.3    229835.6
Is projected: TRUE
proj4string :
[+init=epsg:2834 +proj=lcc +lat_1=41.7 +lat_2=40.43333333333333
+lat_0=39.66666666666666 +lon_0=-82.5 +x_0=600000 +y_0=0 +ellps=GRS80
+units=m +no_defs]
Number of points: 25357
Data attributes:
price               yrbuilt             stories             TLA
Min.: 2000          Min.: 1835          one: 12954          Min.: 120
1st Qu.: 41900      1st Qu.: 1924       bilevel: 509        1st Qu.: 1070
Median : 65500      Median: 1950        multilvl: 723       Median: 1318
Mean   : 79018      Mean: 1945          one+half: 3125      Mean: 1462
3rd Qu.: 97000      3rd Qu.: 1964       two: 8042           3rd Qu.: 1682
Max.   :875000      Max.:1998           two+half: 2         Max.: 7616
...                 ...                 ...                 ...
```

The data includes the following 24 variables:
price: a numeric vector
yrbuilt: a numeric vector
stories: a factor with levels {one, bilevel, multilvl, one+half, two, two+half, three}
TLA: a numeric vector

wall: a factor with levelsstucdrvt ccbtile metlvnyl brick stone wood partbrk
beds: a numeric vector
baths: a numeric vector
halfbaths: a numeric vector
frontage: a numeric vector
depth: a numeric vector
garage: a factor with levels {no garage, basement, attached, detached, carport}
garagesqft: a numeric vector
rooms: a numeric vector
lotsize: a numeric vector
sdate: a numeric vector
avalue: a numeric vector
s1993: a numeric vector
s1994: a numeric vector
s1995: a numeric vector
s1996: a numeric vector
s1997: a numeric vector
s1998: a numeric vector
syear: a factor with levels {1993, 1994, 1995, 1996, 1997, 1998}
age: a numeric vector

7.3 R package for spatial features: sf

R packages for spatial data analysis have been developed mainly on the **sp** package. However, a newly developed **sf** package is becoming the core package for spatial data analysis. The main focus of **sf** package is to deal with the current mainstream GIS data standard (simple feature access, SFA) in R. Currently, the transition from **sp** package to **sf** package is proposed by developers of **sp** package because **sp** can deal with the SFA format only partially. Many packages related to special data analysis approaches still use **sp** as the core package, but **sf** has already taken advantages in data manipulation. Hence in this section, we introduce **sf** package and the newly developed R packages for spatial data handling and visualization, **leaflet** and **ggplot2**. **leaflet** is flexible and interactive visualization package based on JavaScript framework for spatial data. **ggplot2** is a general and popular visualization package in R, not just for spatial data. One of the main advantages of the **sf** package is that it is perfectly compatible with **ggplot2**.

First, install and load packages with the following commands (Fig. 7.3.1 and 7.3.2).

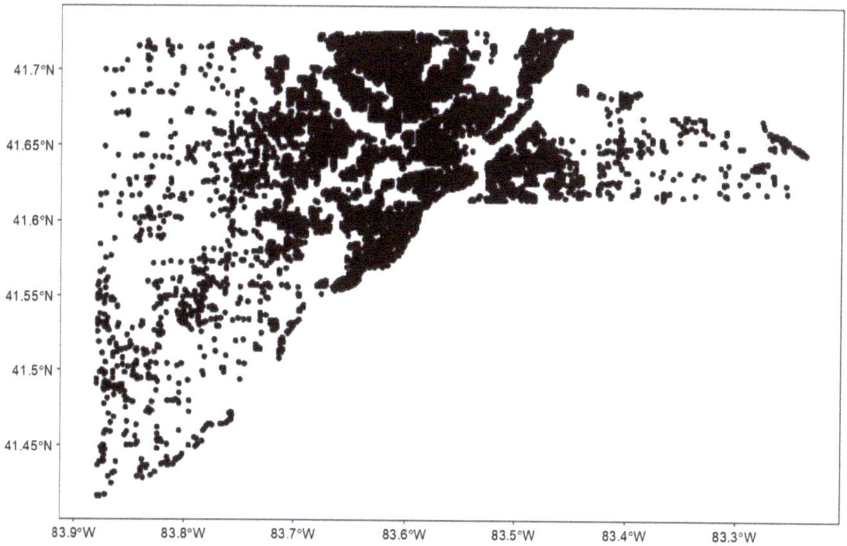

Figure 7.3.1 Plotting Lucas housing price dataset with the ggplot2 package.

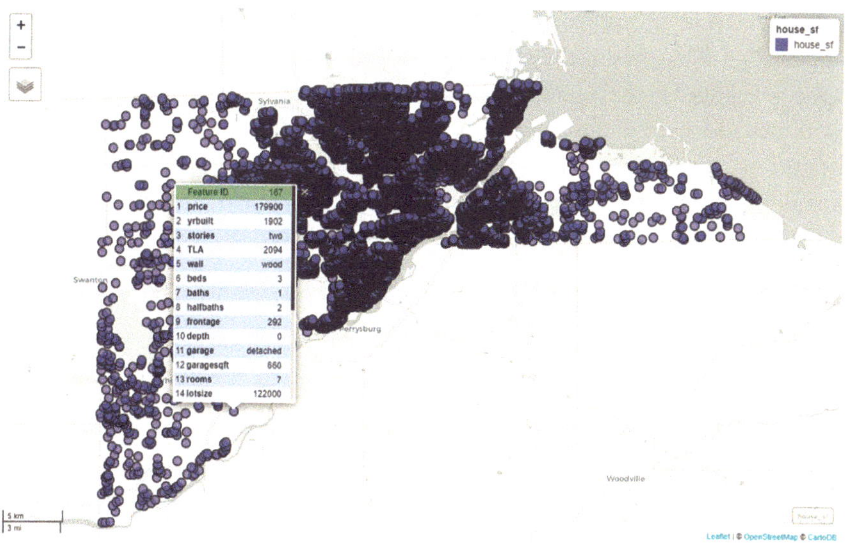

Figure 7.3.2 Plotting Lucas housing price dataset with leaflet package.

```
install.packages("sf",dep=T)
install.packages("leaflet",dep=T)
install.packages("ggplot2",dep=T)
library(sf)
library(leaflet)
library(ggplot2)
```

To visualize Lucas County housing data, type:

```
data(house)
house_sf <- st_as_sf(house)
plot(house_sf[1])

## Figure 7.3.1
ggplot(house_sf) + geom_sf(aes(fill=price))+ theme_bw()
## Figure 7.3.2
leaflet(house_sf)
```

7.4 Global and local indicators of spatial associations

7.4.1 Define spatial weight matrix

Defining the spatial relationship is a critical step to evaluate indicators of spatial association. As Bivand et al. (2013) mentioned, "the first step is to define which relationships between observations are to be given a non-zero weight, that is to choose the neighbour criterion to be used; the second is to assign weights to the identified neighbour links." In this subsection, we introduce how to define spatial neighbors and how to give weight to them. For this purpose, we depend on the **spdep** package. After defining spatial weight matrices, we will proceed with the implementation of global indicators of spatial association and local indicators of spatial association (LISA).

Let us install and load **spdep** and **dplyr** (for data handling) packages.

```
install.packages("spdep",dep=T)
install.packages("dplyr",dep=T)
library(spdep)
library(dplyr)
```

To define spatial neighbors, we first extract coordinate information—"longitude and latitude" as

```
coords <- coordinates(house)
```

Convert sp object (house) to sf object (house_sf), with the `st_as_sf` function.

```
house_sf <- st_as_sf(house)
```

The "*k*-nearest neighbours (kNN)" based **W** can be defined as

```
house.knn <- knearneigh(coords, k=3)
house.knn.nb <- knn2nb(house.knn)
```

`knearneigh` function returns a matrix with the indices of points belonging to the set of the *k* nearest neighbors of each other. This example shows the case of three nearest neighbors. Then, `knn2nb` function converts a knn object returned by `knearneigh` into a neighbors list of class nb with a list of integer vectors containing neighbor region number ids.

Instead, nb for inverse distance-based **W** (with/without cutoff) can be constructed as

```
house.dist.nb <- dnearneigh(coords,d1=0,d2=100,longlat =T)
dlist <- nbdists(house.dist.nb,coords)
idlist <- lapply(dlist,function(x) 1/x^2)
```

The function `dnearneigh` identifies neighbors of region points by Euclidean distance between lower (greater than) (d1) and upper (less than or equal to) (d2) bounds. The function `nbdists` returns the Euclidean distances along the links in a list of the same form as the neighbors list. Here we assume the inverse squared distance.

To check spatial neighbors, it is useful to map the spatial relationships as follows:

```
plot(st_geometry(house_sf))
plot(house.knn.nb, coords, add=TRUE, col="red")
```

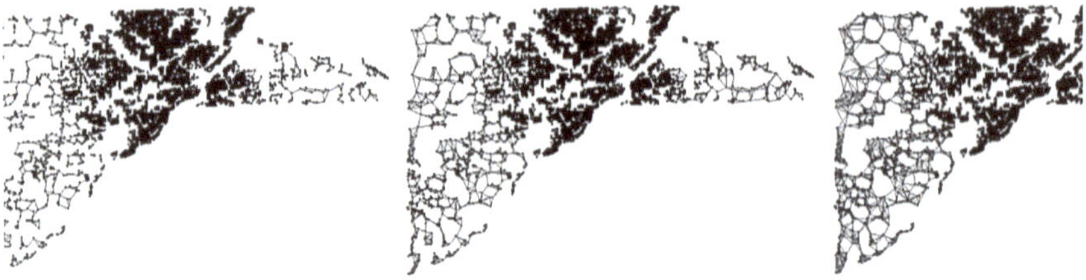

Figure 7.4.1 Mapping spatial neighbors defined by kNN (left) k = 2; (middle) k = 5; (right) k = 8.

Fig. 7.4.1 shows kNN relationships of house data, for different number of k ($k = 2$, 5, and 8). Note that when we have isolation point(s), functions (e.g., `nb2listw`) in the spdep package display a warning message.

After defining spatial neighbor relationships, the next step is putting spatial weights. The `nb2listw` function returns a neighbors list with spatial weights. We can change the standardization schema of **W** with "`style`" argument in the `nb2listw` function. For example, `style = "W"` represents row-standardized form.

For kNN-based **W**,

```
house.knn.w <- nb2listw(neighbours=house.knn.nb, style="W")
```

And for inverse distance-based **W**,

```
house.dist.w <- nb2listw(neighbours=house.dist.nb,glist=idlist,style="W")
```

Note that when readers would like to construct **W** from their shape files, we can easily read shape files with the `st_read` function in the sf package. After reading data, the aforementioned commands can be used for kNN and inverse-distance based **W**. For contiguity based **W**, refer to Bivand (2019).

7.4.2 Testing for global spatial autocorrelation

Here, we illustrate how to calculate Moran's I and Geary's C as global indicators of spatial association on spatial autocorrelation by using Lucas data. Moran's *I* is perhaps the most common global test (Bivand et al., 2013; Bivand and Wong, 2018). By using the `moran.test` function in the **spdep** package, we can get Moran's *I* value. By default setting, the hypothesis testing of `moran.test` will be conducted by randomization assumption.

```
### Moran's I

moran.test(house_sf$price, listw=house.w) # randomization assumption

        Moran I test under randomization
data:  house_sf$price
weights: house.w
Moran I statistic standard deviate = 165.68, p-value <2.2e-16
alternative hypothesis: greater
sample estimates:
Moran I statistic   Expectation   Variance
0.7937264     -0.00003943840      0.00002295395
```

To test under normality assumption, you need to add the `randomization = FALSE` argument in the `moran.test` function. If the variable (in this case, `price`) is normally distributed, the two assumptions yield the same variance. If the variable departs from normality, the randomization assumption compensates by increasing the variance and decreasing the standard deviate (Bivand et al., 2013; see Chapter 3).

```
moran.test(house_sf$price, listw=house.w, randomisation=FALSE) # normality
assumption

        Moran I test under normality
data:  house_sf$price
weights: house.w
Moran I statistic standard deviate = 165.64, p-value <2.2e-16
alternative hypothesis: greater
sample estimates:
Moran I statistic  Expectation     Variance
0.7937264370       -0.0000394384   0.0000229642
```

We can calculate Geary's *C* statistic in a manner similar to Moran's I as follows:

```
### Geary C
geary.test(house_sf$price, listw=house.w)

        Geary C test under randomisation
data:  house_sf$price
weights: house.w

Geary C statistic standard deviate = 114.63, p-value <2.2e-16
alternative hypothesis: Expectation greater than statistic
sample estimates:
Geary C statistic   Expectation   Variance
0.1924420           1.000000      0.00004963286
```

7.4.3 Testing for local spatial autocorrelation

LISA on spatial autocorrelation are used to detect clusters: observations with similar neighbors with high value are called "hotspots". The Moran scatter plot (Fig. 7.4.2) is with observed value on the x-axis and the spatially lagged value on the y-axis. Global Moran's I is a linear relationship between these and is drawn as a slope in Fig. 7.4.2. The plot is further partitioned into

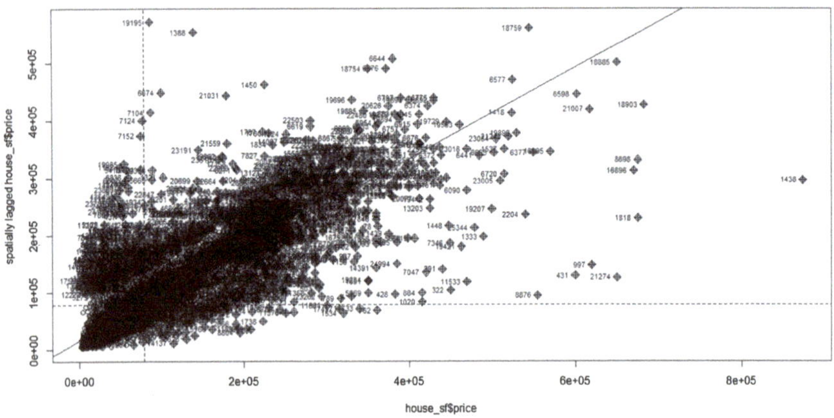

Figure 7.4.2 Moran-scatter plot.

quadrants at the mean values of the x-axis and the y-axis: low-low (cool spot), low-high, high-low, and high-high (e.g., Bivand et al., 2013).

```
### Locan Moran I
LocalI <- as.data.frame(localmoran(house_sf$price, listw=house.w))

str(LocalI)
'data.frame': 25357 obs. of 5 variables:
 $ Ii:          num   5.768 0.591 0.502 0.986 1.598 ...
 $ E.Ii:        num   -3.94e-05 -3.94e-05 -3.94e-05 -3.94e-05-3.94e-05 ...
 $ Var.Ii:      num   0.333 0.333 0.333 0.333 0.333 ...
 $ Z.Ii:        num   9.99 1.02 0.87 1.71 2.77 ...
 $ Pr(z > 0):   num   8.06e-24 1.53e-01 1.92e-01 4.38e-02 2.81e-03 ...

moran.plot(house_sf$price, listw=house.w) # Figure 7.3.2
### check local clusters (if needed)
#house_LocalI_sf <- bind_cols(house_sf,LocalI)
#plot(house_LocalI_sf["Ii"])
```

For Local Geary, we can use GeoDa. As explained in Chapter 3, the local G_i statistic is calculated for each zone based on the spatial weights object used. The value returned is a Z-value, and may be used as a diagnostic tool. High positive values indicate the possibility of a local cluster of high values of the variable being analyzed, and very low relative values, a similar cluster of low values. In the `localG` function, we need to check whether G_i or G_i^* are used. If `attr(output of LocalG function, "gstari")` is `true`, the G_i^* variant, including the self-weight $w_{ii} > 0$, is calculated and returned. And then, to get values on the testing-related values on G_i and G_i^*, we need to add an argument `return_internals = TRUE`.

```
### Local Gi
Local.G.Zvalue <- localG(house_sf$price, listw=house.w, return_internals=TRUE)
attr(Local.G.Zvalue,"gstari") #False
Local.G.values <- bind_cols(as.data.frame(attr(Local.G.Zvalue,"internals")),Z=Local.G.Zvalue)
summary(Local.G.values)

### Local Gi*
house.w.self <- nb2listw(neighbours=include.self(house.nb), style="B")
Local.G.Zvalue.self <- localG(house_sf$price, listw=house.w.self, return_internals=TRUE)
attr(Local.G.Zvalue.self,"gstari") # True
Local.G.valuses.self <-
        bind_cols(as.data.frame(attr(Local.G.Zvalue.self,"internals")),Z=Local.G.Zvalue.self)
summary(Local.G.valuses.self)
```

7.4.4 Testing for local spatial heterogeneity

The H_i statistics proposed by Ord and Getis (2012) can be calculated by `LOSH.cs` and `LOSH.mc` functions in the **spdep** package. `LOSH.cs` and `LOSH.mc` use a Chi-square-based test (Ord and Getis, 2012) and randomization with the Monte-Carlo bootstrap—based test (Xu et al., 2014), respectively.

```
Local.H_cs <- LOSH.cs(house_sf$price, listw=house.w) # Chi2
summary(Local.H_cs)

  Hi                     E.Hi          Var.Hi              Z.Hi
  Min.:      0.00005     Min.:     1   Min.:      14.55    Min.:     0.000007
  1st Qu.:   0.07554     1st Qu.:  1   1st Qu.:   14.55    1st Qu.:  0.010386
  Median:    0.19053     Median:   1   Median:    14.55    Median:   0.026194
  Mean:      0.88261     Mean:     1   Mean:      14.55    Mean:     0.121340
  3rd Qu.:   0.46499     3rd Qu.:  1   3rd Qu.:   14.55    3rd Qu.:  0.063926
  Max.:      207.178     Max.:     1   Max.:      14.55    Max.:     28.48250

 x_bar_i                ei                       Pr()
  Min.:     3233        Min.:      0.000e+00     Min.:     0.0000
  1st Qu.:  44767       1st Qu.:   2.157e+07     1st Qu.:  0.1836
  Median:   66333       Median:    1.068e+08     Median:   0.2312
  Mean:     78778       Mean:      9.065e+08     Mean:     0.2275
  3rd Qu.:  98333       3rd Qu.:   3.862e+08     3rd Qu.:  0.2782
  Max.:     571833      Max.:      3.352e+11     Max.:     0.5651

Local.H_mc <- LOSH.mc(house_sf$price, listw=house.w,nsim=1000) # bootstrap
summary(Local.H_mc)
```

7.5 Geostatistics

7.5.1 Assumptions

There are many R packages for geostatistical modeling. The packages include gstat, geoR, fields, and automap for non-Bayesian modeling and spBayes and ramps for Bayesian modeling. Among them, gstat, which we will introduce in the following section, has widely been used. For spatial large (big) data modeling, in Sections 7.5.3 and 7.5.4, we introduce low-rank and sparse approximation approaches.

Throughout Section 7.5, we illustrate spatial predictions using the Lucas housing data. Let us load the data, and log-transform the price data as follows:

```
library(spData)
data(house)
dat                <- house
dat@data$ln_price <- log(dat@data$price)
```

We split the dataset into two. Specifically, we use 10,000 randomly selected samples as observation data (`odat`) for the model estimation and the remaining samples as unobserved data (`mdat`) at prediction sites. `odat` and `mdat` are generated as follows:

```
n      <-dim(dat)[1]
oid    <- sample(n,10000)
odat   <- dat[ oid,]
mdat   <- dat[-oid,]
```

Exceptionally, in Section 7.5.2, we use 2000 samples randomly selected from `odat` considering the computational burden. `odat2` is extracted as follows:

```
oid     <- sample(n,2000)
odat2   <- dat[ oid,]
```

Following many studies in geostatistics, we assume that there are no explanatory variables in this section.

7.5.2 Classical geostatistical modeling

This section introduces gstat using `odat2` as observed data and `mdat` as missing data. First, let us load the gstat package.

```
library(gstat)
```

Classical geostatistical modeling can be conducted, generally, in the following two steps:

1. estimation of variogram
2. spatial prediction

In the first step, the empirical variogram $\gamma^*(h_\tau)$ (see Chapter 4) is calculated using the `variogram` function as follows.

```
evario          <-  variogram(ln_price~1, odat2)
```

Here, `ln_price~1` specifies that the dependent variable is `ln_price`, and the explanatory variable is only an intercept (1).

The evaluated empirical variogram can be plotted as follows (Fig. 7.5.1):

```
plot(evario)
```

The variogram crowd is displayed if `cloud = TRUE` is added to the `variogram` function. By default, sample pairs whose distances in between are within one-third of the diagonal length of the box containing the sample sites is considered in the `variogram` function. This is because the empirical variogram between distant samples are in general large variations that make estimation unstable (see Cressie, 1993). The threshold distance can be changed by specifying an argument `cutoff` by the distance that the user wants. Another argument `width` with default equals `cutoff/15`, specifies the width of the distance intervals separating empirical variograms. Another important argument is `cressie`. The classical estimator (4.3.3) is used to evaluate the empirical variogram if `cressie = FALSE` (default) while the Cressie-Hawkin's robust estimator (4.3.4) is used if `cressie = TRUE`. These arguments can be determined through a visual assessment. For instance, Fig. 7.5.1 shows a clear pattern that variogram gradually increases as distance increases. Such a tendency, which is assumed in the variogram model, is preferable to stably fit a variogram model.

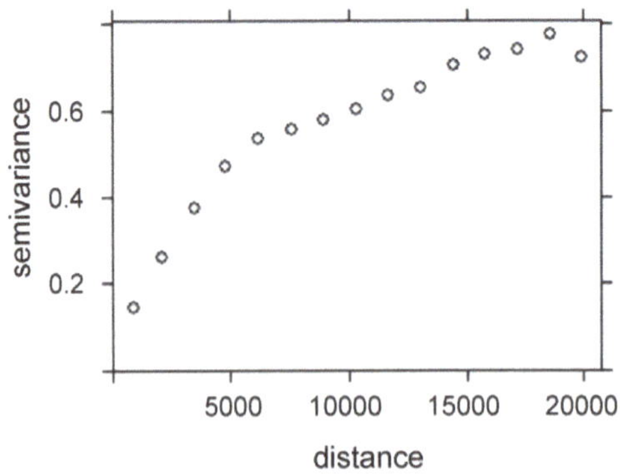

Figure 7.5.1 Empirical variogram.

A variogram model is fitted to the empirical variogram by the nonlinear weighted least squares (WLS) method using the `fit.variogram` function as follows:

```
vmod    <- fit.variogram(evario, vgm(0.5, "Exp", 10000, 0.1))
```

The `vgm` function specifies the model type. "`Exp`" means that the exponential variogram model is assumed. It can be replaced with `Sph` for the spherical model, `Gau` for the Gaussian model, and `Mat` for the Matern model. The three numbers in the vgm function specify the initial values for the partial-sill, range, and nugget parameters. Variogram model and the initial parameter values may be determined through a visual assessment. In the case of Fig. 7.4.1, the exponential model is a reasonable choice considering the quick increase of variogram near the distance equals zero and the absence of the distance that spatial dependence disappears (i.e., variogram values keep increasing). The initial parameter values for the partial-sill, range, and nugget can be 0.5, 0.1, and 10,000, respectively, based on the visual assessment.

The fitted variogram model is plotted by the following command:

```
plot(evario, vmod)
```

Fig. 7.5.2, which plots the output, suggests that the exponential model fits the empirical variogram quite well:

The estimated variogram model is used to construct a geostatistical model. This is done by the `gstat` function as follows:

```
odat2@data$id <-1:(dim(odat2)[1])
gmod          <- gstat(id = "id", formula = ln_price~1, data = odat2,model=vmod)
```

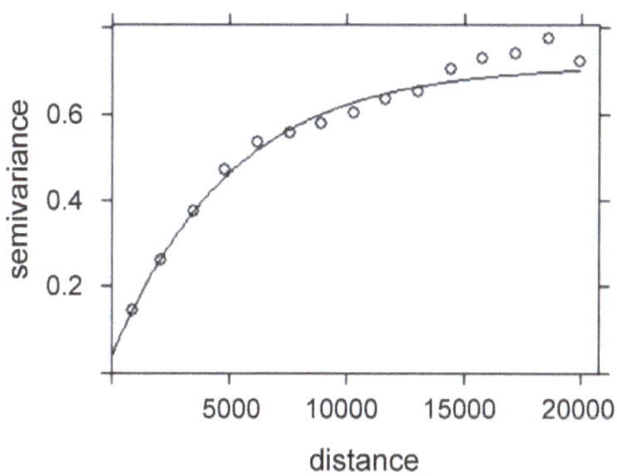

Figure 7.5.2 Fitted exponential variogram model.

In the first line, data id is added in `odat2`. The second line constructs a geostatistical model using the data id (`id = "id"`), the formula (`ln_price ~ 1`), the input data (`odat2`), and the estimated variogram model (`vmod`).

A spatial prediction is implemented using the `predict` function. The arguments are the constructed model (`gmod`) and the data (spatial coordinates and explanatory variables) at unobserved sites (`mdat`). The first line below performs the prediction while the second line extracts the first five rows in the output:

```
pred              <- predict(gmod, mdat)
pred[1:5,]
            coordinates       id.pred        id.var
1 (484875.6, 195301.3)     11.09830     0.4460452
2   (485525.7, 196660)     10.98984     0.1963588
3   (488008.9, 196987)     11.31673     0.1518186
4   (486022, 197032.9)     10.96207     0.1364576
5 (489111.9, 197044.1)     12.20328     0.1549977
```

The output includes the predicted logged price (`id.pred`) and the predicted error variance (`id.var`).

The predicted values can be plotted using the `spplot` function as follows:

```
library(RColorBrewer)
nc     <- 9
cols   <- brewer.pal(n = nc, name = "YlOrRd")
cuts   <- quantile(pred@data$id.pred, probs=seq(0,1,len=9))
spplot(pred, "id.pred",cuts=cuts, col.regions = cols, cex=0.4)
```

We used a color called `YlOrRd`, whose color gradually changes across yellow, orange, and red. This pallet is available from an R package RColorBrewer. The package was loaded in the first line of the code. The list of all available pallets in this package is displayed by commanding `display.brewer.all()`. The color is now divided by 9 (`nc < -9`), which is the maximum number for `YlOrRd`. The third line defines the break points of the nine colors. Here, the nine quantiles of the predicted values `pred@data$id.pred` in `pred` are used. The `spplot` function draws a spatial plot of the predicted value using the color pallets (`cols`) and the break points (`cuts`), where "`cex = 0.4`" specifies the size of each sample site (large value means bigger dots).

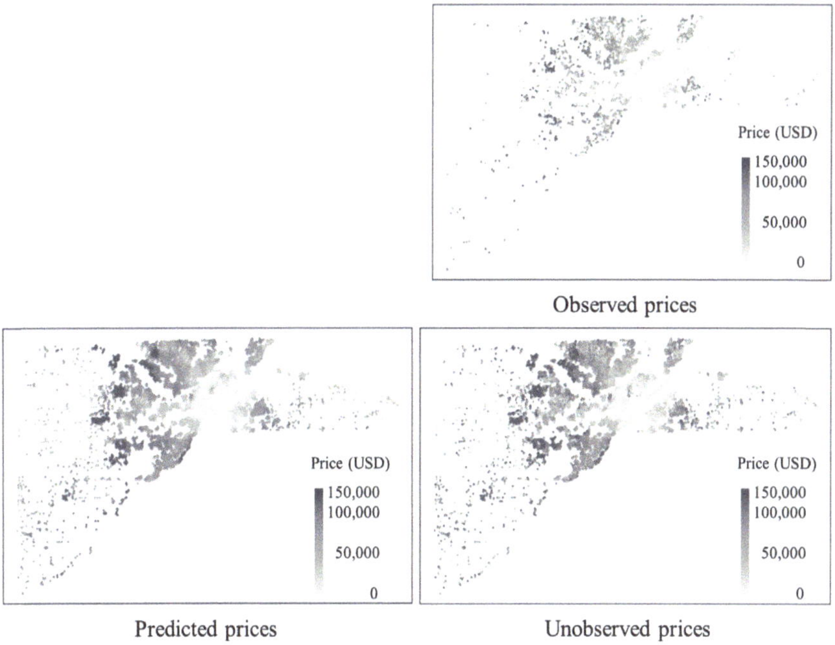

Figure 7.5.3 Spatial prediction result (gstat).

The break points can be defined in other ways. For example, they can be defined by equal intervals using the first line below by manually using the second line:

```
cols  <- seq(0.19,len=nc+1)
cuts  <- c(0, 10, 10.5, 11, 11.2 15)
```

Fig. 7.5.3 plots the observed housing prices in `odat2` and predicted prices using the `spplot` function with the nine quantile-based coloring. This plot confirms the prediction accuracy.

The `gstat.cv` function that implements a *K*-fold cross validation is useful to quantitatively evaluate the predictive accuracy. The implementation in the case of a fivefold cross validation is as follows:

```
cvres  <- gstat.cv(gmod, nfold=5)
```

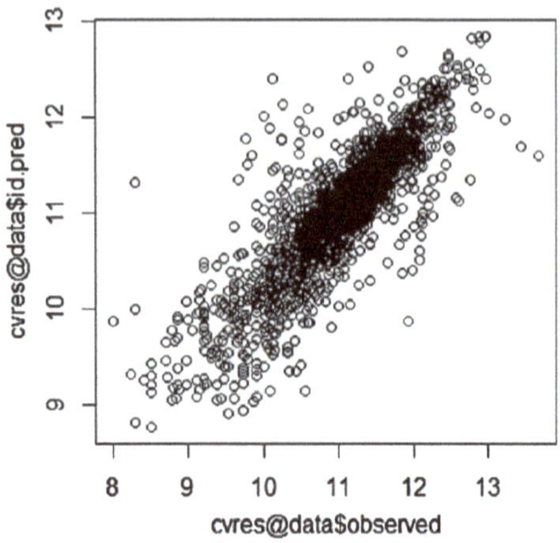

Figure 7.5.4 Five-fold cross-validation result. The x- and y-axes denote observed and predicted values.

The output, whose first five rows are returned as follows, includes predicted values (`id.pred`), predictive variances (`id.var`), observations (`observed`), residuals (`residual`), z score of the residuals (i.e., residuals divided by the predictive standard errors; `zscore`), and which folds each sample is in (`fold`):

```
cvres[1:5,]
           coordinates   id.pred   id.var   observed  residual    zscore  fold
1 (507419.6, 226131.9) 11.22659 0.057588 11.22524 -0.00134 -0.00562    5
2 (508959.8, 224686.7) 10.70004 0.062590 10.75577  0.05573  0.22277    4
3 (498504.1, 227157.4) 11.95987 0.079574 11.86710 -0.09277 -0.32888    4
4 (505273.1, 216626.1) 11.71051 0.073049 11.65269 -0.05781 -0.21392    5
5 (523171.8, 220961.4) 11.05815 0.252869 11.60824  0.55008  1.09390    4
```

Fig. 7.5.4 shows a plot whose x and y axes are the observed and predicted values. This plot is drawn by the following command:

```
plot(cvres@data$observed, cvres@data$id.pred)
```

where `cvres@data$observed` extracts "`observed`" in the data frame `cvres@data` in `cvres` that is a SpatialPointDataFrame object. This plot confirms the accurateness of the Kriging prediction.

Unfortunately, the standard geostatistical approach is available only if the sample size is not large, say $N < 10{,}000$. The next two sections introduce low-rank and sparse approximations to break this bottleneck.

7.5.3 Low-rank approximations

R packages for low-rank approximation includes fixed-rank Kriging (FRK) and autoFRK for, spBayes implementing the predictive process approach, and LatticeKrig for the multiresolution Gaussian process (MGP). Among them, we illustrate an FRK implementation using autoFRK and an MGP implementation using LatticeKrig. We focus these two packages because of their simplicity and computationally efficiency.

Before the calculation, we extract required variables from `odat` with sample size of 10,000 (`mdat` comprises of 15,357 locations):

```
y       <- odat@data$ln_price      # logged land price (odat)
coords  <- coordinates(odat)       # spatial coordinates (odat)
n       <- length(y)               # sample size
mcoords <- coordinates(mdat)       # spatial coordinates (mdat)
```

autoFRK implements FRK quite easily as follows:

```
library(autoFRK)
mod    <- autoFRK(Data=y, loc=coords, maxK=sqrt(n))
pred   <- predict(mod ,newloc=mcoords)
```

where the `autoFRK` function estimates the model, and the `predict` function applied the spatial prediction. Following the manual in this package, the maximum number of spatial basis functions being used to the GP approximation is specified by `maxK=sqrt(n)`.

Likewise, LatticeKrig implements MGP, just several lines, as follows:

```
library(LatticeKrig)
mod    <- LatticeKrig( x= coords,y=y, nlevel=3)
pred   <- predict(mod, xnew= mcoords)
```

where the `LatticeKrig` function estimates the three-level (`nlevel = 3`) MGP in which the internal parameters are estimated by a likelihood maximum, and the `predict` function performs a spatial prediction. A command `surface(mod)` displays a predicted map.

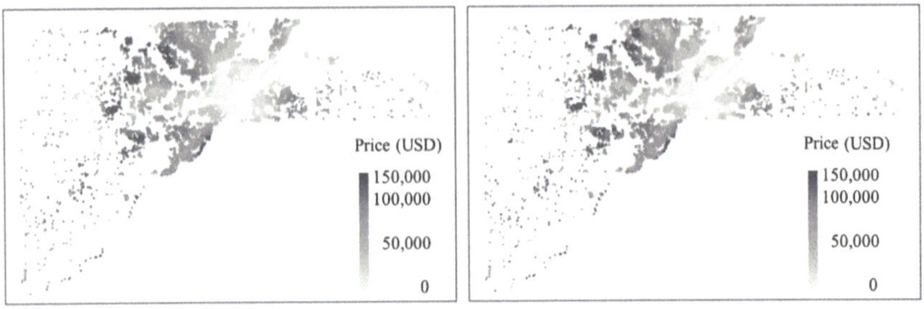

FRK (autoFRK) MGP (LatticeKrig)

Figure 7.5.5 Spatial prediction result (FRK and MGP).

Fig. 7.5.5 plots the land prices interpolated by the FRK and MGP. This figure suggests that, although MGP considers spatial variations in three scales and is advantageous to capture small-scale variations, results from FRK and MGP are similar, at least in this case.

7.5.4 Sparse approximations

While low-rank approximation tends to miss small-scale variations, sparse approximations effectively capture local variations. R packages for sparse approximations include spNNGP for NNGP, laGP for a local approximate GP (Gramacy, 2016), and integrated nested Laplace approximation for the Stochastic Partial Differential Equations (SPDE)-based GP approximation. This section introduces spNNGP, which constricts a valid (i.e., positive definite) GP quite accurately with a small computing cost.

The full Bayes implementation for the NNGP is implemented using the following code:

```
library(spNNGP)
n.samples<- 500  # For this example. Larger value such as 10000 is preferable.
starting <- list("phi"=1/10000, "sigma.sq"=0.3, "tau.sq"=0.3)
tuning   <- list("phi"=1/10000, "sigma.sq"=0.2, "tau.sq"=0.2)
priors   <- list("phi.Unif"=c(1/100000, 1/1000),"sigma.sq.IG"=c(1,0.5), "tau.sq.IG"=c(1,0.5))
cov.model<- "exponential"
mod      <- spNNGP(y~1, coords=coords, starting=starting, tuning=tuning, priors=priors,
                cov.model=cov.model, n.samples=n.samples)
mx       <- as.matrix(rep(1,dim(mcoords)[1]))
pred0    <- spPredict(mod, X.0=mx, coords.0 = mcoords)
mpred    <- apply(pred0$p.y,1,mean)
```

The spNNGP function estimates the model parameters. The arguments include "start", specifying the initial values for the {phi, sigma.sq, tau.sq} parameters that equal {1/range, partial-sill, tau.sq}, and "priors", determining hyperparameter values for these three parameters. In the preceding code, a uniform distribution (phi.Unif) is assumed for phi, while inverse Gamma distributions are assumed for sigma.sq and tau.sq (sigma.sq.IG and tau.sq.IG). cov.model specifies the covariance model, and n.sample specifies the number of Markov chain Monte Carlo (MCMC) iterations. The spNNGP function performs the NNGP-based spatial prediction, and the prior means for the predicted samples are calculated and stored in mpred in the last line.

Unfortunately, the fully Bayesian approach, which relies on MCMC, is slow for large samples. For faster computation, the spNNGP package provides a cross-validation-based spNNGP, which is called conjugate NNGP. Roughly speaking, this approach derives closed form posterior distributions of each parameter using the conjugate Normal inverse Gamma prior distributions, and estimates the parameters minimizing the cross-validation score using a cross validation. This approach is implemented as follows:

```
sigma.sq      <- 0.3
tau.sq        <- 0.3
phi           <- 1/10000
sigma.sq.IG   <- c(1, 0.5)
theta.alpha   <- cbind(seq(phi,1/1000,length.out=10), seq(tau.sq/sigma.sq,3,length.out=10))
colnames(theta.alpha) <- c("phi", "alpha")
modC          <- spConjNNGP(y~1, coords=coords, n.neighbors = 10, cov.model = cov.model,
                  X.0 = mx, coords.0 = mcoords, k.fold = 5,
                  theta.alpha = theta.alpha, sigma.sq.IG = sigma.sq.IG)
mpred         <- modC$y.0.hat
```

theta.alpha and sigma.sq.IG specify initial values for phi, alpha, and sigma.sq. parameters.

Fig. 7.5.6 displays prediction results. This result suggests that both NNGP and conjugate NNGP finish similar results.

Finally, we compare the computational (CP) time and the root mean squared error (RMSE) of the predicted values in Table 7.5.1. In this comparison, we used Windows 10 Pro with a 64-bit operating system (memory: 8.0 GB). This table shows the computational efficiency of the low rank approximates (FRK and MGP). They would be preferable for very

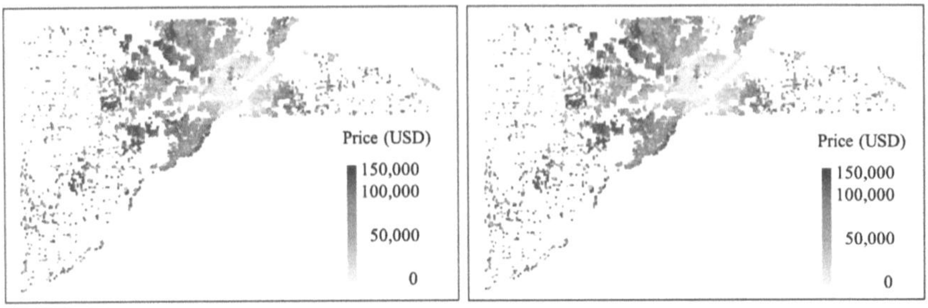

NNGP Conjugate NNGP

Figure 7.5.6 Spatial prediction result (NNGP and conjugate NNGP).

Table 7.5.1 Computational time and root mean squared error of the prediction results.

	FRK	MGP	NNGP (iteration:500)	Conjugate NNGP
CP time (sec)	36.7	38.3	415.2	6.3
RMSE	0.436	0.366	0.347	0.357

CP, computational; *FRK*, fixed-rank Kriging; *MGP*, multiresolution Gaussian process; *NNGP*, nearest-neighbor Gaussian process; *RMSE*, root-mean-square error.

large samples. Although the MCMC-based NNGP, which assumes 500 iterations for this toy example, is slower than the opponents, its RMSE is the smallest. NNGP can be parallelized for faster computation. NNGP will be great in a high-performance computing environment. In contrast, conjugate NNGP indicates the shortest CP time with small RMSE. This approach will be useful for large data modeling even in a standard computing environment.

7.6 Spatial econometrics

7.6.1 Spatial econometric models in R

The **spdep** package has taken the role of the core package on spatial data analysis, including spatial data handling, modeling, and also testing. Therefore, the **spdep** is currently a very huge package with a lot of functions. To maintain the package easily, the developers are moving functions on fitting spatial regression models to the new **spatialreg** package from April 2019 (https://github.com/r-spatial/spatialreg). In this section, we introduce spatial econometric modelings by using the **spatialreg** package considering such situations. In the following, we introduce some methods for large spatial data, explained in Section 5.7.

We use the same data and setting in Section 7.4 (kNN ($k = 3$)-based $\mathbf{W}$ with row-standardization). The dependent variable is log of price, and explanatory variables are age, log of lotsize, and the number of rooms. First, let us install and load related packages.

```
install.packages("spatialreg", dep=T)
library(spatialreg)
library(spdep)
library(sf)
```

Extract longitude and latitude as

```
coords <- coordinates(house)
```

If the object is sf class, we can do that by converting it to sp class with the as function:

```
coords <- coordinates(as(house_sf,"Spatial"))
```

Then define spatial weight matrix $\mathbf{W}$ as

```
house.knn <- knearneigh(coords, k=3)
house.nb <- knn2nb(house.knn)
house.w <- nb2listw(neighbours=house.nb, style="W")
```

and the regression model formula is given as

```
form <- formula(log(price) ~ age + log(lotsize) + rooms)
```

7.6.2 Generalized spatial two-stage least squares method

The spatial two-stage least squares (S2SLS) method for the spatial lag model (SLM) is implemented using the stsls function (S2SLS; see Chapter 5) as follows:

```
model.STSLS <- stsls(formula=form, data=house_sf, listw=house.w)
```

The arguments include formula (`form`), data (`house_sf`), and a list object (listw) summarizing spatial relationships (`house.w`). The estimated coefficients are returned using the `summary` function as follows:

```
summary(model.STSLS)
Call: stsls(formula = form, data = house_sf, listw = house.w)
Residuals:
        Min        1Q          Median     3Q         Max
        -2.4013    -0.1417     0.0389     0.2057     2.388220
Coefficients:
                Estimate       Std. Error     t value     Pr(>|t|)
Rho             0.5049491      0.0088964      56.759      < 2.2e-16
(Intercept)     4.2281180      0.0862316      49.032      < 2.2e-16
age             -0.7686884     0.0152862      -50.286     < 2.2e-16
log(lotsize)    0.1195953      0.0038621      30.966      < 2.2e-16
rooms           0.0927680      0.0018802      49.340      < 2.2e-16
Residual variance (sigma squared): 0.12007, (sigma: 0.34651)
```

For spatial error model (SEM), the `GMerrorsar` function implementing the generalized method of moments (GMM) estimation is available. Just like SLM, we need to specify formula, data, and listw. Here is a code for the GMM estimation:

```
model.SEM <- GMerrorsar(formula=form, data=house_sf, listw=house.w)
```

The estimates are displayed again using the summary function as

```
summary(model.SEM)

Call: GMerrorsar(formula = form, data = house_sf, listw = house.w)
Residuals:
       Min        1Q          Median     3Q         Max
       -3.1989    -0.2053     0.0975     0.3177     2.565637
Type: GM SAR estimator
Coefficients: (GM standard errors)
                 Estimate       Std. Error     z value        Pr(>|z|)
(Intercept)      8.6769468      0.0475724      182.395        < 2.2e-16
age              -0.9982721     0.0134675      -74.125        < 2.2e-16
log(lotsize)     0.2478833      0.0050168      49.411         < 2.2e-16
rooms            0.1063338      0.0020643      51.510         < 2.2e-16
Lambda: 0.57698 (standard error): 0.0085528 (z-value): 67.461
Residual variance (sigma squared): 0.13047, (sigma: 0.3612)
GM argmin sigma squared: 0.13192
Number of observations: 25357
Number of parameters estimated: 6
```

where Lambda is the estimated spatial error parameter.

Finally, we introduce the generalized spatial two-stage least squares (GS2SLS) estimation (Kelejian and Prucha, 1998) of the spatial autoregressive combined (SAC) model, which has both the spatial lag and the spatial error terms (i.e., SLM + SEM). The GS2SLS is implemented using the gstsls function[4] as follows.

```
model.GSTSLS <- gstsls(formula=form, data=house_sf, listw=house.w)
```

whereas the estimates are returned as

```
summary(model.GSTSLS)

Call:gstsls(formula = form, data = house_sf, listw = house.w)
Residuals:
        Min        1Q        Median    3Q        Max
        -2.3793    -0.1410   0.0366    0.2000    2.477103
Type: GM SARAR estimator
Coefficients: (GM standard errors)
               Estimate      Std. Error    z value     Pr(>|z|)
Rho_Wy         0.5043347     0.0088410     57.045      < 2.2e-16
(Intercept)    4.1488234     0.0869285     47.727      < 2.2e-16
age            -0.7461782    0.0148762     -50.159     < 2.2e-16
log(lotsize)   0.1260527     0.0041763     30.183      < 2.2e-16
rooms          0.0953724     0.0018920     50.409      < 2.2e-16
Lambda: 0.17179
Residual variance (sigma squared): 0.11684, (sigma: 0.34182)
GM argmin sigma squared: 0.11835
Number of observations: 25357
Number of parameters estimated: 7
```

4 As explained in Chapter 5, we need to set initial parameters. By default (or missing), gstsls function use values approximated from the initial two-stage least squares model as the autocorrelation coefficient corrected for spatial weights and the model sigma squared as initial values.

Fig. 7.6.1 shows the violin plot of residuals of the three models as follows:

```
x <- data.frame(
      resids = c(rep("SLM", length(model.STSLS$residuals)),
             rep("SEM", length(model.SEM$residuals)),
             rep("SAC", length(model.GSTSLS$residuals))),
            model   =   c(model.STSLS$residuals,   model.SEM$residuals,
model.GSTSLS$residuals)
)
ggplot(x, aes(x = resids, y = model))+
  geom_violin()
```

The results of SEM seem not to be normally distributed and zero-mean. In these models for the Lucas data, the results suggest the spatial lag term included in the SLM and SAC would improve the model accuracy.

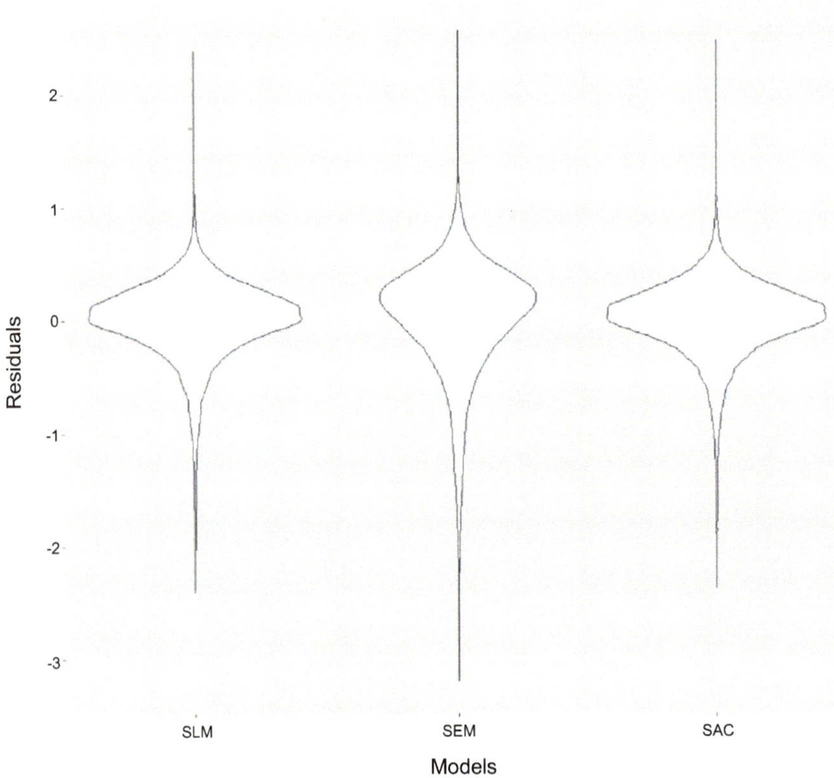

Figure 7.6.1 Violin plots on residuals of SLM (left), SEM (middle), and SAC (right).

7.6.3 Maximum likelihood–based methods

7.6.3.1 Approximation of log of Jacobian

The maximum likelihood (ML) estimation of SLM (spatial Durbin model with `Durbin = TRUE`) and SEM are possible with the functions `lagsarlm` and `errorsarlm`, respectively. Ord (1975)'s approximation or log-determinant term is possible with the option `method = "eigen"`. Note that other schemas such as `"Chebyshev"` and `"MC"` (Monte Carlo approximation) can easily be used by replacing the `"eigen"` of `method`.

```
model.SLM.ML <- lagsarlm (formula=form, data=house_sf, listw=house.w, method="eigen")
model.SEM.ML <- errorsarlm (formula=form, data=house_sf, listw=house.w, method="eigen")
## Note: this functions are computationally heavy for over 10 thousand size data.
```

Also, the Cholesky decomposition method proposed by Suesse (2018) can be implemented in the following manner. Note that R code is available at

```
source("https://www.uow.edu.au/~tsuesse/R/Measurement%20Error/SAR.M.sparse.r")
```

Suesse's (2018) approach is based on the (restricted) ML estimation method and considers measurement error. The SLM and SEM with measurement errors can be estimated as

```
## SAR(SLM) and SEM with mesurement error_ML/REML (Suesse, 2017)
hmm0    <-    model.matrix(form, data = house)
Y       <-    log(house$price)
hlw     <-    nb2listw(house.nb) #
hsn     <-    listw2sn(hlw)
W       <-    as(hlw, "CsparseMatrix")
X       <-    hmm0
n       <-    dim(X)[1]
rownames(W)<-colnames(W)  <-    1:n
rownames(X)<-1:n
W       <-    as(W, "CsparseMatrix")
```

To enable fast computation, Suesse uses the `listw2sn` function, making the listw object to spatial neighbor sparse representation. And then, the `as (object, "CsparseMatrix")` function makes a compressed sparse matrix object.

```
model    <-    "SAR" ## or "SARerr"
resREML <-     try(AR.error(Y,W,X,model=model,
                 se=TRUE, # se: TRUE or FALSE, if FALSE no standard errors
                 REML=FALSE, # REML: TRUE or FALSE, if FALSE then ML
                 rho0=0.5, # rho0 starting value
                 omega.eps0=NULL,  #  omega.eps0:starting value of sigma2.eps
                 omega.Y0=NULL)) # alternatively omega.Y0: starting value of sigma2.y

# Estimation results
beta.hat          <-    resREML$beta           # beta
beta.hat.se       <-    resREML$beta.se        # s.e. of beta
rho.hat           <-    resREML$rho            # rho
rho.hat.se        <-    resREML$rho.se         # s.e. of rho
sigma2.y.hat      <-    resREML$omega.Y        # SAR model variance
sigma2.y.hat.se   <-    resREML$omega.Y.se     # s.e. of SAR model variance
sigma2.eps.hat    <-    resREML$omega.eps      # measurement error variance
omega.eps.hat.se  <-    resREML$omega.eps.se # s.e. of measurement error variance
L                 <-    resREML$L              # log-likelihood

### estimation result
                  Estimate          Std. Error
(intercept)       1.0588            0.0122
age               -0.2145           0.0034
log(lotsize)      0.0243            0.0012
rooms             0.0302            0.0007
rho: 0.8777;      Std. Error: 0.0001
sigma^2: 0.0120;  Std. Error: 0.0002
Measurement error variance: 0.0752; Std. Error: 0.0008
Loglik:       -9649.301
```

7.6.3.2 Matrix exponential spatial specification approach

The computational problems emerging when analyzing very large datasets derive from the inversion of the term $(\mathbf{I} - \rho\mathbf{W})^{-1}$ (see Chapter 5). The specification of the matrix $\mathbf{S} = (\mathbf{I} - \rho\mathbf{W})^{-1}$ in different ways has an effect on the variance-covariance matrix and produces the specification of different spatial econometric models. LeSage and Pace (2007) proposed the following matrix exponential specification for the matrix $\mathbf{S}$:

$$\mathbf{S} = \exp(\alpha\mathbf{W}) = \sum_{t=0}^{\infty} \frac{\alpha^t \mathbf{W}^t}{t!}$$

By introducing the power series expansion, we can take computational advantages. In particular, we can write the inverse of the matrix **S** by $\mathbf{S}^{-1} = \exp(-\alpha\mathbf{W})$; that is, the matrix $\boldsymbol{S}$ can be calculated in a very simple manner. Details are provided in Chapter 5, as well as Chiu et al. (1996), LeSage and Pace (2007), Arbia (2014), and so on.

In R, the matrix exponential spatial specification (MESS) for SLM is implemented in the `lagmess` function of the **spatialreg** package. The model setting is coherent to the models explained in Subsection 7.5.1.

```
## SLM_MESS
model.MESS <- lagmess(formula=form, data=house_sf, listw=house.w)
summary(model.MESS)

Matrix exponential spatial lag model:
Call:
lagmess(formula = form, data = house_sf, listw = house.w)
Residuals:
       Min       1Q        Median    3Q        Max
       -2.5269   -0.1521   0.0386    0.2152    2.430175
Coefficients:
              Estimate     Std. Error   t value    Pr(>|t|)
(Intercept)   4.0631328    0.0326904    124.291    < 2.2e-16
age           -0.7479991   0.0093191    -80.265    < 2.2e-16
log(lotsize)  0.1146137    0.0033438    34.276     < 2.2e-16
rooms         0.0938114    0.0018133    51.735     < 2.2e-16
Residual standard error: 0.36448 on 25353 degrees of freedom
Multiple R-squared:  0.42488,     Adjusted R-squared:  0.42481
F-statistic: 6243.3 on 3 and 25353 DF,  p-value: < 2.22e-16
Alpha: -0.73895, standard error: 0.0065904
    z-value: -112.12, p-value: < 2.22e-16
LR test value: 13865, p-value: < 2.22e-16
Implied rho: 0.5223858
```

Comparing the estimation result of MESS with S2SLS for SLM, the SLM is more accurate from the range of `residuals` of the results, since the MESS uses approximation of $(\boldsymbol{I} - \rho\boldsymbol{W})^{-1}$.

7.7 Quantitative geography

7.7.1 Geographically weighted regression-based approaches

The GWmodel package provides a wide variety of R functions for geographically weighted regression (GWR) and other geographically weighted (GW) modeling, such as GW principal component analysis and GW discriminate analysis. While GWR can be slow for large samples in the R environment, Lu et al. (2014) embedded the main code into C++ code via the Rcpp package. Thus the GWmodel packages allow estimating GWR large samples.

This section illustrates an implementation of GWR and multiscale geographically weighted regression (MGWR) using 2000 samples randomly selected from the Lucas housing data using the following code:

```
library(GWmodel); library(spData)
data(house)
dat    <- house
dat@data$ln_price <- log(dat@data$price)        # Logged housing price
n      <-dim(dat)[1]
dat    <- dat[ sample(n,2000),]
```

We estimate GWR models explaining logged housing prices using lot size (lotsize) and age of individual residences. The bandwidth selection for GWR with the Gaussian kernel is implemented as follows:

```
dMat   <- gw.dist(dp.locat=coordinates(dat))
bw     <- bw.gwr(ln_price~lotsize+age, data=dat, kernel = "gaussian", approach = "CV",
                 adaptive = FALSE, dMat=dMat)
```

where `gw.dist` constructs a distance matrix in which `coordinates(dat)` extracts spatial coordinates from the database. The `bw.gwr` function estimates the bandwidth parameter. By default, the leave-one-out cross validation is used (`approach = "CV"`); it is replaced with a corrected Akaike's information criterion minimization-based bandwidth optimization by specifying `approach = "AIC"`. The Gaussian kernel is used by specifying `kernel = "gaussian"` that can be replaced with "`exponential`" for the exponential kernel, "`bisquare`" for the bisquare kernel, "`tricube`" for the tricube kernel, and "`boxcar`" for the boxcar kernel. The bandwidth is given by a fixed distance when `adaptive = FALSE` (default). If `adaptive = TRUE`, the bandwidth is given by an adaptive bandwidth.

After the bandwidth selection, the optimized bandwidth `bw`, which equals 1602.502 in our case, is used to estimate the GWR model using the `gwr.basic` function. The command is as follows:

```
res   <-  gwr.basic(ln_price~lotsize+age, data=dat, bw=bw, kernel = "gaussian")
```

The GWR modeling including the bandwidth selection takes 20.2 s. Even for 5000 samples it takes 237.8 s (91.47 s for the bandwidth selection and 146.3 s for the model estimation).

The estimated spatially varying coefficients (SVCs) and their diagnostic statistics are summarized in `res$SDF`. The first three rows are as

```
> res$SDF[1:3,]
         coordinates       Intercept    lotsize         age           y           yhat
(   485585, 206636.3)    11.71385    8.912457e-07   -0.7222761   11.69525   11.78794
(505491.6, 213952.4)     11.35312    2.223057e-05   -0.4228965   11.05089   11.83266
(515744.4, 219512.4)     11.15147    3.916140e-05   -1.1901087   10.31228   10.38390

  residual      CV_Score     Stud_residual  Intercept_SE   lotsize_SE     age_SE
  -0.09269550   -0.12615544  -0.2862176     0.39481794     1.464349e-06   0.5974685
  -0.78176645   -0.86377088  -2.1095957     0.09495451     4.659749e-06   0.1631915
  -0.07162278   -0.07234353  -0.1820175     0.11791091     5.956935e-06   0.1264124

  Intercept_TV   lotsize_TV   age_TV      Local_R2
  29.66899       0.6086294    -1.208894   0.9823016
  119.56375      4.7707644    -2.591413   0.7190586
  94.57542       6.5740863    -9.414497   0.7629379
```

where `Intercept, lotsize, age` are estimated SVCs, `Intercept_SE, lotsize_SE, age_SE` are their standard errors, and `Intercept_TV, lotsize_TV, age_TV` are their t-values.

Fig. 7.7.1 plots the estimated SVCs. The spatially varying intercept suggests high price in the suburban area. This figure also suggests strong impact of building lot size and age in the center of the study area. The estimated bandwidth is 1613.9.

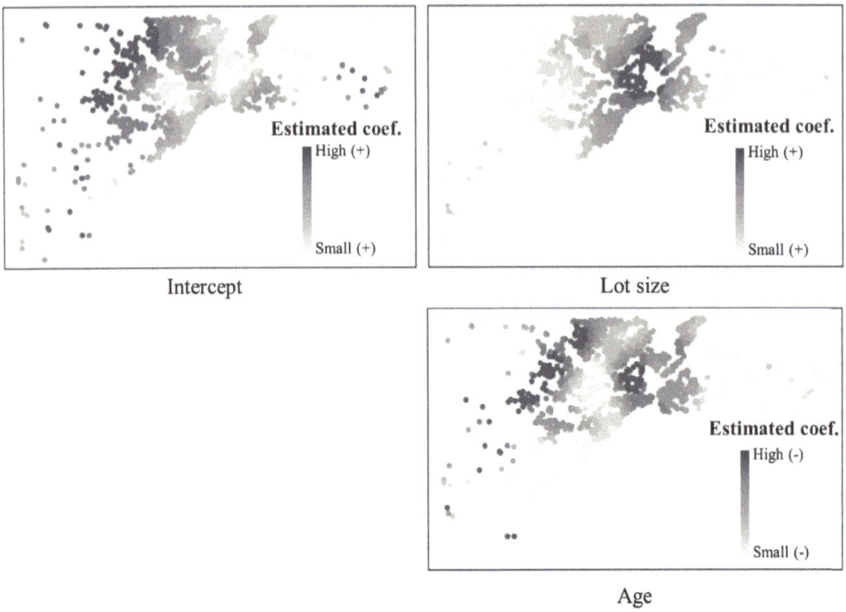

Figure 7.7.1 Estimated spatially varying coefficients (GWR).

The MGWR, which estimates the bandwidth parameter for each coefficient, can also be implemented using the GWmodel package as follows:

```
bws0  <- mean(dMat[,1])
res2  <- gwr.multiscale(ln_price~lotsize+age, data=dat, kernel="gaussian",max.iterations=20,
                        bws0=rep(bws0, bws0, bws0), dMats=list(dMat, dMat, dMat))
```

In this illustration, we assume the maximum of 20 iterations (`max.iterations = 20`) for the backfitting procedure (see Chapter 6). The computational time is 2936 s for the iterations. The estimated bandwidths are 322.8 (intercept), 1048.7 (lotsize), and 485.4 (age), suggesting a large-scale spatial effect from lot size and small-scale effects from age (and intercept). The estimated coefficients are plotted in Fig. 7.7.2. Intercept and the coefficients on age have considerably small-scale spatial variations compared to the basic GWR. The result confirms the importance of considering scales for individual coefficients.

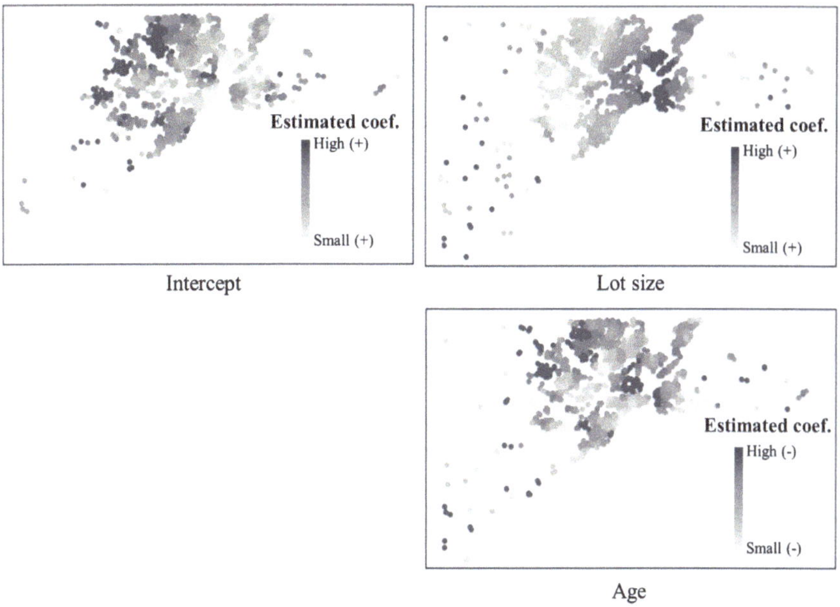

Figure 7.7.2 Estimated spatially varying coefficients (MGWR).

The estimated SVCs are summarized in `res2$SDF` just like the basic GWR:

```
res2$SDF[1:3,]
      coordinates          Intercept  lotsize         age          yhat      residual
 ( 485585, 206636.3 )  11.782686  1.157227e-06  -3.93736204  11.39897  0.2962809
 (505491.6, 213952.4)  11.506962  8.416478e-07  -0.73781335  11.25083  -0.1999426
 (515744.4, 219512.4)  9.974508   1.103923e-04  0.03599578   10.42172  -0.1094349
```

Unlike the output from the `gwr.basic` function, estimation of the standard errors and t-values for the SVCs are not implemented.

Unfortunately, GWR and MGWR are computationally inefficient, and difficult to handle large samples. Outside R, Oshan et al. (2018) implemented a fast GWR algorithm of Li et al. (2019) that is available for millions of samples. Although it implements the basic GWR quite computationally efficiently, MGWR is still slow even if we use this package. One useful way to estimate multiscale SVCs is using the resf_vc function in the spmoran package, which is introduced in the next section.

7.7.2 Spatial filtering approaches

Spatial filtering is another approach in quantitative geography. While the classical eigenvector spatial filtering (ESF) is among popular specifications, its estimation involves two heavy computations: (1) eigen-decomposition of a spatial connectivity matrix, and (2) stepwise eigenvector selection (see Chapter 6). Besides, it has often alluded that extended ESF modeling becomes unstable (e.g., SVC modeling; see Oshan and Fotheringham, 2018).

The spmoran package overcomes these limitations by applying the Nystrom approximation, which is an eigen-approximation technique, for (1) fast eigen-decomposition whereas (2) the stepwise selection step is replaced with a fast shrinkage estimation. This package implements the basic ESF and random-effects ESF (RE-ESF), which is a stabilized ESF.

The spmoran package implements ESF, RE-ESF, and its extension for SVC modeling (Murakami et al., 2017, 2019a), a spatial unconditional quantile regression modeling (Murakami and Seya, 2017), and spatial econometric modeling. Among them, this section illustrates implementation of the basic RE-ESF and the SVC modeling approach.

In this section, we use all the samples in the Lucas housing dataset. Dependent variables (y), explanatory variables (x), and spatial coordinates (coords) are prepared as follows:

```
library(spmoran); library(spData)
data(house)
dat    <- house
y      <- log(dat@data$price)
x      <- dat@data[, c("lotsize", "age")]
coords <- coordinates(dat)
```

The exact Moran eigenvectors are extracted using the meigen function as follows.

```
### Note: this will not work for the large samples
meig     <- meigen(coords, model = "exp", threshold = 0 )
```

By default with `model = "exp"`, the exponential function is used to defined spatial connectivity. Alternatively, the spherical function (`model = "sph"`) or the Gaussian model (`model = "gau"`) is available (see Eq. (6.2.3)−(6.2.6)). Another argument threshold specifies the `threshold` for the eigenvalues being considered. The default of `threshold = 0`, which is the standard setting in ecology, extracts all the eigenvectors. These eigenvectors are the full basis functions explaining positive spatial dependence. `threshold = 0.25` is another setting widely used in regional science; in this case, eigenvectors whose eigenvalues are greater than one-fourth of the first eigenvalue is considered.

Unfortunately, its computational complexity is of order N^3. It is prohibitable for large samples. Instead, the meigen_f function approximates the eigenvectors using the Nystrom approximation. It is implemented as follows:

```
meigf <- meigen_f(coords, model="exp")
```

The meigen_f extracts the first 200 eigenvectors by default. The number of eigenvectors can be reduced by specifying an argument "`enum`" by a value smaller than 200 (see later).

Here, we compared the exact and approximate eigenvectors extracted from 5000 spatial coordinates generated from two independent standard normal distributions. Computational times of the meigen function, and the meigen_f function with enum = 200, 100, and 50, are as follows. This result confirms that the meigen_f function considerably reduces the computational time.

```
-----------------CP time (without approximation) -----------------
> system.time( meig_test     <- meigen( coords = coords_test ) )
   user  system  elapsed
 242.28    1.44   243.79

-----------------CP time (with approximation) ----------------------
> system.time( meig_test200 <- meigen_f( coords = coords_test )
   user  system  elapsed
   0.37    0.00     0.38
> system.time( meig_test100 <- meigen_f( coords = coords_test, enum = 100 ) )

   user  system  elapsed
   0.15    0.00     0.16
> system.time( meig_test50  <- meigen_f( coords = coords_test, enum = 50 ) )
   user  system  elapsed
   0.08    0.00     0.08
```

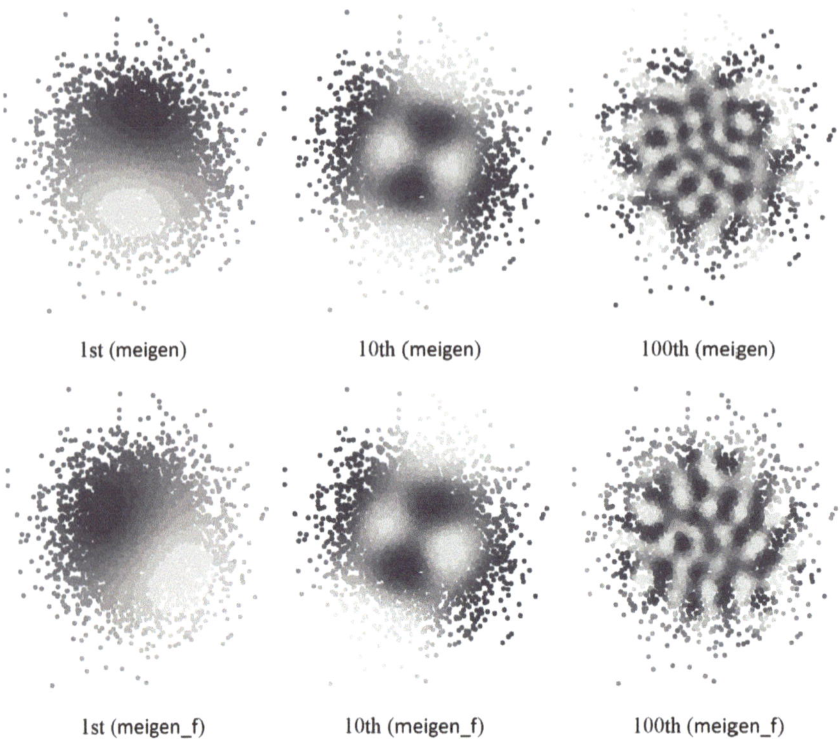

Figure 7.7.3 The 1st, 10th, and 100th eigenvectors extracted from meigen and meigen_f.

Fig. 7.7.3 plots the 1st, 10th, and 100th eigenvectors extracted from the meigen and meigen_f functions, respectively. It is important to note that, while approximated and exact eigenvectors can have different map patterns, respectively, both of them describe patterns in similar spatial scales. In other words, in both cases, 1st eigenvectors describe global map patterns, 10th medium-scale patterns, and 100th local patterns.

The approximate eigenvectors are available to both the basic ESF and RE-ESF models, which eliminate residual spatial dependence (just like the spatial error model). The ESF model is implemented as

```
res1  <- esf( y=y, x=x, meig=meigf, fn = "all")
```

Given `fn = "all"` as above, all the eigenvectors are considered without the stepwise selection. This setting is acceptable for large samples (see Murakami and Griffith, 2018; Murakami and Griffith, 2019) while `fn = "r2"` (default) performs the adjusted R^2 maximization-based eigenvector selection, which has widely been used (Tiefelsdorf and Griffith, 2007). Akaike's information criterion (AIC)-maximization-based eigenvector selection (`fn = "aic"`) and Bayesian information criterion (BIC)-based selection (`fn = "bic"`) are other options.

The estimated coefficients and error statistics are returned as follows:

```
res1$b
             Estimate       SE            t_value      p_value
 (Intercept) 1.143665e+01   8.186584e-03  1396.99944   0.000000e+00
 lotsize     1.969645e-06   1.066775e-07  18.46355     1.283275e-75
 age        -8.249162e-01   1.448967e-02  -56.93134    0.000000e+00

res1$e
 stat
 resid_SE     3.704724e-01
 adjR2        7.641966e-01
 logLik      -1.069922e+04
 AIC          2.180643e+04
 BIC          2.346716e+04
```

where the error statistics include the residual standard error (resid_SE), the adjusted R^2, the log-likelihood (logLik), AIC, and BIC.

On the other hand, the basic RE-ESF is estimated as follows.

```
res2  <- resf( y=y, x=x, meig=meigf, method ="reml")
```

This function is by default computationally efficient. Actually, it took only 4.01 s for the 25,357 housing dataset while the `esf` function with `fn = "all"` took 2.75 s. By default, the estimation is done by a restricted likelihood maximization (`method = "reml"`) that can be replaced with an ML maximization by specifying `method = "ml"`. Note that they perform Type II likelihood (or h-likelihood) maximizations, which are identical to empirical Bayes maximum a posteriori estimation.

The estimated coefficients and error statistics are extracted just like the `esf` function as follows:

```
res2$b
              Estimate        SE              t_value      p_value
(Intercept)  1.143858e+01   8.140265e-03   1405.18500     0
lotsize      1.975890e-06   1.061653e-07   18.61144       0
age         -8.286599e-01   1.440433e-02   -57.52851      0

res2$e
 stat
 resid_SE      3.690478e-01
 adjR2(cond)   7.659605e-01
 rlogLik      -1.125548e+04
 AIC           2.252496e+04
 BIC           2.258195e+04
```

In the outputs, `adjR2(cond)` is the conditional adjusted R^2 value and `rlogLik` is the restricted log-likelihood. As expected, estimated coefficients and error statistics obtained from the two specifications are quite similar.

Table 7.7.1 compares coefficients estimated using the `esf` and `resf` functions to those estimated by the basic linear model (LM). This table shows that coefficients and their t-values estimated from ESF and RE-ESF are quite different from those estimated from LM. This result highlights the importance of considering spatial dependence in a regression analysis. Consideration of spatial dependence leads to a significant improvement of model accuracy as is conceivable from the residual standard errors (SEs) in the table.

RE-ESF, which is identical to a rank-reduced GP (see Murakami and Griffith, 2015), is applicable for spatial interpolation. Following Section 7.5 illustrating spatial prediction using geostatistical approaches, this section randomly selects 10,000 samples, and they are considered as observations. Then the remaining samples are predicted. The code for the prediction is as

```
meig0  <- meigen0( meig= meigf, coords0=coords0 )
pred   <- predict0( mod=res2, meig0=meig0, y=y, x0= x0 )
```

where coords0 and x0 are spatial coordinates and explanatory variables at the prediction sites.

Table 7.7.1 Regression coefficients estimated from the LM, ESF, and RE-EFS models.

	LM			ESF			RE-ESF		
	Estimates	**t-value**		**Estimates**	**t-value**		**Estimates**	**t-value**	
Constant	12.0	1520	***	11.4	1397	***	11.4	1405	***
Lot size	3.16×10^{-6}	26.5	***	1.97×10^{-6}	18.5	***	1.98×10^{-6}	18.6	***
Age	−1.85	−149	***	-8.25×10^{-1}	−56.9	***	-8.29×10^{-1}	−57.5	***
Residuals SE	0.540			0.370			0.369		

*** and ** represent statistical significance at the 1% and 5% levels, respectively. *LM*, linear regression model; *ESF*, eigenvector spatial filtering; *RE-ESF*, random-effects ESF; *SE*, standard error.

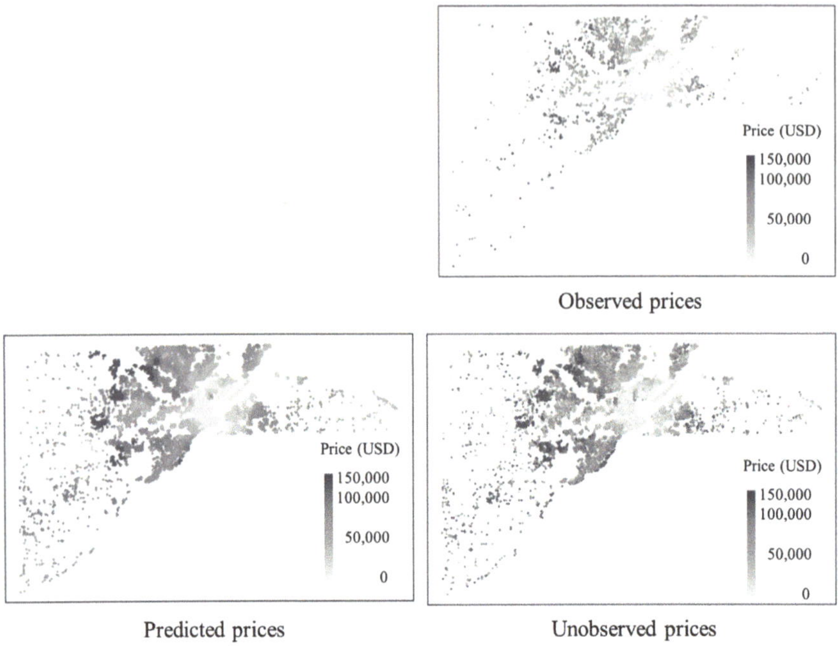

Figure 7.7.4 Spatial prediction result (RE-ESF).

The spatial prediction result is shown in Fig. 7.7.4. The result is quite similar to the prediction result obtained from geostatistical models (see Section 7.4). The parameter estimation and interpolation took only 3.1 s, which is faster than all the fast geostatistical approximations used in Section 7.5. The RMSE for the predicted value becomes 0.395, which is compatible to these geostatistical approaches. RE-ESF would be a useful alternative for spatial interpolation.

The computational efficiency of the RE-ESF holds even if it is extended to SVC modeling, spatial quantile regression modeling, or a spatial econometric modeling. In the case of SVC modeling, the resf_vc function estimates SVCs in which their spatial scales can be different from each other. In other words, the RE-ESF-based approach is an alternative of the MGWR approach. It is implemented as

```
res3   <- resf_vc( y=y, x=x, meig=meigf)
```

The model estimation took only 35.7 s whereas the MGWR is not feasible because of the computational cost. See Murakami et al. (2019a) and Murakami et al. (2019b) for a comparison with MGWR. Unlike `gwr.multiscale` function in the GWmodel package, this function returns not just the SVC estimates (`res3$b_vc`), but also their t-values (`res3$t_vc`) and p-values (`res3$p_vc`). The first five elements of these three are returned as follows:

```
res3$b_vc[1:5,]              ###### Estimated SVCs
   (Intercept)     lotsize          age
1    11.49473 3.047056e-06 -0.2928574
2    11.49732 2.950317e-06 -0.2891090
3    11.50187 2.781844e-06 -0.2825014
4    11.52037 2.034577e-06 -0.2596299
5    11.53843 1.349793e-06 -0.2356380

res3$t_vc[1:5,]              ###### t-values
   (Intercept)  lotsize         age
1    160.8401   7.332346   -3.421325
2    157.6194   7.034060   -3.311386
3    152.3331   6.520565   -3.129204
4    134.2076   4.383220   -2.531326
5    125.4113   2.798886   -2.149436

res3$p_vc[1:5,]              ###### p-values
  (Intercept)  lotsize      age
1        0     2.331468e-13 0.0006241681
2        0     2.057909e-12 0.0009296698
3        0     7.138445e-11 0.0017548263
4        0     1.174164e-05 0.0113693060
5        0     5.131861e-03 0.0316094754
```

The error statistics, which suggest improvement of model accuracy relative to the basic ESF and RE-ESF models, are displayed by the following command:

```
res3$e
  stat
  resid_SE           0.3380231
  adjR2(cond)        0.8036332
  rlogLik        -9584.6346056
  AIC            19189.2692111
  BIC            19270.6773122
```

Finally, Fig 7.7.5 plots the estimated coefficients. The result has similar tendency to the coefficients estimated from GWR and MGWR.

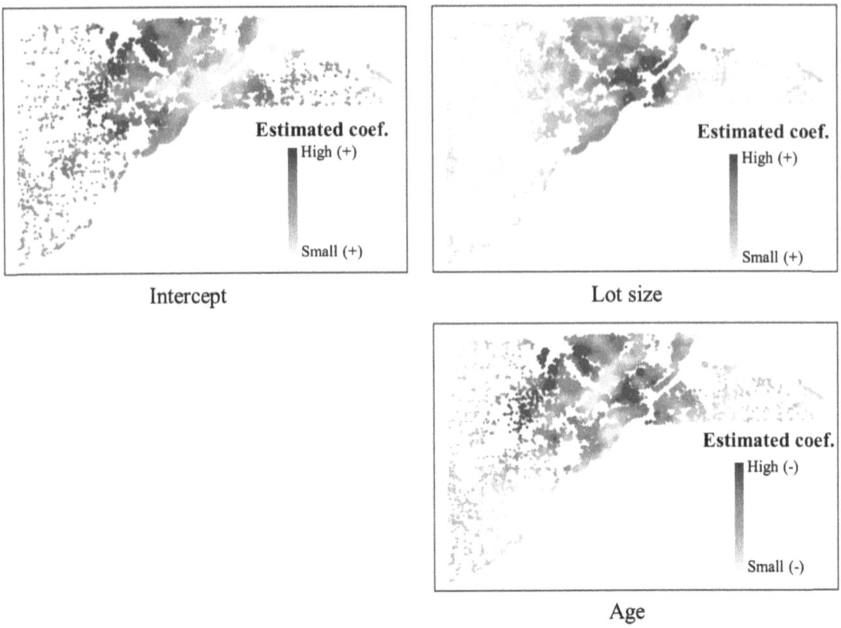

Figure 7.7.5 Estimated spatially varying coefficients (RE-ESF).

References

Arbia, G., 2014. A Primer for Spatial Econometrics: With Applications in R. Palgrave Mcmilan.

Bivand, R., 2019. Creating Neighbours. https://cran.r-project.org/web/packages/spdep/vignettes/nb.pdf.

Bivand, R., Wong, D.W., 2018. Comparing implementations of global and local indicators of spatial association. Test 27, 716–748.

Bivand, R., Pebesma, E.J., Gomez-Rubio, V., 2013. Applied Spatial Data Analysis with R. Springer.

Chiu, T.Y., Leonard, T., Tsui, K.W., 1996. The matrix-logarithmic covariance model. Journal of the American Statistical Association 91 (433), 198–210.

Cressie, N.A., 1993. Statistics for spatial data. Wiley, New York.

Filzmoser, P., Hron, K., Templ, M., 2018. Analyzing compositional data using R. In: Applied Compositional Data Analysis. Springer.

Gramacy, R.B., 2016. laGP: large-scale spatial modeling via local approximate Gaussian processes in R. Journal of Statistical Software 72 (1), 1–46.

Kelejian, H.H., Prucha, I.R., 1998. A generalized spatial two-stage least squares procedure for estimating a spatial autoregressive model with autoregressive disturbances. The Journal of Real Estate Finance and Economics 17 (1), 99–121.

LeSage, J.P., Pace, R.K., 2007. A matrix exponential spatial specification. Journal of Econometrics 140 (1), 190–214.

Li, Z., Fotheringham, A.S., Li, W., Oshan, T., 2019. Fast Geographically Weighted Regression (FastGWR): a scalable algorithm to investigate spatial process heterogeneity in millions of observations. International Journal of Geographical Information Science 33 (1), 155–175.

Lovelace, R., Nowosad, J., Muenchow, J., 2019. Geocomputation with R. CRC Press.
Lu, B., Harris, P., Charlton, M., Brunsdon, C., 2014. The GWmodel R package: further topics for exploring spatial heterogeneity using geographically weighted models. Geo-Spatial Information Science 17 (2), 85–101.
Murakami, D., Griffith, D.A., 2015. Random effects specifications in eigenvector spatial filtering: a simulation study. Journal of Geographical Systems 17 (4), 311–331.
Murakami, D., Griffith, D.A., 2018. Eigenvector spatial filtering for large data sets: fixed and random effects approaches. Geographical Analysis 51 (1), 23–49.
Murakami, D., Griffith, D.A., 2019. Spatially varying coefficient modeling for large datasets: Eliminating N from spatial regressions. Spatial Statistics 30, 39–64.
Murakami, D., Seya, H., 2017. Spatially filtered unconditional quantile regression. Environmetrics. https://doi.org/10.1002/env.2556.
Murakami, D., Yoshida, T., Seya, H., Griffith, D.A., Yamagata, Y., 2017. A Moran coefficient-based mixed effects approach to investigate spatially varying relationships. Spatial Statistics 19, 68–89.
Murakami, D., Lu, B., Harris, P., Brunsdon, C., Charlton, M., Nakaya, T., Griffith, D.A., 2019a. The importance of scale in spatially varying coefficient modeling. Annals of the Association of American Geographers 109 (1), 50–70.
Murakami, D., Tsutsumida, N., Yoshida, T., Nakaya, T., Lu, B., 2019b. Scalable GWR: A linear-time algorithm for large-scale geographically weighted regression with polynomial kernels. arXiv preprint arXiv:1905.00266.
Ord, J.K., 1975. Estimation methods for models of spatial interaction. Journal of the American Statistical Association 70, 120–126.
Ord, J.K., Getis, A., 2012. Local spatial heteroscedasticity (LOSH). The Annals of Regional Science 48 (2), 529–539.
Oshan, T., Fotheringham, A.S., 2018. A comparison of spatially varying regression coefficient estimates using geographically weighted and spatial–filter–based techniques. Geographical Analysis 50 (1), 53–75.
Oshan, T., Li, Z., Kang, W., Wolf, L., Fotheringham, A.S., 2018. mgwr: a Python implementation of multiscale geographically weighted regression for investigating process spatial heterogeneity and scale. OSF preprints. https://doi.org/10.31219/osf.io/bphw9.
Suesse, T., 2018. Estimation of spatial autoregressive models with measurement error for large data sets. Computational Statistics 33 (4), 1627–1648. https://doi.org/10.1007/s00180-017-0774-7.
Tiefelsdorf, M., Griffith, D.A., 2007. Semiparametric filtering of spatial autocorrelation: the eigenvector approach. Environment and Planning 39 (5), 1193–1221.
Xu, M., Mei, C.L., Yan, N., 2014. A note on the null distribution of the local spatial heteroscedasticity (LOSH) statistic. The Annals of Regional Science 52 (3), 697–710.

PART THREE

Applications

CHAPTER EIGHT

Spatial heat-wave assessments using geotagged Twitter data

Daisuke Murakami[1], Yoshiki Yamagata[2]
[1]The Institute of Statistical Mathematics, Tachikawa, Tokyo, Japan
[2]Center for Global Environmental Research, National Institute for Environmental Studies, Tsukuba, Ibaraki, Japan

Contents

8.1 Introduction

As an increasing number of geospatial data are available, analysis combining data from multiple sources is becoming more and more important. How to combine low-quality sensor data (e.g., remotely sensed data, mobile GNSS data, geotagged Twitter data) with conventional high-quality data (e.g., census data, officially monitored temperature data) is an especially important issue. A large number of studies have addressed this issue under keywords including change of support problem (COSP; e.g., Gotway and Young, 2002), which is a problem to change the support (e.g., aggregation unit, sample site) of a given spatial data to different supports; data fusion (e.g., Hilker et al., 2009), which combines data from multiple sources (e.g., for spatial interpolation and data assimilation; e.g., Evensen, 2009), which balance model and observations for accurate spatial and temporal prediction.

Spatial Analysis using Big Data
ISBN: 978-0-12-813127-5
https://doi.org/10.1016/B978-0-12-813127-5.00008-4

These topics have actively been studied in geostatistics. In fact, the basic Kriging can be viewed as a method for COSP converting data given at monitoring sites to data at prediction sites (see Gotway and Young, 2002). Kriging has been extended to area-to-point Kriging (Kyriakidis, 2004), which converts areal data into point or fine grid data (e.g., point-level disease risk estimation using multiple disease risk index), area-to-area Kriging (see Goovaerts, 2006) to convert areal data to another aggregation unit (e.g., conversion from municipality to grids), and others. Data fusion methods for spatial data, including co-Kriging and linear model of coregionalization, have also been developed in geostatistics, mainly for spatial prediction using multiple spatial data. More recently, Bayesian geostatistical modeling has actively been used to combine multiple spatial data with different supports though data assimilation (see Cressie and Wikle, 2011).

In relation to these advances, this section introduces the result of Murakami et al. (2016), which combined geotagged Twitter data and monitored temperature data for urban heat modeling to illustrate studies on COSP and data fusion.

As global warming progresses, it is increasingly important to monitor and manage urban heat. Actually, roughly 70,000 people were sacrificed by the major European heat wave in 2003; 56,000 people were sacrificed in the Russian heat wave in 2010; in India, 2300 people died from the 2015 heat wave; and so on. Even worse, Fuss et al. (2014) projected that global temperatures will increase 3.2–5.4 degrees by 2100 relative to 1850–1900 in a high-emission scenario (representative concentration pathways (RCP) 8.5). In this scenario, people in deadly heat areas, which is currently 30% of the global population, is projected to increase up to 74% in 2100 (Mora et al., 2017). Even in a low-emission scenario (RCP 2.6) the temperature increases 0.9–2.3 degrees, and the people in deadly heat areas are projected to increase by 18%.

Unfortunately, adaptation to heat-wave risk is not necessarily straightforward. This is partly because intensity of heat changes rapidly across space and time. For instance, crowded streets might be hotter than paths shaded by many trees. Temperatures might also change depending on materials of ambient buildings and roads, real-time population density, and so on. Accordingly, real-time and street-level temperature monitoring is needed to cope with heat-wave risks. Unfortunately, weather monitoring stations are very often sparsely distributed over space. For example, there are only eight monitoring stations in Tokyo, Japan. Although remote sensors such as MODIS (MODerate resolution Imaging Spectroradiometer) reveal ground surface temperatures with spatial resolution of 1 km, we cannot acquire real-time climate information from such satellite images 24 h a day. In the case of Japan, MODIS imagery is available only at four time points: approximately 11:30 a.m., 1:30 p.m., 8:30 p.m., and 10:30 p.m. each day. Thus street-level and (near) real-time heat monitoring is quite difficult to implement in terms of both cost and human resources.

Given the challenges faced by sparsity (in space) of ground-based weather and climate monitoring stations and the sparsity (in time) of remote sensing data to monitor in real-time intraurban climates, we seek an alternative approach that can supplement these accurate data sources with a less accurate—but prevalent in time and space—lower quality data source. Hence, to provide real-time district-level climate information for adaptive public urban management of extreme climate events, we need to explore a novel solution to supplement the missing data in regions far from monitoring sensor sites. We will demonstrate in this chapter how to begin to utilize Twitter (http://twitter.com) as an auxiliary information source to help to explain and extrapolate in an informed manner the local urban climate, especially, in this study, the local intraurban temperatures of Tokyo city. Twitter is a social media that allows users to post short messages (up to 140 characters in Japanese) called "tweets." Since a large amount of tweets are posted at arbitrary times and locations, we investigate whether they may provide real-time and high spatial resolution information relating to temperature and in particular extreme temperature events such as heat waves. It is unknown as to what extent such data would be useful in helping to resolve this issue of estimation in the presence of scarce data from real climate monitoring sensor networks. Therefore, we aim to study the utility of this additional Twitter data in forming an estimation of temperature in local urban environments to supplement the results obtained from sensor monitoring station recordings.

Application of tweets to such estimation problems is an active topic; for instance Thelwall et al. (2011) show that major events significantly change the sentiment of tweets (see also Go et al., 2009). Biever (2010) mapped happiness in the United States and showed that the eastern part is happier at noon. Bollen et al. (2011) utilized Twitter data to estimate public mood, and then applied the results to financial market analysis. Bermingham and Smeaton (2011), Sang and Bos (2012), and Gayo-Avello (2012) used tweets to predict election results. Ritterman et al. (2009) and Achrekar et al. (2011) employed tweets for pandemic predictions. Tweets have also been applied for event detection including crimes (e.g., Wang et al., 2012; Gerber, 2014), car accidents (Li et al., 2012), and earthquakes (Sakaki et al, 2010).

Most relevant to the study we undertake, An et al. (2014) demonstrated that tweets change depending on climate events; the information content in tweets and the topic of tweets is causally affected by climate conditions of the tweeter. They also show that tweets concerning climate change are increasing. However, most Twitter studies, including these studies just mentioned, ignore the spatial dimension and structure of the data, likely because of the difficulty of obtaining geotagged data on such tweet data records.

It is starting to be demonstrated that spatial data associated with tweets may also be significant and informative when utilizing Twitter data. For instance, some studies suggest significant influence of location on tweets; see, for example, Hahmann et al. (2014), who show that intensity of tweets about facilities (airports, bakeries, cinemas, etc.) change depending on the distance to the facility, while Li et al. (2012) demonstrate that tweets effectively reveal important information relating to local events such as car accidents and earthquakes. Tweets might also effectively describe local urban climate; it is this premise that we aim to investigate here.

As a first step to utilizing tweets in urban climate monitoring, we first analyze statistical relationships between tweets and temperatures of their corresponding locations at intraurban resolutions. In particular we focus on unpleasant hotness and heat waves as the target of our extreme climate study.

8.2 Geotagged Twitter data

We acquired data for tweets that included the following important attributes: text message; user id code; spatial coordinates; and time of tweeting. Such Twitter databases are known as geotagged tweets; the particular data set we utilized is commercially available and was collected by Nightley Inc. and purchased for this research project. The dataset consists of tweets posted in Tokyo between August 1 and August 31 in 2012. As a privacy policy, this data does not include all the recorded tweets posted but instead accounts for only approximately 1% of a randomly sampled set of the geotagged tweets.

Following An et al. (2014), we exclude retweets, which involve data that comes as a consequence of a reposting of someone else's tweet. The reason for this choice is that it is difficult to detect sentiment from a retweet. The resulting sample size we utilized involves 130,331 geotagged tweets, which are plotted in Fig. 8.2.1.

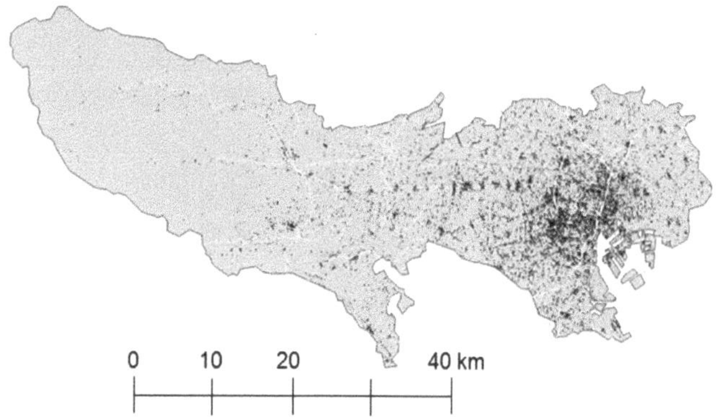

Figure 8.2.1 Spatial distribution of the tweeter data in Tokyo in August 2012. *From Murakami, D., Peters, G.W., Yamagata, Y., Matsui, T., 2016. "Participatory sensing data tweets for micro-urban real-time resiliency monitoring and risk management." IEEE Access 4 347–372.*

8.2.1 Extraction of heat-related tweets: heat-tweets

In this study we extracted tweets that specifically related to unpleasant heat using an approach known as keygram (http://kizasi.jp/labo/keygram/keygram.py/), which utilizes a Japanese synonyms dictionary to associate words (characters) to heat-related words. Table 8.2.1 summarizes synonyms of "heat" or "heat + uncomfortable", which were extracted through the use of the keygram.

In this chapter we propose a heat-related sentiment index, which is formulated as follows:

$$\text{Heat} - \text{tweet}_i = \begin{cases} \left|\text{Sent}_i^{\text{Heat}}\right| I_i^{\text{Heat}} & \text{if } \text{Sent}_i^{\text{Heat}} < 0 \\ 0 & \text{otherwise} \end{cases} \tag{8.2.1}$$

where $i \in \{1, \cdots, N\}$ is an index of tweet, I_i^{Heat} is the dummy indicating 1 if i-th tweet includes any synonyms of heat summarized in Table 8.2.1 and 0 otherwise, and $\text{Sent}_i^{\text{Heat}}$ is the strength score of the negative sentiment in the tweet (see Go et al., 2009). The index takes a value between 0 and 1, which approaches 1 if i-th tweet is a heat-related tweet with strong negative sentiment, 0 if the tweet is a heat-related tweet with weak negative sentiment, and 0 if it is not related to heat. Namely, Heat-tweet$_i$ estimates discomfort resultant from local urban heat.

Spatial distribution of tweets including synonyms of heat for each week in August 2012 are shown in Fig. 8.2.2. This figure suggests that heat-tweets

Table 8.2.1 Extracted synonyms of "heat" and/or "heat + uncomfortable".

Japanese	English	Japanese	English
あつい	Hot	熱い	Hot
猛暑	Heat wave	炎天下	Blazing sun
残暑	Lingering summer heat	熱中症	Heat illness
寝苦しい	Cannot sleep well	夏本番	Midsummer
照り	Reflected heat	湿度	Humid
ジメジメ	Damp	ムシムシ	Humid
汗	Sweat	蒸し	Muggy
体調管理	Health management	猛烈に	Furious
死ぬ	Dying	異常	Abnormal
不快	Discomfort	イヤ	Unpleasant
クソ	Damn	Orz	Discourage
辛い	Hard	大変	Hard
厳しい	Severe	苦手	Weak

From Murakami, D., Peters, G.W., Yamagata, Y., Matsui, T., 2016. "Participatory sensing data tweets for micro-urban real-time resiliency monitoring and risk management." IEEE Access 4 347–372.

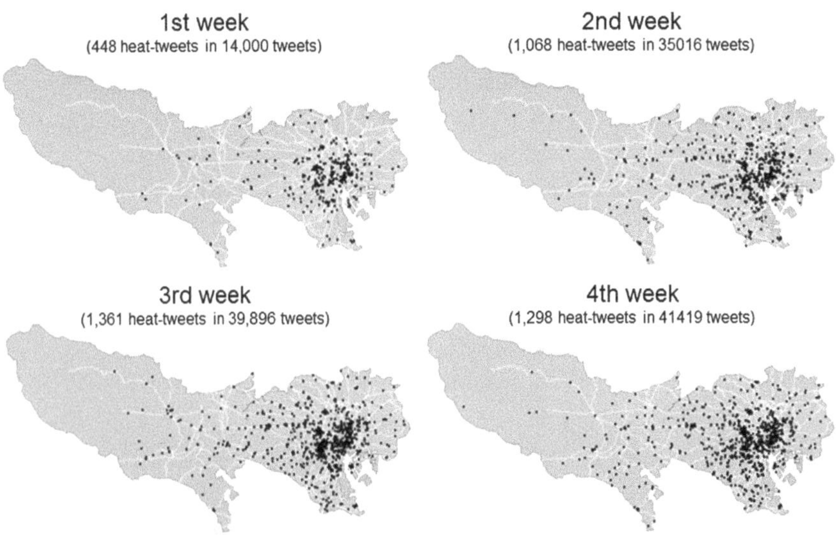

Figure 8.2.2 Spatial distribution of tweets including any synonyms of heat for each week in August 2012. *From Murakami, D., Peters, G.W., Yamagata, Y., Matsui, T., 2016. "Participatory sensing data tweets for micro-urban real-time resiliency monitoring and risk management." IEEE Access 4 347–372.*

increase in nearby station areas and that they increase in the second and third week, which correspond to our dataset to the periods of the middle of the summer in Japan, and decrease in the fourth week, which is the end of the summer.

8.3 Spatial field reconstruction of intraurban high-resolution temperature profiles using heat-tweet geotagged Twitter data

Based on the features observed in the geotagged heat-tweet data, we now undertake an application that utilizes this data to perform intraurban temperature profile analysis. Hence in this part of the analysis we utilize heat-tweet data as auxiliary information to capture local temperature interpolation and combine it with more accurate sparse weather/climate monitoring data as well as remote sensing MODIS data for Tokyo prefecture.

This will require us to first develop a spatiotemporal temperature interpolation model considering both monitored temperatures and heat-tweet data. Since heat-tweet data occur at any time and at any place, the idea is that they should provide greater spatial coverage for spatial temperature profile reconstruction in areas without any local sensor monitoring stations. Therefore, the aim of this section is to assess the utility of such geotagged heat-tweet data in informing such spatial temperature map reconstruction for intraurban scale analysis.

We use two data for the temperature modeling; one is the temperature data observed by Japan Meteorological Agency (JMA) and the other is the heat-tweet data. Section 8.3.1 explains the JMA data modeling and Section 8.3.2 explains the heat-tweet modeling.

8.3.1 Model for weather monitoring data

Both models that we develop in this section are based on a spatiotemporal Gaussian process (*GP*) in which we express the detrended temperature at the *i*-th location. The spatial coordinates and monitoring time are denoted $\mathbf{s}$ and t, respectively. The JMA temperature data monitored at location $\mathbf{s}$ at time t, which is denoted as $y(\mathbf{s}, t)$, is modeled as follows:

$$y(\mathbf{s}, t) = \mu + u(\mathbf{s}, t) + v(\mathbf{s}, t), \quad v(\mathbf{s}, t) \sim N\left(0, \sigma^2\right), \tag{8.3.1}$$

where μ is a constant, and σ^2 is a variance parameter. $u(\mathbf{s}, t)$ is a *GP*, which we express as follows:

$$u(\mathbf{s}, t) \sim N(0, C(\mathbf{h_s}, \mathbf{h}_t)), \tag{8.3.2}$$

where $C(\mathbf{h_s}, h_t) = E[u(\mathbf{s}, t)u(\mathbf{s} + \mathbf{h_s}, t + h_t)]$ is a covariance (kernel) function.

We specify the spatiotemporal covariance function using a covariance function $C(\mathbf{h_s})$ depending on geographic distance $\mathbf{h}_s$ and the covariance function $C(h_t)$ depending on the time-lag h_t. The resulting *GP* describes both spatial and temporal dependencies.

Here, we have to pay particular attention to the form of the kernel in terms of how space and time features may interact in the temperature profile reconstruction. In this analysis we adopt the product-sum model proposed in De Iaco et al. (2001), which provides a popular spatiotemporal modeling specification that is formulated as follows according to the spatiotemporal covariance function (see Chapter 4):

$$C(\mathbf{h_s}, h_t) = \sigma_s^2 C(\mathbf{h_s}) + \sigma_t^2 C(h_t) + \sigma_{st}^2 C(\mathbf{h_s})C(h_t), \tag{8.3.3}$$

where σ_s^2, σ_t^2, and σ_{st}^2 are unknown variance parameters. The spatial and temporal covariance functions are defined using exponential function as follows:

$$C(\mathbf{h_s}) = exp\left(-\frac{\mathbf{h_s}}{r_s}\right); \tag{8.3.4}$$

$$c(h_t) = exp\left(-\frac{h_t}{r_t}\right) \tag{8.3.5}$$

where r_s and r_t are range parameters.

8.3.2 Model for heat-tweet geotagged Twitter data

While the previous section introduced a model for the JMA temperature observations, this section introduces another model for heat-tweets.

Suppose that $y_{ht}(\mathbf{s}, t)$ is a dummy variable indicating 1 if the tweet at location $\mathbf{s}$ at time t is a heat-tweet, and 0 otherwise. We describe the probability of $y_{ht}(\mathbf{s}) = 1$ using Eqs. (8.3.6) and (8.3.7), which are defined as

$$\begin{aligned} p(y_{ht}(\mathbf{s}, t) = 1|u(\mathbf{s}, t)) &= \sum_{p=0}^{1} p\big(y_{ht}(\mathbf{s}, t) \\ &= 1\big|\widetilde{y}_{ht}(\mathbf{s}, t) = p\big)p(y_{ht}(\mathbf{s}, t) = p|u(\mathbf{s}, t)) \end{aligned} \tag{8.3.6}$$

$$\widetilde{y}_{ht}(\mathbf{s}, t) = \begin{cases} 1 & \text{if } u(\mathbf{s}, t) - \mu_{ht} \geq 0 \\ 0 & \text{otherwise} \end{cases} \tag{8.3.7}$$

where μ_{ht} is a predetermined threshold. $\widetilde{y}_{ht}(\mathbf{s}, t)$ is a dummy variable indicating 1 if $u(\mathbf{s}, t)$ exceeds the threshold temperature μ_{ht}, and 0 otherwise. Eq. (8.3.6) assumes that one tends to comment about heat when $u(\mathbf{s}, t)$ exceeds T.

8.3.3 Spatial prediction combining the weather monitoring data and heat-tweets

In this section we develop a *GP*-based approach to predict the temperature at an unobserved location $\mathbf{s}*$ by minimizing the mean squared error (see Chapter 4). The predictor is given in Chapter 4 as follows:

$$\begin{aligned}\widehat{y}(s*) &= E\left[u*\boldsymbol{u}\prime, u*\boldsymbol{u}_{ht}'\right]E^{-1}\begin{bmatrix}\boldsymbol{u}\boldsymbol{u}' & \boldsymbol{u}\boldsymbol{u}_{ht}' \\ \boldsymbol{u}_{ht}\boldsymbol{u}' & \boldsymbol{u}_{ht}\boldsymbol{u}_{ht}'\end{bmatrix}\begin{bmatrix}\boldsymbol{y}-\mu\mathbf{1} \\ \boldsymbol{y}_{ht}-\mu_{ht}\mathbf{1}\end{bmatrix} \\ &= \left[c_*', E\left[\boldsymbol{u}_{ht}'\right]\right]\begin{bmatrix}\sigma^2\mathbf{I}+\mathbf{C} & E\left[\boldsymbol{u}\boldsymbol{u}_{ht}'\right] \\ E\left[\boldsymbol{u}_{ht}\boldsymbol{u}'\right] & E\left[\boldsymbol{u}_{ht}\boldsymbol{u}_{ht}'\right]\end{bmatrix}^{-1}\begin{bmatrix}\boldsymbol{y}-\mu\mathbf{1} \\ \boldsymbol{y}_{ht}-\mu_{ht}\mathbf{1}\end{bmatrix}.\end{aligned} \tag{8.3.8}$$

Suppose $\boldsymbol{y}$ is a vector of JMA temperature observations, and $\boldsymbol{u}$ is the latent *GP* at the monitored location and time. $\boldsymbol{y}_{ht}$ and $\boldsymbol{u}_{ht}$ are similarly defined for the heat-tweets. $\mathbf{1}$ is a vector of ones, $\mathbf{I}$ is an identity matrix, $\boldsymbol{c}*$ is a column vector whose i-th element is $C(\mathbf{s}_i, \mathbf{s}*)$, and $\mathbf{C}$ is a matrix whose (i, j)-th element is $C(\mathbf{s}_i, \mathbf{s}_j)$. Fortunately, Eq. (8.3.8) can be evaluated analytically (see Murakami et al., 2016).

8.4 Application to temperature interpolation

8.4.1 Assumptions

This section applies the proposed approach to a spatiotemporal temperature interpolation in Tokyo in August 25, 2012. The data considered here is the temperature monitoring data at eight monitoring stations in Tokyo and the Twitter data. Because computational efficiency is crucially important in real-time risk management, which is our focus, we apply the basic function approach for the covariance function estimation (see Chapter 4).

The spatial prediction result considering only the hourly temperature monitoring data ($GP_{without}$) and *GP* considering both data and heat-tweets (GP_{with}) are shown in Fig. 8.4.1. Here, the results at 6 a.m., 12 p.m., and 6 p.m. are displayed. A significant difference between the with and without approaches are found at 12 p.m. The northern area is the hottest based on $GP_{without}$; the center of Tokyo area, where heat-tweets are densely distributed at around 12 p.m., is the hottest based on GP_{with}. Considering the severe heat island effect in the central Tokyo area, the latter result is intuitively more reasonable.

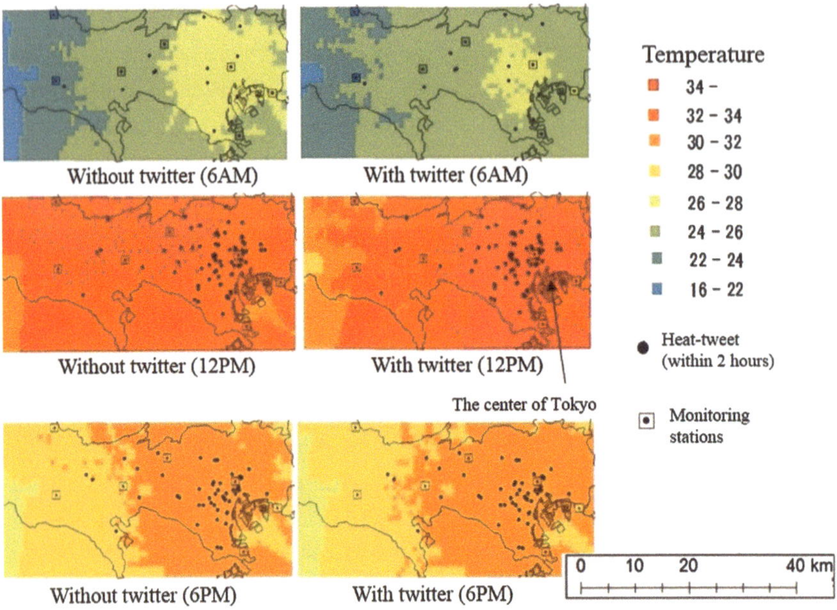

Figure 8.4.1 Interpolated temperatures at 6 a.m., 12 p.m., and 6 p.m. on August 25, 2012 using GP_{with} (right) and $GP_{without}$ (left). Here, temperatures interpolated in Tokyo area are plotted and the border of Tokyo is drawn. The Tokyo central area is in an eastern part indicated in the right-middle of the figure. In each figure, *square dots* denote the monitoring stations and *round dots* denote tweets including synonyms of heat. *From Murakami, D., Peters, G.W., Yamagata, Y., Matsui, T., 2016. "Participatory sensing data tweets for micro-urban real-time resiliency monitoring and risk management." IEEE Access 4 347–372.*

Accuracy of GP_{with} and $GP_{without}$ are compared by a cross-validation. Since consideration of heat-tweets must be significant for temperature interpolation at unmonitored sites, temperatures monitored at seven stations (and heat-tweets) are applied to interpolate temperatures at the remaining station site, and it is iterated for all eight cases. Then predictive accuracy is evaluated by root-mean-square error (RMSE).

RMSE of GP_{with} and $GP_{without}$ are 3.85 and 3.89 only at the monitoring sites, respectively, verifying that consideration of tweets increases local temperature interpolation accuracy marginally. Though due to the calibration of the models at these sites, it is not unreasonable to expect similar performance. However, more importantly, as shown in Fig. 8.4.1, we see that the incorporation with the geotagged Twitter data can significantly change the estimated spatial resolution accuracy for local area analysis. This finding would be valuable as a first step of utilizing Twitter and other social media in urban climate analysis. We believe this is the first step in the incorporation of participatory sensing data with a ground-based sensor. As with all first attempts, this can also be improved with remote satellite sensing data. We believe the study of the Twitter data and the approach of extracting heat-related tweets can be enhanced further in future analysis.

8.5 Concluding remarks

We first demonstrated how to construct a model in space and time for a geotagged Twitter dataset in which we first selected heat-related tweets and then developed a statistical model that could be utilized as a heat-related sentiment index in space and time for an urban environment. This index was then studied to see if had similar statistical features to actual observed spatial and temporal heat recordings, with particular focus on extreme hot temperature periods such as would occur during a heat wave. The focus of this study was on Tokyo metropolitan region.

Our discussion suggests the potential of Twitter in real-time management of temperature-related risks, including the risk of urban heat wave. Considering the trend of global warming and the fact that some past heat waves have caused many deaths, real-time risk management of heat waves must be an urgent task. Fortunately, tweets reflect not only ambient temperatures, but also conditions of each person. A risks analysis using both temperature information and human condition information in tweets (participatory sensing data) would be an important study toward real-time urban heat-wave management utilizing social media data.

References

Achrekar, H., Gandhe, A., Lazarus, R., Yu, S.-H., Liu, B., Apr. 2011. Predicting flu trends using Twitter data. In: Proceedings of IEEE Commutating Communications Workshops. INFOCOM WKSHPS, pp. 702–707.

An, X., Ganguly, A.R., Fang, Y., Scyphers, S.B., Hunter, A.M., Dy, J.G., 2014. Tracking climate change opinions from Twitter data. In: Proceedings Workshop on Data Science and Social Good, pp. 1–5.

Bermingham, A., Smeaton, A.F., Apr. 2011. On using Twitter to monitor political sentiment and predict election results. In: Proceedings of the IEEE Computer Communications Workshops. INFOCOM WKSHPS), pp. 1–9.

Biever, C., Jul. 2010. Twitter mood maps reveal emotional states of America. New Scientist 207 (14), 2771.

Bollen, J., Mao, H., Zeng, X., Mar. 2011. Twitter mood predicts the stock market. Journal of Computational Science 2 (1), 1–8.

Cressie, N., Wikle, C.K., 2011. Statistics for Spatio-Temporal Data. John Wiley & Sons.

De Iaco, S., Myers, D.E., Posa, D., 2001. Spacetime analysis using a general product-sum model. Statistical Probability Letters 52 (1), 21–28.

Evensen, G., 2009. Data Assimilation: The Ensemble Kalman Filter. Springer Science & Business Media.

Fuss, S., Canadell, J.G., Peters, G.P., Tavoni, M., Andrew, R.M., Ciais, P., et al., 2014. Betting on negative emissions. Nature Climate Change 4, 850–853.

Gayo-Avello, D., 2012. No, you cannot predict elections with Twitter. IEEE Internet Computing 6 (16), 91–94. Nov./Dec.

Gerber, M.S., May 2014. Predicting crime using Twitter and kernel density estimation. Decision Support Systems 61, 115–125.

Go, A., Bhayani, R., Huang, L., 2009. Twitter Sentiment Classification using Distant Supervision. Stanford University. CS224N-Final Project Report. [Online]. Available: http://hughchristensen.co.uk/papers/socialNetworking/Twitter%20Sentiment%20Analysis.pdf.

Goovaerts, P., 2006. Geostatistical analysis of disease data: accounting for spatial support and population density in the isopleth mapping of cancer mortality risk using area-to-point Poisson kriging. International Journal of Health Geographics 5 (1), 52.

Gotway, C.A., Young, L.J., 2002. Combining incompatible spatial data. Journal of the American Statistical Association 97 (458), 632–648.

Hahmann, S., Purves, R., Burghardt, D., Feb. 2014. Twitter location (sometimes) matters: exploring the relationship between georeferenced tweet content and nearby feature classes. Journal of Spatial Information Science 9, 1–36.

Hilker, T., Wulder, M.A., Coops, N.C., Linke, J., McDermid, G., Masek, J.G., Gao, F., White, J.C., 2009. A new data fusion model for high spatial-and temporal-resolution mapping of forest disturbance based on Landsat and MODIS. Remote Sensing of Environment 113 (8), 1613–1627.

Kyriakidis, P.C., 2004. A geostatistical framework for area–to–point spatial interpolation. Geographical Analysis 36 (3), 259–289.

Li, R., Lei, K.H., Khadiwala, R., Chang, K.C.-C., Apr. 2012. TEDAS: a Twitterbased event detection and analysis system. In: Proceedings of IEEE 28th International Nonconference on Data Engineering. ICDE), pp. 1273–1276.

Mora, C., Dousset, B., Caldwell, I.R., Powell, F.E., Geronimo, R.C., Bielecki, C.R., et al., 2017. Global risk of deadly heat. Nature Climate Change 7, 501–506.

Murakami, D., Peters, G.W., Yamagata, Y., Matsui, T., 2016. Participatory sensing data tweets for micro-urban real-time resiliency monitoring and risk management. IEEE Access 4, 347–372.

Ritterman, J., Osborne, M., Klein, E., 2009. Using prediction markets and Twitter to predict a swine u pandemic. In: Proceedings of the 1st International Workshop on Mining Social Media, pp. 1–8.

Sakaki, T., Okazaki, M., Matsuo, Y., 2010. Earthquake shakes Twitter users: real-time event detection by social sensors. In: Proceedings of the 19th International Conference on World Wide Web, pp. 851–860.

Sang, E.T.K., Bos, J., 2012. Predicting the 2011 Dutch senate election results with Twitter. In: Proceedings of the Workshop Semantic Analysis in Social Media, pp. 53–60.

Thelwall, M., Buckley, K., Paltoglou, G., Feb. 2011. Sentiment in twitter events. Journal of the American Society for Information Science and Technology 62 (2), 406–418.

Wang, X., Gerber, M.S., Brown, D.E., 2012. Automatic crime prediction using events extracted from Twitter posts. In: Yang, S., Greenberg, A.M., Endsley, M. (Eds.), Social Computing, Behavioral-Cultural Modeling and Prediction. Springer, Berlin, Germany, pp. 231–238.

CHAPTER NINE

Evaluating walkability using mobile GPS data

Yoshiki Yamagata[1], Daisuke Murakami[2], Takahiro Yoshida[1]
[1]Center for Global Environmental Research, National Institute for Environmental Studies, Tsukuba, Ibaraki, Japan
[2]The Institute of Statistical Mathematics, Tachikawa, Tokyo, Japan

Contents

9.1 Introduction

Walkability is a key concept toward sustainable urban development. Walkable neighborhoods have a great potential to contribute to creating low-carbon (green), climate-resilient, and high well-being communities (Jabareen, 2006; Leyden, 2003; Frumkin et al., 2004). The influence of walkability on sustainability has been evaluated in urban studies literature. For example, improving walkability decreases CO_2 and NO emissions in the block (Frank et al., 2006; Marshall et al., 2009). However, there are still many issues that need to be addressed as to what is real walkability and how

Spatial Analysis using Big Data
ISBN: 978-0-12-813127-5
https://doi.org/10.1016/B978-0-12-813127-5.00009-6

we can evaluate it with measurable indicators (Hanibuchi et al., 2011, 2012, 2015; Kikuchi et al. 2018; Koohsari et al. 2019a, 2019b; Inoue et al., 2011; Du Toit et al., 2007). For example, Leadership in Energy and Development for Neighborhood Development, which is a standard environmental certification system of urban districts, certifies neighborhood's sustainability considering walkability; however, the index was basically developed to be applied to cities in the United States, and therefore we need to adjust the system to fit with specific city environments if applied to other countries such as Japan (Hanibuchi et al., 2012).

As a first step to establish urban systems design with walkable green neighborhoods and smart communities, we analyze the relationship between walkability indicators and pedestrian flows (estimated from mobile GPS data). Namely, conventional walkability indicators (e.g., centrality, betweenness, angularity) are evaluated using micro–road network data, and pedestrian flows are estimated by a GPS dataset (every 30 min, mobile phone location data during July–December in 2016). Walking environment might have a considerable spatial heterogeneity. For example, in the case of Tokyo, which is our target area, the central area includes a business district (CBD), commercial districts, historical districts, and others. Walking environment in each of these areas will be quite different. Actually, there are regular road networks in the CBD whereas there are many winding paths in the historical areas. Given this background, this section applies geographically weighted regression (GWR) to quantify district-level walkability considering spatial heterogeneity (e.g., Fotheringham et al., 2003).

9.2 Data and methods

9.2.1 Mobile GPS data

Our target area is the six central wards of Tokyo: Chuo, Chiyoda, Taito, Bunkyo, and Sumida. The target area includes some of the main stations in Tokyo (Tokyo, Akihabara, Ueno, Asakusa, and Hikifune stations as shown in Fig. 9.2.1). Each area has different land uses such as business areas (around Tokyo station), tourist areas (around Akihabara and Asakusa stations), and downtown-residential areas (around Ueno and Hikifune stations).

To evaluate walkability indices, it is necessary to collect data on pedestrian behaviors. We used mobile GPS data (around 2% samples of whole

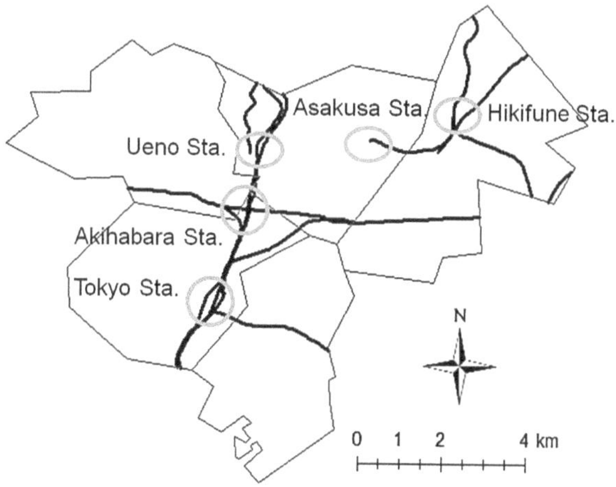

Figure 9.2.1 Target area: six main wards in Tokyo (*black lines*: train networks except for subway).

mobile phone users) in 2016 from July to December. The data records the coordinate location of users registered in a specific smartphone application every 30 min. Unfortunately, the mobile GPS data are not tagged with a traffic mode. Therefore, we need to classify the data into three traffic modes (walk, car, train use, etc.) by considering pedestrian flows as the movement between two points meeting the following two criteria:

1. The average moving speed between two points is less than 6 km/h.
2. One or more of the two points are located at a point 50 m or more away from the railway lines.

Fig. 9.2.2 shows the spatial distribution of estimated pedestrian density for weekdays and holidays in July. From this figure, it is confirmed that the spatial distribution of pedestrians on weekdays and holidays is quite different. On weekdays, pedestrians are globally concentrated around Tokyo station where offices are concentrated. On holidays, pedestrians are concentrated around local subcenters, including areas around Asakusa and Akihabara stations. The difference between weekday and holiday is also conceivable from [number of holiday pedestrians/number of weekday pedestrians] (see Fig. 9.2.2).

Fig. 9.2.3 plots the number pedestrians in each day between July and December 2016. From this figure, we can find that there are more pedestrians on weekdays than holidays; on weekdays, pedestrians decrease in the winter season; on holidays, the largest number of pedestrians are in the end of July.

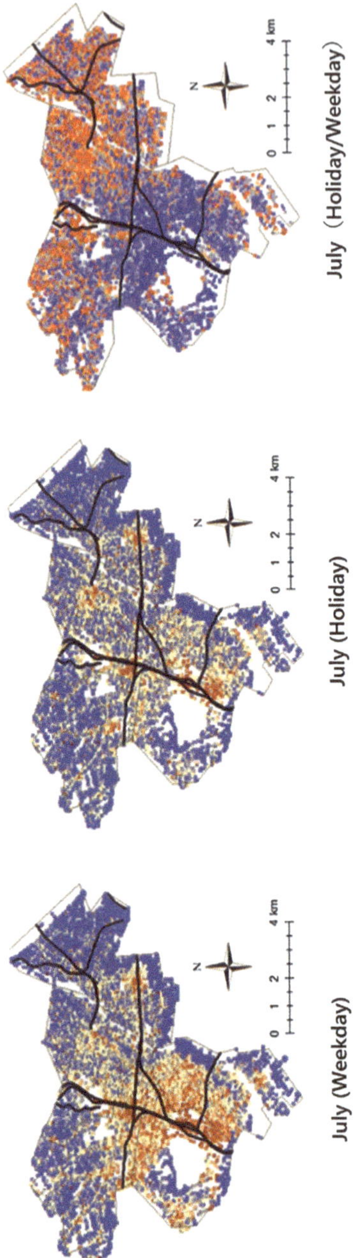

Figure 9.2.2 Pedestrian densities in July on Weekday (left), Holiday (middle), and ratio (right).

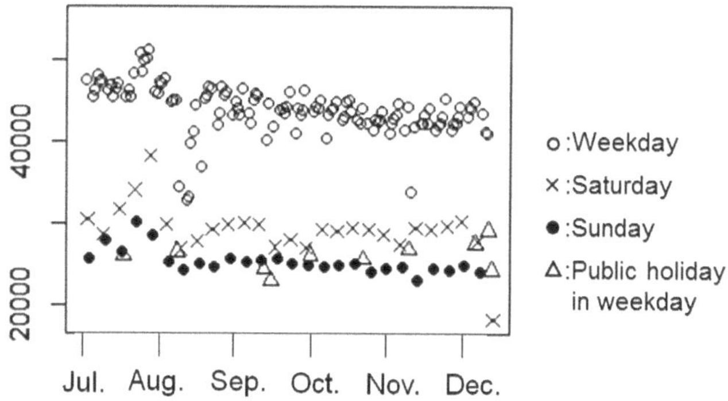

Figure 9.2.3 Temporal variations of the number of pedestrians.

9.2.2 Walkability indices

Many walkability indices have been proposed in urban studies. We examine usefulness of such indices for assessing actual walkability estimated from GPS data. Fig. 9.2.4 shows the calculation results of representative walkability indices. Table 9.2.1 shows the description of the walkability indices. The indices can be categorized into four groups. In the first group, the link

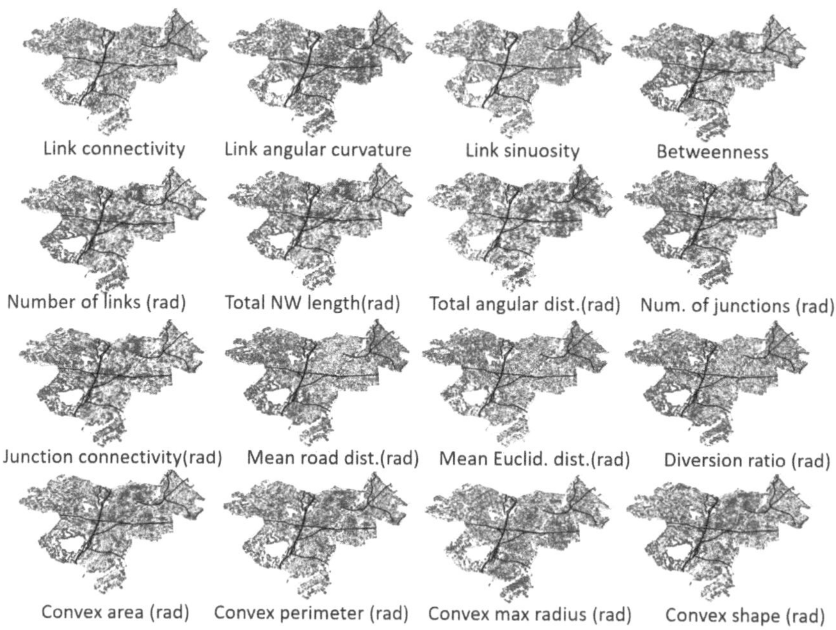

Figure 9.2.4 Walkability indices (the indices get higher as the colors become red).

Table 9.2.1 Walkability indices (regarding buffer radius *d*, we assume some cases: 100 m, 200 m, …, 1000 m).

Indices	Description
Link connectivity	Number of links connected the *i*-th link
Link angular curvature	Cumulative angular curvature of the *i*-th link
Link sinuosity	The ratio of [network distance of the *i*-th link]/[direct distance of the *i*-th link]
Betweenness	The ratio of the shortest path through the *i*-th link
Number of links	Number of links in a circle with radius *d*
Total network distance	Total distance of the links in a circle with radius *d*
Total angular distance	Total angular distance of the links in a circle with radius *d*
Number of junctions	Number of junctions in a circle with radius *d*
Junction connectivity	Number of links connected to junctions in a circle with radius *d*
Mean road distance	Mean road distance from the *i*-th link to each link in a circle with radius *d*
Mean direct distance	Mean direct distance from the *i*-th link to each link in a circle with radius *d*
Diversion ratio	The ratio of [direct distance from the *i*-th link]/[direct distance from the *j*-th link] in a circle with radius *d*
Convex area	Convex area covering road network in a circle with radius *d*
Convex perimeter	Convex perimeter covering road network in a circle with radius *d*
Convex max radius	Convex max radius covering road network in a circle with radius *d*
Convex shape	Convex shape index covering road network in a circle with radius *d*: (convex perimeter)^2/($4\pi \times$ convex area)

connectivity, the link angular curvature, and the link sinuosity represent the characteristics of each road link. In the second group, the betweenness, number of links, total network length, total angular distance, number of junctions, and junction connectivity are indicators of the street environment around each link. In the third group, the mean road distance, the mean Euclid distance, and the deviation ratio are indices of the goodness of access from each link to the surroundings. In the fourth group, the convex area, the convex perimeter, the convex radius, and the convex shape are two-dimensional shape indices of walkable environments.

Each index is evaluated for each road link. When evaluating each index (other than the first three), a buffer is generated from each link center of gravity point and evaluated based on the link containing the center of gravity in the buffer. Since the radius of the appropriate buffer is unknown, the walkability indices were evaluated for each case of 100 m, 200 m, ..., and 1000 m buffers.

9.2.3 Averaging of geographically weighted regression models

We estimate the explanatory power of the walkability indices on the local pedestrian density. We employ the GWR to estimate the impact in each district. The large number of walkability indices implies a large number of possible models. Specifically, given K indices being used as explanatory variables, there are 2^K possible models depending on whether or not each variable is included in the model. Consideration of such a model uncertainty is required in our setting. Thus we combine GWR with Bayesian model averaging (BMA), which flexibly accommodates model uncertainties (Hoeting et al., 1999; Ley and Steel, 2007) and stabilizes model estimation.

BMA evaluates the posterior probability of a model M_v ($v \in 1, \ldots, V$) as follows:

$$p(M_v|\mathbf{y}) = \frac{p(\mathbf{y}|M_v)p(M_v)}{\sum_v p(\mathbf{y}|M_v)p(M_v)}, \tag{9.2.1}$$

where $\mathbf{y} = [y(\mathbf{s}_1)\cdots y(\mathbf{s}_N)]'$ ($N \times 1$) is a vector of dependent variables that are given by the logged pedestrian density in each road link.

Each submodel M_v is specified by the GWR model with a different set of explanatory variables. Specifically, $p(\mathbf{y}|M_v)$ is given by the likelihood of the following GWR model:

$$y(s_i) = \sum_{K=1}^{K} \mathbf{x}_{k(v)}(s_i)\beta_{k(v)}(s_i) + \varepsilon(s_i) \quad \varepsilon(s_i) \sim N\left(0, \sigma_v^2\right), \tag{9.2.2}$$

where $\mathbf{x}_{k(v)}(s_i)$ is the k-th explanatory variable in the v-th submodel, and σ_v^2 is the error variance of the v-th model. The explanatory variables are given by a set of walkability indices shown in Fig. 9.2.4: number of passengers in the nearest railway station (Number of passengers), number of restaurants within 500 m (Number of restaurants), and number of offices within 100 m (Number of offices). The walkability indices are evaluated while changing the buffer radius (100 m, 200 m, ..., 1000 m) and are selected using BMA.

The local coefficient $\boldsymbol{\beta}_{k(v)}(\mathbf{s}_i)$ is estimated using GWR. In this section we use the boxcar kernel, which is a non-distance-decay-type kernel specified as

$$\text{Boxcar kernel: } g(\mathbf{s}_i, \mathbf{s}_j; b) = \begin{cases} 1 & \text{if } d(\mathbf{s}_i, \mathbf{s}_j) < b \\ 0 & \text{Otherwise} \end{cases} \tag{9.2.3}$$

Following Ley and Steel (2007), we assumed the prior distribution of M_v, $p(M_v)$ as the random theta prior. From the above, the posterior distribution of $\boldsymbol{\beta}_k(s_i)$ is given as follows:

$$p(\boldsymbol{\beta}_k(s_i)|\mathbf{y}) = \sum_v p\left(\boldsymbol{\beta}_{k(v)}|M_v, \mathbf{y}\right)p(M_v|\mathbf{y}). \tag{9.2.4}$$

BMA considers model uncertainties by using Eq. (9.2.4), which averages the coefficient estimates of submodels. We estimate the bandwidth b a priori. Then, we used Markov chain Monte Carlo method for the BMA (iteration: 10,000 times; burn-in period: the first 1000 times).

9.3 Estimation results

We apply the BMA + GWR approach to quantify the impact of each walkability index around stations shown in Fig. 9.2.1 between the number of pedestrians and walkability indices by using road links within 1 km from the station. Table 9.3.1 shows regression analysis results that neighborhood curvature indices were positive (Ueno and Asakusa stations) because enjoyable curvy districts tend to be preferred, and negative (Tokyo station) because mobility efficient straight networks tend to not be preferred. Moreover, the sign of the number of links and total link length were changed by districts because desirable network structure changes depending on districts.

Fig. 9.3.1 shows the influence of walkability on pedestrian density evaluated by sum of each [walkability index] × [GWR coefficients]. The holiday result was more interpretable because old districts (Asakusa, North Sumida, Yanesen area, etc.) were more influenced by walkability. This is a useful result for creating walkable green communities.

9.4 Individual level walkability evaluation considering heat-wave stress

9.4.1 Walkability evaluation at individual personal level considering heat-wave stress

In this section, we introduce the results of individual personal level walkability evaluation considering heat-wave stress. As we explained in

Table 9.3.1 Regression analysis result (Holiday).

Explanatory variables	Tokyo station			Akihabara station			Ueno station			Asakusa station			Hikifune station		
	Coefficient	Distance	PIP	Coefficient	Distance	PIP	Coefficient	Distance	PIP	Coefficient	Distance	PIP	Coefficient	Distance	PIP
Number of passengers				2.77×10^{-9}		1***				1.39×10^{-8}		1***	1.25×10^{-8}		1***
Number of offices										3.72×10^{-2}		1***			
Number of restaurants							5.87×10^{-3}		0.96**						
Number of links	−46.8	200	0.97**	9.25×10^{-2}	600	0.93*				2.46×10^{-2}	1000	0.94*			
Total NW length	9.95×10^{-4}	300	0.95*	1.10×10^{-3}	600	1***	−36	1000	1***						
Total angular distance	−20.5	1000	1***	2.54×10^{-3}	100	0.94*	1.05×10^{-3}	700	1***	5.42×10^{-4}	1000	1***			
Number of junctions							2.82×10^{-1}	500	1***				8.77×10^{-2}	700	1***
Mean road distance													−94.8	700	0.96**
Mean euclid distance													3.02×10^{-2}	600	0.94*
Diversion rate	55.31	800	1***				−5.88	1000	0.92*						
Convex area							4.59×10^{-5}	300	1 ***						
Convex perimeter				9.17×10^{-3}	500	0.93*	−12.2	300	1***						
Convex max radius	2.51×10^{-2}	600	1***												
Convex shape	8.34×10^{-1}	200	1***							61.59	900	1***			
Adj-R^2	0.734			0.438			0.528			0.416			0.286		

*, **, and *** represent statistical significance at 10%, 5%, and 1%, respectively. PIP: the posterior inclusion probabilities.

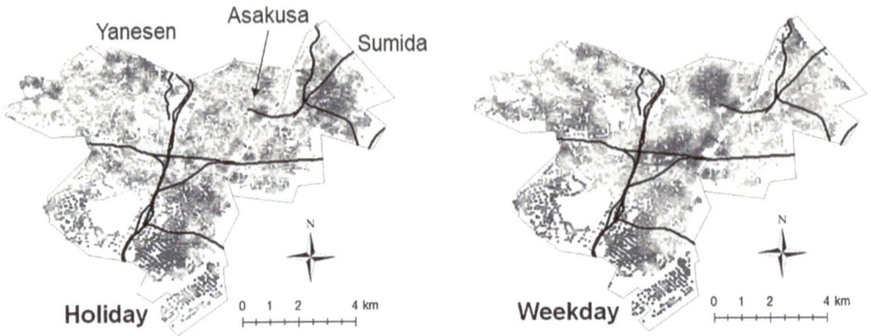

Figure 9.3.1 Pedestrian increase rates by improving walkability indices.

this chapter, conventional walkability studies have focused on aggregate "road" level. In the Internet of Things and big data era, "individual personal" level data such as mobile GPS data and twitter data (e.g., Murakami et al., 2016) has become available for use. For recent examples, Wheeler et al. (2010) and Carlson et al. (2015) attempt to use GPS data to evaluate walkability at individual personal level for neighborhood and greenspace effects, respectively. Walkability analysis at the "individual personal" level would be useful to know the relationships between actual human preferable street/place and its street layout including road width, wooden cover ratio, the number of shops, distance to station, heat environment, and so on. It will enable the urban policy maker and planner to design landscapes more comfortable for humans. Additionally, by combining spatially detailed surface temperature data from aircraft observations (Fig. 9.4.1), we can evaluate

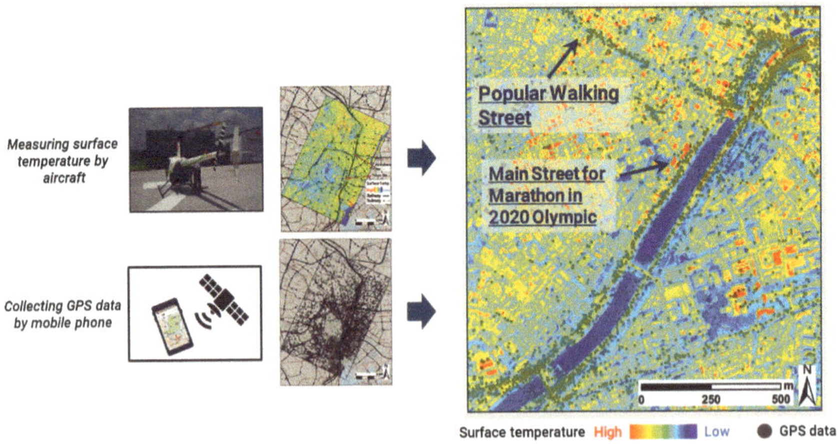

Figure 9.4.1 Combining surface temperature data and GPS data around a main street for the 2020 Olympic Games marathon at Tokyo.

heat-wave stress at an individual level. The purpose of this section is to describe heat stress evaluation at the individual personal level as a walkability index. Subsection 9.4.2 introduces an example of how to quantify heat stress of each person by employing ground surface temperature data and mobile sensing data. Next, subsection 9.4.3 explains how to detect pedestrian movement from mobile GPS data. Subsection 9.4.4 describes spatial data analysis approach for people flow data. Spatial hots spots of people's heat stress are detected using an approach based on the G star (G^*) statistic (Getis and Ord, 1992), which is a cluster detection approach well-known in spatial statistics (Fischer and Getis, 2009). Finally, subsection 9.4.5 shows the case study result of the spatial data analysis of heat stress evaluation in the central Tokyo area.

9.4.2 Background: serious heat-wave stress

Due to the urban heat island effect and global warming, health damage caused by heat waves are rising in the world as well as in Japan. In fact, heat strokes caused by large-scale heat waves have been reported in recent years (Rooney et al., 1998; Beniston, 2004; Le Tertre et al., 2006; Hajat et al., 2006; Clark et al., 2010; Klinenberg, 2015; Lemonsu et al., 2015; Mora et al., 2017; Zampieri et al., 2017; Sailor et al., 2019). Improving urban resilience against heat stress is an urgent task (Solecki et al., 2005; Gill et al., 2007; Milan and Creutzig, 2015). It is especially important to take measures against heat risks during the summer Olympic Games in 2020 Tokyo.

The impact of heat waves on human health, such as dehydration and dysfunction, becomes serious when people are exposed to heat for a long time (Rooney et al., 1998; Richardson, 2015). To evaluate the heat stress of individuals, it is necessary to know not only heat intensity (hazard) but also how people were exposed to the heat (exposure). As temperature changes greatly by location due to the surrounding surface conditions and individual walking patterns are different, it is not easy to evaluate both heat hazard and exposure of each individual at the same time with conventional methods.

Regarding hazard, the ground surface temperature data is useful to know the heat environment in each place. Ground surface temperatures reflect heating on concrete and cooling on parks/grassland more sensitively than air temperatures (Richardson, 2015). The ground surface temperature data observed by a satellite, such as ASTER (Advanced Spaceborne Thermal

Emission and Reflection radiometer; Spatial Resolution: 90 m) and MODIS (MODerate resolution Imaging Spectroradiometer; Spatial Resolution: 1 km), are publicly available these days. These data would be valuable to analyze thermal condition on a local spatial scale.

Regarding exposure, collecting and managing location information of people has been done through mobile sensing in recent years. For example, Agoop Co., Ltd. (https://www.agoop.co.jp/) provides location information logs obtained from applications of smartphones. The logs are acquired in 30 min intervals or 500 m to 1 km moves. This GPS information will be useful to know movement of individual people, which determines exposure to heat. To find an area in which people are highly exposed to heat hazard, it is necessary to consider the spatial cluster of people flows.

9.4.3 Transportation mode detection from low sample rate mobile GPS data

For ground surface temperatures data, we used thermal images observed from a helicopter (spatial resolution: 5 m; observation period: 11:30–13:00, August 5, 2016, a sunny day), shown in Fig. 9.4.1. For data of individual people's movement, we used Agoop's Point type floating population data. We analyzed individual level heat stress by applying the approach we developed in the next subsection. The target area is the center of Tokyo shown in Fig. 9.4.1.

Regarding exposure, our targets are pedestrians. This is because pedestrians are directly exposed to high temperatures and solar radiations. Unfortunately, because these people flow data do not have attributes such as traffic modes, we need to classify the GPS data into walk and other transportation modes (see Fig. 9.4.2). The criterion of walk is that the average moving speed is less than 6 km/h in each movement. Six km/h is equivalent to 1.5 times faster than 4 km/h, which is often assumed as average walking speed. In addition, when the movement before and after movement at 6 km/h is less than 6 km/h, it is divided into two people flows data (Yamagata et al., 2019a). In this research, we analyze only people flow tagged by walk extracted by the above assumption. Refinement of the pedestrian identification method, for example, extreme gradient boosting approach (Chen and Guestrin, 2016), is an important research subject in the future.

9.4.4 LISA analysis for people flow data

9.4.4.1 G* *statistic*

The G^* statistic, explained in Chapter 3, is a popular test statistic to detect hot spots, such as a high-risk area, economically agglomerated area, and

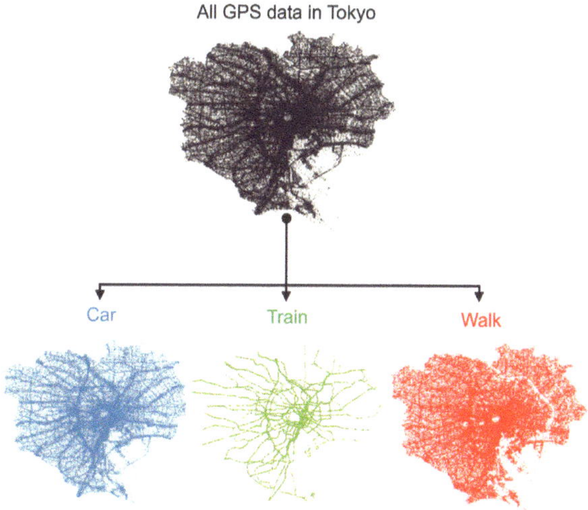

Figure 9.4.2 The mobile GPS data and transportation mode detection results in Tokyo.

ecological community, on a geographical space (Getis and Ord, 1992). The G^* statistic for a sample site $i \in \{1, \ldots, n\}$ is defined as follows:

$$G_i^* = \frac{\sum_{j=1}^{n} w_{i,j} y_j}{\sum_{j=1}^{n} y_j} \tag{9.4.1}$$

where y_j represents the observation at the j-th site. $w_{i,j}$ represents the spatial proximity between the sample sites i and j. The proximity can be defined by a variable indicating 1 if the distance between the sites i and j is shorter than a threshold distance and 0 otherwise. Alternatively, the proximity may be given by a distance-decay function.

The G_i^* takes a nonnegative value. A large G_i^* suggests a concentration of large y_j values near the site j. For example, if y_j represents ground temperatures at the site j, the large G_i^* value means a considerably high ground temperatures near that site. See Chapter 3 for further details.

9.4.4.2 G statistic for people flow data*

The original G_i^* statistic assumes samples distributed over a two-dimensional space. In other words, the statistic is not readily applicable to our GPS data (Fig. 9.4.3). The GPS data we use is a collection of people locations (2D coordinates) every 30 min (see Fig. 9.4.3), or by 500 m or 1000 m of movement for moving people. We focus not on individual GPS points but on

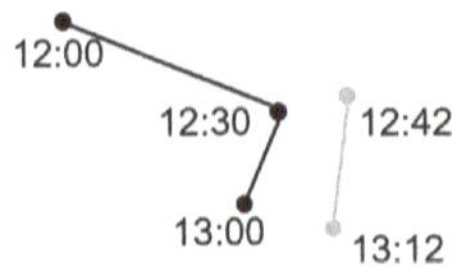

Figure 9.4.3 Image of the GPS data.

flow of individual people indexed by $I \in \{1, ..., N\}$. The I-th flow is composed of a set of n_I spatial coordinates, which we will index by $i \in \{1, ..., n_I\}$.

To apply the G^* statistic to our data, we need to define the proximity $W_{I,J}$ between the flow I and J. Statistical papers such as Tao and Thill (2016) and Ermagun and Levinson (2018) have studied proximity between people flows. Based on their discussions, we defined the proximity $W_{I,J}$ as follows:

$$W_{I,J} = \frac{1}{n_I n_J} \sum_{i \in I} \sum_{j \in J} w_{I,J} \tag{9.4.2}$$

In Eq. (9.4.2), $w_{i,j}$ denotes the spatial proximity between a GPS point i, which is in I-th flow, and a point j, which is in J-th flow. We defined the proximity using an exponential decay function $\exp(-d_{i,j})$, where $d_{i,j}$ is the Euclidean distance separating these points. Eq. (9.4.2) evaluates the proximity between flows I and J by averaging the proximities between GPS points in the I-th flow and those in the J-th flow (see Fig. 9.4.4).

Spatial concentration of large y_I values can be quantified using Eq. (9.4.3), which is given by substituting Eq. (9.4.2) into Eq. (9.4.1):

$$G_I^* = \frac{\sum_{J=1}^{N} W_{I,J} y_J}{\sum_{J=1}^{N} y_J} \tag{9.4.3}$$

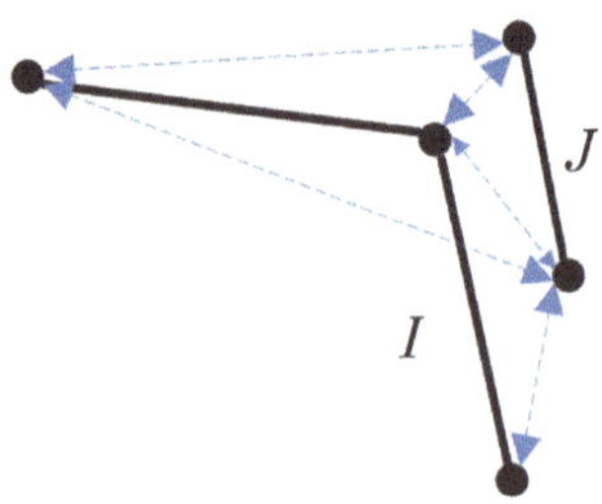

Figure 9.4.4 Image of the proximity between people flow I and J.

In our analysis, the G^* statistic for flow data (Eq. 9.4.3) is used to detect hot spots of people's heat stress. The heat stress of J-th people is defined by Eq. (9.4.4):

$$y_J = \sum_{j \in J} t_j \delta\left[g_j > 30\right]\left(g_j - 30\right) \tag{9.4.4}$$

where g_j is the ground temperature at the j-th GPS point and t_j is the estimated time spent at the point, which we assume 0.5 (= 30 min). $\delta[\bullet]$ is an indicator returning 1 if $[\bullet]$ is satisfied, and 0 otherwise. y_J quantifies how long J-th people walk on hazardous heat areas, which are defined as areas with mean ground temperatures more than 30°C at the target period. Eq. (9.4.3) indicates a large value in areas with many people suffering from hazardous heat. That is, Eq. (9.4.3) detects high risk heat areas considering individual people's behavior. Because Eq. (9.4.3) is identical to the standard G^* statistic, the statistical inference for the original G^* statistic is readily available.

9.4.5 Result

Fig. 9.4.5 shows spatial clusters of pedestrians with heat stress evaluated by G_I^* in Eq. (9.4.3). In this result, G_I^* is small in popular walking streets and main streets for the 2020 Olympic Games marathon.

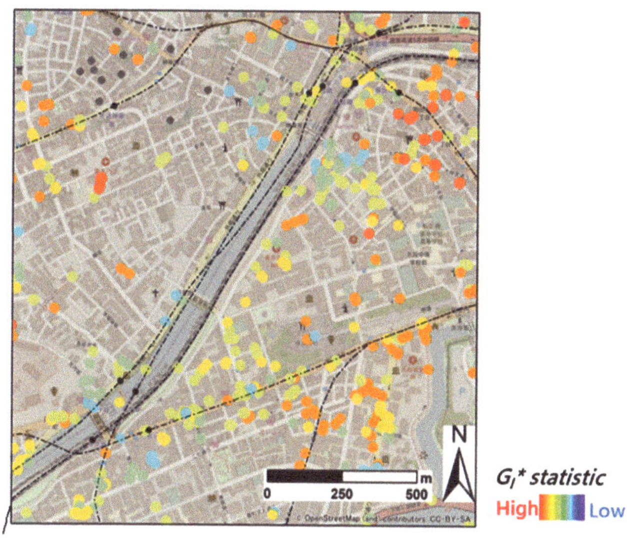

Figure 9.4.5 Evaluated G_I^* statistic.

This is probably because the walking distance tends to become longer in these streets where the station density is relatively high. The result suggests that considering the traveling time of pedestrians is important to properly evaluate the heat stress.

9.5 Discussion and concluding remarks

In this study, the relationship between the walkability indicators and pedestrian flow were analyzed for major districts near the center of Tokyo using GPS data. A spatial BMA technique was used to explain pedestrian behavior using a hedonic approach with walkability indicators. The analysis suggested that some indicators specifically corresponding to the traditional region (near train stations) are correlated with long-distance pedestrian behaviors. In the future, it would be important to see the induced effect of improving the walkability from the restriction of cars in green, low-carbon communities. Furthermore, it would also be important to consider community-scale effects around roads including health indices (Smith et al., 2008; Brown et al., 2009; Yamada et al., 2012) and greenness indices (Lwin and Murayama, 2011). The finding also has useful implications for planning vibrant streets using the indicators for design of walkable future green smart communities in Japan (Yamagata et al., 2019a).

Furthermore, as we described in Section 9.4, to estimate comprehensive walkability at an individual personal level, it is also important to consider spatially and temporally changeable environmental factors such as heat wave. First, we need to estimate spatial and temporal distribution of heat-wave hazard in detail, which would require the use of multiscale observations: by satellite (spatially global range, low resolution, and temporally low frequency), aircraft (spatially local range, high resolution, and temporally one shot), and high tower (spatially local range, middle resolution, and temporally high frequency). Yamagata et al. (2019b) and Murakami et al. (2019) describe how to combine those multiscale observations in a study area around the central Tokyo area, Japan.

Second, we need to use people flow data collected by mobile GPS data. Even if we get the GPS data, we would need to attach transportation mode tags to the GPS data: walk, bicycle, car, train, and so on. And then, after we classify pedestrian people flow data from GPS data, we need to use map-matching methods like Hidden-Markov model (Newson and Krumm, 2009). As an example for individual people movement detection, Yamagata et al. (2019b) and Yoshida et al. (2019) used Agoop's Point type floating population data and detected pedestrian flows from the mobile GPS data by using machine-learning techniques like Extreme Gradient boosting classification (Chen and Guestrin, 2016). It was initially useful to use a criterion of walk that the average moving speed is less than 6 km/h in each movement. The speed 6 km/h is equivalent to 1.5 times faster than 4 km/h, which is often assumed as average walking speed. Refinement of the pedestrian identification method using machine-learning techniques is an important research subject for the future (Yamagata et al., 2019b).

References

Beniston, M., 2004. The 2003 heat wave in Europe: a shape of things to come? An analysis based on Swiss climatological data and model simulations. Geophysical Research Letters 31 (2), L02202.

Brown, B.B., Yamada, I., Smith, K.R., Zick, C.D., Kowaleski-Jones, L.R., Fan, J.X., 2009. Mixed land use and walkability: variations in land use measures and relationships with BMI, overweight, and obesity. Health & Place 15, 1130–1141.

Carlson, J.A., Saelens, B.E., Kerr, J., Schipperijn, J., Conway, T.L., Frank, L.D., Sallis, J.F., 2015. Association between neighborhood walkability and GPS-measured walking, bicycling and vehicle time in adolescents. Health & Place 32, 1–7.

Chen, T., Guestrin, C., 2016. XGBoost: a scalable tree boosting system. In: Proceedings of the 22nd ACM SIGKDD: International Conference on Knowledge Discovery and Data Mining, pp. 785–794. https://doi.org/10.1145/2939672.2939785.

Clark, R.T., Murphy, J.M., Brown, S.J., 2010. Do global warming targets limit heatwave risk? Geophysical Research Letters 37 (17), L17703.

Du Toit, L., Cerin, E., Leslie, E., Owen, N., 2007. Does walking in the neighbourhood enhance local sociability? Urban Studies 44, 1677–1695.

Ermagun, A., Levinson, D., 2018. An introduction to the network weight matrix. Geographical Analysis 50, 76–96.

Fischer, M.M., Getis, A. (Eds.), 2009. Handbook of Applied Spatial Analysis: Software Tools, Methods and Applications. Springer, Berlin.

Fotheringham, A.S., Brunsdon, C., Charlton, M., 2003. Geographically Weighted Regression: The Analysis of Spatially Varying Relationships. John Wiley & Sons.

Frank, L.D., Sallis, J.F., Conway, T.L., Chapman, J.E., Saelens, B.E., Bachman, W., 2006. Many pathways from land use to health: associations between neighborhood walkability and active transportation, body mass index, and air quality. Journal of the American Planning Association 72, 75–87.

Frumkin, H., Frank, L.D., Jackson, R., 2004. The Public Health Impacts of Sprawl. Island Press.

Getis, A., Ord, J.K., 1992. The analysis of spatial association by use of distance statistics. Geographical Analysis 24, 189–206.

Gill, S.E., Handley, J.F., Ennos, A.R., Pauleit, S., 2007. Adapting cities for climate change: the role of the green infrastructure. Built Environment 33 (1), 115–133.

Hajat, S., Armstrong, N., Baccini, M., Biggeri, A., Bisanti, L., Russo, A., Paldy, A., Menne, B., Kosatsky, T., 2006. Impact of high temperatures on mortality: is there an added heat wave effect? Epidemiology 17 (6), 632–638.

Hanibuchi, T., Kawachi, I., Nakaya, T., Hirai, H., Kondo, K., 2011. Neighborhood built environment and physical activity of Japanese older adults: Results from the Aichi Gerontological Evaluation Study (AGES). BMC Public Health 11 (1), 657. https://doi.org/10.1186/1471-2458-11-657.

Hanibuchi, T., Kondo, K., Nakaya, T., Shirai, K., Hirai, H., Kawachi, I., 2012. Does walkable mean sociable? Neighborhood determinants of social capital among older adults in Japan. Health & Place 18, 229–239.

Hanibuchi, T., Nakaya, T., Yonejima, M., Honjo, K., 2015. Perceived and objective measures of neighborhood walkability and physical activity among adults in Japan: A multilevel analysis of a nationally representative sample. International Journal of Environmental Research and Public Health 12 (10), 13350–13364. https://doi.org/10.3390/ijerph121013350.

Hoeting, J.A., Madigan, D., Raftery, A.E., Volinsky, C.T., 1999. Bayesian model averaging: a tutorial. Statistical Science 14, 382–401.

Inoue, S., Ohya, Y., Odagiri, Y., Takamiya, T., Kamada, M., Okada, S., Shimomitsu, T., 2011. Perceived Neighborhood Environment and Walking for Specific Purposes Among Elderly Japanese. Journal of Epidemiology 21 (6), 481–490. https://doi.org/10.2188/jea.je20110044.

Jabareen, Y.R., 2006. Sustainable urban forms: their typologies, models, and concepts. Journal of Planning Education and Research 26, 38–52.

Kikuchi, H., Nakaya, T., Hanibuchi, T., Fukushima, N., Amagasa, S., Oka, K., Inoue, S., 2018. Objectively measured neighborhood walkability and change in physical activity in older Japanese adults: A five-year cohort study. International Journal of Environmental Research and Public Health 15 (9). https://doi.org/10.3390/ijerph15091814.

Klinenberg, E., 2015. Heat Wave: A Social Autopsy of Disaster in Chicago. Univ. of Chicago Press, Chicago.

Koohsari, M.J., Kaczynski, A.T., Nakaya, T., Shibata, A., Ishii, K., Yasunaga, A., et al., 2019a. Walkable Urban Design Attributes and Japanese Older Adults' Body Mass Index: Mediation Effects of Physical Activity and Sedentary Behavior. American Journal of Health Promotion 33 (5), 764–767. https://doi.org/10.1177/0890117118814385.

Koohsari, M.J., McCormack, G.R., Nakaya, T., Shibata, A., Ishii, K., Yasunaga, A., et al., 2019b. Urban design and Japanese older adults' depressive symptoms. Cities 87 (April 2018), 166–173. https://doi.org/10.1016/j.cities.2018.09.020.

Lemonsu, A., Viguie, V., Daniel, M., Masson, V., 2015. Vulnerability to heat waves: impact of urban expan- sion scenarios on urban heat island and heat stress in Paris (France). Urban Climate 14, 586–605.

Le Tertre, A., Lefranc, A., Eilstein, D., Declercq, C., Medina, S., Blanchard, M., Chardon, B., Fabre, P., Filleul, L., Jusot, J.F., Pascal, L., Prouvost, H., Cassadou, S., Ledrans, M., 2006. Impact of the 2003 heatwave on all-cause mortality in 9 French Cities. Epidemiology 17 (1), 75–79.

Ley, E., Steel, M.F., 2007. Jointness in Bayesian variable selection with applications to growth regression. Journal of Macroeconomics 29, 476–493.

Leyden, K.M., 2003. Social capital and the built environment: the importance of walkable neighborhoods. American Journal of Public Health 93, 1546–1551.

Lwin, K.K., Murayama, Y., 2011. Modelling of urban green space walkability: eco-friendly walk score calculator. Computers, Environment and Urban Systems 35, 408–420.

Marshall, J.D., Brauer, M., Frank, L.D., 2009. Healthy neighborhoods: walkability and air pollution. Environmental Health Perspectives 117, 1752–1759.

Milan, B.F., Creutzig, F., 2015. Reducing urban heat wave risk in the 21st century. Current Option Environmental Sustainability 14, 221–231.

Mora, C., Dousset, B., Caldwell, I.R., Powell, F.E., Geronimo, R.C., Bielecki, C.R., Counsell, C.W., Dietrich, B.S., Johnston, E.T., Louis, L.V., Lucas, M.P., McKenzie, M.M., Shea, A.G., Tseng, H., Giambelluca, T.W., Leon, I.R., Hawkins, E., Trauernicht, C., 2017. Global risk of deadly heat. Nature Climate Change 7, 501–506.

Murakami, D., Peters, G.W., Yamagata, Y., Matsui, T., 2016. Participatory sensing data tweets for micro-urban real-time resiliency monitoring and risk management. IEEE Access 4, 347–372.

Murakami, D., Yamagata, Y., Yoshida, T., 2019. Spatiotemporal heatwave risk modeling combining multiple observations. Proceedings of the 2019 IEEE Geoscience and Remote Sensing Society Symposium (July 28–August 2; Yokohama, Japan), in press.

Newson, P., Krumm, J., 2009. Hidden Markov map matching through noise and sparseness. In: Proceedings of the 17th ACM SIGSPATIAL: International Conference on Advances in Geographic Information Systems, pp. 336–343. https://doi.org/10.1145/1653771.1653818.

Rooney, C., McMichael, A.J., Kovats, R.S., Coleman, M.P., 1998. Excess mortality in England and Wales, and in greater London, during the 1995 heatwave. Journal of Epidemiology & Community Health 52 (8), 482–486.

Sailor, D.J., Baniassadi, A., O'Lenick, C.R., Wilhelmi, O.V., 2019. The growing threat of heat disasters. Environmental Research Letters 14 (5), 054006.

Smith, K.R., Brown, B.B., Yamada, I., Kowaleski-Jones, L.R., Zick, C.D., Fan, J.X., 2008. Walkability and body mass index: density, design, and new diversity measures. American Journal of Preventive Medicine 35, 237–244.

Solecki, W.D., Rosenzweig, R., Parshall, L., Pope, G., Clark, M., Cox, J., Wiencke, M., 2005. Mitigation of the heat island effect in urban New Jersey. Global Environmental Change B: Environmental Hazards 6 (1), 39–49.

Steffen, W., Hughes, L., Perkins, S., 2014. Heatwaves: Hotter, Longer, More Often. Climate Council, Australia.

Tao, R., Thill, J., 2016. Spatial cluster detection in spatial flow data. Geographical Analysis 48, 355–372.

Wheeler, B.W., Cooper, A.R., Page, A.S., Jago, R., 2010. Greenspace and children's physical activity: a GPS/GIS analysis of the PEACH project. Preventive Medicine 51 (2), 148–152.

Yamada, I., Brown, B.B., Smith, K.R., Zick, C.D., Kowaleski-Jones, L.R., Fan, J.X., 2012. Mixed land use and obesity: an empirical comparison of alternative land use measures and geographic scales. The Professional Geographer 64, 157–177.

Yamagata, Y., Murakami, D., Wu, Y., Yang, P.P.J., Yoshida, T., Binder, R., 2019a. Big-data analysis for carbon emission reduction from cars: Towards walkable green smart community. Energy Procedia 158, 4292–4297. https://doi.org/10.1016/j.egypro.2019.01.795.

Yamagata, Y., Murakami, D., Yoshida, T., 2019b. Spatiotemporal heatwave risk evaluation: Considering hazard, exposure, and vulnerability. Proceedings of the 2019 IEEE Geoscience and Remote Sensing Society Symposium (July 28–August 2; Yokohama, Japan), in press.

Yoshida, T., Yamagata, Y., Murakami, D., 2019. Individual level heat risk evaluation using GPS towards smart navigation system. Proceedings of the International Cartographic Association 2, 152. https://doi.org/10.5194/ica-proc-2-152-201.

Zampieri, M., Ceglar, A., Dentener, F., Toreti, A., 2017. Wheat yield loss attributable to heat waves, drought and water excess at the global, national and subnational scales. Environmental Research Letters 12, 064008.

CHAPTER TEN

Spatial scenario creation based on downscale methods

Daisuke Murakami[1], **Yoshiki Yamagata**[2]
[1]The Institute of Statistical Mathematics, Tachikawa, Tokyo, Japan
[2]Center for Global Environmental Research, National Institute for Environmental Studies, Tsukuba, Ibaraki, Japan

Contents

10.1 Introduction

Socioeconomic scenarios are needed to project carbon dioxide (CO_2) emissions, disaster risks, and other factors affecting sustainability from a long-term perspective. The Intergovernmental Panel on Climate Change published Shared Socioeconomic Pathways (SSPs; O'Neill et al., 2014, 2017) that describe future socioeconomic conditions under various scenarios, including SSP1-3. SSP1 makes relatively good progress toward sustainability under an open and globalized world. SSP2 is a middle-of-the-road scenario assuming that the typical trends in the last decades will continue, and in SSP3, the world is closed and fragmented into regions, and it fails to achieve sustainability.

While the SSPs are devised in terms of country scenarios, finer scenarios (e.g., scenarios in terms of 0.5-degree grids) are required to analyze regional/city-level sustainability and resiliency. A number of studies have downscaled country-level socioeconomic scenarios into finer spatial units

Spatial Analysis using Big Data
ISBN: 978-0-12-813127-5
https://doi.org/10.1016/B978-0-12-813127-5.00010-2

(e.g., Bengtsson et al., 2006; Asadoorian, 2007; Grübler et al., 2007; van Vuuren et al., 2007; Gaffin et al., 2004; Hachadoorian et al., 2011; Jones and O'Neill, 2013; Nam and Reilly, 2013; McKee et al., 2015; Yamagata et al., 2015; Jones and O'Neill, 2016).

Yet, these studies have several limitations. First, they do not consider interactions among cities. It is likely that spatial interactions, that is, interactions depending on geographical distance, are significant locally, while economic interactions are significant globally. These local and global interactions among cities must be considered in addition to spill-over from cities to their neighbors, as done by Jones and O'Neill (2013). Second, many previous studies did not utilize auxiliary variables (e.g., land use, road network, location of airports), which seem useful for the consideration of urban form and functions, but rather, simply extrapolated past trends using a logistic-of-growth model (e.g., Gaffin et al., 2004), share-of-growth model (e.g., Yamagata et al., 2015), gravity-type model (e.g., Grübler et al., 2007; Jones and O'Neill, 2016), and so on. Mc Kee et al. (2015) study is an exception, as it considers land-use data, road-network data, and so on. Nevertheless, their target area is limited to the United States. Also, they determine weights exogenously for each auxiliary variable. It is desirable to estimate the importance of each auxiliary variable endogenously.

Given this background, this section introduces the results of Murakami and Yamagata (2019), which estimates fine-scale socioeconomic scenarios using a spatial econometric approach considering spatial and economic interactions. In this chapter, we downscaled the country-level SSP1-3 scenarios into 0.5-degree grids while overcoming these two limitations. Specifically, our downscale approach estimates the intensity of interactions among cities and the importance of auxiliary variables, from data. Although Jones and O'Neill (2016) already published gridded SSP population scenarios (https://www2.cgd.ucar.edu/sections/tss/iam/ssp-projections), they apply a simple approach ignoring auxiliary variables. Our study, considering these two estimates would be beneficial in developing more sophisticated gridded scenarios.

10.2 Downscaling approach

10.2.1 Overview

This study downscales the urban population, nonurban population, and gross domestic productivity (GDP; purchasing power parity, billion USD in 2005 year rate) by country under SSP1-3 (source: SSP database: https://

tntcat.iiasa.ac.at/SspDb/dsd?Action=htmlpage&page=about) into 0.5-degree grids.[1] The target years are from 2010 to 2100, every 5 years.

We assume the following: (1) city population changes over time; (2) urban area expands or shrinks according to the city population change; (3) city population, urban expansion/shrinkage, and other auxiliary variables determine gridded populations and gross productivities. Differences in SSPs are considered in steps (1) and (2) as we will explain later.

Under these assumptions, populations and GDPs are downscaled as summarized in Fig. 10.2.1. Urban populations by country are downscaled into cities based on a city growth model, which considers (1). The estimated city populations are used to project (2) urban expansion/shrinkage. The city populations are further downscaled into 0.5-degree grids considering projected urban expansion and auxiliary variables summarized in Table 10.2.1.

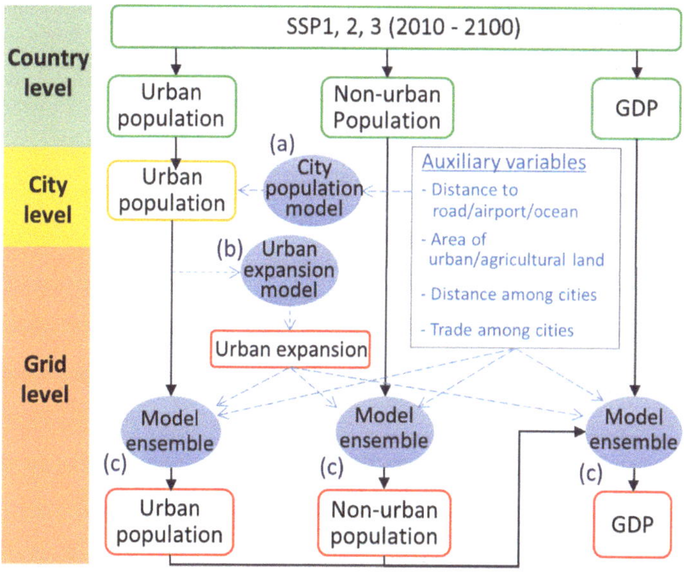

Figure 10.2.1 Procedure for population and GDP downscaling. Variables by countries, cities, and grids are colored by green, yellow, and red, respectively. The *black arrows* represent the downscaling procedure while the *blue arrows* represent subprocessing to consider auxiliary variables. As this figure shows, urban population is downscaled from countries to cities to grids, while nonurban population is downscaled from countries to grids. GDP is downscaled from countries to grids by utilizing downscaled populations. See Murakami and Yamagata (2019) for further detail

[1] The urban and nonurban populations are obtained by dividing the SSP country population scenarios using share of urban populations projected by Jiang and O'Neill (2015).

Table 10.2.1 Auxiliary variables.

Variables	Description	Unit	Source	Year
City pop	City population	67,934 cities	GRUMP[1]	1990, 1995, 2000
Urban area	Urban area (km^2)	0.5-degree grids	Schneider et al., 2009 [2]	2001–02
Agri area	Agricultural area (km^2)			
Road dens	Total length (km) of principal roads		Natural Earth[3]	2012
Airport dist	Distance (km) to the nearest airport	N.A.		
Ocean dist	Distance (km) to the nearest ocean			2010
Trade amount	Amount of bilateral trade (current US dollars)	Country	CoW[4]	2009

[1]Settlement Points, v1 (http://sedac.ciesin.columbia.edu/data/set/grump-v1-settlement-points; Balk et al., 2006) of Global Rural-Urban Mapping Project (GRUMP), SEDAC (Socioeconomic Data and Applications Center; http://sedac.ciesin.columbia.edu/).
[2]Global maps of urban extent from satellite data (https://nelson.wisc.edu/sage/data-and-models/schneider.php), which is estimated from MODIS (MODerate resolution Imaging Spectroradiometer; https://modis.gsfc.nasa.gov/).
[3]Natural Earth (http://www.naturalearthdata.com/).
[4]CoW (The Correlates of War project; http://www.correlatesofwar.org/).

On the other hand, nonurban populations by country are downscaled into 0.5-degree grids considering projected urban expansion and the auxiliary variables. GDP is also downscaled considering urban expansion, the auxiliary variables, and downscaled urban and nonurban populations.

Hereafter, the city population model, the urban expansion/shrinkage model, and the downscaling model will be explained in Sections 10.2.2 and 10.2.3, Section 10.2.4, and Section 10.2.5, respectively.[2]

10.2.2 City growth model: estimation with current data

This section estimates the impacts of local spatial interactions, global economic interactions, and auxiliary variables {*Road dense*, *Airport dist*, *Ocean dist*} on city population change between 1995 and 2000 (source: GRUMP

[2] Our calculations are implemented in a Windows 10 64-bit system with 48 GB of memory. It takes about 1.0 h for all the calculations to be completed.

Figure 10.2.2 GRUMP population data in 67,934 cities (2000).

Settlement Point dataset version 1; see Fig. 10.2.2) by fitting a city growth model, which is formulated as

$$\Delta \mathbf{p}_{t+5}^{(log)} = \left(\rho_{geo}\mathbf{W}_{geo} + \rho_{e1}\mathbf{W}_{e1} + \rho_{e2}\mathbf{W}_{e2}\right)\Delta \mathbf{p}_t^{(log)} + \alpha \Delta \mathbf{p}_t^{(log)} \\ + \mathbf{X}_t \boldsymbol{\beta} + \boldsymbol{\varepsilon}_t \quad E[\boldsymbol{\varepsilon}_t] = \mathbf{0} \quad Var[\boldsymbol{\varepsilon}_t] = \sigma^2 \mathbf{I}, \tag{10.2.1}$$

$\Delta \mathbf{p}_t^{(\log)}$ is an $N \times 1$ vector whose c-th element equals $\log(p_{c,t}/p_{c,t\text{-}5})$, where $p_{c,t}$ is the population of city c in year t. $\boldsymbol{\varepsilon}_t$ is an $N \times 1$ vector of disturbance with variance σ^2, $\mathbf{0}$ is an $N \times 1$ vector of zeros, $\mathbf{I}$ is an $N \times N$ identity matrix, and α is a coefficient (scalar). $\mathbf{X}_t$ is an $N \times K$ matrix of explanatory variables, including road density (*Road dens*), distance to the nearest airport (*Airport dist*), and distance to the nearest ocean (*Ocean dist*; see Table 10.2.1), whose coefficients are denoted by β_{road}, β_{ocean}, and β_{airport}, respectively (i.e., $\boldsymbol{\beta} = [\beta_{\text{road}}, \beta_{\text{ocean}}, \beta_{\text{airport}}]'$).

$\mathbf{W}_{geo}$, $\mathbf{W}^{e1}$, and $\mathbf{W}^{e2}$ are given by row-standardizing $\mathbf{W}_{geo}^0$, $\mathbf{W}_{e1}^0$, and $\mathbf{W}_{e2}^0$, which describe connectivity among cities. $\mathbf{W}_{geo}^0$ is a spatial connectivity matrix whose (c, c')-th element is $\exp(-d_{c,c'}/h)$, where $d_{c,c'}$ is the arc distance between cities c and c', and h is an unknown range parameter. $\mathbf{W}_{e1}^0$ and $\mathbf{W}_{e2}^0$ describe economic connectivity. Since we could not find any data on economic connectivity among cities, we approximated it with Eq. (10.2.2), which represents an estimate of trade amount between cities c and c':

$$\hat{t}_{c,c'} = \frac{p_c}{P_C}\frac{p_{c'}}{P_{C'}} T_{C,C'} \tag{10.2.2}$$

where P_C is the population of the country, including the c-th city, and $T_{C,C'}$ is the amount of trade between countries C and C' (source: CoW data set; see Table 10.2.1). Eq. (10.2.2) simply distributes the amount of trade, $T_{C,C'}$, in proportion to city populations. The (c, c')-th element of $\mathbf{W}_{e1}^0$ is given by

Table 10.2.2 Parameter estimates.

		Estimate	*t*-Value	
Intercept		-6.19×10^{-4}	-8.12	***
α		1.87×10^{-3}	8.98	***
ρ^{geo}		9.56×10^{-1}	188.57	***
ρ^{e1}		1.83×10^{-3}	24.95	***
ρ^{e2}		4.10×10^{-4}	0.84	
β_{road}		1.21×10^{-3}	3.46	***
β_{ocean}		2.10×10^{-4}	2.19	***
$\beta_{airport}$		-1.66×10^{-4}	-0.47	
h		209		
Quasi-adjusted R^2	For $\Delta\mathbf{p}_{t+5}$	0.405		
	For $\mathbf{p}_{t+5}$	0.998		

*** Statistical significance at the 1% level.

$\widehat{t}_{c,c\prime}$ if cities c and $c\prime$ are in different countries (i.e., $C \neq C\prime$), and 0 otherwise. By contrast, the (c, $c\prime$)-th elements of $\mathbf{W}_{e2}^{0}$ are given by $\widehat{t}_{c,c\prime}$ if these cities are in the same country (i.e., $C = C\prime$), and 0 otherwise. Finally, $\mathbf{W}_{e1}$ and $\mathbf{W}_{e2}$ describe international and national economic connectivity, respectively. We use the spatial two-stage least squares (2SLS) method for the estimation. Specifically, to estimate h in $\mathbf{W}_{geo}$, 2SLS is iterated while varying h values, and the optimal h value maximizing the adjusted R^2, is identified.

Table 10.2.2 summarizes the estimated parameters. The table suggests that population rapidly increases in areas with dense road network and good access to airports. These results are intuitively consistent. Also, city growth in inland areas tends to be faster than that in coastal cities. This might be because coastal cities are already matured, and their populations are more stable than those of inland cities. Regarding the interaction parameters $\{\rho^{geo}$, ρ^{e1}, $\rho^{e2}\}$, it is estimated that both (local) spatial interaction and (global) economic interaction encourage population increase.

10.2.3 City growth model: application for city population projections

Since SSP1−3 are globalization, business as usual (BAU), and fragmentation scenarios, respectively, different levels of socioeconomic interactions are assumed in each scenario. Specifically, we assume that the intensity of the economic interaction doubles by 2100 in comparison with 2000 in SSP1, stays constant in SSP2, and halves in SSP3. In each scenario, the intensity of the economic interaction between 2010 and 2100 is linearly interpolated.

Under these assumptions, city populations in 2005, 2010, ..., 2100 are estimated by sequentially applying the city growth model, which projects the 5-year-after populations.

10.2.4 Downscale approach

The downscaling is done through a gradient boosting–based ensemble learning of subdownscaling models. Each submodel distributes population or GDP in proportion to weights, which are defined by (baseline variable) × (control variable). Baseline variables capture the difference in urban expansion/shrinkage assumed in each scenario whereas control variables capture the influence from auxiliary variables. City population projected using the spatial econometric model is used as a baseline variable. These variables are given in Table 10.2.3.

First, we downscale country-level urban populations into 0.5-degree grids using 12 (3 × 4; see Table 10.2.3) submodels and distribute urban populations proportionally to (baseline variable) × (control variable). Likewise, the nonurban populations are downscaled using 12 submodels. After that, country GDPs are downscaled using 16 submodels in which downscaled population is now used as a baseline variable. In each case, downscaling is done by a weighted average of the submodels whose weights are determined using the gradient boosting (Freidman, 2002), which is an ensemble learning method.

Table 10.2.3 Baseline and control variables for the urban population, nonurban population, and GDP downscaling. Baseline variables are projected under each SSP. Control variables are constant across years.

Baseline				Control
Urban population	**Nonurban population**	**GDP**		**(Common)**
City pop_{ag}	City pop_{ag}	City pop_{ag}	×	Constant
Urban pot	Urban pot	Urban pot		Road dens
Urban area	Agri area	UAgri Area		Airport dist
		SSP pop		Ocean dist

Agri area, agricultural area; *City* pop_{ag}, city populations, which are projected and aggregated into grids; *SSP pop.*, downscaled urban + nonurban SSP populations; *UAgri area*, urban area + agricultural area; *Urban pot*, urban potential, which is defined by a kernel density of city populations (see Murakami and Yamagata, 2019). For control variables, see Table 10.2.1.

10.3 Downscaling results

Fig. 10.3.1 plots the estimated population distributions in 2080 under SSP1-3. Compared with SSP3, SSP1 and SSP2 show higher population density around megacities, including London, Paris, and New York. By contrast, SSP3 has a higher and dispersed population density in Africa and west-middle Asia. Thus the populations in SSP1 are concentrated while those in SSP3 are dispersed. The concentration and dispersed patterns are

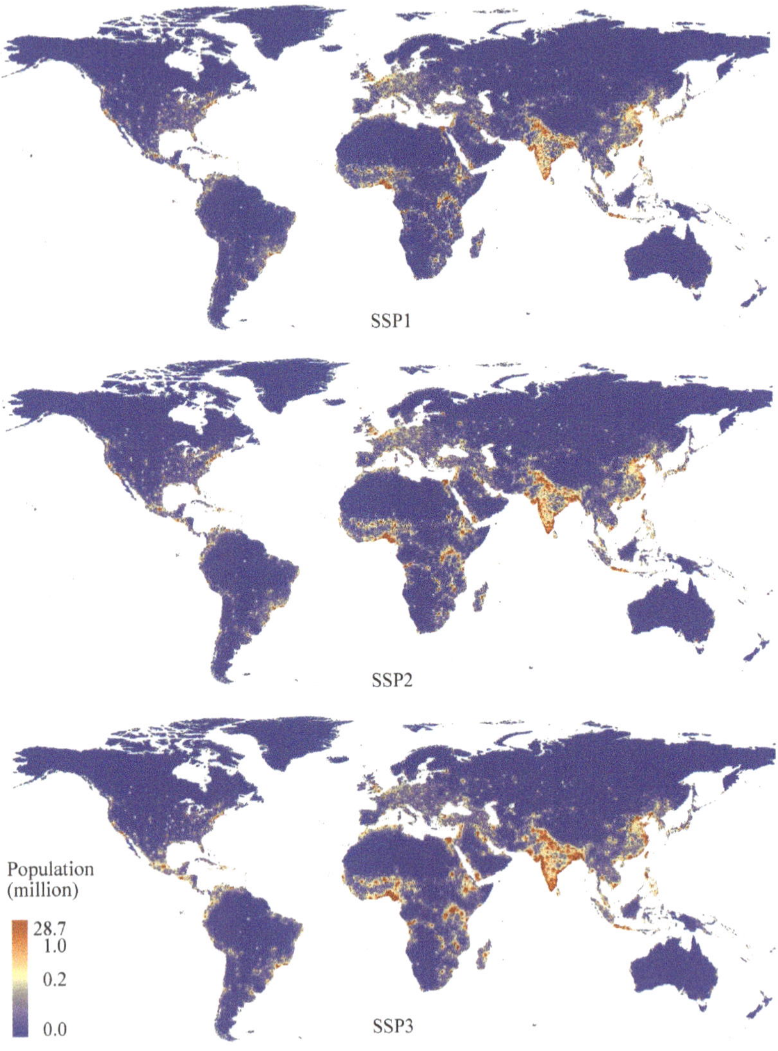

Figure 10.3.1 Downscaled population distributions in 2080.

thought to be due to the spatial range parameter *r* that is set in Section 10.2.4 following scenario assumptions. It is verified that these parameters are useful to control urban expansion/shrinkage following scenario assumptions.

Fig. 10.3.2 displays the distributions of gross productivity in 2080. The results in SSP1 and SSP2 are relatively similar; both show considerable economic productivity around megacities (e.g., London and New York). By contrast, economic productivity is small and dispersed in SSP3.

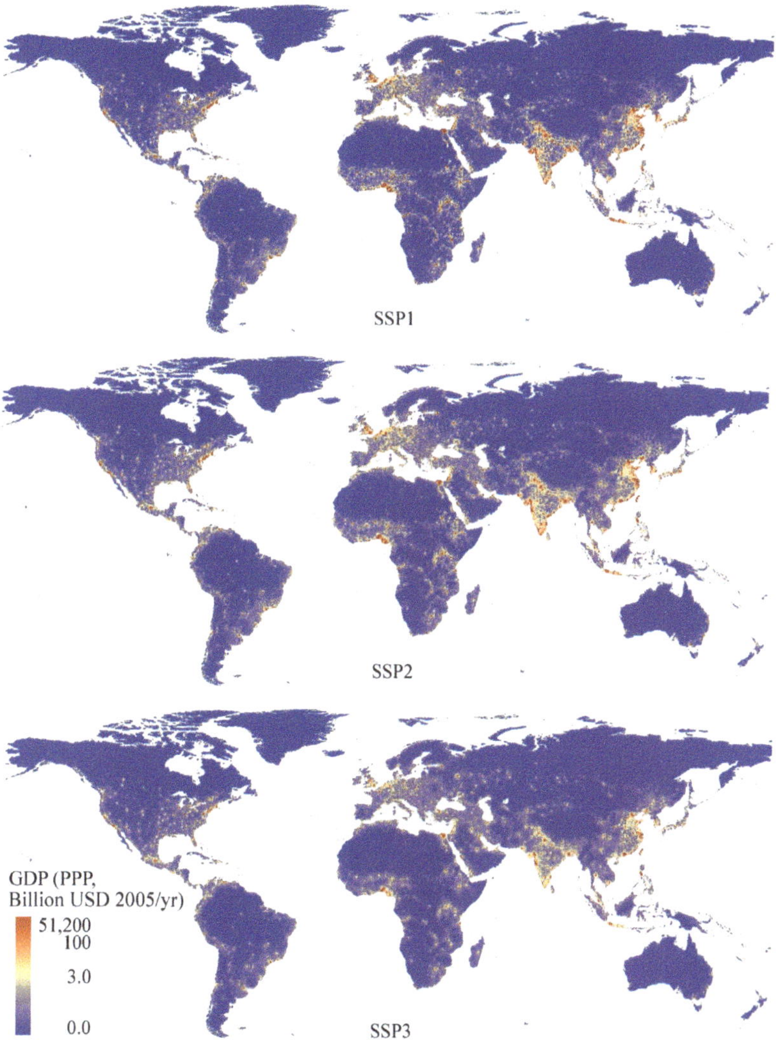

Figure 10.3.2 Downscaled gross productivities in 2080.

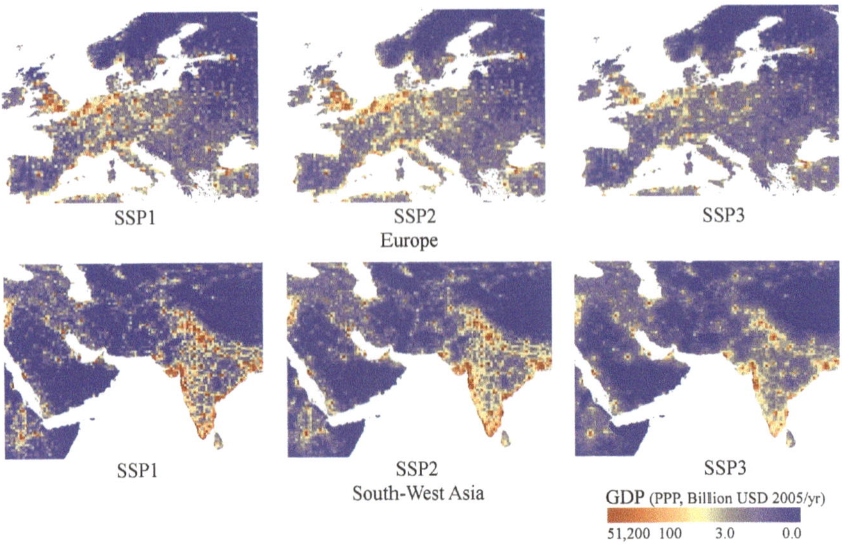

Figure 10.3.3 Downscaled gross productivities in 2080 (south and west Asia, and Europe).

Fig. 10.3.3 displays the results of the GDP downscaling in Europe and Southwest Asia. In Europe, economic productivity around major cities (e.g., London and Paris) changes significantly depending on SSPs. In Southwest Asia, compared with SSP1-2, SSP3 shows lower productivity in urban areas but higher productivity in nonurban areas. In other words, SSP3 results in dispersed economic growth. Considering such differences among SSPs would be important for analyzing future climate risks on socioeconomic activities.

Fig. 10.3.4 compares our population estimates in 2080 in SSP2 with those of Jones and O'Neill (2016). Estimates of Jones and O'Neill (2016) tend to be overly smooth (e.g., populations are uniformly distributed in

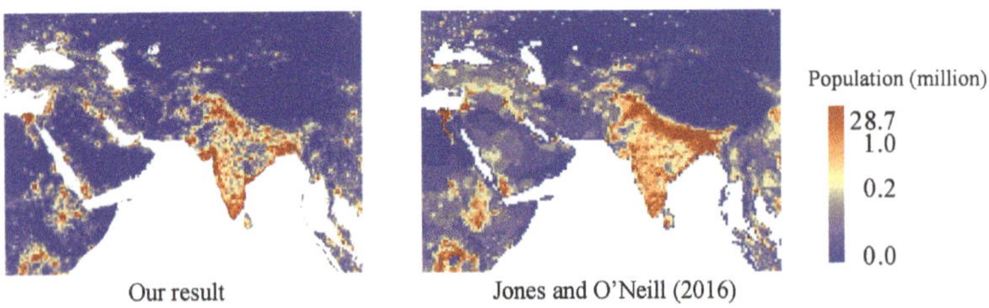

Figure 10.3.4 Comparison of estimated populations in Southwest Asia in 2080 (SSP2).

desert areas in Saudi Arabia). It might be because the authors apply a gravity-based approach, which ignores auxiliary variables. In our results, such over-smoothing is not conceivable. It is verified that consideration of auxiliary variables is also needed to avoid oversmoothing.

10.4 Concluding remarks

This section introduces the study by Murakami and Yamagata (2019), which downscales SSP scenarios into 0.5-degree grids. In the calculation, a spatial econometric model is used to project future population growth, and the spatial interaction parameter is used to describe spatial and economic interactions under the globalization, BAU, and fragmentation scenarios. Thus a spatial econometric model is useful for scenario creation although spatial econometrics has never been used for such purposes. Extension of spatial econometric modeling for spatially fine scenario creation will be helpful to estimate not only local population and productivity, but also CO_2 emissions, disaster risks, energy demand, and other variables determining future sustainability and resiliency.

The downscaling results are available from "Global Dataset of Gridded Population and GDP Scenarios," which is provided by the Global Carbon Project, National Institute of Environmental Studies (http://www.cger.nies.go.jp/gcp/population-and-gdp.html). This dataset summarizes population and GDP scenarios in 0.5×0.5-degree grids between 1980 and 2100, every 10 years. The gridded data in 2020–2100 are estimated by downscaling country-level SSP1-3 scenarios (SSP database: https://secure.iiasa.ac.at/web-apps/ene/SspDb/dsd?Action=htmlpage&page=about) as explained in this chapter, whereas those in 1980–2010 are estimated by applying the same downscaling method to actual populations and GDPs by country (source: IMF data; http://www.imf.org/data).

References

Asadoorian, M.O., 2007. Simulating the spatial distribution of population and emissions to 2100. Environmental and Resource Economics 39 (3), 199–221.

Balk, D.L., Deichmann, U., Yetman, G., Pozzi, F., Hay, S.I., Nelson, A., 2006. Determining global population distribution: methods, applications and data. Advances in Parasitology 62, 119–156.

Bengtsson, M., Shen, Y., Oki, T., 2006. A SRES-based gridded global population dataset for1990–2100. Population and Environment 28 (2), 113–131.

Friedman, J.H., 2002. Stochastic gradient boosting. Computational Statistics and Data Analysis 38 (4), 367–378.

Gaffin, S.R., Rosenzweig, C., Xing, X., Yetman, G., 2004. Downscaling and geo-spatial gridding of socio-economic projections from the IPCC special report one missions scenarios (SRES). Global Environmental Change 14 (2), 105–123.

Grübler, A., O'Neill, B., Riahi, K., Chirkov, V., Goujon, A., Kolp, P., Prommer, I., Scherbov, S., Slentoe, E., 2007. Regional, national, and spatially explicit scenarios of demographic and economic change based on SRES. Technol Forecast Soc 74 (7), 980–1029.

Hachadoorian, L., Gaffin, S., Engelman, R., 2011. Projecting a gridded population of the world using ratio methods of trend extrapolation. In: Cincotta, R., Gorenflo, L. (Eds.), Human Population. Springer, New York, pp. 13–25.

Jiang, L., O'Neill, B.C., 2015. Global urbanization projections for the shared socioeconomic pathways. Global Environmental Change 42, 193–199.

Jones, B., O'Neill, B.C., 2013. Historically grounded spatial population projections for the continental United States. Environmental Research Letters 8 (4), 044021.

Jones, B., O'Neill, B.C., 2016. Spatially explicit global population scenarios consistent with the shared socioeconomic pathways. Environmental Research Letters 11 (8), 084003.

McKee, J.J., Rose, A.N., Bright, E.A., Huynh, T., Bhaduri, B.L., 2015. Locally adaptive, spatially explicit projection of US population for 2030 and 2050. Proceedings of the National Academy of Sciences United States of America 112 (5), 1344–1349.

Murakami, D., Yamagata, Y., 2019. Estimation of gridded population and GDP scenarios with spatially explicit statistical downscaling. Sustainability 11 (7), 2106.

Nam, K.-M., Reilly, J.M., 2013. City size distribution as a function of socioeconomic conditions: an eclectic approach to downscaling global population. Urban Studies 50 (1), 208–225.

O'Neill, B.C., Kriegler, E., Riahi, K., Ebi, K.L., Hallegatte, S., Carter, T.R., et al., 2014. A new scenario framework for climate change research: the concept of shared socioeconomic pathways. Climatic Change 122 (3), 387–400.

O'Neill, B.C., Kriegler, E., Ebi, K.L., Kemp-Benedict, E., Riahi, K., Rothman, D.S., van Ruijven, B.J., van Vuuren, D.P., Birkmann, J., Kok, K., Levy, M., Solecki, W., 2017. The roads ahead: narratives for shared socioeconomic pathways describing world futures in the 21st century. Global Environmental Change 42, 169–180.

Schneider, A., Friedl, M.A., Potere, D., 2009. A new map of global urban extent from MODIS satellite data. Environmental Research Letters 4 (4), 044003.

van Vuuren, D.P., Lucas, P.L., Hilderink, H., 2007. Downscaling drivers of global environmental change. Global Environmental Change 17 (1), 114–130.

Yamagata, Y., Murakami, D., Seya, H., 2015. A comparison of grid-level residential electricity demand scenarios in Japan for 2050. Applied Energy 158 (15), 255–262.

CHAPTER ELEVEN

Quasi real-time energy use estimation using Google's Popular Times data

Takahiro Yoshida, Yoshiki Yamagata
Center for Global Environmental Research, National Institute for Environmental Studies, Tsukuba, Ibaraki, Japan

Contents

11.1 Introduction

The smart community concept attracts considerable attention as a system to increase energy resilience, support/manage smart life, and reduce carbon emissions (Zautra et al., 2008). Managing energy demands on a local scale is an important issue for accurate and highly effective smart community design. Fortunately, in recent years, data on individual buildings are increasingly available due to the development of IoT (Internet of Things) sensor technologies (Li et al., 2013; Yamagata et al., 2017; 2018). These data allow us to monitor building conditions, human movements, market transactions, and many other activities in real time in cities that will offer new useful insights (Batty et al., 2012; Batty, 2013, 2016). Yet, the use of these data for local-scale monitoring is still limited and these demonstration experiments applied to real cities have just begun. Toward smart community design, it is increasingly important to clarify to what extent

Spatial Analysis Using Big Data
ISBN: 978-0-12-813127-5
https://doi.org/10.1016/B978-0-12-813127-5.00011-4

these IoT sensor technologies related to human activity help visualize and support energy resilience (Li et al., 2013).

As the first step of creating such an energy-resilient smart community, Yoshida et al. (2019) attempted to estimate quasi-real-time energy demand on an individual building scale by using compositional Kriging, which is a geostatistical interpolation technique, has been developed in the field of compositional data analysis (CODA), and with Google's Popular Times data. This study briefly introduces the result of Yoshida et al. (2019). According to CODA WEB,[1] CODA refers to the analysis of compositional data that have been defined historically as random vectors with strictly positive components whose sum is constant (e.g., 100, and 1). Because we focus on rate data (from 0% to 100%), we need to consider such compositional characteristics of data when we conduct any interpolation (Yoshida and Tsutsumi, 2018). Poisson Kriging (Goovaerts, 2005) is one of the methods to attain this, but in this chapter, we focus on a much simpler method, termed compositional Kriging, where we can depend on conventional universal (or regression) Kriging.

Our target area is Sumida-ward, Tokyo, Japan. Sumida-ward includes a popular commercial district, Kinshi-cho; a recent redeveloped area, around Tokyo SkyTree tower; and many downtown residential districts such as Kyojima.

11.2 Materials and methods

11.2.1 Energy use estimation by hour in monthly average

To our knowledge, only the Japan Institute of Energy provides hourly electricity intensity data (kWh/m2/h) for each of th category including residential, office, hospital, hotel, store, and sport facility for the year 2008 (Yamagata and Seya, 2014). Fig. 11.2.1 shows this hourly electricity intensity data for residential and office buildings in April (shown as the ratio to daily maximum value). Note that in office buildings, intensity value is higher in the daytime, whereas in residential buildings, it is higher during hours 18–20. The left-hand side of Fig. 11.2.2 represents the type of building (residential or commercial/office) and the right-hand side represents the floor

[1] http://www.compositionaldata.com/

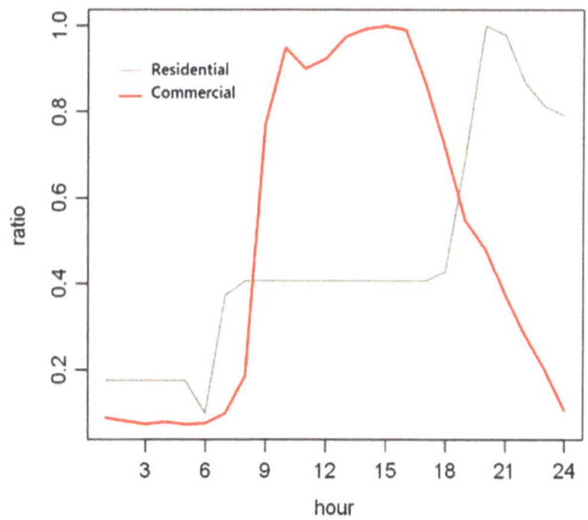

Figure 11.2.1 Average energy demand in April (relative value to the peak hour).

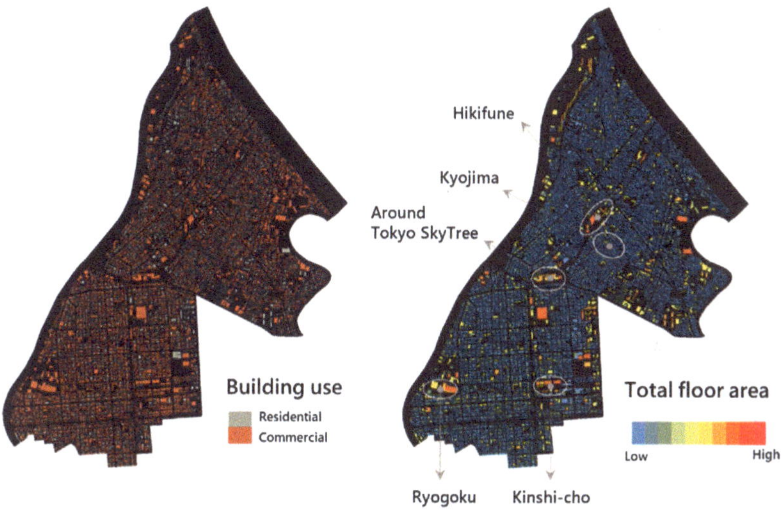

Figure 11.2.2 Building data: use (left) and total floor area (right).

area of each building. From this information (Figs. 11.2.1 and 11.2.2) we can estimate hourly electricity demand of each building for each month.

However, this intensity data captures only the typical (average) relationship between energy demand and total floor area of each building use; we cannot know the variation of the relationship from the intensity data. To confront, we use the spatial big data as a weight, so that we can estimate energy demand in more realistic manner.

11.2.2 Energy use estimation by hour and by day of the week

11.2.2.1 Google's Popular Times data

For the energy demand estimation by hour and by day of the week, we used Google's Popular Times data (Riedmaph, 2018) in Sumida-ward in Tokyo, which was collected by a web-scraping of Google Maps via its application programming interface in April 2018. The Popular Times data is a collection of aggregated and anonymized Google location history of smartphone (Google's Android and Apple's iOS) users.[2] The Popular Times data represents how popular an individual shop is under a typical situation during different times of the day, based on average popularity over the last several weeks.[2] Popularity for any given hour is shown relative to the typical peak popularity for the business for the week. The popularity will be useful to monitor quasi-real-time people/urban activities and the resulting energy/electricity consumption depends on the activities.

The sample size collected in Sumida-ward is $N = 945$. Fig. 11.2.3 shows the collected sample's locations and its popularity rate, which represents relative value of Google's Popular Times, to the most congested hour of the week, from 3:00 to 21:00 every 3 h on Friday as an example. Popularity rate rapidly increases at a typical work start time (9:00). At lunch time (12:00), the rate becomes totally peak and active. At night time (21:00 and 24:00), high popularity is only for a main commercial area (e.g., near train stations).

11.2.2.2 Compositional Kriging approach

The popularity rate is limited only to places with points of interest on Google Maps. To interpolate the popularity rate for all office (commercial) buildings, we used compositional Kriging, which is a geostatistical spatial interpolation technique for compositional data (see Pawlowsky-Glahn et al., 2015), assuming there is a spatial dependence.

Because popularity rate takes the value from zero to one (or 100%), we need to consider such a boundary constraint when we build a model. In fact, with data transformation developed in the field of CODA (Aitchison, 1986), we can use the conventional Kriging technique for interpolation. To be more concrete, the first data is transformed by relaxing the unit sum constraint, and then we perform conventional universal (or regression) Kriging (see Chapter 4). Lastly, the interpolated values are back-transformed to the

[2] https://support.google.com/business/answer/6263531?hl=en

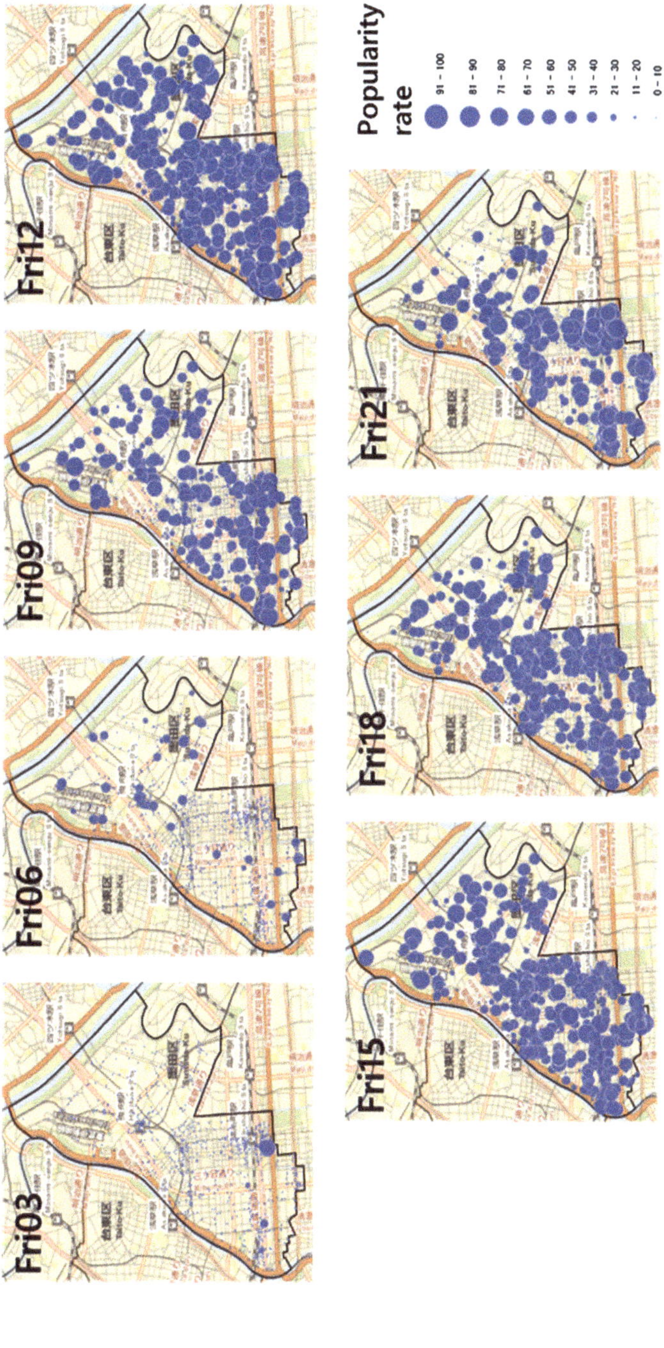

Figure 11.2.3 Mapping of popularity rate on Friday every 3 h.

original 0–100 (percentage) scale. For Kriging, the following three explanatory variables are employed—distance to the nearest train stations, total floor area for each building, and office use ratio in each building. Details about the compositional Kriging procedure are explained as follows.

For the first transformation step, the isometric log-ratio (ilr) transformation (Egozcue et al., 2003), which is well used in CODA literature and provides a reasonable translative relationship from a simplex geometry of the compositional data to the ordinary Euclidean geometry, is conducted as

$$z_{i,t,d} = \frac{1}{\sqrt{d(d+1)}} \ln\left(\frac{\prod_d y_{i,t,d}}{\left(y_{i,t,d+1}\right)^d}\right) \text{ for } d = 1, \ldots, D-1 \tag{11.1}$$

where $z_{i,t,d}$ is the ilr-transformed popularity rate of the i-th building ($i = 1, \ldots, N$) in t-th time ($t = 1, \ldots, 168$), respectively; D is the dimension of the original compositional data $\boldsymbol{y}_{i,t}$, and in our case, $D = 2$: popular ($y_{i,t,1}$) and not popular ($y_{i,t,2}$).

11.3 Estimation results

We estimate the energy demand of each building with the energy demand intensity data, total floor area of each building, office use ratio in each building, and the (interpolated) popularity, assuming that the energy demand depends on human activity in the shop. The popularity data are used as a *weight* for the energy demand intensity. Although the intensity data capture only the typical (average) relationship between energy demand and total floor area by building use, we cannot know the variation of the relationship from the intensity data. By using the popularity data as a weight, we can estimate energy demand in a more realistic manner.

Fig. 11.3.1 shows estimated energy demand from 3:00 to 21:00 on Friday every 3 h as an example of daily changes. As the color of polygons changes to red from blue, demand from individual buildings increases. Energy demand increased and continued to be high between 6:00 and 21:00. Since we considered human activity using Google's Popular Times data, commercial areas, especially around Tokyo SkyTree, Kinshi-cho Station and Ryogoku Station, were high during working hours. Demand of large condominiums in north parts of the area and around Hikifune Station were high all day long. For smart community design including energy sharing at a local scale, the results suggest that large grids would be

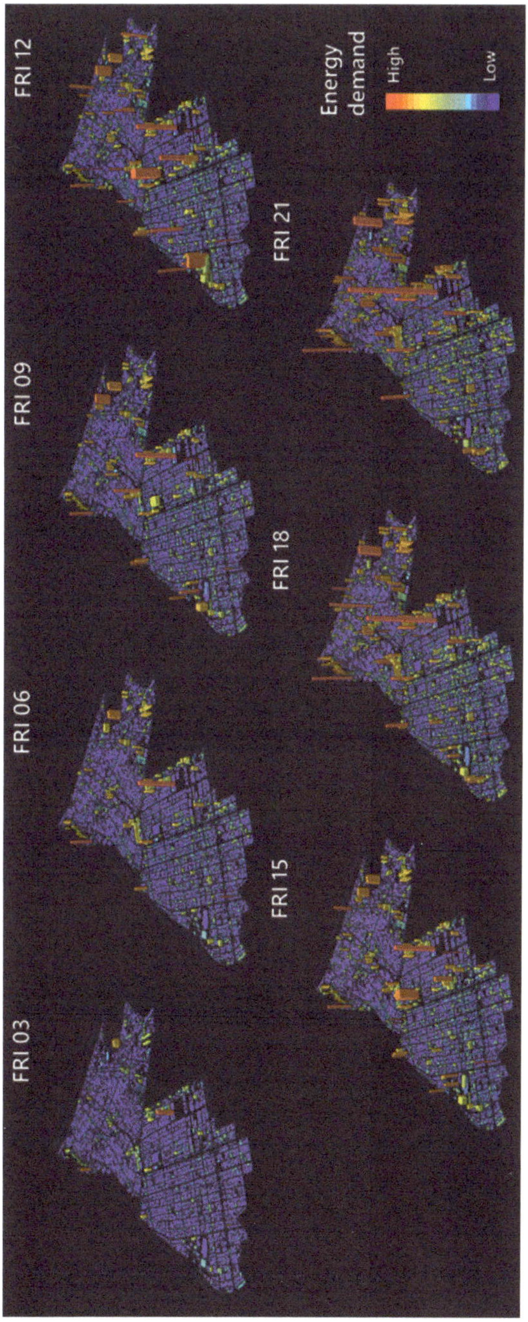

Figure 11.3.1 Estimated energy demand on Friday every 3 h.

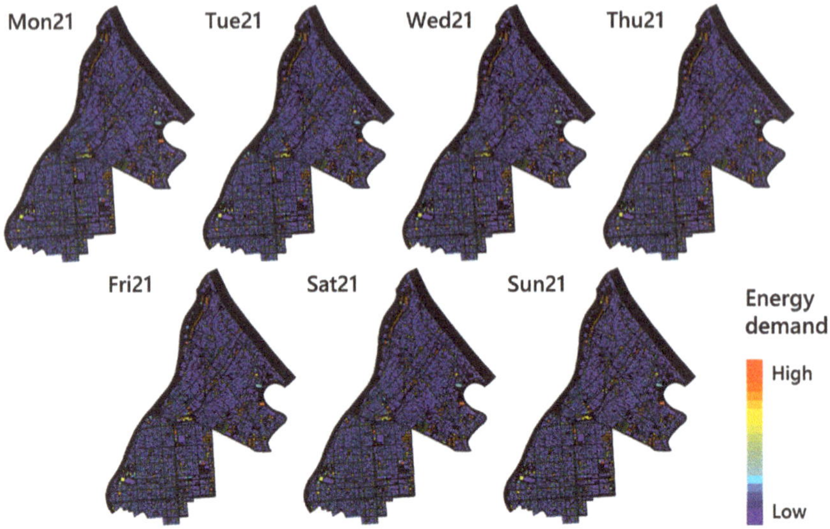

Figure 11.3.2 Estimated energy demand at 21:00 by day of the week.

needed to cover high energy demand in these areas. Fig. 11.3.2 shows the estimated energy demand at 21:00 by day of the week. Although the changes of demand were very few, demand of the commercial areas above were increased on weekends (Friday, Saturday, and Sunday). Since the energy demands depend on human activity, especially in commercial areas, the results suggest that we would need to consider their uncertainty for smart community design. To evaluate the uncertainty of the interpolation by compositional Kriging, Fig. 11.3.3 shows the prediction error variance of the transformed popularity rate (Eq. 11.1) on 21:00, Friday, as an example. The result is high in areas with few observation points of the popularity rate.

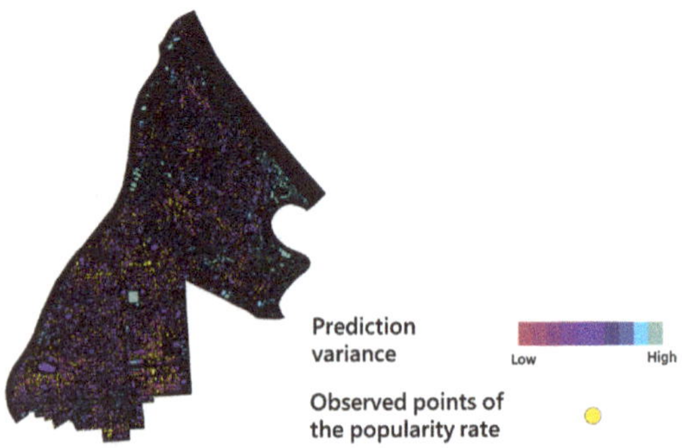

Figure 11.3.3 The predicted error variance of the compositional Kriging at 21:00 on Friday.

It is verified that our results of energy demand estimation are intuitive. Such a demand for estimation using location and activity sensors in real time would increase in the near future as our results would be beneficial to know changes of energy demands depending on human activity by hour and by day of the week.

11.4 Concluding remarks

We showed that spatial analysis of Google's Popular Times data are useful to estimate energy consumption from individual commercial buildings as quasi-real-time human activity data. To consider the characteristics of the Popular Times data, which can be viewed as compositional time-series and nonexhaustive, we explained isometric log-ratio transformation (compositional data analysis technique) and Kriging (spatial statistical interpolation techniques). In the near future, more advanced GPS and IoT sensors would be available in cities, which would make it possible to grasp human activity as well as the environment. With the application of spatial analytical techniques explained in this chapter, spatial and temporal energy demand-supply matching that considers human activity could be achieved. This would allow us to estimate and predict building energy demand in real time.

References

Aitchison, J., 1986. The Statistical Analysis of Compositional Data. Chapman & Hall.

Batty, M., Axhausen, K.W., Giannotti, F., Pozdnoukhov, A., Bazzani, A., Wachowicz, M., Portugali, Y., 2012. Smart cities of the future. The European Physical Journal Special Topics 214, 481–518.

Batty, M., 2013. Big data, smart cities and city planning. Dialogues in Human Geography 3, 274–279.

Batty, M., 2016. Big Data and the City 42, 321–337.

Egozcue, J.J., Pawlowsky-Glahn, V., Mateu-Figueras, G., Barcelo-Vidal, C., 2003. Isometric logratio transformations for compositional data analysis. Mathematical Geology 35, 279–300.

Goovaerts, P., 2005. Geostatistical analysis of disease data: estimation of cancer mortality risk from empirical frequencies using Poisson Kriging. International Journal of Health Geographics 4 (1), 31.

Li, M., Li, Z., Vasilakos, A.V., 2013. A survey on topology control in wireless sensor networks: taxonomy, comparative study, and open issues. Proceedings of the IEEE 101, 2538–2557.

Pawlowsky-Glahn, V., Egozcue, J.J., Tolosana-Delgado, R., 2015. Modeling and Analysis of Compositional Data. John Wiley & Sons.

Riedmaph, M., 2018. Populartimes. GitHub Repository. Available at: https://github.com/m-wrzr/populartimes/blob/master/LICENSE.md.

Yoshida, T., Tsutsumi, M., 2018. On the effects of spatial relationships in spatial compositional multivariate models. Letters in Spatial and Resource Sciences 11 (1), 57–70. https://doi.org/10.1007/s12076-017-0199-5.

Yamagata, Y., Murakami, D., Yoshida, T., 2017. Dynamic urban carbon mapping with spatial big data. Energy Procedia 142, 2461–2466.

Yamagata, Y., Seya, H., 2014. Proposal for a local electricity-sharing system: a case study of Yokohama city, Japan. IET Intelligent Transport Systems 9, 38–49.

Yoshida, T., Yamagata, Y., Murakami, D., 2019. Energy demand estimation using quasi-real-time people activity data. Energy Procedia 158, 4172–4177.

Yamagata, Y., Yoshida, T., Murakami, D., Matsui, T., Akiyama, Y., 2018. Seasonal urban carbon emission estimation using spatial micro big data. Sustainability 10 (12), 4472. https://doi.org/10.3390/su10124472.

Zautra, A., Hal, J., Murray, K., 2008. Community development and community resilience: an integrative approach. Community Development 39, 130–147.

Index

Note: 'Page numbers followed by "f" indicate figures, "t" indicates tables'.

H

I

K

L

M

FSC
www.fsc.org
MIX
Papier | Fördert gute Waldnutzung
FSC® C083411

Kolibri 360 GmbH
Ferdinand-Jühlke-Straße 7
99095 Erfurt, Deutschland
produktsicherheit@kolibri360.de